【英汉对照全译本】

AN INQUIRY INTO THE NATURE AND CAUSES OF THE WEALTH OF NATIONS

国民财富的性质与原理

[英]亚当·斯密 著

赵东旭 丁 毅 译

(四)

中国社会科学出版社

CHAPTER II

Of Restraints Upon The Importation From Foreign Countries Of Such Goods As Can Be Produced At Home

<small>High duties and prohibitions giving a monopoly to a particular home industry are very common.</small>

By restraining, either by high duties, or by absolute prohibitions, the importation of such goods from foreign countries as can be produced at home, the monopoly of the home market is more or less secured to the domestic industry employed in producing them. Thus the prohibition of importing either live cattle or salt provisions from foreign countries secures to the graziers of Great Britain the monopoly of the home market for butcher's meat. The high duties upon the importation of corn, which in times of moderate plenty amount to a prohibition, give a like advantage to the growers of that commodity. The prohibition of the importation of foreign woollens is equally favourable to the woollen manufacturers. ① The silk manufacture, though altogether employed upon foreign materials, has lately obtained the same advantage. ②The linen manufacture has not yet obtained it, but is making great strides towards it. ③ Many other sorts of manufacturers have, in the same manner, obtained in Great Britain, either altogether, or very nearly a monopoly against their countrymen. The variety of goods of which the importation into Great Britain is prohibited, either absolutely, or under certain circumstances, greatly exceeds what can easily be suspected by those who are not well acquainted with the laws of the customs.

---

① [11 and 12 Ed. III., c. 3; 4Ed. IV., c. 7.]
② [6 Geo. III., c. 28.]
③ [By the additional duties, 7 Geo. III., c. 28.]

第二章 论对从外国进口的、在国内能生产的货物的限制

以征收高额关税或绝对禁止进口的办法限制从外国进口国内能够生产的货物,可以使国内从事生产这些货物的产业或多或少确保国内市场的垄断地位。例如,禁止从外国进口活牲畜和腌制食品的结果,就是确保英国牧畜业者对国内肉类市场的垄断。对谷物进口课以高额关税,就给予谷物生产者以同样的利益,因为在适当丰收的时候对谷物的进口课以高额关税,就等于禁止它的进口。对外国毛纺织品进口的禁止,同样有利于毛织品制造业。① 丝绸制造业所用的材料虽然全部产自国外,但近来也已取得了同样的利益。② 麻布制造业还没有取得这样的利益,但正在大踏步向这一目标迈进。③ 还有其他许多种类的制造业同样地在英国完全取得或几乎取得了不利于同胞们的垄断地位。英国所绝对禁止进口或在某些条件下禁止进口的货物,其种类之繁多,对那些关税法律不很熟悉的人来说很难猜想出来。

这种国内市场的独占,对享有独占权的各种产业往往给予很

---

① 爱德华三世十一、十二年第 3 号法令。乔治三世七年第 28 号法令。
② 乔治三世六年第 28 号法令。
③ 根据乔治三世七年第 27 号法令的附加税。

They encourage the particular industry, but neither increase general industry nor give it the best direction.	That this monopoly of the home-market frequently gives great encouragement to that particular species of industry which enjoys it, and frequently turns towards that employment a greater share of both the labour and stock of the society than would otherwise have gone to it, cannot be doubted. But whether it tends either to increase the general industry of the society, or to give it the most advantageous direction, is not, perhaps, altogether so evident.
The number of persons employed cannot exceed a certain proportion to the capital of the society,	The general industry of the society never can exceed what the capital of the society can employ. As the number of workmen that can be kept in employment by any particular person must bear a certain proportion to his capital, so the number of those that can be continually employed by all the members of a great society, must bear a certain proportion to the whole capital of that society, and never can exceed that proportion. No regulation of commerce can increase the quantity of industry in any society beyond what its capital can maintain. It can only divert a part of it into a direction into which it might not otherwise have gone; and it is by no means certain that this artificial direction is likely to be more advantageous to the society than that into which it would have gone of its own accord.
and every man's interest leads him to seek that employment of capital which is most advantageous to the society.	Every individual is continually exerting himself to find out the most advantageous employment for whatever capital he can command. It is his own advantage, indeed, and not that of the society, which he has in view. But the study of his own advantage naturally, or rather necessarily leads him to prefer that employment which is most advantageous to the society.
(I) He tries to employ it as near home as possible.	First, every individual endeavours to employ his capital as near home as he can, and consequently as much as he can in the support of domestic industry; provided always that he can thereby obtain the ordinary, or not a great deal less than the ordinary profits of stock. Thus, upon equal or nearly equal profits, every wholesale merchant naturally prefers the home-trade to the foreign trade of consumption, and the foreign trade of consumption to the carrying trade. In the home-trade his capital is never so long out of his sight as it frequently is in the foreign trade of consumption. He can know better the character and situation of the persons whom he trusts, and if he should happen to be deceived, he knows better the laws of the country

大的鼓励,并往往使社会在这种情况下有较大部分的劳动和资财转用到这方面来,那是毫无疑问的。但这个办法会不会增进社会的全部产业,会不会引导全部产业走上最有利的方向,也许并不是十分明显的。

社会全部的劳动绝不会超过社会资本所能维持的限度。任何个人所能雇用的工人人数必定和他的资本成一定比例,同样的,社会的一切成员所能够继续雇用的工人人数,也一定同这个社会的全部资本成一定比例,绝不会超过这个比例。任何商业法规都不可能使任何社会的产业量的增加超过其资本所能维持的限度。它只能够使本来没有纳入某一方向的一部分产业转到这个方向来。至于这个人为的方向是否比自然的方向更有利于社会,却不能确定。

各个人都不断地努力为他自己所能支配的资本找到最有利的用途。诚然,他所考虑的不是社会的利益,而是他自身的利益;但他对自身利益的研究自然或者极其必然地会引导他去选择一种最有利于社会的用途。

第一,每个人都想把他的资本投在尽可能接近他家乡的地方,因而都尽可能把资本用来维持国内产业;如果这样做他能够取得资本的正常利润,或稍微比正常利润少一些的利润。

所以,如果利润均等或几乎均等,每一个批发商人就都自然宁愿经营国内贸易而不愿经营消费品的国外贸易,宁愿经营消费品国外贸易而不愿经营运送贸易。投资经营消费品国外贸易,资本往往不在自己的监控之下,但投在国内贸易上的资本却常在自己的监控之下。他能够对所授信的人的品性和地位有更好的了解,即使偶然受骗,他也比较清楚地了解取得赔偿所必须依据的

from which he must seek redress. In the carrying trade, the capital of the merchant is, as it were, divided between two foreign countries, and no part of it is ever necessarily brought home, or placed under his own immediate view and command. The capital which an Amsterdam merchant employs in carrying corn from Konnigsberg to Lisbon, and fruit and wine from Lisbon to Konnigsberg, must generally be the one-half of it at Konnigsberg and the other half at Lisbon. No part of it need ever come to Amsterdam. The natural residence of such a merchant should either be at Konnigsberg or Lisbon, and it can only be some very particular circumstances which can make him prefer the residence of Amsterdam. The uneasiness, however, which he feels at being separated so far from his capital, generally determines him to bring part both of the Konnigsberg goods which he destines for the market of Lisbon, and of the Lisbon goods which he destines for that of Konnigsberg, to Amsterdam: and though this necessarily subjects him to a double charge of loading and unloading, as well as to the payment of some duties and customs, yet for the sake of having some part of his capital always under his own view and command, he willingly submits to this extraordinary charge; and it is in this manner that every country which has any considerable share of the carrying trade, becomes always the emporium, or general market, for the goods of all the different countries whose trade it carries on. The merchant, in order to save a second loading and unloading, endeavours always to sell in the home-market as much of the goods of all those different countries as he can, and thus, so far as he can, to convert his carrying trade into a foreign trade of consumption. A merchant, in the same manner, who is engaged in the foreign trade of consumption, when he collects goods for foreign markets, will always be glad, upon equal or nearly equal profits, to sell as great a part of them at home as he can. He saves himself the risk and trouble of exportation, when, so far as he can, he thus converts his foreign trade of consumption into a hometrade. Home is in this manner the center, if I may say so, round which the capitals of the inhabitants of every country are continually circulating, and towards which they are always tending, though by particular causes they may sometimes be driven off and repelled from it towards more distant employments. But a capital employed in the home-trade, it has already been shown, necessarily puts into motion a greater quantity of domestic industry, and gives revenue and employment to a greater number of the inhabitants of the country, than an equal capital employed in the foreign trade of con-

本国法律。至于运送贸易,商人的资本可以说分散在两个外国,任何一部分都没有必要带回本国或者必须由他自己亲自监控和支配。比如,阿姆斯特丹商人从克尼斯堡运送谷物至里斯本,从里斯本运送水果和葡萄酒至克尼斯堡,通常必须把他的资本的一半投在克尼斯堡,另一半投在里斯本。没有任何部分有流入阿姆斯特丹的必要。这样的商人自然应当住在克尼斯堡或里斯本,只有在某种非常特殊的情况下才会使他选择阿姆斯特丹作为他的住处。然而,由于远离资本而感到的不放心,往往促使他把本来要运往里斯本的克尼斯堡货物和要运往克尼斯堡的里斯本货物的一部分,不计装货卸货的双重费用,也不计税金和关税的支付,运往阿姆斯特丹。为了亲身监控和支配资本的若干部分,他自愿担负这种额外的费用。也正是由于这种情况,运送贸易占相当份额的国家才经常成为它通商各国货物的中心市场或总市场。为了免除第二次装货卸货的费用,商人总是尽量设法在本国市场售卖各国的货物,从而在可能的范围内尽量使运送贸易变为消费品国外贸易。同样,经营消费品国外贸易的商人,当收集货物准备运往外国市场时,总会愿意以均等或几乎均等的利润尽可能在国内售卖货物的一大部分。当他这样尽可能地使他的消费品国外贸易变为国内贸易时,他就可以避免承担出口的风险和麻烦。这样一来,要是我可以这样说的话,本国总是每一国家居民的资本不断绕之流通并经常趋向的中心,虽然由于特殊原因,这些资本有时从那些中心被赶出来,在更遥远地方使用。可是,我已经指出,投在国内贸易上的资本,同投在消费品国外贸易上的等量资本相比,必能推动更大规模的国内产业,使国内有更多的居民能够由此取得收入和就业机会。投在消费品国外贸易上的资本,同投在运送

国民财富的性质与原理

sumption; and one employed in the foreign trade of consumption has the same advantage over an equal capital employed in the carrying trade. Upon equal, or only nearly equal profits, therefore, every individual naturally inclines to employ his capital in the manner in which it is likely to afford the greatest support to domestic industry, and to give revenue and employment to the greatest number of people of his own country.

(2) He endeavours to produce the greatest possible value.

Secondly, every individual who employs his capital in the support of domestic industry, necessarily endeavours so to direct that industry, that its produce may be of the greatest possible value.

The produce of industry is what it adds to the subject or materials upon which it is employed. In proportion as the value of this produce is great or small, so will likewise be the profits of the employer. But it is only for the sake of profit that any man employs a capital in the support of industry; and he will always, therefore, endeavour to employ it in the support of that industry of which the produce is likely to be of the greatest value, or to exchange for the greatest quantity either of money or of other goods.

But the annual revenue of every society is always precisely equal to the exchangeable value of the whole annual produce of its industry, or rather is precisely the same thing with that exchangeable value. As every individual, therefore, endeavours as much as he can both to employ his capital in the support of domestic industry, and so to direct that industry that its produce may be of the greatest value; every individual necessarily labours to render the annual revenue of the society as great as he can. He generally, indeed, neither intends to promote the public interest, nor knows how much he is promoting it. By preferring the support of domestic to that of foreign industry, he intends only his own security; and by directing that industry in such a manner as its produce may be of the greatest value, he intends only his own gain, and he is in this, as in many other cases, led by an invisible hand to promote an end which was no part of his intention. Nor is it always the worse for the society that it was no part of it. By pursuing his own interest he frequently promotes that of the society more effectually than when he really intends to promote it. I have never known much good done by those who affected to trade for the public good. It is an affectation, indeed, not very common among merchants, and very few words need be employed in dissuading them

贸易上的等量资本相比,也有同样的优点。所以,在利润均等或几乎均等的情况下,每个个人自然会运用他的资本来给国内产业提供最大的援助,使本国尽量多的居民获得收入和就业机会。

第二,每个个人把资本用以支持国内产业,必然会努力指导那种产业,使其生产物尽可能有最大的价值。

(2)他会努力提供生产最大可能的价值。

劳动的结果是劳动对其对象或对施以劳动的原材料所增加的东西。劳动者利润的大小,同这些生产物的价值大小成比例。但是,把资本用来支持产业的人,即以牟取利润为唯一目的,他自然总会努力使他用其资本所支持的产业的生产物能具有最大价值,换言之,能交换最大数量的货币或其他货物。

但每个社会的年收入,总是与其产业的全部年产出的交换价值恰好相等,或者更恰当地说,与那种交换价值恰好是同一种东西。所以,由于每个人都努力把他的资本尽可能用来支持国内产业,都努力经营管理国内产业,以便使其产出价值能达到最大化;他就必然努力促使社会年收入尽可能地大。确实,他通常既不打算促进公共利益,也不知道他自己是在什么程度上促进这种公共利益。由于宁愿投资支持国内产业而不支持国外产业,他只是盘算他自己的安全;由于他经营管理产业的方式目的在于使其产出价值能够最大化,他所盘算的也只是他自己的利益。在这种情况下,像在其他许多情况一样,他受着一只看不见的手的支配,去尽力达到一个并非他本意所想要达到的目的。也并不因为事非出于本意,就对社会有害。他追求自己的利益,往往使他能比在真正出于本意的情况下更有效地促进社会的利益。我从来没有听说过,那些假装为公众福祉而经营贸易的人做了多少好事。事实上,这种装模作样的神态在商人中间并不普遍,用不着多费口舌

国民财富的性质与原理

from it.

<small>He can judge of this much better than the statesman.</small> What is the species of domestic industry which his capital can employ, and of which the produce is likely to be of the greatest value, every individual, it is evident, can, in his local situation, judge much better than any statesman or lawgiver can do for him. The statesman, who should attempt to direct private people in what manner they ought to employ their capitals, would not only load himself with a most unnecessary attention, but assume an authority which could safely be trusted, not only to no single person, but to no council or senate whatever, and which would no-where be so dangerous as in the hands of a man who had folly and presumption enough to fancy himself fit to exercise it.

<small>High duties and prohibitions direct people to employ capital in producing at me what they could buy cheaper from abroad.</small> To give the monopoly of the home-market to the produce of domestic industry, in any particular art or manufacture, is in some measure to direct private people in what manner they ought to employ their capitals, and must, in almost all cases, be either a useless or a hurtful regulation. If the produce of domestic can be brought there as cheap as that of foreign industry, the regulation is evidently useless. If it cannot, it must generally be hurtful. It is the maxim of every prudent master of a family, never to attempt to make at home what it will cost him more to make than to buy. The taylor does not attempt to make his own shoes, but buys them of the shoemaker. The shoemaker does not attempt to make his own clothes, but employs a taylor. The farmer attempts to make neither the one nor the other, but employs those different artificers. All of them find it for their interest to employ their whole industry in a way in which they have some advantage over their neighbours, and to purchase with a part of its produce, or what is the same thing, with the price of a part of it, whatever else they have occasion for.

What is prudence in the conduct of every private family, can scarce be folly in that of a great kingdom. If a foreign country can supply us with a commodity cheaper than we ourselves can make it,

第四篇 第二章

去劝阻他们。

关于可以把资本用在什么类型的国内产业，其产出价值才能够取得最大化这一问题上面，每一个人根据他所处的位置，显然比政治家或立法者能够更好地做出判断。如果政治家企图指导私人应如何运用他们的资本，那不仅是自寻烦恼地去关注那些并不需要他们关注的问题，而且僭取了一种不能放心地委托给任何个人、也不能放心地委托给与任何委员会或参议院的权力。把这种权力交给一个大言不惭地、荒唐地自认为有资格行使的人，那是再危险不过的。

> 他可以比政治家做出更好的判断。

在任何特定的工艺或制造业里，为了赋予国内产业的产品在国内市场的垄断地位，就是在某种程度上指导私人应如何运用他们的资本，而这种指导管制几乎毫无例外的必定是无用的或有害的。如果本国产业的产品在国内市场上的价格同外国产业的产品一样低廉，这种管制显然无用。如果价格不能一样低廉，那么一般地说，这种管制必定是有害的。如果一件物品在购买时所花费的代价比在家内生产时所花费的小，那么就永远不会想要在家内生产，这是每一个精明的家长都知道的格言。裁缝不想制作他自己的鞋子，而向鞋匠购买。鞋匠不想制作他自己的衣服，而雇用裁缝制作。农场主不想缝衣，也不想制鞋，而宁愿雇用那些不同的工匠去做。他们都感到，为了他们自身的利益，应当把他们的全部精力集中使用到比邻人处于某种有利地位的方面，而以劳动生产物的一部分或同样的东西，即其一部分的价格，购买他们所需要的其他任何物品。

> 高税上制人资在从购国产品比国产品宜的生产上。收关禁止管口进和征额的指导把用那些外国买内更有便商品的指那

在每一个私人家庭的行为中是精明的事情，在一个大国的行为中就很少成为荒唐的事情。如果外国供应给我们的商品比我

— 977 —

国民财富的性质与原理

<small>It is as foolish for a nation as for an individual to make what can be bought cheaper.</small> better buy it of them with some part of the produce of our own industry, employed in a way in which we have some advantage. The general industry of the country, being always in proportion to the capital which employs it, will not thereby be diminished, no more than that of the above-mentioned artificers; but only left to find out the way in which it can be employed with the greatest advantage. It is certainly not employed to the greatest advantage, when it is thus directed towards an object which it can buy cheaper than it can make. The value of its annual produce is certainly more or less diminished, when it is thus turned away from producing commodities evidently of more value than the commodity which it is directed to produce. According to the supposition, that commodity could be purchased from foreign countries cheaper than it can be made at home. It could, therefore, have been purchased with a part only of the commodities, or, what is the same thing, with a part only of the price of the commodities, which the industry employed by an equal capital would have produced at home, had it been left to follow its natural course. The industry of the country, therefore, is thus turned away from a more, to a less advantageous employment, and the exchangeable value of its annual produce, instead of being increased, according to the intention of the lawgiver, must necessarily be diminished by every such regulation.

<small>a manufacture may be established earlier than it would otherwise have been, but this would make capital accumulate slower.</small> By means of such regulations, indeed, a particular manufacture may sometimes be acquired sooner than it could have been otherwise, and after a certain time may be made at home as cheap or cheaper than in the foreign country. But though the industry of the society may be thus carried with advantage into a particular channel sooner than it could have been otherwise, it will by no means follow that the sum total, either of its industry, or of its revenue, can ever be augmented by any such regulation. The industry of the society can augment only in proportion as its capital augments, and its capital can augment only in proportion to what can be gradually saved out of its revenue. But the immediate effect of every such regulation is to diminish its revenue, and what diminishes its revenue is certainly not very likely to augment its capital faster than it would have augmented of its own accord, had both capital and industry been left to find out their natural employments.

Though for want of such regulations the society should never acquire the proposed manufacture, it would not, upon that account, necessarily be the poorer in any one period of its duration. In every period of its duration its whole capital and industry might still have

们自己制造的还便宜,我们最好还是使用那些我们在生产上有利的自己产业的一部分物品向他们购买。国家的总劳动既然总是与维持它的产业资本成比例,也就绝不会因此减少,正如上述工匠的劳动并不减少一样,只不过顺其自然寻找最有利的用途而已。要是把劳动用在生产那些购买比自己制造还便宜的商品上,那一定不是最为有利的使用。劳动不用在明显比政府指导的生产用途更有价值的商品的生产上,那么一定或多或少会减少其年产出的价值。根据假设,向外国购买这种商品,所花费比国内制造便宜。所以,如果听其自然,仅以等量资本雇用劳动,在国内所生产商品的一部分或其价格的一部分,就可以把这些商品购买进来。因此,上述管制的结果使国家的劳动由较有利的用途转移到较为不利的用途上;其年产出的交换价值不但没有按照立法者的意愿有所增加,而且一定还会减少下去。

个人与国家一样,自己能生产的那些商品都可以从外购买更便宜是明智的。

诚然,由于有了这种管制,特定制造业有时能比没有此种管制时更加迅速地成长起来,而且经过一段时间,能在国内以同样低廉或更低廉的费用制造这些特定商品。不过,由于有了此种管制,尽管社会的劳动可以更为迅速地流入有利的特定用途上,但劳动和收入总额却都不能增加。社会的劳动只能按社会资本增加的比例而增加;社会资本的增加又与社会能够从社会收入中逐渐节省的多少成比例。而上述那种管制的直接结果是减少社会的收入;凡是减少社会收入的措施,一定不会迅速增加社会资本;要是听任资本和劳动寻找自然的用途,社会的资本自然会迅速地增加。

有了这种管制,它比没有管制能更快地成长起来,资本很,

没有那种管制,特定制造业虽然不能在这社会上确立起来,但在其发展的任何时期内,社会并不因此而更为贫穷。在社会发

and the country might always be just as rich if it never acquired the manufacture. been employed, though upon different objects, in the manner that was most advantageous at the time. In every period its revenue might have been the greatest which its capital could afford, and both capital and revenue might have been augmented with the greatest possible rapidity.

No one proposes that a country should strive against great natural advantages, but it is also absurd to strive against smaller advantages whether natural or acquired. The natural advantages which one country has over another in producing particular commodities are sometimes so great, that it is acknowledged by all the world to be in vain to struggle with them. By means of glasses, hotbeds, and hotwalls, very good grapes can be raised in Scotland, and very good wine too can be made of them at about thirty times the expence for which at least equally good can be brought from foreign countries. Would it be a reasonable law to prohibit the importation of all foreign wines, merely to encourage the making of claret and burgundy in Scotland ? But if there would be a manifest absurdity in turning towards any employment, thirty times more of the capital and industry of the country, than would be necessary to purchase from foreign countries an equal quantity of the commodities wanted, there must be an absurdity, though not altogether so glaring, yet exactly of the same kind, in turning towards any such employment a thirtieth, or even a three hundredth part more of either. Whether the advantages which one country has over another, be natural or acquired, is in this respect of no consequence. As long as the one country has those advantages, and the other wants them, it will always be more advantageous for the latter, rather to buy of the former than to make. It is an acquired advantage only, which one artificer has over his neighbour, who exercises another trade; and yet they both find it more advantageous to buy of one another, than to make what does not belong to their particular trades.

Merchants and manufacturers get the most benefit from high duties and prohibitions. Merchants and manufacturers are the people who derive the greatest advantage from this monopoly of the home-market. The prohibition of the importation of foreign cattle, and of salt provisions, together with the high duties upon foreign corn, which in times of moderate plenty amount to a prohibition, are not near so advantageous to the graziers and farmers of Great Britain, as other regulations of the same kind are to its merchants and manufacturers. Manufactures, those of the finer kind especially, are more easily transported from one country

展的任何时期内,虽然社会全部资本与劳动使用的对象并不相同,但仍有可能使用在当时最有利的用途上。在每一个时期内,其收入可能是资本所能提供的最大收入,而资本与收入也许以可能快的速度增加。

> 如果国家并不扶持制造业,那么国家也会一样富裕。

有时,在某些特定商品的生产上,某一国拥有非常大的自然优势,以致全世界都认为,跟这种优势进行斗争全无用处。通过安装玻璃、建设温床和暖壁,苏格兰也能栽种出很好的葡萄,并酿造出很好的葡萄酒,其费用大约 30 倍于从外国购买的品质至少同样好的葡萄酒。仅仅为了要奖励苏格兰酿造波尔多和布冈迪红葡萄酒,便以法律禁止一切外国葡萄酒进口,这难道合理吗?但是,如果苏格兰不向外国购买它所需要的一定数量的葡萄酒,而用比购买所需的多 30 倍的资本和劳动来自己制造,显然是不合理的,那么即使所使用的资本与劳动,仅仅多 1/30,或甚至仅多 1/300,那也是不合理的,不合理的程度虽然没有那么惊人,但同样是完全不合理的。至于一国比另一国所拥有的优势地位,无论是固有的还是后来获得的,在这个方面无关紧要。只要甲国拥有这种优势,乙国没有这种优势,乙国向甲国购买,总是比自己制造有利。一种技艺的工匠比另一种技艺的工匠所拥有的优越地位,只是后来获得的,但他们两者都认为,互相交换彼此产品比自己制造更有利。

> 没有人应该对那些拥有明显较大优势的国家进行的手工业进行较小数量荒唐可笑的,无论这种优势是固有还是后天获得的。

从垄断国内市场取得最大好处的是商人与制造业者。禁止外国牲畜和腌制食品的进口,以及对外国谷物课以高额关税(这在正常丰收年份就等于禁止进口),虽然有利于英国牧畜业者和农场主,但其有利程度比不上商人和制造业者从同类限制中所获取的利益。制造品,尤其是精细制造品,比谷物和牲畜更容易于

> 商人和制造业者从征收高额关税和禁止进口的管制中收益最大。

to another than corn or cattle. It is in the fetching and carrying manufactures, accordingly, that foreign trade is chiefly employed. In manufactures, a very small advantage will enable foreigners to undersell our own workmen, even in the home market. It will require a very great one to enable them to do so in the rude produce of the soil. If the free importation of foreign manufactures were permitted, several of the home manufactures would probably suffer, and some of them, perhaps, go to ruin altogether, and a considerable part of the stock and industry at present employed in them, would be forced to find out some other employment. But the freest importation of the rude produce of the soil could have no such effect upon the agriculture of the country.

<small>The free importation of foreign cattle would make no great difference to British graziers.</small>   If the importation of foreign cattle, for example, were made ever so free, so few could be imported, that the grazing trade of Great Britain could be little affected by it. Live cattle are, perhaps, the only commodity of which the transportation is more expensive by sea than by land. By land they carry themselves to market. By sea, not only the cattle, but their food and their water too, must be carried at no small expence and inconveniency. The short sea between Ireland and Great Britain, indeed, renders the importation of Irish cattle more easy. But though the free importation of them, which was lately permitted only for a limited time, were rendered perpetual, it could have no considerable effect upon the interest of the graziers of Great Britain. Those parts of Great Britain which border upon the Irish sea are all grazing countries. Irish cattle could never be imported for their use, but must be drove through those very extensive countries, at no small expence and inconveniency, before they could arrive at their proper market. Fat cattle could not be drove so far. Lean cattle, therefore, only could be imported, and such importation could interfere, not with the interest of the feeding or fattening countries, to which, by reducing the price of lean cattle, it would rather be advantageous, but with that of the breeding countries only. The small number of Irish cattle imported since their importation was permitted, together with the good price at which lean cattle still continue to sell, seem to demonstrate that even the breeding countries of Great Britain are never likely to be much affected by the free importation of Irish

从一个国家运至另一个国家。所以,国外贸易通常以贩卖制造品为主要业务。在制造品方面,只要有一点点利益,甚至在国内市场上,也能使外国人以低于我国工人的产品价格出售。但在土地原产物方面,只有很大的好处才能做到这种地步。如果在这种情况下准许外国制造品自由进口,也许有几种国内制造业会受其损害,也许有几种国内制造业会完全毁灭,结果大部分资本与劳动将离开现在用途,被迫寻找其他用途。但土地原产物最自由的进口却不能对本国农业发生这样的影响。

例如,即使牲畜的进口也变得那么自由,但由于能够进口的很少,所以对英国牧畜业没有多大影响。活牲畜,恐怕是海运比陆路运输费用昂贵的唯一商品。因为牲畜能够行走,陆运时牲畜能自己搬运自己。但通过海运则被输运的不仅是牲畜,而且还有牲畜所需的食料和饮料,需要花费许多钱,还有许多不方便之处。由于爱尔兰和不列颠之间的海上距离很短,所以爱尔兰牲畜的进口比较容易。最近仅仅允许爱尔兰牲畜在有限时期内自由进口,但如果允许其永久地自由进口,对不列颠畜牧业者的利益也不会有很大影响。不列颠靠近爱尔兰海的地方都是牧场。进口的爱尔兰牲畜很少,因为必须赶过广大的地方才能到达适当的市场,所费不菲,而且还有很多麻烦。肥胖的牲畜不能行走那么远,所以只有干瘦的牲畜可以进口;这种进口不会损害饲养牲畜或育肥牲畜的地方的利益,因为瘦牲畜的价值有所降低,所以对这些地方是有利的,这种进口只会损害繁育牲畜地方的利益。自从爱尔兰牲畜准许进口以来,爱尔兰牲畜运入不多,而瘦牲畜售价依然高昂这一事实,似乎足以证明,就连不列颠繁育牲畜的地方也不一定会受到爱尔兰牲畜自由进口很大的影响。据说,爱尔兰的普

牲畜自由进口对英国牧畜业者影响不大。

cattle. The common people of Ireland, indeed, are said to have sometimes opposed with violence the exportation of their cattle. But if the exporters had found any great advantage in continuing the trade, they could easily, when the law was on their side, have conquered this mobbish opposition.

It might even benefit the cultivated plains at the expense of the rugged mountainous districts

Feeding and fattening countries, besides, must always be highly improved, whereas breeding countries are generally uncultivated. The high price of lean cattle, by augmenting the value of uncultivated land, is like a bounty against improvement. To any country which was highly improved throughout, it would be more advantageous to import its lean cattle than to breed them. The province of Holland, accordingly, is said to follow this maxim at present. The mountains of Scotland, Wales and Northumberland, indeed, are countries not capable of much improvement, and seem destined by nature to be the breeding countries of Great Britain. The freest importation of foreign cattle could have no other effect than to hinder those breeding countries from taking advantage of the increasing population and improvement of the rest of the kingdom, from raising their price to an exorbitant height, and from laying a real tax upon all the more improved and cultivated parts of the country.

The free importation of salt provisions also would make little difference to the graziers,

The freest importation of salt provisions, in the same manner, could have as little effect upon the interest of the graziers of Great Britain as that of live cattle. Salt provisions are not only a very bulky commodity, but when compared with fresh meat, they are a commodity both of worse quality, and as they cost more labour and expence, of higher price. They could never, therefore, come into competition with the fresh meat, though they might with the salt provisions of the country. They might be used for victualling ships for distant voyages, and such like uses, but could never make any considerable part of the food of the people. The small quantity of salt provisions imported from Ireland since their importation was rendered free, is an experimental proof that our graziers have nothing to apprehend from it. It does not appear that the price of butcher's-meat has ever been sensibly affected by it.

Even the free importation of foreign corn could very little affect the interest of the farmers of Great Britain. Corn is a much more bulky commodity than butcher's-meat. A pound of wheat at a penny is as

通人民，对于牲畜的出口有时曾加以强烈地反对。但是，出口者如果觉得继续出口牲畜有很大利益，那么在有法律支持他们时，他们要克服爱尔兰群众的反对是很容易的。

此外，饲养和育肥牲畜的地方，必定都是那些已经大加改良的地方，而繁殖牲畜的地方却通常是未加开垦的地方。由于提高瘦畜的价格增加了未加开垦土地的价值，这等于是反对土地改良的奖金。对于全境都已经大加改良的地方，进口瘦牲畜比繁殖瘦畜更为有利。因此，现在的荷兰据说遵循了这个原理。苏格兰、威尔士及诺森伯兰的山地，都是些不能够进行多大改良的地方，并且看来先天注定要作为不列颠的繁畜场。准许外国牲畜自由进口，其唯一结果不过是禁止那些国内繁育牲畜的地方利用联合王国其他地方人口日益增加与土地改良的好处，使他们不能把牲畜价格抬高到非常高的水平，不能对国内土地改良较好和已经开垦过的地方课征一种真实的税收。

牲畜自由进口牲畜不山区益，对改平来畜的进口在崎岖的牺牲利平前提下，已经良的原带处。

像活牲畜一样，腌制食品最自由的进口，也不能对不列颠畜牧业者的利益有多大影响。腌制食品，不仅是笨重的商品，而且与鲜肉比较，其品质较差；其价格又因所需劳动和费用较多而比较昂贵。所以，这种腌制食品，虽然能够与本国的腌制食品相竞争，但绝不能与本国的鲜肉相竞争。它虽然可以用作远洋航轮上的食品和类似用途，但在人民的食品中毕竟不占很大部分。自从准许腌制食品自由进口以来，从爱尔兰进口的腌制食品数量仍然不多这一事实，是我国牧畜业者丝毫不用恐惧这种自由进口的实证。家畜的价格似乎不曾显著地受到它的影响。

腌制食品的自由进口对畜牧业者的影响不大。

即使进口了外国谷物，也不会对不列颠农场主的利益产生多大影响。谷物是比家畜肉类笨重得多的商品。四便士一磅的家

dear as a pound of butcher's-meat at four-pence. The small quantity of foreign corn imported even in times of the greatest scarcity, may satisfy our farmers that they can have nothing to fear from the freest importation. The average quantity imported one year with another, amounts only, according to the very well informed author of the tracts upon the corn trade, to twenty-three thousand seven hundred and twenty-eight quarters of all sorts of grain, and does not exceed the five hundredth and seventy-one part of the annual consumption. ① But as the bounty upon corn occasions a greater exportation in years of plenty, so it must of consequence occasion a greater importation in years of scarcity, than in the actual state of tillage would otherwise take place. By means of it, the plenty of one year does not compensate the scarcity of another, and as the average quantity exported is necessarily augmented by it, so must likewise, in the actual state of tillage, the average quantity imported. If there were no bounty, as less corn would be exported, so it is probable that, one year with another, less would be imported than at present. The corn merchants, the fetchers and carriers of corn between Great Britain and foreign countries, would have much less employment, and might suffer considerably; but the country gentlemen and farmers could suffer very little. It is in the corn merchants accordingly, rather than in the country gentlemen and farmers, that I have observed the greatest anxiety for the renewal and continuation of the bounty.

Country gentlemen and farmers are, to their great honour, of all people, the least subject to the wretched spirit of monopoly. The undertaker of a great manufactory is sometimes alarmed if another work of the same kind is established within twenty miles of him. The Dutch undertaker of the woollen manufacture at Abbeville stipulated, that no work of the same kind should be established within thirty leagues of that city. Farmers and country gentlemen, on the contrary, are generally disposed rather to promote than to obstruct the cultivation and improvement of their neighbours farms and estates. They have no secrets, such as those of the greater part of manufacturers, but are generally rather fond of communicating to their neighbours, and of

---

① [Charles Smith, *Three Tracts on the Corn-Trade and Corn-Laws*, pp. 144-145. The same figure is quoted below, vol. ii.]

畜肉与一便士一磅的小麦一样昂贵。甚至在大灾荒年份里,进口的外国谷物为数也不多这一事实,可消除我国农场主对外国谷物自由进口的恐惧。根据知识渊博的谷物贸易研究者的论文,平均每年进口的各种谷物量,总共不过 23,729 夸特,只占本国消费额的 1/571。① 但由于谷物奖金在丰收年份导致了超过实际耕种水平所能够容许的出口量,所以在歉收年份,必然导致超过实际耕种水平所容许的进口量。这样一来,今年的丰收不能补偿明年的歉收。平均出口量一定因为这种奖金而增大,所以平均进口量也必定因为这种奖金而增大,超过实际耕种水平所需要进口的程度。要是没有奖金,那么出口的谷物将比现在少,因此逐年平均计算,进口量也许比现在少。换句话说,谷物商人与在英国和其他国家之间贩运谷物的人,将因此而失去许多生意,遭受很大损失,但就乡绅和农业家来说,吃亏却极其有限,所以我曾说,最希望奖金制度继续实行下去的人,不是乡绅与农业家,而是谷物商人。

在所有人民中,乡绅与农场主算是卑劣的垄断精神最少的一类人,这对他们来说是莫大的光荣。如果大制造业主发觉附近20英里内新建了一个同类工厂,有时会惊慌起来。在阿比维尔经营毛纺织品制造业的荷兰人,规定在该城市周围 60 英里内不许建设同类工厂。相反的是,农场主与乡绅却通常愿意促进邻近各个田庄的开垦与改良,不会加以阻止。大部分制造业者都有要严守的秘密,而他们却没有什么秘密,如果他们发现了有利的新方法,

---

① 查理·史密斯:《谷物贸易和谷物法的三契约》,第 144~145 页。这个数字还在第 2 卷中引用了。

extending as far as possible any new practice which they have found to be advantageous. *Pius Questus*, says old Cato, *stabilissimusque, minimeque invidiosus*; *minimeque male cogitantes sunt, qui in eo studio occupati sunt*. Country gentlemen and farmers, dispersed in different parts of the country, cannot so easily combine as merchants and manufacturers, who being collected into towns, and accustomed to that exclusive corporation spirit which prevails in them, naturally endeavour to obtain against all their countrymen, the same exclusive privilege which they generally possess against the inhabitants of their respective towns. They accordingly seem to have been the original inventors of those restraints upon the importation of foreign goods, which secure to them the monopoly of the home-market. It was probably in imitation of them, and to put themselves upon a level with those who, they found, were disposed to oppress them, that the country gentlemen and farmers of Great Britain so far forgot the generosity which is natural to their station, as to demand the exclusive privilege of supplying their countrymen with corn and butcher's-meat. They did not perhaps take time to consider, how much less their interest could be affected by the freedom of trade, than that of the people whose example they followed.

<small>The prohibition of foreign corn and cattle restrains the population.</small>

To prohibit by a perpetual law the importation of foreign corn and cattle, is in reality to enact, that the population and industry of the country shall at no time exceed what the rude produce of its own soil can maintain.

<small>There are two cases which are exceptional,</small>

There seem, however, to be two cases in which it will generally be advantageous to lay some burden upon foreign, for the encouragement of domestic industry.

The first is, when some particular sort of industry is necessary for the defence of the country. The defence of Great Britain, for example, depends very much upon the number of its sailors and shipping. The act of navigation,① therefore, very properly endeavours to give the sailors and shipping of Great Britain the monopoly of the trade of their own country, in some cases, by absolute prohibitions, and in others by heavy burdens upon the shipping of foreign countries. The following are the principal dispositions of this act.

<small>(1) when a particular industry is necessary for the defence of the country, like shipping, which is properly encouraged by the act of navigation,</small>

First, all ships, of which the owners, masters, and three-fourths of the mariners are not British subjects, are prohibited, upon pain of

---

① [12 Car. Ⅱ., c. 18, 'An act for the encouraging and increasing of shipping ano navigation.']

他们一般都喜欢把这方法告诉他们邻人,并与他们交流,而且尽可能来推广它。老伽图曾说:这是最受人尊敬的职业,从事这种职业的人生活最为稳定,最不为人忌恨,他们也最没有不满的思想。乡绅与农业家,散居在国内各地,不易于联合起来;商人与制造业者却聚居于城内,容易联合。他们都沾染有城市所盛行的同业专营的习气,他们一般都取得了违反各城市居民利益的专营特权,自然竭力设法取得违反所有本国人利益的专营特权。确保对国内市场的垄断和限制外国货物进口的方法,似乎就是他们的发明。乡绅和农场主忘却他们本人自然所应有的宽大心怀,起来要求谷物和家畜肉供应的专营权;也许是模仿商人和制造业者,而且鉴于他们有意强迫自己要和他们居于同等的地位。至于自由贸易对他们利益的影响比对商人和制造业者利益的影响小得多这一问题上,他们也许没花工夫去考虑。

<small>禁止谷物和牲畜进口会限制人口的增加。</small>

以永久的法律禁止谷物和牲畜的进口,实际上等于规定,一国的人口与产业永远不得超过本国土地原产物所能维持的限度。

<small>有两种情况例外,</small>

但是,给外国产业增加若干负担来奖励国内产业,似乎一般只在下述两种情况下是有利的。

第一,为国防所必需的特定产业。例如,大不列颠的国防,在很大程度上取决于它有多少海员与船只。所以,大不列颠的航海法,①当然力图通过绝对禁止或对外国航船课以重税来使本国海员和船舶垄断本国航运业。航海法的规定内容大致如下:

<small>(1)当这项特殊的产业是国防所需的产业时,如航海法所鼓励的航运业,</small>

一、凡是与大不列颠本土和殖民地通商或在大不列颠沿岸经商的船舶,其船主、船长及3/4船员必须为英国国籍臣民,违反者

---

① 查理二世十二年第18号法令"鼓励和扩大船运和航海的法令"。

forfeiting ship and cargo, from trading to the British settlements and plantations, or from being employed in the coasting trade of Great Britain.

Secondly, a great variety of the most bulky articles of importation can be brought into Great Britain only, either in such ships as are above described, or in ships of the country where those goods are produced, and of which the owners, masters, and three-fourths of the mariners, are of that particular country; and when imported even in ships of this latter kind, they are subject to double aliens duty. If imported in ships of any other country, the penalty is forfeiture of ship and goods. ① When this act was made, the Dutch were, what they still are, the great carriers of Europe, and by this regulation they were entirely excluded from being the carriers to Great Britain, or from importing to us the goods of any other European country.

Thirdly, a great variety of the most bulky articles of importation are prohibited from being imported, even in British ships, from any country but that in which they are produced; under pain of forfeiting ship and cargo. ② This regulation too was probably intended against the Dutch. Holland was then, as now, the great emporium for all European goods, and by this regulation British ships were hindered from loading in Holland the goods of any other European country.

Fourthly, salt fish of all kinds, whale-fins, whale-bone, oil, and blubber, not caught by and cured on board British vessels, when imported into Great Britain, are subjected to double aliens duty. The Dutch, as they are still the principal, were then the only fishers in Europe that attempted to supply foreign nations with fish. By this regulation, a very heavy burden was laid upon their supplying Great Britain.

a wise act, though dictated by animosity,

When the act of navigation was made, though England and Holland were not actually at war, the most violent animosity subsisted between the two nations. It had begun during the government of the long

---

① [Eds. 1 and 2 read 'ship and cargo'. The alteration was probably made in order to avoid wearisome repetition of the same phrase in the three paragraphs.]

② [which, however, applies to all such goods of foreign growth and manufacture as were forbidden to be imported except in English ships, not only to bulky goods. The words 'great variety of the most bulky articles of importation' occur at the beginning of the previous paragraph, and are perhaps copied here by mistake.]

第四篇　第二章

将被没收船舶及其装载的货物。

二、大量大宗进口品只能由上述船舶或由商品出产国的船舶（其船主、船长及 3/4 船员为该国人民）进口到大不列颠，但由后一类船舶进口必须征收加倍的外籍税。若由其他船舶进口，则处以没收船舶及其所装载商品[①]的惩罚。该法令颁布时，荷兰人是欧洲的大宗货物运输者，它现在仍是欧洲的大宗运输者。但这项法令公布以后，他们再不能做大不列颠的大宗货物运输者，再也不能把欧洲其他各国的货物进口到我国。

三、有许多大宗笨重进口品，只允许由货物出产国船舶进口，连使用英国船舶运送也在禁止之列，违反者将被没收船舶及其所装载货物。[②] 这项规定可能也是专为荷兰人而设。荷兰那时与现在一样，是欧洲各种货物的大市场，有了这个条例，英国船舶就不能在荷兰国境内启运欧洲其他各国的货物。

四、各种腌鱼、鲸须、鲸鳍、鲸油、鲸脂，如果不是由英国船只捕获和调制，在输入不列颠时必须征收加倍的外籍税。那时欧洲以捕鱼业所提供的鱼来供应其他国家的，只有荷兰人，现在主要仍然是荷兰人。有了这个条例，他们向英国供应鱼，就必须缴纳极重的税收。

这部航海法制定的时候，英、荷两国虽然没有处于交战状态，但两国之间的仇恨已经到了极点。在制定这部法律的长期议会尽管是出于仇恨而颁布的，但也是一部明智的法律，

---

① 在第一版和第二版是"船只和货物"。更改的目的在于在这三段里避免重复。

② 不仅适用于笨重物品，也适用于那些除了用英国船只运输以外被禁止的外国制造产品。"大量大宗笨重物品的输入"一词在前一段的开始印刷有误，在这里又再一次印刷错误。

— 991 —

parliament, which first framed this act,① and it broke out soon afterin the Dutch wars during that of the Protector and of Charles the Second. It is not impossible, therefore, that some of the regulations of this famous act may have proceeded from national animosity. They are as wise, however, as if they had all been dictated by the most deliberate wisdom. National animosity at that particular time aimed at the very same object which the most deliberate wisdom would have recommended, the diminution of the naval power of Holland, the only naval power which could endanger the security of England.

<small>and unfavourable to foreign commerce;</small> The act of navigation is not favourable to foreign commerce, or to the growth of that opulence which can arise from it. The interest of a nation in its commercial relations to foreign nations is, like that of a merchant with regard to the different people with whom he deals, to buy as cheap and to sell as dear as possible. But it will be most likely to buy cheap, when by the most perfect freedom of trade it encourages all nations to bring to it the goods which it has occasion to purchase; and, for the same reason, it will be most likely to sell dear, when its markets are thus filled with the greatest number of buyers. The act of navigation, it is true, lays no burden upon foreign ships that come to export the produce of British industry. Even the ancient aliens duty, which used to be paid upon all goods exported as well as imported, has, by several subsequent acts, been taken off from the greater part of the articles of exportation.② But if foreigners, either by prohibitions or high duties, are hindered from coming to sell, they cannot always afford to come to buy; because coming without a cargo, they must lose the freight from their own country to Great Britain. By diminishing the number of sellers, therefore, we necessarily diminish that of buyers, and are thus likely not only to buy foreign goods dearer, but to sell our own cheaper, than if there was a more perfect freedom of trade. As defence, however, is of much more importance

---

① [In 1651, by 'An act for the increase of shipping and encouragement of the navigation of this nation,' p. 1, 449 in the collection of Commonwealth Acts.]

② [By 25 Car. Ⅱ., c. 6, § 1, except on coal. The plural 'acts' may refer to renewing acts. Anderson, *Commerce*, A. D. 1672.]

统治时期①,这种仇恨已经开始,不久在克伦威尔王朝及查理二世王朝的荷兰战争中爆发了出来。所以,说这个有名的法令有几款法条是从民族仇恨出发的,也不是不可能的。但这些法条却是像深思熟虑的结果一样明智。当时的民族仇恨,以削弱唯一可能危害英格兰安全的荷兰海军力量为其目的,这和经过最冷静的深思熟虑所想出来的恰好相同。

航海法对国外贸易或对引起的财富增长是不利的。在一国对外国的通商贸易关系中,与个别商人对他所交易的人的关系一样,以贱买贵卖为有利。但是,在贸易完全自由的情况下,一个国家最可能有贱买的机会,因为贸易完全自由,鼓励一切国家把它所需要的物品运到它那边去。由于同一原因,它也最可能贵卖,因为买者聚集于它的市场,货物售价尽可能地提高。诚然,航海法不对来到英国并出口英国产出的外国船只征税。甚至过去出口货物和进口货物通常都要缴纳的外籍税,由于以后颁布的若干法令,大部分出口品就不再缴纳该项税收;但这一切都不足减轻航海法对国外贸易的有害倾向。② 外国人如果因为受到禁止或被课以高额关税,不能来到本国销售,也不能来购买。空船来我国装货的外国人,势必损失从他们国家到大不列颠的船费。所以减少销售者人数也就是减少购买者人数。这样,与贸易完全自由的时候相比较,我们不仅在购买外国货物时要买得更贵,而且在销售本国货物时要卖得更加便宜。但是,由于国防比国富要重要

和不利于国外贸易;

---

① 在 1651 年,依据"国家航海鼓励和船运增长法案",收在英联邦法律集里。

② 根据查理二世二十五年第 6 号法令第 1 节,煤炭除外。其他后来的法令可能指的是重新更定的法律。见安德森的《商业》,1672 年。

— 993 —

than opulence, the act of navigation is, perhaps, the wisest of all the commercial regulations of England.

<small>and (2) when there is a tax on the produce of the like home manufacture.</small>

The second case, in which it will generally be advantageous to lay some burden upon foreign for the encouragement of domestic industry, is, when some tax is imposed at home upon the produce of the latter. In this case, it seems reasonable that an equal tax should be imposed upon the like produce of the former. This would not give the monopoly of the home market to domestic industry, nor turn towards a particular employment a greater share of the stock and labour of the country, than what would naturally go to it. It would only hinder any part of what would naturally go to it from being turned away by the tax, into a less natural direction, and would leave the competition between foreign and domestic industry, after the tax, as nearly as possible upon the same footing as before it. In Great Britain, when any such tax is laid upon the produce of domestic industry, it is usual at the same time, in order to stop the clamorous complaints of our merchants and manufacturers, that they will be undersold at home, to lay a much heavier duty upon the importation of all foreign goods of the same kind.

<small>Some people say that this principle justifies a general imposition of duties on imports to counterbalance taxes levied at home on necessaries,</small>

This second limitation of the freedom of trade according to some people should, upon some occasions, be extended much farther than to the precise foreign commodities which could come into competition with those which had been taxed at home. When the necessaries of life have been taxed in any country, it becomes proper, they pretend, to tax not only the like necessaries of life imported from other countries, but all sorts of foreign goods which can come into competition with any thing that is the produce of domestic industry. Subsistence, they say, becomes necessarily dearer in consequence of such taxes; and the price of labour must always rise with the price of the labourers subsistence. Every commodity, therefore, which is the produce of domestic industry, though not immediately taxed itself, becomes dearer in consequence of such taxes, because the labour which produces it becomes so. Such taxes, therefore, are really equivalent, they say, to a tax upon every particular commodity produced at home. In order to put domestic upon the same footing with foreign industry, therefore, it becomes necessary, they think, to lay some duty upon

得多,所以,在英国各种通商条例中,航海法也许是最明智的一种。

给外国产业增加若干负担来奖励国内产业的做法有利的第二种情况是,在国内对国内产出物品课税时。在这种情况下,对外国同样产出物品课以同等金额的税收,似乎也算合理。这种办法不会给国内产业以国内市场的垄断权,也不会使流入某种特殊用途的资财和劳动比自然流入的多。征税的结果,仅仅使本来要流入这种用途的任何一部分资财与劳动,不再流向较不自然的用途;而本国产业与外国产业,在课税后仍能在和课税前大约相同的条件下互相竞争。在大不列颠,当国内产业的生产物课税时,通常同时也对同类外国商品的进口课以更高水平的关税,免得国内商人和制造业者吵吵嚷嚷地埋怨说,此等商品要在国内贱卖了。

关于对自由贸易的第二种限制,有人认为,在一些情况下不应该局限于输入本国的、与本国课税产出物品相竞争的那些外国商品,应该扩大到许许多多外国商品。他们说,要是在国内对生活必需品课税,那么不仅对外国输入的同种生活必需品课税是正当的,而且也对输入本国能和本国任何产业的产出物品相竞争的各种外国商品课税也是正当的。他们说,这种课税的结果必然会抬高生活必需品价格,劳动者生活品价格抬高的结果,劳动价格一定跟着提高。所以,虽然对本国产业生产的每一种商品没有直接课税,但其价格都将由于该种课税而上升,因为生产各种商品的劳动的价格上升。所以,他们说,这种课税虽然仅仅以生活必需品为课税对象,但实际上等于对国内一切产出物品课税。他们认为,为了使国内产业与国外产业处于同等地位,对输入本国而

(2)在对国内同类产出物品征税时。

有些人认为,为了抵消国内需税项就了国普的。

every foreign commodity, equal to this enhancement of the price of the home commodities with which it can come into competition.

but there is a difference, Whether taxes upon the necessaries of life, such as those in Great Britain upon soap, salt, leather, candles, &c. necessarily raise the price of labour, and consequently that of all other commodities, I shall consider hereafter, when I come to treat of taxes. Supposing, however, in the mean time, that they have this effect, and they have it undoubtedly, this general enhancement of the price of all commodities, in consequence of that of labour, is a case which differs in the two following respects from that of a particular commodity, of which the price was enhanced by a particular tax immediately imposed upon it.

since (a) the effect of taxes on necessaries cannot be exactly known, First, it might always be known with great exactness how far the price of such a commodity could be enhanced by such a tax: but how far the general enhancement of the price of labour might affect that of every different commodity about which labour was employed, could never be known with any tolerable exactness. It would be impossible, therefore, to proportion with any tolerable exactness the tax upon every foreign, to this enhancement of the price of every home commodity.

and (b) taxes on necessaries are like poor soil or bad climate: they cannot justify an attempt to give capital an unnatural direction. Secondly, taxes upon the necessaries of life have nearly the same effect upon the circumstances of the people as a poor soil and a bad climate. Provisions are thereby rendered dearer in the same manner as if it required extraordinary labour and expence to raise them. As in the natural scarcity arising from soil and climate, it would be absurd to direct the people in what manner they ought to employ their capitals and industry, so is it likewise in the artificial scarcity arising from such taxes. To be left to accommodate, as well as they could, their industry to their situation, and to find out those employments in which, notwithstanding their unfavourable circumstances, they might have some advantage either in the home or in the foreign market, is what in both cases would evidently be most for their advantage. To lay a new tax upon them, because they are already overburdened with taxes, and because they already pay too dear for the necessaries of life, to make them likewise pay too dear for the greater part of other commodities, is certainly a most absurd way of making amends.

与本国任何商品竞争的任何外国商品,必须一律课以与本国商品价格增高额相等的税收。

对生活必需品征税,如英国的石碱税、盐税、皮革税、蜡烛税等等,是否必然提高劳动价格,从而提高一切其他商品的价格,我将在后面论及税收时再加以研究。但是,假定这种赋税具有这种后果(它无疑有这种后果),一切商品价格就像这样由于劳动价格上涨而普遍上涨的情况,在以下两个方面与特定商品由于直接课征特种赋税而涨价的情况有所不同。_{但会存在不同的情况。}

该特种赋税能使这种特定商品的价格提高到什么程度,总可以很准确地知道。但劳动价格普遍地提高,可以在什么程度上影响各种不同劳动产出物品的价格,却不能相当准确地加以判定。所以,要按各种国内商品价格上涨的比例,对各种外国商品课以相当水平的赋税,不可能做得相当准确。_{(1)并不能够准确地掌握对生活必需品的影响。}

第二,对生活必需品征税给人民生活状况所产生的影响,与贫瘠土壤和不良气候所产生的影响大致相同。粮食价格因此变得比从前昂贵,正如在土壤贫瘠和气候不良的情况下生产粮食一样,需要额外更多的劳动和费用。在土壤和气候引起天然贫乏时,指导人民如何使用其资本与劳动是不合理的;在对生活必需品课税所引起人为的缺乏时,指导人民应该如何使用其资本与劳动也是不合理的。很明显,在这两种情况之下,对人民最有利的是,让他们尽可能适应自己的环境,寻找劳动的用途,使他们在不利的情况下能在国内或国外市场占有稍稍优越的地位。他们负担的税收已经太重,再给他们课征新税,他们已经对生活必需品支付过高的价格;作为补救办法,要他们对其他大部分物品也支付过高的价格无疑是最不合理的。_{(2)对必需品征税与贫瘠的土地和不良的气候所带来的影响一样:税收不能证明企图给予资本一个不指导其合理性自然。}

Taxes on necessaries are commonest in the richest countries because no others could support them.

Such taxes, when they have grown up to a certain height, are a curse equal to the barrenness of the earth and the inclemency of the heavens; and yet it is in the richest and most industrious countries that they have been most generally imposed. No other countries could support so great a disorder. As the strongest bodies only can live and enjoy health, under an unwholesome regimen; so the nations only, that in every sort of industry have the greatest natural and acquired advantages, can subsist and prosper under such taxes. Holland is the country in Europe in which they abound most, and which from peculiar circumstances continues to prosper, not by means of them, as has been most absurdly supposed, but in spite of them.

There are two other possible exceptions to the general principle:

As there are two cases in which it will generally be advantageous to lay some burden upon foreign, for the encouragement of domestic industry; so there are two others in which it may sometimes be a matter of deliberation; in the one, how far it is proper to continue the free importation of certain foreign goods; and in the other, how far, or in what manner, it may be proper to restore that free importation after it has been for some time interrupted.

(1) Retaliation

The case in which it may sometimes be a matter of deliberation how far it is proper to continue the free importation of certain foreign goods, is, when some foreign nation restrains by high duties or prohibitions the importation of some of our manufactures into their country. Revenge in this case naturally dictates retaliation, and that we should impose the like duties and prohibitions upon the importation of some or all of their manufactures into ours. Nations accordingly seldom fail to retaliate in this manner. The French have been particularly forward to favour their own manufactures by restraining the importation of such foreign goods as could come into competition with them. In this consisted a great part of the policy of Mr. Colbert, who, notwithstanding his great abilities, seems in this case to have been imposed upon by the sophistry of merchants and manufacturers, who are always demanding a monopoly against their countrymen. It is at present the opinion of the most intelligent men in France that his operations of this kind have not been beneficial to his country. That minister, by the tarif of 1667, imposed very high duties upon a great number of foreign manu-

这类赋税在达到一定高度时所造成的损害,等于土壤贫瘠和天时险恶所造成的损害。但最普遍征收这类赋税的地方却是最富裕和最勤勉的国家。其他国家都经不起这么剧烈的折腾。只有最强健的身体才能在不卫生的饮食条件下生存并处在健康状态;所以,只有在各种产业都具有最大先天优势和后天获得优势的国家里,才能在这类赋税下存在和繁荣。在欧洲,这一类赋税最多的国家要数荷兰,而荷兰之所以可以持续繁荣,并不像不合理的想象那样,不是由于有了这一类赋税,而是由于荷兰有了特殊情况,使得这种赋税不能阻止其持续繁荣下去。

<small>对生活必需品普遍征税,在裕富的国家里最原因在其他国家不征税</small>

给外国产业加上若干负担来奖励本国产业,在上述两种情况下是一般有利的,而在下述两种情况下则必须要慎重考虑。(一)一种情况是,在什么程度上继续准许某种外国货物的自由输入,是适当的;(二)另一个情况是,在什么程度上或使用什么方式,在自由进口已经中断一段时间之后,恢复自由进口是适当的。

<small>一般原则之外还存在两种情况:</small>

在什么程度上继续准许某种外国商品的自由进口是适当的,有时成为值得考虑的情况是,在某一外国以高关税或禁止的方法限制我国某些制造品输入该国的情况。在这种情况下,复仇心理自然要驱使我们报复,我们对他们某些或一切制造品,课以同样高的关税或禁止其输入我国。各国通常都是如此进行报复的。法国人为了保护本国的制造业,对于一切能和他们竞争的外国商品,特别喜欢用限制进口的方法。这似乎构成科尔伯特政策的大部分内容。虽然科尔伯特才能卓越,但在这种情况下,却似乎为商人和制造业者的诡辩所欺骗;这些商人和制造业者总是要求拥有一种有损于同胞的垄断权。现在,法国最有才能的人都认为,他的这种行为对法国没有好处。这位大臣于1667年公布关税

<small>(1)报复</small>

factures. Upon his refusing to moderate them in favour of the Dutch, they in 1671 prohibited the importation of the wines, brandies and manufactures of France. The war of 1672 seems to have been in part occasioned by this commercial dispute. The peace of Nimeguen put an end to it in 1678, by moderating some of those duties in favour of the Dutch, who in consequence took off their prohibition. It was about the same time that the French and English began mutually to oppress each other's industry, by the like duties and prohibitions, of which the French, however, seem to have set the first example. The spirit of hostility which has subsisted between the two nations ever since, has hitherto hindered them from being moderated on either side. In 1697 the English prohibited the importation of bonelace, the manufacture of Flanders. The government of that country, at that time under the dominion of Spain, prohibited in return the importation of English woollens. In 1700, the prohibition of importing bonelace into England, was taken off upon condition that the importation of English woollens into Flanders should be put on the same footing as before.

<small>may be good policy where it is likely to secure the abolition of foreign restraints.</small>   There may be good policy in retaliations of this kind, when there is a probability that they will procure the repeal of the high duties or prohibitions complained of. The recovery of a great foreign market will generally more than compensate the transitory inconveniency of paying dearer during a short time for some sorts of goods. To judge whether such retaliations are likely to produce such an effect, does not, perhaps, belong so much to the science of a legislator, whose deliberations ought to be governed by general principles which are always the same, as to the skill of that insidious and crafty animal, vulgarly called a statesman or politician, whose councils are directed by the momentary fluctuations of affairs. When there is no probability that any such repeal can be procured, it seems a bad method of compensating the injury done to certain classes of our people, to do another injury ourselves, not only to those classes, but to almost all the other classes of them. When our neighbours prohibit some manufacture of ours, we generally prohibit, not only the same, for that alone would seldom affect them considerably, but some other manufacture of theirs. This may no doubt give encouragement to some particular class

法，对大多数外国制造品课以极高的关税。荷兰人请求减轻关税未果，于 1671 年开始禁止进口法国葡萄酒、白兰地以及制造品。1672 年战争一部分可以归因于这次商业上的争论。1678 年尼麦格恩和约，受荷兰人的关切才减轻了这种关税，荷兰人于是也撤销了他们自己有关的进口禁令。英法两国大约是在同时开始互相采用同样的高关税与禁止政策来压制对方的产业，但首先采用措施的似乎是法兰西。从那时以来两国都怀有仇恨心理，使得它们都不肯减轻关税。在 1697 年，英国禁止进口佛兰德制造的束腰骨架花边。那时佛兰德为西班牙附属地，作为报复，西班牙政府禁止从英国进口毛纺织品。在 1700 年，英国撤销了有关禁止进口佛兰德束腰骨架花边的禁令，前提条件是佛兰德撤销禁止从英国进口毛纺织品的禁令。

　　为了要撤销大家所抱怨的高关税或禁令而采用的报复政策，如果能达到撤销的目的，就可以说是好政策。一般来说，一个庞大外国市场的恢复，可以足以补偿由于某些物品价格暂时昂贵而蒙受暂时的不便。要判断这种报复政策能否产生这种效果，与其说与立法者的知识有关，不如说与所谓政治家或政客的技巧有关，因为立法者的考虑应受不变的一般原理指导；而潜伏和狡猾的动物即世俗所称的政治家或政客，他们的考虑则应受事件暂时波动所支配。在没有可能撤销这种禁令时，为了补偿本国某些阶级所遭受的损失，从而使用另一种损害我们自己利益的办法，似乎不是一个好办法；因为这不仅会损害那些阶级的利益，而且还会损害几乎所有其他阶级的利益。在我们邻国禁止我国某种制造品时，我们通常不但禁止他们同种制造品，而且禁止他们其他几种制造品，因为仅仅禁止前者很少能给他们带来显著的影响。

<small>报复政策如果能够使禁令取消的话，可能是一项好政策。</small>

of workmen among ourselves, and by excluding some of their rivals, may enable them to raise their price in the home-market. Those workmen, however, who suffered by our neighbours prohibition will not be benefited by ours. On the contrary, they and almost all the other classes of our citizens will thereby be obliged to pay dearer than before for certain goods. Every such law, therefore, imposes a real tax upon the whole country, not in favour of that particular class of workmen who were injured by our neighbours prohibition, but of some other class.

(2) It may be desirable to introduce freedom of trade by slow gradations.

The case in which it may sometimes be a matter of deliberation, how far, or in what manner, it is proper to restore the free importation of foreign goods, after it has been for some time interrupted, is, when particular manufactures, by means of high duties or prohibitions upon all foreign goods which can come into competition with them, have been so far extended as to employ a great multitude of hands. Humanity may in this case require that the freedom of trade should be restored only by slow gradations, and with a good deal of reserve and circumspection. Were those high duties and prohibitions taken away all at once, cheaper foreign goods of the same kind might be poured so fast into the home market, as to deprive all at once many thousands of our people of their ordinary employment and means of subsistence. The disorder which this would occasion might no doubt be very considerable. It would in all probability, however, be much less than is commonly imagined, for the two following reasons:

But the disorder occasioned by its sudden introduction would be less than is supposed since

First, all those manufactures, of which any part is commonly exported to other European countries without a bounty, could be very little affected by the freest importation of foreign goods. Such manufactures must be sold as cheap abroad as any other foreign goods of the same quality and kind, and consequently must be sold cheaper at home. They would still, therefore, keep possession of the home market, and though a capricious man of fashion might sometimes prefer foreign wares, merely because they were foreign, to cheaper and better goods of the same kind that were made at home, this folly could, from the nature of things, extend to so few, that it could make no sensible impression upon the general employment of the people. But a great part of all the different branches of our woollen manufacture, of our tanned leather, and of our hard-ware, are annually exported to

(a) no manufacture which is now exported would be affected;

这无疑给我国某些部门的工人以鼓励，替他们排除了一些竞争者，使他们能在国内市场上抬高他们的价格。不过，由于邻国禁令而蒙受损失的我国工人，绝不会从我国的禁令得到利益。反之，他们和我国几乎所有其他阶级人群，在购买某些货物时，都不得不支付比从前更为昂贵的价格。所以，像这一类的法律对全国课征了真实的税收，受益的不是受邻国禁令损害的那一部分阶级工人，却是另一部分阶级人民。

在中止外国货物自由进口一段时间以后，多大程度或者以什么样的方式恢复自由进口才妥当，这或许也是一个值得深思的问题。本国的某些制造业，通过对一切能和它们的制造品竞争的外国货物课以高关税或被禁止输入而扩大起来，从而能雇用许许多多工人的情况。在这种情况下，人道主义也许要求，只能一步一步地、小心翼翼地恢复自由贸易。如果突然取消高额关税和有关禁止进口禁令，那么价格相对低廉的同类外国货物将迅速流入国内市场，迅速使我国千千万万人民失去日常就业岗位和生活资料；由此而起的混乱肯定不小。但依据下面两个理由，这些混乱也许比一般所想象的要小得多。

（2）必须逐渐地开放自由贸易。

第一，在没有奖金时，制造品一般也可以出口到欧洲其他各国，受到外国商品最自由进口的影响不大。这种输往外国的制造品，其销售价格一定与同品质同种类的其他外国商品一样低廉。因此，在国内的销售价格必定更加低廉，因而仍然能够占有国内市场。即使有一些时尚人士有时喜爱外国货，仅仅因为它们是外国货；本国制造的同种类货物，虽然价廉物美，也不被他们所看中，然而这种愚蠢的行为一般不会那么普遍，所以对人民的一般就业并没有显著影响。我国毛纺织品制造业、皮鞍制造业和铁器

但是这种突然开放自由贸易形成的混乱状况要比想象的要小，因为

（1）对制造业出口并没有影响；

other European countries without any bounty, and these are the manufactures which employ the greatest number of hands. The silk, perhaps, is the manufacture which would suffer the most by this freedom of trade, and after it the linen, though the latter much less than the former.

(b) the of one employment would easily find another,

Secondly, though a great number of people should, by thus restoring the freedom of trade, be thrown all at once out of their ordinary employment and common method of subsistence, it would by no means follow that they would thereby be deprived either of employment or subsistence. By the reduction of the army and navy at the end of the late war, more than a hundred thousand soldiers and seamen, a number equal to what is employed in the greatest manufactures, were all at once thrown out of their ordinary employment; but, though they no doubt suffered some inconveniency, they were not thereby deprived of all employment and subsistence. The greater part of the seamen, it is probable, gradually betook themselves to the merchant-service as they could find occasion, and in the meantime both they and the soldiers were absorbed in the great mass of the people, and employed in a great variety of occupations. Not only no great convulsion, but no sensible disorder arose from so great a change in the situation of more than a hundred thousand men, all accustomed to the use of arms, and many of them to rapine and plunder. The number of vagrants was

especially if the privileges of corporations and the law of settlement were abolished.

scarce any-where sensibly increased by it, even the wages of labour were not reduced by it in any occupation, so far as I have been able to learn, except in that of seamen in the merchant-service. But if we compare together the habits of a soldier and of any sort of manufacturer, we shall find that those of the latter do not tend so much to disqualify him from being employed in a new trade, as those of the former from being employed in any. The manufacturer has always been accustomed to look for his subsistence from his labour only: the soldier to expect it from his pay. Application and industry have been familiar to the one; idleness and dissipation to the other. But it is surely much easier to change the direction of industry from one sort of labour to another, than to turn idleness and dissipation to any. To the greater part of manufactures besides, it has already been observed, there are other collateral manufactures of so similar a nature, that a workman can easily transfer his industry from one of them to another. The greater part of such workmen too are occasionally employed in country labour. The stock which employed them in a particular manufacture before, will still remain in the country to employ an equal

业中，有很大一部分制造品，每年不依赖奖金而输往欧洲其他各国；而雇用职工最多的制造业也就是这几类制造业。受到自由贸易损害最大的也许是丝织制造业；其次是麻布制造业，但后者所受损失比前者要少得多。

第二，虽然恢复贸易自由将使许多人突然失去他们正常的职业和普通的谋生方法，但不能得出他们就会因此失业或失去生计。上次战争结束时，海陆军裁员10万人以上，所裁减的人数等于大型制造业所雇用的人数，这样他们就突然失去了他们平日的职业；尽管他们会遇到一些困难，但他们并不会因此便被剥夺了一切职业与谋生的办法。较大一部分水兵也许会逐渐转移到商船上去服务；此时被遣散的海陆军士兵都被吸收在广大的人民群众中并受雇于各种职业。10万多人习惯使用武器，而且其中有许多惯于抢劫掠夺的人，他们的地位发生了如此大的变化，却不曾引起大的动乱，也不曾引起显著的混乱。任何地方，流氓的数目并没有因此而剧烈增加；而且据我所知，除了商船海员以外，无论何种职业的劳动工资也没有减少。要是我们把兵士和任何一种类制造业工人之间的习惯进行比较，我们就可以发现，后者改行的可能性比前者要大，因为士兵一向以军饷为生，而制造业工人则仅仅以出卖自身劳动为生。前者常常懒惰和散漫，后者则总是勤勉和刻苦。由一种辛勤劳动改为另一种辛勤劳动，当然比由懒惰闲散改为勤劳刻苦容易得多。此外，根据观察可知，大部分制造业都有性质类似的附属制造业，所以，工人很容易从一种制造业转到另一种制造业。而且这类工人中的相当一部分，有时还被雇佣从事农村劳动。以前在特定制造业上雇用他们的资财，仍然将留在国内，按另一个方式雇用相同数量的人。国家的资本和

（2）失业的人会容易再找到另外一份职业。

尤其在同业专营特权和居住法案被废止以后。

number of people in some other way. The capital of the country remaining the same, the demand for labour will likewise be the same, or very nearly the same, though it may be exerted in different places and for different occupations. Soldiers and seamen, indeed, when discharged from the king's service, are at liberty to exercise any trade, within any town or place of Great Britain or Ireland. Let the same natural liberty of exercising what species of industry they please, be restored to all his majesty's subjects, in the same manner as to soldiers and seamen; that is, break down the exclusive privileges of corporations, and repeal the statute of apprenticeship, both which are real encroachments upon natural liberty, and add to these the repeal of the law of settlements, so that a poor workman, when thrown out of employment either in one trade or in one place, may seek for it in another trade or in another place, without the fear either of a prosecution or of a removal, and neither the public nor the individuals will suffer much more from the occasional disbanding some particular classes of manufacturers, than from that of soldiers. Our manufacturers have no doubt great merit with their country, but they cannot have more than those who defend it with their blood, nor deserve to be treated with more delicacy.

Private interests are too strong to allow of the restoration of freedom of trade in Great Britain

To expect, indeed, that the freedom of trade should ever be entirely restored in Great Britain, is as absurd as to expect that an Oceana or Utopia should ever be established in it. Not only the prejudices of the public, but what is much more unconquerable, the private interests of many individuals, irresistibly oppose it. Were the officers of the army to oppose with the same zeal and unanimity any reduction in the number of forces, with which master manufacturers set themselves against every law that is likely to increase the number of their rivals in the home market; were the former to animate their soldiers, in the same manner as the latter enflame their workmen, to attack with violence and outrage the proposers of any such regulation; to attempt to reduce the army would be as dangerous as it has now become to attempt to diminish in any respect the monopoly which our manufacturers have obtained against us. This monopoly has so much increased the number of some particular tribes of them, that, like an overgrown standing army, they have become formidable to the government, and upon many occasions intimidate the legislature. The mem-

从前相同,劳动的需要也和从前相同或大致相同,只不过是在不同地方和不同职业上使用。当然,海陆军士兵如果被遣散,他们有在不列颠或爱尔兰的任何都市或任何地方从事任何职业的自由。让我们恢复国王陛下的一切臣民拥有选择任何职业的天然自由,与海陆军士兵所享受的那样;也就是说,打破同业联合的专营特权和废除学徒法令(这二者都是对天然自由真正造成侵害),再撤废居住法,使贫穷工人在一个地方或某种行业失业,能在另外一个地方或另一个行业就业,不用担心被人检举,也不用担心被迫迁徙;由于某特定制造业工人的偶然遣散而使个人和社会遭受的损失,就不会比士兵遣散使他们所遭受的损失大。我国的制造业工人无疑对国家做出很大的贡献,但与以血肉之躯保卫国家的那些人相比,他们的功绩就显得小,对于他们用不着有更好的待遇。

不能期望在不列颠完全恢复自由贸易,正如不能期望在不列颠建立世外桃源或乌托邦一样。完全恢复自由贸易的不可抗拒的阻力不仅来自于公众的偏见,还有更难以克服的许多个人私利。如果军队的军官,都像制造业者那样强烈和一致地反对在国内市场增加竞争对手人数的每一部法律的方式来反对缩小兵力;都像制造业者鼓动他们工人,以暴力攻击和侵犯任何这类法律的提议者一样激烈和一致的方式去鼓动他们士兵,以暴力攻击和侵犯缩减兵力的提议者,那么要想缩编军队,正如现在试图在任何方面减少我国制造业者所拥有的、与我们同胞利益相违背的垄断权一样危险。这种垄断权,已经在很大的程度上增加了某些制造业的人数,他们就像一个过于庞大臃肿的常备军一样,不但可以胁迫政府,而且往往还可以胁迫立法机构。对加强这种垄断权提

<small>不列颠私人利最难以克服,以至于不允许恢复自由贸易。</small>

ber of parliament who supports every proposal for strengthening this monopoly, is sure to acquire not only the reputation of understanding trade, but great popularity and influence with an order of men whose numbers and wealth render them of great importance. If he opposes them, on the contrary, and still more if he has authority enough to be able to thwart them, neither the most acknowledged probity, nor the highest rank, nor the greatest public services, can protect him from the most infamous abuse and detraction, from personal insults, nor sometimes from real danger, arising from the insolent outrage of furious and disappointed monopolists.

<small>The fact that equitable regard is due to the manufacturer who has fixed capital in his business is an argument against the establishment of new monopolies.</small> The undertaker of a great manufacture, who, by the home markets being suddenly laid open to the competition of foreigners, should be obliged to abandon his trade, would no doubt suffer very considerably. That part of his capital which had usually been employed in purchasing materials and in paying his workmen, might, without much difficulty, perhaps, find another employment. But that part of it which was fixed in workhouses, and in the instruments of trade, could scarce be disposed of without considerable loss. The equitable regard, therefore, to his interest requires that changes of this kind should never be introduced suddenly, but slowly, gradually, and after a very long warning. The legislature, were it possible that its deliberations could be always directed, not by the clamorous importunity of partial interests, but by an extensive view of the general good, ought upon this very account, perhaps, to be particularly careful neither to establish any new monopolies of this kind, nor to extend further those which are already established. Every such regulation introduces some degree of real disorder into the constitution of the state, which it will be difficult afterwards to cure without occasioning another disorder.

<small>Customs duties imposed for revenue remain to be considered hereafter.</small> How far it may be proper to impose taxes upon the importation of foreign goods, in order, not to prevent their importation, but to raise a revenue for government, I shall consider hereafter when I come to treat of taxes. Taxes imposed with a view to prevent, or even to diminish importation, are evidently as destructive of the revenue of the customs as of the freedom of trade.

案表示支持的国会议员，不仅可以获得理解贸易的佳誉，而且还可以在那个以人数众多和财富庞大而地位显赫的阶级当中受到欢迎与拥护。反过来，如果他反对这类提案，要是他有权利阻止这类提案的通过，那么，即使他被公认为是最正直的人，即使他的社会地位最高或他的社会功绩最大，恐怕也难免不受到最无耻的侮辱与诽谤，难免不受人身的攻击；而且有时面临实际的危险，因为愤怒异常和极端失望的垄断者，有时会以无理的暴力行径加害于他。

大制造业经营者，如果由于在国内市场上突然面对外国人的竞争，不得不放弃他的老本行，他所遭受的损失肯定不小。通常用来购买原材料和支付工资的那一部分资本，要想寻找另外用途也许困难不会太大。但固定在工厂厂房和加工机具上的那一部分资本，处置它们不免会形成相当大的损失。因此，公平地对待他的个人利益就要求：进行这种变革不要操之过急，而要缓慢地、逐渐地进行，要在发出警告很久以后才可实行。要是立法机关的考虑不为带有片面利益的吵吵嚷嚷的要求所左右，而为广大人民的普遍幸福思想所指引，那么它就要特别小心，不再批准任何新的这一类型的垄断，也不要进一步推广已经建立的垄断。在一定程度上这样的每一部法规给国家政治制度带来紊乱，而后来的补救措施也难免会引起另一种紊乱。

至于对进口的外国商品课税在什么程度上合适，不是为了禁止进口，而是为了增加政府收入，我在以后考察赋税时再加以研究。出于禁止进口或减少进口的目的而征税，显然是既有损于贸易自由，也会不利于关税收入。

CHAPTER III

Of the Extraordinary Restraints Upon The Importation Of Goods Of Almost All Kinds, From Those Countries With Which The Balance Is Supposed To Be Disadvantageous

PART I

Of The Unreasonableness Of Those Restraints Even Upon The Principles Of The Commercial System

British restraints on imports from France are an example.

To lay extraordinary restraints upon the importation of goods of almost all kinds, from those particular countries with which the balance of trade is supposed to be disadvantageous, is the second expedient by which the commercial system proposes to increase the quantity of gold and silver. Thus in Great Britain, Silesia lawns may be imported for home consumption, upon paying certain duties. But French cambrics and lawns are prohibited to be imported, except into the port of London, there to be warehoused for exportation. [1] Higher duties are imposed upon the wines of France than upon those of Portugal, or indeed of any other country. By what is called the impost 1692, [2] a duty of five and twenty per cent. , of the rate or value, was laid upon all French goods; while the goods of other nations were, the greater part of them, subjected to much lighter duties, seldom exceeding five per cent. The wine, brandy, salt and vinegar of France were indeed

---

[1] [18 Geo. II. , c 36; 7 Geo. III. , c. 43.]
[2] [4 W. and M. , c. 5, § 2.]

第三章　论把与那些国家之间发生的贸易差额看作是不利的而对那些国家的各种货物的进口所施加的特别限制

第一节　即使是依据重商主义原理也不合理的一些限制

重商主义所提倡的增加金银数量的第二个方法,就是对于那些贸易差额会认为不利于我国的国家,对它们几乎所有的货物的进口施加特别的限制。例如,在西利西亚的细竹布缴纳了一定关税以后,就可以输入英国以供本国国内消费;但法国的细棉布和细竹布,却除了输入伦敦港入库再等待出口以外,禁止输入英国销售。① 对进口的法国葡萄酒所征收的关税,也比对葡萄牙或其他任何国家进口的葡萄酒所征收的关税要重。依照1692年所谓进口税,②一切法国商品都必须缴纳其价值的25%的税;尽管其他各国的货物所缴纳的关税大部分要轻得多,很少超过5%。当然,法国葡萄酒、白兰地、食盐和醋除外,但这些商品却要按照其他法

英国对法国货物进行就是一例。

---

① 乔治二世十八年第36号法令;乔治三世七年第43号法令。
② 威廉和玛利四年第5号法令第2节。

<small>Such restraints are unreasonable on the principles of the mercantile system, since</small> excepted; these commodities being subjected to other heavy duties, either by other laws, or by particular clauses of the same law. In 1696, a second duty of twenty-five per cent., the first not having been thought a sufficient discouragement, was imposed upon all French goods, except brandy; together with a new duty of five and twenty pounds upon the ton of French wine, and another of fifteen pounds upon the ton of French vinegar. ① French goods have never been omitted in any of those general subsidies, or duties of five per cent., which have been imposed upon all, or the greater part of the goods enumerated in the book of rates. If we count the one third and two third subsidies as making a complete subsidy between them, there have been five of these general subsidies; so that before the commencement of the present war seventy-five per cent. may be considered as the lowest duty, to which the greater part of the goods of the growth, produce, or manufacture of France were liable. But upon the greater part of goods, those duties are equivalent to a prohibition. The French in their turn have, I believe, treated our goods and manufactures just as hardly; though I am not so well acquainted with the particular hardships which they have imposed upon them. Those mutual restraints have put an end to almost all fair commerce between the two nations, and smugglers are now the principal importers, either of British goods into France, or of French goods into Great Britain. The principles which I have been examining in the foregoing chapter took their origin from private interest and the spirit of monopoly; those which I am going to examine in this, from national prejudice and animosity. ② They are, accordingly, as might well be expected, still more unreasonable. They are so, even upon the principles of the commercial system.

First, though it were certain that in the case of a free trade be-

---

① [7 and 8 W. Ⅲ, c. 20; but wine and vinegar were excepted from the general increase of 25 per cent. as well as brandy, upon which the additional duty was £ 30 per ton of single proof and £ 6o per ton of double proof.]

② [Nearly all the matter from the beginning of the chapter to this point appears first in Additions and Corrections and ed. 3. Eds. 1 and 2 contain only the first sentence of the chapter and then proceed, 'Thus in Great Britain higher duties are laid upon the wines of France than upon those of Portugal. German linen may be imported upon paying certain duties; but French linen is altogether prohibited. The principles which I have been examining took their origin from private interest and the spirit of monopoly; those which I am going to examine from national prejudice and animosity.']

律或同一法令的特殊条款,缴纳其他税率更重的税。在 1696 年又认为这第一个 25% 还不够阻止法国商品进口,于是又对除白兰地以外的法国货物再课以 25% 的税收;同时对法国葡萄酒每大桶新征税 25 镑并对法国每大桶醋新征税收为 15 镑。① 上面列举的各种货物或大部分货物必须缴纳的那些一般附加税或 5% 的税从来没有对法国货物免征过。要是把 1/3 附加税和 2/3 附加税也计算在内,作为全部要缴纳的附加税,那么开征的附加税就有五种。因此,在这次战争开始以前,法国绝大部分农产品和制造品至少必须负担 75% 的税;对它们征收这样重的税无异于禁止其进口。我相信,法国也针锋相对地以同样对我们的货物及制造品征收重税;虽然我不清楚法国所征收的税具体重到什么程度。但这种相互的限制几乎断绝了两国间一切公平贸易,走私者成为把法国货物运至英国和把英国货物运至法国的主要进口者。我在上一章所考察的原理,发源于私人利害关系和垄断精神;在这章所要考察的各条原则,却发源于国家的偏见与敌意。② 因此,我在这章所要考察的原理更不合理。甚至根据重商主义的原理来说,也是不合理的。

第一,即使在英、法之间自由贸易的情况下,所产生的贸易差额

---

① 威廉三世七年、八年第 20 号法令,但是对葡萄酒和醋,还有白兰地都免征 25% 的税;对一个标准酒精度征收 30% 额外税收,对两个标准酒精精度要征收 60% 的额外税收。

② 几乎从本章开始到现在几乎所有的内容似乎出现在添加部分和更正部分以及第三版之中。在第一版和第二版中仅包括本章第一句,接着后面就是:"英国对法国的葡萄酒征收的税收高于葡萄牙。对进口的德国亚麻布征收少许税;但禁止进口法国亚麻布。我是从个人私利和垄断权的角度考察这些原理;现在我将从国家偏见和敌意的角度来研究它们。"

(1) if free trade with France did lead to an unfavourable balance with France, it might yet not do so with the world in general,

tween France and England, for example, the balance would be in favour of France, it would by no means follow that such a trade would be disadvantageous to England, or that the general balance of its whole trade would thereby be turned more against it. If the wines of France are better and cheaper than those of Portugal, or its linens than those of Germany, it would be more advantageous for Great Britain to purchase both the wine and the foreign linen which it had occasion for of France, than of Portugal and Germany. Though the value of the annual importations from France would thereby be greatly augmented, the value of the whole annual importations would be diminished, in proportion as the French goods of the same quality were cheaper than those of the other two countries. This would be the case, even upon the supposition that the whole French goods imported were to be consumed in Great Britain.

(2) a part of French imports might be re-exported and bring back gold and silver,

But, secondly, a great part of them might be re-exported to other countries, where, being sold with profit, they might bring back a return equal in value, perhaps, to the prime cost of the whole French goods imported. What has frequently been said of the East India trade might possibly be true of the French; that though the greater part of East India goods were bought with gold and silver, the re-exportation of a part of them to other countries, brought back more gold and silver to that which carried on the trade than the prime cost of the whole amounted to. One of the most important branches of the Dutch trade, at present, consists in the carriage of French goods to other European countries. Some part even of the French wine drank in Great Britain is clandestinely imported from Holland and Zealand. If there was either a free trade between France and England, or if French goods could be imported upon paying only the same duties as those of other European nations, to be drawn back upon exportation, England might have some share of a trade which is found so advantageous to Holland and

(3) the balance cannot be certainly known:

Thirdly, and lastly, there is no certain criterion by which we can determine on which side what is called the balance between any two countries lies, or which of them exports to the greatest value. National prejudice and animosity, prompted always by the private interest of particular traders, are the principles which generally direct our judgment upon all questions concerning it. There are two criterions, however, which have frequently been appealed to upon such occasions, the custom-house books and the course of exchange. The customhouse books, I think, it is now generally acknowledged, are a very uncertain criterion, on account of the inaccuracy of the valuation at which

的确对法国有利,也不能因此就下断言这样一种贸易将对英国不利,或者也不能就断定英国全部贸易总差额就将更不利于英国。如果法国葡萄酒比葡萄牙葡萄酒价廉物美,其麻布也比德意志的麻布价廉物美,那么英国所需的葡萄酒与外国麻布,向法国购买的好处要大于向葡萄牙和德意志购买。每年从法国进口货物的价值肯定将大大增加,但与葡萄牙、德意志两国的同质货物相比,由于从法国进口的货物物美价廉,所以全部进口物品的价值必会减少,而减少的数量与其低廉程度成比例。即使进口的法国货物完全在英国消费,情况也是如此。

(1)如果英法之间贸易自由,由此导致的不利贸易差额的产生,一般会有限制,

第二,有大部分从法国进口的货物可能再出口到其他国家去做牟取利润的销售。这种再出口也许会带回与法国全部进口品的原始成本价值相同的收益。东印度贸易事例也适用于对法国贸易的说明;就是说,虽然大部分东印度货物是用金银购买,但其中一部分的货物再出口所带回到本国来的金银,比全部货物的原始成本还要多。现在,荷兰最重要贸易部门之一就是把法国货物运到欧洲其他各国。英国人饮用的法国葡萄酒,也有一部分秘密由荷兰和新西兰进口。如果英法之间贸易自由,或法国货物在进口时与欧洲其他各国缴纳同样水平的税收,并在出口时收回,那么英国就可能分享到那些对荷兰十分有利的贸易所带来的好处。

(2)可以把从法国进口的一部分货物再出口带回金银,

第三,没有一个明确的标准让我们做出判断,两国之间的贸易差额究竟对哪一个国家有利,或哪一个国家出口的价值最大。对于这一类问题,我们的判断往往根据由个别商人的私利所驱使的国民偏见与敌意。在这种情况下,人们往往使用两个标准,即关税账簿与汇率情况。由于关税账簿对大部分各种商品所做估

(3)以及不能准确知道贸易差额:

the greater part of goods are customhouse books are useless, and the course of exchange is little better.

rated in them. The course of exchange① is, perhaps, almost equally so.

When the exchange between two places, such as London and Paris, is at par, it is said to be a sign that the debts due from London to Paris are compensated by those due from Paris to London. On the contrary, when a premium is paid at London for a bill upon Paris, it is said to be a sign that the debts due from London to Paris are not compensated by those due from Paris to London, but that a balance in money must be sent out from the latter place; for the risk, trouble, and expence of exporting which, the premium is both demanded and given. But the ordinary state of debt and credit between those two cities must necessarily be regulated, it is said, by the ordinary course of their dealings with one another. When neither of them imports from the other to a greater amount than it exports to that other, the debts and credits of each may compensate one another. But when one of them imports from the other to a greater value than it exports to that other, the former necessarily becomes indebted to the latter in a greater sum than the latter becomes indebted to it: the debts and credits of each do not compensate one another, and money must be sent out from that place of which the debts over-balance the credits. The ordinary course of exchange, therefore, being an indication of the ordinary state of debt and credit between two places, must likewise be an indication of the ordinary course of their exports and imports, as these necessarily regulate that state.

But though the ordinary course of exchange should be allowed to be a sufficient indication of the ordinary state of debt and credit between any two places, it would not from thence follow, that the balance of trade was in favour of that place which had the ordinary state of debt and credit in its favour. The ordinary state of debt and credit between any two places is not always entirely regulated by the ordina-

---

① [Ed. I reads 'The course of exchange, at least as it has hitherto been estimated, is, perhaps, almost equally so.']

价并不准确，所以现在大家都承认这种标准靠不住。至于汇率标准，①恐怕也是同样不可靠。

当伦敦与巴黎两地之间的汇率为平价时，据说那就表明，伦敦欠巴黎的债务恰好被巴黎欠伦敦的债务所抵消。反之，购买巴黎汇票，若必须在伦敦升水支付，据说那就表明伦敦欠巴黎的债务没有被巴黎欠伦敦的债务所抵消。因此，伦敦必须以一定差额的货币送往巴黎。因为出口货币既危险又麻烦，并且必须支付费用，所以代汇者要求汇水，汇兑人亦须给付汇水。据说，两个都市之间债权与债务的普遍状态，必然受到彼此之间正常商务来往情况的支配。如果由甲方进口乙方的数额小于等于由乙方出口到甲方的数额，由乙方进口甲方的数额小于等于由甲方出口到乙方的数额，则彼此之间债务与债权可以抵消。但若甲方从乙方进口的价值大于甲方向乙方出口的价值，则甲方负乙方的数额必大于乙方负甲方的数额。债权债务不能互相抵消，于是债务大于债权的方面，必须出口货币。汇兑的普通情况，既标示两地间债务与债权的普通状态，亦必然标示两地间出口与进口的普通情况，因为两地间债权债务的普通状态，必然受两地间进出口普通情况的支配。

可是，即使汇率的一般情况可以充分表示两地之间债务和债权的普通状态，但也不能就此断言，如果债务债权的普通状态有利于一个地方，贸易差额也就对它有利。两地之间债务和债权的一般状态，不一定完全取决于两地之间贸易来往的一般情况，而

---

① 第一版为"至于汇率标准，由于至少是估计出来的，也与账薄记录一样。"

| 国民财富的性质与原理

<small>A favourable exchange with a particular country does not prove a favourable balance with that country.</small> ry course of their dealings with one another; but is often influenced by that of the dealings of either with many other places. If it is usual, for example, for the merchants of England to pay for the goods which they buy of Hamburgh, Dantzic, Riga, &c. by bills upon Holland, the ordinary state of debt and credit between England and Holland will not be regulated entirely by the ordinary course of the dealings of those two countries with one another, but will be influenced by that of the dealings of England with those other places. England may be obliged to send out every year money to Holland, though its annual exports to that country may exceed very much the annual value of its imports from thence; and though what is called the balance of trade may be very much in favour of England.

<small>Besides, the ordinary computation of exchange is often misleading, since,</small> In the way, besides, in which the par of exchange has hitherto been computed, the ordinary course of exchange can afford no sufficient indication that the ordinary state of debt and credit is in favour of that country which seems to have, or which is supposed to have, the ordinary course of exchange in its favour: or, in other words, the real exchange may be, and, in fact, often is so very different from the computed one, that from the course of the latter, no certain conclusion can, upon many occasions, be drawn concerning that of the former. ①

When for a sum of money paid in England, containing, according to the standard of the English mint, a certain number of ounces of pure silver, you receive a bill for a sum of money to be paid in France, containing, according to the standard of the French mint, an equal number of ounces of pure silver, exchange is said to be at par between England and France. When you pay more, you are supposed to give a premium, and exchange is said to be against England, and in favour of France. When you pay less, you are supposed to get a premium, and exchange is said to be against France, and in favour of England.

---

① [In place of this paragraph ed. I reads, 'But though this doctrine, of which some part is, perhaps, not a little doubtful, were supposed ever so certain, the manner in which the par of exchange has hitherto been computed renders uncertain every conclusion that has ever yet been drawn from it'.]

常常受到两地之间任何一地对其他各地贸易的一般情况支配。例如,英国购买了汉堡、但泽、里加等处的货物,如果常常用荷兰汇票支付货物价格,那么英荷之间债务和债权的普通状态,不完全受这两个国家之间贸易的一般情况所支配,而却受英国对那些其他地方一般贸易情况的影响。在这种情况下,即使英格兰每年向荷兰的出口远远超过英国每年从荷兰进口的价值,即使所谓贸易差额非常有利于英国,但英国仍然每年必须出口货币到荷兰去。

此外,按照计算汇率平价的方法,汇率的一般情况也不能充分表明,如果汇兑的一般情况似乎或假定有利于一个国家,那么债务和债权的一般情况也对它有利。或换句话说,真实的汇率情况与计算的汇率情况可能差异很大,而且事实上差异往往也很大;所以,在许多情况下,关于债务债权的一般情况,我们绝不能根据汇率的一般情况得到确实的结论。①

假设你在英国支付一笔货币,按照英国造币厂的标准,[2]包含若干盎司的纯银,而你在法国所得到的汇票,按照法国造币厂标准,在法国兑付的货币额含有等量盎司的纯银,人们就说英法两国以平价进行汇兑。如果你所支付的多于兑付所得,人们就认为你升水支付,并说汇率对英国不利,对法国有利。如果你所支付的少于兑付所得,人们就认为你得到升水,并说汇率对法国不利,对英国有利。

---

① 在第一版里本段为:"尽管对这个存在一点怀疑的观点还是被假定为叫靠的,但是汇率平价的计算方式使得从该观点得出的结论具有不确定性。"

〔2〕 第一版在这里和往下7行是"标准"。

(1) money is often below its nominal standard.

But, first, we cannot always judge of the value of the current money of different countries by the standard① of their respective mints. In some it is more, in others it is less worn, clipt, and otherwise degenerated from that standard. But the value of the current coin of every country, compared with that of any other country, is in proportion not to the quantity of pure silver which it ought to contain, but to that which it actually does contain. Before the reformation of the silver coin in king William's time, exchange between England and Holland, computed, in the usual manner, according to the standard of their respective mints, was five and twenty per cent. against England. But the value of the current coin of England, as we learn from Mr. Lowndes, was at that time rather more than five and twenty per cent. below its standard value. The real exchange, therefore, may even at that time have been in favour of England, notwithstanding the computed exchange was so much against it; a smaller number of ounces of pure silver, actually paid in England, may have purchased a bill for a greater number of ounces of pure silver to be paid in Holland, and the man who was supposed to give, may in reality have got the premium. The French coin was, before the late reformation of the English gold coin, much less worn than the English, and was, perhaps, two or three per cent. nearer its standard. If the computed exchange with France, therefore, was not more than two or three per cent. against England, the real exchange might have been in its favour. Since the reformation of the gold coin, the exchange has been constantly in favour of England, and against France.

(2) coin is sometimes raised by seignorage above the value of the bullion contained in it.

Secondly, in some countries, the expence of coinage is defrayed by the government; in others, it is defrayed by the private people who carry their bullion to the mint, and the government even derives some revenue from the coinage. In England, it is defrayed by the government, and if you carry a pound weight of standard silver to the mint, you get back sixty-two shillings, containing a pound weight of the like standard silver. In France, a duty of eight per cent. is deducted for the coinage, which not only defrays the expence of it, but affords a small revenue to the government. In England, as the coinage costs nothing, the current coin can never be much more valuable than the quantity of bullion which it actually contains. In France, the workmanship, as you pay for it, adds to the value, in the same manner as

---

① [Ed. I reads 'standards' here and seven lines lower.]

但是,第一,我们不能常常按照各国造币厂的标准①来判断各国通货的价值。各国通货磨损与剪蚀的程度低于标准的程度多少不一。一国通用铸币与其他国家通用铸币的相对价值,并不看各自规定所含的纯银量,而是要看各自实际含有的纯银量来决定。在威廉王朝时代银币改革以前,按照普通计算方法,按照各自造币厂的标准,英荷之间的汇率英国要贴水25%。但从朗兹先生所做的研究就可以知道,英国当时通用铸币的价值却低于其标准价值25%。所以,按照通常计算方法得出当时两国之间的汇率,虽然对英国十分不利,而实际汇率却有利于英国。实际上在英国支付较小量纯银所购得的汇票,却可以在荷兰兑得较大量纯银。被认为是支付升水的人,实际上可能得到升水。在英国最近金币铸造改革以前,法国铸币比英国铸币的磨损程度小得多,而法国铸币接近其标准的程度也许比英国铸币高出2%或3%。如果英法之间的汇率按计算不利于英国的程度,如果没有超过2%或3%,真实的汇率便可能对英国有利。而自从金币铸造改革以来,汇率总是有利于英国而不利于法国。

(1) 货币常常低于名义标准以下。

第二,有些国家的造币费用由政府支付;有些国家则由私人支付。在后一种情况下,持有银块到造币厂铸造银币,不仅要支付铸币的费用,有时政府还会从中取得一定的收入。在英国,造币费用由国家支付,如果你持有1磅的标准银块到造币厂铸造货币,你可取回62先令,内含同样的标准银1磅。在法国,铸币必须扣除8%的税,这不仅足够支付造币费用,而且可给政府提供一笔小的收入。在英国,由于铸造不收费,所以铸币的价值绝不可能大大超过铸币实际内含的银块的价值。在法国,货币铸造工艺增加铸币的价值,正如加工技术增加精制金银器皿的价值一样。

(2) 铸币的价值有时有税而增加,超过所含银块价值。

---

① 第一版在这里和往下7行是"标准"。

to that of wrought plate. A sum of French money, therefore, containing a certain weight of pure silver, is more valuable than a sum of English money containing an equal weight of pure silver, and must require more bullion, or other commodities, to purchase it. Though the current coin of the two countries, therefore, were equally near the standards of their respective mints, a sum of English money could not well purchase a sum of French money, containing an equal number of ounces of pure silver, nor consequently a bill upon France for such a sum. If for such a bill no more additional money was paid than what was sufficient to compensate the expence of the French coinage, the real exchange might be at par between the two countries, their debts and credits might mutually compensate one another, while the computed exchange was considerably in favour of France. If less than this was paid, the real exchange might be in favour of England, while the computed was in favour of France.

and (3) bank money bears an agio.

Thirdly, and lastly, in some places, as at Amsterdam, Hamburgh, Thirdly, and lastly, in some placesVenice, &c. foreign bills of exchange are paid in what they call bank money; while in others, as at London, Lisbon, Antwerp, Leghorn, &c. they are paid in the common currency of the country. What is called bank money is always of more value than the same nominal sum of common currency. A thousand guilders in the bank of Amsterdam, for example, are of more value than a thousand guilders of Amsterdam currency. The difference between them is called the agio of the bank, which, at Amsterdam, is generally about five per cent. Supposing the current money of two countries equally near to the standard of their respective mints, and that the one pays foreign bills in this common currency, while the other pays them in bank money, it is evident that the computed exchange may be in favour of that which pays in bank money, though the real exchange should be in favour of that which pays in current money; for the same reason that the computed exchange may be in favour of that which pays in better money, or in money nearer to its own standard, though the real exchange should be in favour of that which pays in worse. The computed exchange, before the late reformation of the gold coin, was generally against London with Amsterdam, Hamburgh, Venice, and, I believe, with all other places which pay in what is called bank money. It will by no means follow, however, that the real exchange was

所以，包含一定重量纯银的一定数额法国货币，比包含等量纯银的一定数额英国货币有更大的价值，必须支付更多的银块或商品来购买它。所以，这两国的铸币，虽然同样接近各自造币厂的标准，但包含等量纯银的一定数额英国货币，不一定就能够购买包含等量纯银的一定数额法国货币，因而未必就能购买在法国兑付等量货币额的汇票。如果为购买一张汇票，英国所支付的超额货币，恰好足以补偿法国的铸币费用，那么两国间的汇率，事实上就是平价汇率。债务和债权可以互相抵消，虽然按照计算的两国之间的汇率十分有利于法国。如果为购买这张汇票，英国所支付的货币少于上述数额，那么两国之间的汇率事实上有利于英国，虽然按计算的汇率对法国有利。

（3）和用银行货币兑付带来贴水。 第三，有些地方，如阿姆斯特丹、汉堡、威尼斯等地，都以他们称之为银行货币来兑付外国汇票；但在有些地方，如伦敦、里斯本、安特卫普、勒格亨等地，则用当地通用货币兑付。所谓银行货币，总是比同一名义金额的通用货币有更大价值，例如，阿姆斯特丹银行货币1000盾，就比阿姆斯特丹地方通用货币1000盾有更大的价值。二者之间的差额，被称为银行的贴水，在阿姆斯特丹，贴水一般是大约5%。假设两国通用的货币，同样接近各自造币厂的标准，但一国以通用货币兑付外国汇票，另一国则以银行货币兑付外国汇票，这两国之间的汇率，即使事实上有利于以通用货币兑付的国家，但按照计算，仍然有利于以银行货币兑付的国家。同样的原因可以知道，尽管实际汇兑有利于以较劣货币兑付外国汇票的国家，但是按照计算的汇率有利于以优良货币或用较为接近自己标准的货币进行兑付的国家。在最近金币铸造改革以前，对阿姆斯特丹、汉堡、威尼斯以及对一切其他以所谓银行货

against it. Since the reformation of the gold coin, it has been in favour of London even with those places. The computed exchange has generally been in favour of London with Lisbon, Antwerp, Leghorn, and, if you except France, I believe, with most other parts of Europe that pay in common currency; and it is not improbable that the real exchange was so too.

Digression Concerning Banks Of Deposit, Particularly Concerning That Of Amsterdam[①]

<small>Small states must admit foreign coin, which is of uncertain value.</small> The currency of a great state, such as France or England, generally consists almost entirely of its own coin. Should this currency, therefore, be at any time worn, clipt, or otherwise degraded below its standard value, the state by a reformation of its coin can effectually re-establish its currency. But the currency of a small state, such as Genoa or Hamburgh, can seldom consist altogether in its own coin, but must be made up, in a great measure, of the coins of all the neighbouring states with which its inhabitants have a continual intercourse. Such a state, therefore, by reforming its coin, will not always be able to reform its currency. If foreign bills of exchange are paid in this currency, the uncertain value of any sum, of what is in its own nature so uncertain, must render the exchange always very much against such a state, its currency being, in all foreign states, necessarily valued even below what it is worth.

In order to remedy the inconvenience to which this disadvantageous exchange must have subjected their merchants, such small states, when they began to attend to the interest of trade, have frequently enacted, that foreign bills of exchange of a certain value should be paid, not in common currency, but by an order upon, or by a transfer in the books of a certain bank, established upon the cre-

---

① [See the preface to the 4th ed., above.]

币兑付的地方与伦敦之间的计算出来汇率,我认为都是不利于伦敦的。但我们绝不能因此就下断言,这种汇兑事实上对伦敦不利。从金币铸造改革以来,甚至与这些地方通汇也对伦敦有利。我相信除了对法国以外,伦敦对里斯本、安特卫普、勒格亨以及对欧洲大多数以通用货币兑付汇票的地方,按照计算的汇兑大都对伦敦有利;事实上的汇兑大抵也是这样。

顺便谈谈存款银行,尤其是阿姆斯特丹的存款银行[①]

像法国和英国那样的大国,其通货几乎全由本国铸币构成。如果这种通货由于磨损、裁削或其他原因,而其价值降到标准价值以下,国家可通过重新铸造来有效地恢复通货的原貌。但是,像热那亚和汉堡那样的小国,其通货很少全部由本国铸币构成,一定有大部分是由与它的居民经常往来的各个邻国的铸币构成。像这样的国家,通过重新铸造的方式只能改良其铸币,却不一定能够改良其通货。这种通货由于其本身性质极不确定,一定数额的这种通货的价值也很不确定,所以在外国,对其所做的估价必然低于其实际价值。所以,如果这种国家以这种通货兑付外国汇票,其汇兑就一定对它十分不利。

这种不利的汇兑必然使商人们带来不便。这些小国一旦注意到了贸易的利益,为了解决商人们面临的困难,往往规定,凡有一定价值的外国汇票不得以通用货币兑付,只允许以某类家银行

小国须那值确铸外
一些必须接受些并不定的国币。

① 参见第四版的序言。

国民财富的性质与原理

Banks are then established to pay in standard money regardless of the condition of the coin, and this money bears an agio.
dit, and under the protection of the state; this bank being always obliged to pay, in good and true money, exactly according to the standard of the state. The banks of Venice, Genoa, Amsterdam, Hamburgh, and Nuremberg, seem to have been all originally established with this view, though some of them may have afterwards been made subservient to other purposes. The money of such banks being better than the common currency of the country, necessarily bore an agio, which was greater or smaller, according as the currency was supposed to be more or less degraded below the standard of the state. The agio of the bank of Hamburgh, for example, which is said to be commonly about fourteen per cent. is the supposed difference between the good standard money of the state, and the clipt, worn, and diminished currency poured into it from all the neighbouring states.

Before 1609 the common currency of Amsterdam was 9 per cent. below the standard.
Before 1609 the great quantity of clipt and worn foreign coin, which the extensive trade of Amsterdam brought from all parts of Europe, reduced the value of its currency about nine per cent. below that of good money fresh from the mint. Such money no sooner appeared than it was melted down or carried away, as it always is in such circumstances. The merchants, with plenty of currency, could not always find a sufficient quantity of good money to pay their bills of exchange; and the value of those bills, in spite of several regulations which were made to prevent it, became in a great measure uncertain.

The bank was then established to receive and pay coin at its intrinsic value in good standard money.
In order to remedy these inconveniencies, a bank was established in 1609 under the guarantee of the city. This bank received both foreign coin, and the light and worn coin of the country at its real intrinsic value in the good standard money of the country, deducting only so much as was necessary for defraying the expence of coinage, and the other necessary expence of management. For the value which remained, after this small deduction was made, it gave a credit in its books. This credit was called bank money, which, as it represented money exactly according to the standard of the mint, was always of the same real value, and intrinsically worth more than current money. It was at the same time enacted, that all bills drawn upon or negotiated at Amsterdam of the value of six hundred guilders and upwards should be paid in bank money, which at once took away all uncertainty in the value of those bills. Every merchant, in consequence

的银票兑付或在银行的账簿上进行转账支付。这类银行是依靠国家的信用和在国家的保护下建立起来的,其兑付汇票肯定完全按照国家的标准,以良好和真正的货币兑付。威尼斯、热那亚、阿姆斯特丹、汉堡、纽伦堡等地的银行,原来似乎都是为了这个目的而设立的,尽管其中有些可能是在后来被迫改变了目的。这种银行的货币既优于这些国家的通用货币,必然会产生贴水,贴水的大小要视通货被认为低于国家标准的程度的大小而定。据说,汉堡银行的贴水一般约为14%,这个14%被认为是国家标准良币与由邻国流入的损削低价的劣币二者之间应有的差额。

在1609年以前,阿姆斯特丹广大的贸易从欧洲各地带回来的大量剪削磨损的外国铸币,使阿姆斯特丹通货的价值比造币厂新出良币的价值约低9%。在这种情况下,新出的良币往往是一经铸造出来,立即就被溶解或被出口。拥有大量通货的商人不能常常找到足够的良币来兑付他们的汇票;此类汇票的价值在很大程度上变得十分不确定,尽管制定了一些法规来防止这种不确定性。

为了纠正这种不利情况,阿姆斯特丹于1609年在全市的担保下设立了一家银行。这家银行既接受外国铸币,也接受本国轻量的和已磨损的铸币,除了在价值中扣除必要的铸造费用和管理费用以外,并按照国家的标准良币计算其内在价值。在扣除这些小额费用以后,所剩余的价值作为存款记在银行账簿上。这种存款信用叫做银行货币,因其所代表的货币恰好按照造币厂标准,所以常有相同的真实价值,并且其内在价值又大于通用货币。同时又规定,凡在阿姆斯特丹兑付或卖出的600盾以上的汇票都必须以银行货币进行兑付。这种规定马上就消除了一切汇票在价

of this regulation, was obliged to keep an account with the bank in order to pay his foreign bills of exchange, which necessarily occasioned a certain demand for bank money.

<small>Money in the bank was not only up to the standard, but also secure and easily transferred, so that it bore an agio.</small> Bank money, over and above both its intrinsic superiority to currency, and the additional value which this demand necessarily gives it, has likewise some other advantages. It is secure from fire, robbery, and other accidents; the city of Amsterdam is bound for it; it can be paid away by a simple transfer, without the trouble of counting, or the risk of transporting it from one place to another. In consequence of those different advantages, it seems from the beginning to have borne an agio, and it is generally believed that all the money originally deposited in the bank was allowed to remain there, nobody caring to demand payment of a debt which he could sell for a premium in the market. By demanding payment of the bank, the owner of a bank credit would lose this premium. As a shilling fresh from the mint will buy no more goods in the market than one of our common worn shillings, so the good and true money which might be brought from the coffers of the bank into those of a private person, being mixed and confounded with the common currency of the country, would be of no more value than that currency, from which it could no longer be readily distinguished. While it remained in the coffers of the bank, its superiority was known and ascertained. When it had come into those of a private person, its superiority could not well be ascertained without more trouble than perhaps the difference was worth. By being brought from the coffers of the bank, besides, it lost all the other advantages of bank money; its security, its easy and safe transferability, its use in paying foreign bills of exchange. Over and above all this, it could not be brought from those coffers, as it will appear by and by, without previously paying for the keeping.

<small>The bank receives bullion as well as coin, giving in exchange a credit in bank money to 95 per cent. of the value</small> Those deposits of coin, or those deposits which the bank was bound to restore in coin, constituted the original capital of the bank, or the whole value of what was represented by what is called bank money. At present they are supposed to constitute but a very small part of it. In order to facilitate the trade in bullion, the bank has been for these many years in the practice of giving credit in its books upon deposits of gold and silver bullion. This credit is generally about five

值上的不确定性。由于有了这种规定,每个商人为了要兑付他们的外国汇票,不得不与这家银行往来;这必然会引起对银行货币的需求。

银行货币,除了它对通用货币所固有的优越性和上述需求所必然产生的增加价值以外,还具有其他几种优点。它不会遭遇到火灾、劫掠以及其他意外事故;阿姆斯特丹市对它负全责,其兑付仅仅需要通过单纯的转账,用不着计算,也用不着冒风险由一个地方运到另一个地方。因为它有这些种种优点,似乎自始就产生了一种贴水;大家都认为,所有原来储存在银行内的货币,都听其留在银行账户上,谁也不想要求银行支付,虽然这种存款在市场上出售,可得到一项贴水。如果要求银行支付,银行存款信用的所有者就会失去此项贴水。刚从造币厂铸造出来的先令,不能在市场上比普通磨损了的先令购得更多的货物,所以,从银行金柜中取出来又进入私人金柜中的良好货币,和通用货币混杂在一起,就不易辨认,其价值也就不高于通用货币。当它存在银行金柜时,它的优越性是为大家所知晓和认可的。当它流入私人金柜时,确认它的优越性所付出的代价可能要大于这两种货币的差额。此外,一旦从银行金柜中提出,银行货币也就必定会失去的其他各种优点,如:安全性、方便、安全的可转移支付性以及可以支付外国汇票的用处。不仅如此,要不是预先支付保管费用,就不可能从银行金柜提出银行货币来。

这种铸币存款或者说银行必须以铸币归还的存款,就是银行当初的资本,或者说就是所谓银行货币所代表事物的全部价值。现在,一般认为这只是银行资本的极小一部分。为了便利用金银块进行贸易,许多年以来,银行采取的办法是在银行账簿里给储

国民财富的性质与原理

It also gives a receipt which entitles the bearer to recover the bullion on repaying the sum advanced a- nd paying $\frac{1}{4}$ percent. for silver and $\frac{1}{2}$ per -cent. for gold.

per cent. below the mint price of such bullion. The bank grants at the same time what is called a recipice or receipt, intitling the person who makes the deposit, or the bearer, to take out the bullion again at any time within six months, upon retransferring to the bank a quantity of bank money equal to that for which credit had been given in its books when the deposit was made, and upon paying one-fourth per cent. for the keeping, if the deposit was in silver; and one-half per cent. if it was in gold; but at the same time declaring, that in default of such payment, and upon the expiration of this term, the deposit should belong to the bank at the price at which it had been received, or for which credit had been given in the transfer books. What is thus paid for the keeping of the deposit may be considered as a sort of warehouse rent; and why this warehouse rent should be so much dearer for gold than for silver, several different reasons have been assigned. The fineness of gold, it has been said, is more difficult to be ascertained than that of silver. Frauds are more easily practised, and occasion a greater loss in the more precious metal. Silver, besides, being the standard metal, the state, it has been said, wishes to encourage more the making of deposits of silver than those of gold. ①

The receipes are generally worth something and are renewed at the end of each six months.

Deposits of bullion are most commonly made when the price is somewhat lower than ordinary; and they are taken out again when it happens to rise. In Holland the market price of bullion is generally above the mint price, for the same reason that it was so in England before the late reformation of the gold coin. The difference is said to be commonly from about six to sixteen stivers upon the mark, or eight ounces of silver of eleven parts fine, and one part alloy. The bank price, or the credit which the bank gives for deposits of such silver (when made in foreign coin, of which the fineness is well known and ascertained, such as Mexico dollars), is twenty-two guilders the mark; the mint price is about twenty-three guilders, and the market price is from twenty-three guilders six, to twenty-three guilders sixteen stivers, or from two to three per cent. above the mint price. ② The proportions between the bank price, the mint price, and the mar-

---

① [Eds. 1-3 have the more correct but awkward reading 'than of those of gold'.]

② The following are the prices at which the bank of Amsterdam at present (September 1775) receives bullion and coin of different kinds:

第四篇　第三章

存金银块的人以存款记入。这种存款货币一般比金银条块的造币厂价格约低5%。同时，银行开具一张接收证书或收据，让储存金银块的人或持证人在6个月内任何时候必须取回所存金银，条件是将与那笔存款等额的银行货币交还银行，并支付25‰（如果存的是白银）或50‰（如果存的是黄金）的保管费用；但同时又规定，若是到期仍然没有进行此种支付，那么所存入的金银块就按收时的价格，或按记入存款时的价格收归银行所有。支付的存款保管费用可以看作是一种仓库租金。至于金的仓库租金为什么要比银的仓库租金高那么多，也有几种不同的理由。据说，金的纯度比银的纯度更难确认。比较贵重的金属比较容易做假，由做假而引起的损失也比较大。此外，银是标准金属；据说国家的意图是鼓励储存银而不怎么鼓励储存金。①

银行还发给收据，使持有收据人在偿付垫支项和缴纳25‰的白银保管费或50‰的黄金保管费后，可以取回金银块。

金银条块的价格比通常略低时的储存情况最为普遍；当价格攀升时，则往往被提出。在荷兰，金银条块的市场价格一般比其造币厂价格高，这与最近英格兰金币铸造改革以前的原因相同。两者差额据说一般每马克6—16斯梯弗，或含纯银与合金比例为11∶1的八盎司银。对于这样的银（在铸为外国铸币时，其成色为一般所周知而且被确认，例如墨西哥银元）的储存，银行所给的价格即银行所给的存款，则为每马克22盾；造币厂价格约为23盾，市场价格则为23盾6斯梯弗，甚至到23盾16斯梯弗，超出造币厂价格2%乃至3%。②金银条块的银行价格、造币厂价格以

银行收据一般具有一个价值，并且重新更换。在六个月末

---

① 第一至第三版都是与本文一样，正确有余而恰当不足。
② 下面是阿姆斯特丹银行现在接收不同类型金银条块和铸币的价格（1775年9月）：

ket price of gold bullion, are nearly the same. A person can generally sell his receipt for the difference between the mint price of bullion and the market price. A receipt for bullion is almost always worth something, and it very seldom happens, therefore, that any body suffers his receipt to expire, or allows his bullion to fall to the bank at the price at which it had been received, either by not taking it out before the end of the six months, or by neglecting to pay the one-fourth or one-half per cent. in order to obtain a new receipt for another six months. This, however, though it happens seldom, is said to happen sometimes, and more frequently with regard to gold, than with regard to silver, on account of the higher warehouse-rent which is paid for the keeping of the more precious metal.

The depositor usually parts with his receipt. The person who by making a deposit of bullion obtains both a bank credit and a receipt, pays his bills of exchange as they become due with his bank credit; and either sells or keeps his receipt according as he judges that the price of bullion is likely to rise or to fall. The receipt and the bank credit seldom keep long together, and there is no occasion that they should. The person who has a receipt, and who wants to take out bullion, finds always plenty of bank credits, or

SILVER.

Mexico dollars ⎫
French crowns ⎬ Guilders.
English silver coin ⎭ B − 22 per mark.

Mexico dollars new coin . . 21 10
Ducatoons 3
Rix dollars 2 8

Bar silver containing $\frac{11}{12}$ fine silver 21 per mark, and in this proportion down to $\frac{1}{4}$ fine, on which 5 guilders are given.

Fine bars, 23 per mark.

GOLD.

Portugal coin ⎫
Guineas ⎬ B − 310 per mark.
Louis dórs new ⎭

Ditto old 300
New ducats . . . . . . 4 19 8 per ducat.

Bar or ingot gold is received in proportion to its fineness compared with the above foreign gold coin. Upon fine bars the bank gives 340 per mark. In general, however, something more is given upon coin of a known fineness, than upon gold and silver bars, of which the fineness cannot be ascertained but by a process of

及市场价格几乎保持着相同的比例。一个人一般可以为了金银条块的造币厂价格与市场价格之间的差额,出售其受领证书。金银条块的受领证书一般具有一些价值。所以,坐等6个月期满,不把储金提出来或忘记支付25‰或50‰的保管费,而获取另6个月的新受领证书,以致银行按收时的价格把储金收为己有,这种情况并不常见。但是,这种现象虽不常见,但也时有发生,而金的情况又比银的情况更经常发生,因为银的保管费用较少,金则因为是比较贵重的金属,其保管也要支付较高的仓库租金。

  由储存金银条块而换得银行存款和收据的人,在其汇票到期时以银行存款兑付。至于收据是出卖还是保留,那要看他对于金银条块价格的涨跌做出的判断如何。但此种银行存款和收据,大都不会两者一起长期保留,也没有长期一起保留的必要。持有收据并要提取金银条块的人,总是发现有许多银行存款或银行货币储存人总是放弃收据。

银 { 墨西哥银圆 / 法国硬币 / 英国银币 }　　每马克 22 盾

墨西哥新铸银圆　　每马克 21 盾 10 斯梯弗
金币　　　　　　　每马克 3 盾
里克司元　　　　　每马克 2 盾 8 斯梯弗

含 11/12 的纯银的条银每马克 21 盾;只含有 1/4 的纯银,相应的价格为 5 盾。纯的条银每马克为 23 盾。

金 { 葡萄牙金铸币 / 几尼 / 路易多新币 }　　每马克 310 盾

路易多旧币　　　　每马克 300 盾
新金币　　　　　　每达克特 4 盾 19 斯梯弗 8 盾

  金条或金块按照纯度与上述外国金铸币进行比较。银行按照每马克 340 盾接收纯金条。然而,一般来说银行给一种著名的金币的接收价格高于由于在熔化和分割过程中纯度不太确定的金条和银条的价格。

melting and assaying. bank money to buy at the ordinary price; and the person who has bank money, and wants to take out bullion, finds receipts always in equal abundance.

<small>The bank money and the receipt together equal in value the bullion deposited.</small> The owners of bank credits, and the holders of receipts, constitute two different sorts of creditors against the bank. The holder of a receipt cannot draw out the bullion for which it is granted, without reassigning to the bank a sum of bank money equal to the price at which the bullion had been received. If he has no bank money of his own, he must purchase it of those who have it. The owner of bank money cannot draw out bullion without producing to the bank receipts for the quantity which he wants. If he has none of his own, he must buy them of those who have them. The holder of a receipt, when he purchases bank money, purchases the power of taking out a quantity of bullion, of which the mint price is five per cent. above the bank price. The agio of five per cent. therefore, which he commonly pays for it, is paid, not for an imaginary, but for a real value. The owner of bank money, when he purchases a receipt, purchases the power of taking out a quantity of bullion of which the market price is commonly from two to three per cent. above the mint price. The price which he pays for it, therefore, is paid likewise for a real value. The price of the receipt, and the price of the bank money, compound or make up between them the full value or price of the bullion.

<small>Receipts for current coin are also given, but these are often of no value and are allowed to expire.</small> Upon deposits of the coin current in the country, the bank grants receipts likewise as well as bank credits; but those receipts are frequently of no value, and will bring no price in the market. Upon ducatoons, for example, which in the currency pass for three guilders three stivers each, the bank gives a credit of three guilders only, or five per cent. below their current value. It grants a receipt likewise intitling the bearer to take out the number of ducatoons deposited at any time within six months, upon paying one-fourth per cent. for the keeping. This receipt will frequently bring no price in the market. Three guilders bank money generally sell in the market for three guilders three stivers, the full value of the ducatoons, if they were taken out of the bank; and before they can be taken out, one-fourth per cent. must be paid for the keeping, which would be mere loss to the holder of the receipt. If the agio of the bank, however, should at any

让他以正常价格购买；同样，拥有银行货币并要提出金银条块的人，也发现有同样多的收据让他购买。

银行存款信用所有者和收据持有者是银行的两种不同债权人。如果收据持有者没有向银行支付与金银条块接收价格相等数额的银行货币，就不能提取收据上所记明的金银条块。如果他自己没有银行货币，他就得向拥有银行货币的人购买银行货币。但有银行货币的人，如果不能向银行提供收据表明自己所需要的数额，他也不能提取金银条块。如果他自己没有收据，他也得向有收据的人购买。有收据的人购买银行货币，其实就是购买提取一定数量金银条块的权力，这种金银条块的造币厂价格比其银行价格高5%。所以，他为购买银行货币而通常支付的那5%贴水，并不是为了一种想象的价值，而是为了一个真实的价值才支付的。有银行货币的人购买收据，其实也就是购买提取一定数量金银条块的权力，这种金银条块的市场价格，一般比其造币厂价格高2%甚至到3%。所以，他为购买收据而支付的价格，也同样是为了一个真实的价值而支付的。收据的价格和银行货币的价格合计起来，便构成金银条块的完全价值或价格。

银行货币和收据的价格加起来等于金银条块的价格。

以国内流通的铸币存入银行，银行既给予银行信贷，也发给收据；但这种收据通常是没有价值的，在市场上也没有价格。例如，以3盾3斯梯弗的达克金币存入银行，所换得的信用只值3盾，或者说比流通价值低了5%。银行虽然也同样发给收据，使收据持有人在6个月内的任何时候，在支付2.5‰的保管费用后，提出存在银行的达克；但这种收据往往在市场上不值钱。3盾银行货币在市场上卖价可以为3盾3斯梯弗；如果在提出以后，可以得到达克的全部价值，但由于在提出以前，必须交纳2.5‰的保管费，所以得失恰好互相抵消。可是，如果银行贴水降为3%，这种

可以给存入铸币的人出具收据，但这些收据常常没有价值，其自到期。

time fall to three per cent. such receipts might bring some price in the market, and might sell for one and three-fourths per cent. But the agio of the bank being now generally about five per cent. such receipts are frequently allowed to expire, or, as they express it, to fall to the bank. The receipts which are given for deposits of gold ducats fall to it yet more frequently, because a higher warehouse-rent, or one-half per cent. must be paid for the keeping of them before they can be taken out again. The five per cent. which the bank gains, when deposits either of coin or bullion are allowed to fall to it, may be considered as the warehouse-rent for the perpetual keeping of such deposits.

<small>So there is a considerable sum of bank money for which the receipts have expired, but it is not a large proportion of the whole.</small> The sum of bank money for which the receipts are expired must be very considerable. It must comprehend the whole original capital of the bank, which, it is generally supposed, has been allowed to remain there from the time it was first deposited, nobody caring either to renew his receipt or to take out his deposit, as, for the reasons already assigned, neither the one nor the other could be done without loss. But whatever may be the amount of this sum, the proportion which it bears to the whole mass of bank money is supposed to be very small. The bank of Amsterdam has for these many years past been the great warehouse of Europe for bullion, for which the receipts are very seldom allowed to expire, or, as they express it, to fall to the bank. The far greater part of the bank money, or of the credits upon the books of the bank, is supposed to have been created, for these many years past, by such deposits which the dealers in bullion are continually both making and withdrawing.

<small>This cannot be drawn out of the bank.</small> No demand can be made upon the bank but by means of a recipice or receipt. The smaller mass of bank money, for which the receipts are expired, is mixed and confounded with the much greater mass for which they are still in force; so that, though there may be a considerable sum of bank money, for which there are no receipts, there is no specific sum or portion of it, which may not at any time be demanded by one. The bank cannot be debtor to two persons for the same thing; and the owner of bank money who has no receipt, cannot demand payment of the bank till he buys one. In ordinary and quiet times, he can find no difficulty in getting one to buy at the market price, which generally corresponds with the price at which he can sell the coin or bullion it intitles him to take out of the bank.

It might be otherwise during a public calamity; an invasion, for example, such as that of the French in 1672. The owners of bank money being then all eager to draw it out of the bank, in

收据便可在市场上以一定的价格出售,比如以1.75%的价格出售。但现在银行贴水大都在5%左右,所以,这种收据往往任其期满,或者像人们所说,听其归属银行所有。至于储存金达克而得到的收据,就更经常任其期满,因为其仓库租金更为昂贵即为0.5%。在这种铸币或条块的储存听任其归属银行所有时,银行往往可获利5%,这个5%可看作是永远保管这种储存物的仓库租金。

收据过期的银行货币的数额肯定不小。收据已经过期的银行货币的数额,必定包含银行当初的全部资本。根据一般假设,银行当初的全部资本,自从第一次存入以来,就没有一个人想要调换更新收据,或把储金提出,因为根据我们上面举出的种种理由,那就无论采用两种方法中任何一种,都必然有损失。但这个数额无论怎样大,在银行货币全额中所占的比例是很小的。在过去好几年里,阿姆斯特丹银行是欧洲最大的金银条块仓库,但其收据却是很少过期的,或很少按一般所说归属银行所有。比这部分大得多的银行货币或银行账簿上的存款信用,都是过去好几年来由金银条块商人不断储存和不断提取而形成的。

尽管这一部分收据过期的银行货币相比,它在银行货币所占比例并不大。

没有收据,就不能向银行有所要求。收据过期的那部分数量比较小的银行货币,和收据仍然有效的那部分数量比较大的银行货币混在一起,所以没有收据的银行货币额显然很可观,但不可能没有人对某一特定部分银行货币永远提出要求。银行不能为同一事物而对两个人承担债务人义务;没有收据的银行货币所有者,在未购得收据以前,绝不可能要求银行付款。在正常时期,按照市场价格他会毫不费力地购得一张收据。这种购买价格和持有收据向银行提取铸币或金银条块能在市场上销售的价格一般是相一致的。

没有收据是不能从银行提取货金块或条块的。

但在国难时期,情形就两样了。例如,在1672年法兰西人侵

国民财富的性质与原理

^{So that if all the holders of bank money desired to exchange it for coin and bullion receipts might comm- and an exorbit- ant price.} order to have it in their own keeping, the demand for receipts might raise their price to an exorbitant height. The holders of them might form extravagant expectations, and, instead of two or three per cent. demand half the bank money for which credit had been given upon the deposits that the receipts had respectively been granted for. The enemy, informed of the constitution of the bank, might even buy them up, in order to prevent the carrying away of the treasure. In such emergencies, the bank, it is supposed, would break through its ordinary rule of making payment only to the holders of receipts. The holders of receipts, who had no bank money, must have received within two or three per cent. of the value of the deposit for which their respective receipts had been granted. The bank, therefore, it is said, ^{but it is supposed in an e- mergency the bank would p- ay out money or bullion without receipts being offered.} would in this case make no scruple of paying, either with money or bullion, the full value of what the owners of bank money who could get no receipts were credited for in its books; paying at the same time two or three per cent. to such holders of receipts as had no bank money, that being the whole value which in this state of things could justly be supposed due to them.

Even in ordinary and quiet times it is the interest of the holders of receipts to depress the agio, in order either to buy bank money (and consequently the bullion, which their receipts would then enable them to take out of the bank) so much cheaper, or to sell their re- ^{Of late years t- he bank has alw- ays sold bank m- oney at 5 per cent. agio and bought at 4 per cent.} ceipts to those who have bank money, and who want to take out bullion, so much dearer; the price of a receipt being generally equal to the difference between the market price of bank money, and that of the coin or bullion for which the receipt had been granted. It is the interest of the owners of bank money, on the contrary, to raise the agio, in order either to sell their bank money so much dearer, or to buy a receipt so much cheaper. To prevent the stock-jobbing tricks which those opposite interests might sometimes occasion, the bank has of late years come to the resolution to sell at all times bank money for currency, at five per cent. agio, and to buy it in again at four per cent. agio. In consequence of this resolution, the agio can never either rise above five, or sink below four per cent. and the proportion between the market price of bank and that of current money, is kept at all times very near to the proportion between their intrinsic values. Before this resolution was taken, the market price of bank money used sometimes to rise so high as nine per cent. agio, and sometimes to

— 1038 —

第四篇　第三章

入时,银行货币所有者都想从银行提出储金,归属自己保存,大家都需要收据。这种收据需求可能使收据的价格提高到过高的水平。有收据的人可能会作非分之想,不再要求各收据所记明的银行货币的2%或3%,却要求50%。了解银行机构的敌人,甚至会把一切收据都收买进来以防止财宝取出。一般认为,在这个非常时期银行会打破只对收据的持有者付款的常规。没有银行货币但有收据的人,一定领取了各自收据所记明的储金价值的2%或3%。所以,有人说,在这种情况下,银行定会毫不犹豫地用货币或金银条块,对有银行货币记在银行账簿上但无收据可向银行提取储金的人支付全部价值;同时,对于有收据但无银行货币的人支付2%或3%,因为这个数目在这个时候已经是他们所应得到的全部价值。

〔所持有银行货币的人想换取金银条块的话,结果对其价格的促高到过高水平。〕

〔一般认为,在非常时期银行会打破只对收据的持有者付款的规定。〕

即在正常和平静的时候,收据持有者的利益在于减低贴水,以至于以较低价格购买银行货币(从而以较低价格购买收据上所记明的可以提取的金银条块),或以较高价格把收据卖给有银行货币并希望提取金银条块的人;收据的价格,一般等于银行货币的市场价格与收据所记明的铸币或金银条块的市场价格之差。反之,银行货币所有者的利益却在于提高贴水,用以高价出售其银行货币,或以低价购买收据。这样相反的利害关系往往会引起投机买卖的欺诈行为。为防止这种欺诈行为,近数年来银行决定,不论什么时候卖出银行货币换取通货要贴水5%,而再度买进银行货币要贴水4%。这种决定的结果使贴水不能上升到5%以上,也不能下降到4%以下;银行货币和流通货币二者市场价格之间的比例,不论在什么时候,都很接近它们内在价值之间的比例。但在没有这个决定以前,银行货币的市场价格高低不一,按照这

〔近些年来银行总是以贴水5%卖出银行货币,以4%的贴水购进银行货币。〕

1039

sink so low as par, according as opposite interests happened to influence the market.

<small>It professes to lend out no part of t- he deposits.</small> The bank of Amsterdam professes to lend out no part of what is deposited with it, but, for every guilder for which it gives credit in its books, to keep in its repositories the value of a guilder either in money or bullion. That it keeps in its repositories all the money or bullion for which there are receipts in force, for which it is at all times liable to be called upon, and which, in reality, is continually going from it and returning to it again, cannot well be doubted. But whether it does so likewise with regard to that part of its capital, for which the receipts are long ago expired, for which in ordinary and quiet times it cannot be called upon, and which in reality is very likely to remain with it for ever, or as long as the States of the United Provinces subsist, may perhaps appear more uncertain. At Amsterdam, however, no point of faith is better established than that for every guilder, circulated as bank money, there is a correspondent guilder in gold or silver to be found in the treasure of the bank. The city is guarantee that it should be so. The bank is under the direction of the four reigning burgomasters, who are changed every year. Each new set of burgomasters visits the treasure, compares it with the books, receives it upon oath, and delivers it over, with the same awful solemnity, to the set which succeeds; and in that sober and religious country oaths are not yet disregarded. A rotation of this kind seems alone a sufficient security against any practices which cannot be avowed. Amidst all the revolutions which faction has ever occasioned in the government of Amsterdam, the prevailing party has at no time accused their predecessors of infidelity in the administration of the bank. No accusation could have affected more deeply the reputation and fortune of the disgraced party, and if such an accusation could have been supported, we may be assured that it would have been brought. In 1672, when the French king was at Utrecht, the bank of Amsterdam paid so readily as left no doubt of the fidelity with which it had observed its engagements. Some of the pieces which were then brought from its repositories appeared to have been scorched with the fire which happened in the town-house soon after the bank was established. ① Those

---

① [*Lectures*, pp. 193、194. and is quoted thence by Anderson, *Commerce*, A. D. 1672.]

两种相反利害关系对市场的影响,有时贴水上升到9%,有时又下跌而与通用货币平价。

阿姆斯特丹银行宣称,不贷出一分储金;储金账簿上每记下一盾,在金库内就保藏有与一盾等价的货币或金银条块。收据尚未失效,随时可以提取,而事实上不断地流出和流入的货币和金银条块部分,肯定全部保藏在金库内;但由于收据到期很久,由于在正常与和平时期不要求提取和实际上大概在联邦国家存在的时期内会永远留在银行里的那一部分资本,是否也是这样却似乎存在疑问。然而,在阿姆斯特丹,有一盾银行货币就有一盾金银存在银行金库里这一信条,在各种信条中它总算是执行得最有力。阿姆斯特丹市做了这个信条的保证人。银行置于四个现任市长的监督之下,这四个市长每年改选一次,新任的四个市长视察银行金库,对照账簿,宣誓接管;后来再以同样庄严的仪式把金库点交给继任者。在这个真诚的宗教国家,宣誓制度至今有效。有了此种更迭,对于一切不正当行为似乎有了充分保障。党派纷争在阿姆斯特丹政治上引起过许多次革命,但在这一切革命中,占据优势的党派都没在银行管理这一点上攻击他们前任的不忠诚。对于失势党派的名誉和信用,再没有第二种事情比这种攻击具有更加深刻的影响;如果这种攻击具有真凭实据的话,我们可以断言那是肯定会被提出来的。在1672年,当时法国国王在乌德勒支,阿姆斯特丹银行付款迅速,人们对它履行契约的忠诚确信不疑。当时,从银行金库中提出的货币,有些还是银行设立后市政厅大火所烧焦的货币。[①] 这些货

旁注:阿姆斯特丹银行宣布不会贷出一分储备金。

[①] 《关于法律、警察、岁入及军备的演讲》,第193、194页。在安德森1672年出版的《商业》里引用过。

pieces, therefore, must have lain there from that time.

<small>The amount of treasure in the bank is a subject of conjecture.</small> What may be the amount of the treasure in the bank, is a question which has long employed the speculations of the curious. Nothing but conjecture can be offered concerning it. It is generally reckoned that there are about two thousand people who keep accounts with the bank, and allowing them to have, one with another, the value of fifteen hundred pounds sterling lying upon their respective accounts (a very large allowance), the whole quantity of bank money, and consequently of treasure in the bank, will amount to about three millions sterling, or, at eleven guilders the pound sterling, thirty-three millions of guilders;① a great sum, and sufficient to carry on a very extensive circulation; but vastly below the extravagant ideas which some people have formed of this treasure.

<small>The city derives a considerable revenue from the various profits of the bank.</small> The city of Amsterdam derives a considerable revenue from the bank. Besides what may be called the warehouse-rent above mentioned, each person, upon first opening an account with the bank, pays a fee of ten guilders; and for every new account three guilders three stivers; for every transfer two stivers; and if the transfer is for less than three hundred guilders, six stivers, in order to discourage the multiplicity of small transactions. The person who neglects to balance his account twice in the year forfeits twenty-five guilders. The person who orders a transfer for more than is upon his account, is obliged to pay three per cent. for the sum overdrawn, and his order is set aside into the bargain. The bank is supposed too to make a considerable profit by the sale of the foreign coin or bullion which sometimes falls to it by the expiring of receipts, and which is always kept till it can be sold with advantage. It makes a profit likewise by selling bank money at five per cent. agio, and buying it in at four. These different emoluments amount to a good deal more than what is necessary for paying the salaries of officers, and defraying the expence of management. What is paid for the keeping of bullion upon receipts,

---

① [N. Magens, *Universal Merchant*, ed. Horsley, pp. 32、33, who also protests against the common exaggeration, gives 3000 as a maximum estimate for the number of accounts, and 60000000 guilders as the utmost amount of the treasure.]

币必定是从那时候起就保存在银行金库内的。

这家银行的金银总额究竟有多少,老早就成为好事者猜测的问题。但至于总额有多少,只能猜测。一般认为,与这家银行有资金账目往来的人约有2000个;假设他们每人平均存有1500镑的价值(那是最大的假设),那么银行货币总额,即银行金银总额大约等于300万镑,以每镑11盾计算,就大约等于3300万盾。① 这样大的一个数额,足以经营极其广泛的流通,但却远远低于一些人熟悉总额所做的夸大的臆测数字。

阿姆斯特丹市从这家银行获得了很大的收入。除了前面提到的仓库租金,凡是第一次在银行开具往来结算账户的,必须交纳费用10盾;每开一次新的账户,要交纳费用3盾3斯梯弗;每转账结算一次,必须交纳费用2斯梯弗;如果转账金额在300盾以下,则必须交纳6斯梯弗,以防止过多的小额转账。每年两次没有结清账目的,罚款25盾。转账的金额如果超过了储存的账户金额,必须交纳超支金额的3%并搁置结算请求。假设银行由收据期满归属为自己所有的外国铸币和金银条块,保存到有利时再出售,也会获得不少利润。此外,银行货币以5%的贴水卖出,以4%的贴水买入,也会给银行带来利润。这些不同的收益大大超过支付职员工薪和管理费用。仅就储存收取的保管费用一项收入,据说有15万盾到20万盾的年纯收入。不过,机关设立的目

——

① 马根斯:《环球商人》,豪斯里出版,第32、33页。马根斯对一般的夸大估计表示反对;他给出的估计为每个账户的金额的最大数为3000镑,那么银行金库所具有最大的金额为6000万盾。

is alone supposed to amount to a neat annual revenue of between one hundred and fifty thousand and two hundred thousand guilders. Public utility, however, and not revenue, was the original object of this institution. Its object was to relieve the merchants from the inconvenience of a disadvantageous exchange. The revenue which has arisen from it was unforeseen, and may be considered as accidental. But it is now time to return from this long digression, into which I have been insensibly led in endeavouring to explain the reasons why the exchange between the countries which pay in what is called bank money, and those which pay in common currency, should generally appear to be in favour of the former, and against the latter. The former pay in a species of money of which the intrinsic value is always the same, and exactly agreeable to the standard of their respective mints; the latter in a species of money of which the intrinsic value is continually varying, and is almost always more or less below that standard. ①

PART II
Of the Unreasonableness of those extraordinary Restraints upon other Principles②

In the foregoing Part of this Chapter I have endeavoured to shew,③ even upon the principles of the commercial system, how unnecessary it is to lay extraordinary restraints upon the importation of goods from those countries with which the balance of trade is supposed to be disadvantageous.

Nothing, however, can be more absurd than this whole doctrine

---

① [Ed. I runs on here as follows, 'But though the computed exchange must generally be in favour of the former, the real exchange may frequently be in favour of the latter.']

② [In place of this part heading ed. I reads, in square-bracketed italics, 'End of the Digression concerning Banks of Deposit'.]

③ [In place of this first line ed. I reads, 'Though the computed exchange between any two places were in every respect the same with the real, it would not always follow that what is called the balance of trade was in favour of that place which had the ordinary course of exchange in its favour. The ordinary course of exchange might, indeed, in this case, be a tolerable indication of the ordinary state of debt and credit between them, and show which of the two countries usually had occasion to send out money to the other. But the ordinary state of debt and credit between any two places is not always entirely regulated by the ordinary course of their dealings with one another, but is influenced by that of the dealings of both with many other countries.]

标原本不是收入,而是公共利益。其目的在于减轻商人由于不利的汇兑带来的不便。由此而产生的收入是预料之外的,简直可以说是一种意外。现在是回归主题的时候了,我偏离主题的原因在于想要说明,是什么原因使得用银行货币进行汇兑的国家比用通用货币进行兑付的国家更加有利。前一种国家用以兑付汇票的货币,其内在价值总是不变,恰好与其造币厂的标准相符;后一种国家用以兑付汇票的货币,其内在价值不断变动,而且几乎总是多多少少低于其造币厂的标准。①

第二节 按照其他原则,② 论这些特殊限制的不合理性

本章的上一节主要说明,③根据重商主义体系原理,我国与某些国家贸易出现逆差时,对其货物的进口加以特别的限制是多么的不必要。

不管怎么说,在这种贸易平衡理论之上建立起的种种限制政策以及几乎所有其他的商业条款,都是再愚蠢不过的东西了。根据这种理论,两个国家贸易时,如果贸易差额持平,则双方都既不

---

① 第一版内容如下:"尽管计算的汇兑有利于前者,但真实汇兑则有利于后者。"

② 在版本1中为加了方括号的斜体字"关于储蓄的最后题外话"。

③ 在第一版中写道:"尽管两地之间估计的交易在每个方面都和真实情况一样,但所谓的贸易平衡也并不总是偏袒于外汇兑换率占有利地位的国家。在这种情况下,外汇兑换率只是二者之间债务和借贷的一种象征,表明一个国家向另一个国家借出了多少钱。但是两地之间正常的债务和借贷之间的关系,并不总是完全由它们之间的兑换率决定,而是还受它们与其他国家之间的汇率影响。"

The whole doctrine of the balance of trade is absurd.
of the balance of trade, upon which, not only these restraints, but almost all the other regulations of commerce are founded. When two places trade with one another, this doctrine supposes that, if the balance be even, neither of them either loses or gains; but if it leans in any degree to one side, that one of them loses, and the other gains in proportion to its declension from the exact equilibrium. Both suppositions are false. A trade which is forced by means of bounties and monopolies, may be, and commonly is disadvantageous to the country in whose favour it is meant to be established, as I shall endeavour to shew hereafter. But that trade which, without force or constraint, is naturally and regularly carried on between any two places, is always advantageous, though not always equally so, to both.

By advantage or gain, I understand, not the increase of the quantity of gold and silver, but that of the exchangeable value of the annual produce of the land and labour of the country, or the increase of the annual revenue of its inhabitants.

Where there is an even balance and the exchange consists wholly of native commodites two countries trading will gain nearly equally.
If the balance be even, and if the trade between the two places consist altogether in the exchange of their native commodities, they will, upon most occasions, not only both gain, but they will gain equally, or very near equally: each will in this ease afford a market for a part of the surplus produce of the other: each will replace a capital which had been employed in raising and preparing for the market① this part of the surplus produce of the other, and which had been distributed among, and given revenue and maintenance to a certain number of its inhabitants. Some part of the inhabitants of each, therefore, will indirectly derive their revenue and maintenance from the other. As the commodities exchanged too are supposed to be of equal value, so the two capitals employed in the trade will, upon most occasions, be equal, or very nearly equal; and both being employed in raising the native commodities of the two countries, the revenue and maintenance which their distribution will afford to the inhabitants of each will be equal, or very nearly equal. This revenue and maintenance, thus mutually afforded, will be greater or smaller in proportion to the extent of their dealings. If these should annually amount to an hundred thousand pounds, for example, or to a million on each side, each of them would afford an annual revenue in the one case of an hundred thousand pounds, in the other, of a million, to the inhabitants of the other.

If their trade should be of such a nature that one of them exported to the other nothing but native commodities, while the returns of

---

① [Ed. I does not contain 'and preparing for the market'.]

亏也不赚;如果贸易差额稍稍有些倾斜,就会一方亏损,一方赢利,赢利与受损的程度成正比。但是,这两种设想都是错误的。某个国家为了赢利,通过奖励和垄断手段而促成的贸易,对本国可能是没有益处的。事实上,通常也的确如此,下面的内容还会讲到。而两国之间自然地、正常地进行的,不受强制和约束的贸易却对双方均有利,虽然不一定同等有利。

_{整个贸易平衡理论都是荒谬的。}

所谓利益或利润,我认为,不是金银量的增加,而是国家的土地和劳动这二者年产品交换价值的增加,或者是国民年收入的增加。

如果两国的贸易额持平,同时两个国家的贸易货物都是各自的国产商品,那么大多数情况下,双方不仅都会赢利,而且赢利相等或几乎相等。双方均为对方的一部分剩余产品提供了一个市场,而为了这个市场①生产和准备这部分剩余产品所用的资本以及分配给某些国民的收入和生计,都由对方来归还。因此,两个国家各有一部分国民将间接地从对方获得他们的收入和生计。假设两国交换的商品价值相等,那么大多数情况下,双方在贸易上的投入也相等或几乎相等。两个国家生产本国商品所用的资本以及支付部分国民的收入和生计,也是相等或几乎相等的。这种为彼此支付的收入和生计根据交易量的大小有多有少。比方说,如果一方给对方的国民支付了10万镑或者100万镑,那么对方也同样给该方国民支付了10万镑或100万镑。

_{贸易额持平且交换的国产商品,两国赢利相等或几乎相等。}

假设两个国家之间进行贸易,一方向另一方出口的全部是国产商品,而另一方的回程货全部为外国商品,在这种以商品支付

---

① 在第一版中没有"为了这个市场准备"。

If one exported. nothing but native commodities, but the other consisted altogether in foreign goods; the balance, in this case, would still be supposed even, commodities being paid for with commodities. They would, in this case too, both gain, but they would not gain equally; and the inhabitants of the country which exported nothing but native commodities would derive the greatest revenue from the trade. If England, for example, should import from France nothing but the native commodities of that country, and, not having such commodities of its own as were in demand there, should annually repay them by sending thither a large quantity of foreign goods, tobacco, we shall suppose, and East India goods; this trade, though it would give some revenue to the inhabitants of both countries, would give more to those of France than to those of England. The whole French capital annually employed in it would annually be distributed among the people of France. But that part of the English capital only which was employed in producing the English commodities with which those foreign goods were purchased, would be annually distributed among the people of England. The greater part of it would replace the capitals which had been employed in Virginia, Indostan, and China, and which had given revenue and maintenance to the inhabitants of those distant countries. If the capitals were equal, or nearly equal, therefore, this employment of the French capital would augment much more the revenue of the people of France, than that of the English capital would the revenue of the people of England. France would in this case carry on a direct foreign trade of consumption with England; whereas England would carry on a round-about trade of the same kind with France. The different effects of a capital employed in the direct, and of one employed in the round-about foreign trade of consumption, have already been fully explained.

Mixed cases conform to the principle. There is not, probably, between any two countries, a trade which consists altogether in the exchange either of native commodities on both sides, or of native commodities on one side and of foreign goods on the other. Almost all countries exchange with one another partly native and partly foreign goods. That country, however, in whose cargoes there is the greatest proportion of native, and the least of foreign goods, will always be the principal gainer.

If it was not with tobacco and East India goods, but with gold and silver, that England paid for the commodities annually imported from France, the balance, in this case, would be supposed uneven, commodities not being paid for with commodities, but with gold and silver. The trade, however, would, in this case, as in the foregoing, give some revenue to the inhabitants of both countries, but more to those of France than to those of England. It would give some revenue to those of England. The capital which had been employed in producing the English goods that purchased this gold and silver, the capital

商品的情况下，贸易额仍然认为是平衡的。此时两国都赢利，不过赢利的大小不等，全部出口国产商品的国家在这种贸易中赢利最大。比方说，英国从法国进口的全部是法国国产货，而英国本国又不生产法国所需要的货品，于是不得不每年出口大量的外国货、烟草以及东印度的货物。这种贸易尽管给两国的国民都带来了收入，但给法国的却比给英国的多。法国每年投入贸易的资本将全部分配给法国人民，而英国每年仅仅是一部分资本在英国人民中间分配，这部分是用来生产商品与外国交换的，大部分资本则用来支付弗吉尼亚、印度和中国这些国家生产商品所需资本以及这些国家的国民的收入和生计。因此，如果英法两国投入贸易的资本相等或几乎相等，那么，法国人民增加的收入要比英国人民的多。因为在这种情况下，法国向英国直接出口消费品，而英国向法国间接出口消费品。这两种贸易方式所产生的不同结果，前面的章节已详细论述了。

如果一方只出口国产商品，另一方只出口外国商品，双方都赢利，但前者赢利更多。

　　两个国家贸易时，不大可能出现双方都是国产商品或者一方全部是国产商品而另一方全部为外国商品。几乎所有的国家都是一部分国产商品一部分外国商品。那些国产商品占较大份额、外国商品占较小份额的国家，赢利最多。

在商品混合的情况下，上述原则仍然适用。

　　假设英国每年从法国进口货物时支付的不是烟草和东印度的货物，而是金银，那么这种情况下，贸易额不再持平，因为不是以商品支付商品，而是以金银来支付商品。其实在这种情况下，正如前面所提到的那样，贸易仍然会给两国人民带来收入，但是给法国人民的要比给英国人民的多。给英国人民的只是部分收入。那些用来生产英国货物以换取金银的资本，以及给部分英国人民提供收入的资本都被偿还，以便能够继续使用。出口金银与

国民财富的性质与原理

<small>It would be no worse for England to pay in gold and silver than in tobacco.</small> which had been distributed among, and given revenue to, certain inhabitants of England, would thereby be replaced, and enabled to continue that employment. The whole capital of England would no more be diminished by this exportation of gold and silver, than by the exportation of an equal value of any other goods. On the contrary, it would, in most cases, be augmented. No goods are sent abroad but those for which the demand is supposed to be greater abroad than at home, and of which the returns consequently, it is expected, will be of more value at home than the commodities exported. If the tobacco which, in England, is worth only a hundred thousand pounds, when sent to France will purchase wine which is, in England, worth a hundred and ten thousand pounds, the exchange will augment the capital of England by ten thousand pounds. If a hundred thousand pounds of English gold, in the same manner, purchase French wine, which, in England, is worth a hundred and ten thousand, this exchange will equally augment the capital of England by ten thousand pounds. As a merchant who has a hundred and ten thousand pounds worth of wine in his cellar, is a richer man than he who has only a hundred thousand pounds worth of tobacco in his warehouse, so is he likewise a richer man than he who has only a hundred thousand pounds worth of gold in his coffers. He can put into motion a greater quantity of industry, and give revenue, maintenance, and employment, to a greater number of people than either of the other two. But the capital of the country is equal to the capitals of all its different inhabitants, and the quantity of industry which can be annually maintained in it, is equal to what all those different capitals can maintain. Both the capital of the country, therefore, and the quantity of industry which can be annually maintained in it, must generally be augmented by this exchange. It would, indeed, be more advantageous for England that it could purchase the wines of France with its own hard-ware and broadcloth, than with either the tobacco of Virginia, or the gold and silver of Brazil and Peru. A direct foreign trade of consumption is always more advantageous than a round-about one. But a round-about foreign trade of consumption, which is carried on with gold and silver, does not seem to be less advantageous than any other equally round-about one. Neither is a country which has no mines, more likely to be exhausted of gold and silver by this annual exportation of those metals, than one which does not grow tobacco by the like annual exportation of that plant. As a country which has where-withal to buy tobacco will never be long in want of it, so neither will one be long in want of gold and silver which has wherewithal to purchase those metals.

  It is a losing trade, it is said, which a workman carries on with the alehouse; and the trade which a manufacturing nation would naturally carry on with a wine country, may be considered as a trade of

出口同等价值的其他货物一样,英国资本的总量都不会减小。相反,在大数情况下,资本将会增加。只有那些海外需求量比国内需求量大,其回程货在国内的价值比出口的商品大的货物才出口。假设在英国烟草仅仅值 10 万英镑,出口到法国后可以从法国购回价值 11 万英镑的酒,那么这种交易就使英国的资本增加了 1 万英镑。如果英国用价值 10 万英镑的金子,也进行上述的交易,那么,它同样可以使英国的资本增加 1 万英镑。一个在地窖里储存了价值 11 万英镑酒水的商人,要比一个在仓库里存放了 10 万英镑烟草的商人富有,同样,他也比一个在保险箱中放了 10 万英镑金子的人富有。与其他两人相比,他可以投入更多的产业生产,给更多的人提供收入、生计和工作。但是国家的资本等于全体人民资本的总和,而国家所维持的产业量等于所有资本所能维持的产业量。所以,国家的资本和其每年所维持的产业量,会因这种交换而增加。就英国而言,用它自己的铁器和宽幅厚呢来购买法国的葡萄酒比用弗吉尼亚烟草或巴西、秘鲁的金银购买获得的利益更多。由自己直接提供的消费品所进行的对外贸易,总比由他人间接提供的消费品所进行的对外贸易更加有利。但是,以金银进行的间接贸易,并不比以其他货物进行的间接贸易更不利。没有矿产的国家不会因为每年出口金银而变得金银匮乏,一个不生产烟草的国家也不会因为每年出口烟草而变得烟草匮乏。因为,有财力购买烟草的国家,其市场不会缺乏烟草;有财力购买金银的国家,也绝不会缺乏金银。用金银支付并不比用烟草更坏。

有人说,工人和麦酒店做买卖会吃亏。同样,以制造业为主的国家和产葡萄酒国家之间的贸易,也是如此。我认为,工人和

trade with the alehouse is not necessarily a losing trade. In its own nature it is just as advantageous as any other, though, perhaps, somewhat more liable to be abused. The employment of a brewer, and even that the same nature. I answer, that the of a retailer of fermented liquors, are as necessary divisions of labour as any other. It will generally be more advantageous for a workman to buy of the brewer the quantity he has occasion for, than to brew it himself, and if he is a poor workman, it will generally be more advantageous for him to buy it, by little and little, of the retailer, than a large quantity of the brewer. He may no doubt buy too much of either, as he may of any other dealers in his neighbourhood, of the butcher, if he is a glutton, or of the draper, if he affects to be a beau among his companions. It is advantageous to the great body of workmen, notwithstanding, that all these trades should be free, though this freedom may be abused in all of them, and is more likely to be so, perhaps, in some than in others. Though individuals, besides, may sometimes ruin their fortunes by an excessive consumption of fermented liquors, there seems to be no risk that a nation should do so. Though in every country there are many people who spend upon such liquors more than they can afford, there are always many more who spend less. It deserves to be remarked too, that, if we consult experience, the cheapness of wine seems to be a cause, not of drunkenness, but of sobriety. The inhabitants of the wine countries are in general the soberest people in Europe; witness the Spaniards, the Italians, and the inhabitants of the southern provinces of France. People are seldom guilty of excess in what is their daily fare. Nobody affects the character of liberality and good fellowship, by being profuse of a liquor which is as cheap as small beer. On the contrary, in the countries which, either from excessive heat or cold, produce no grapes, and where wine consequently is dear and a rarity, drunkenness is a common vice, as among the northern nations, and all those who live between the tropics, the negroes, for example, on the coast of Guinea. When a French regiment comes from some of the northern provinces of France, where wine is somewhat dear, to be quartered in the southern, where it is very cheap, the soldiers, I have frequently heard it observed, are at first debauched by the cheapness and novelty of good wine; but after a few months residence, the greater part of them become as sober as the rest of the inhabitants. Were the duties upon foreign wines, and the excises upon malt, beer, and ale, to be taken away all at once, it might, in the same manner, occasion in Great Britain a pretty general and temporary drunkenness among the middling and inferior ranks of people, which would probably be soon followed by a permanent and almost universal sobriety. At present drunkenness is by no means the vice of people of fashion, or of those who can easily afford the most

麦酒店做买卖并不一定吃亏。就这种交易本身的性质来说,其得失和其他任何交易相同,当然,这种交易可能会更广泛一些。酿酒者和酒零售商,与其他职业一样,同是社会劳动的必要分工。工人需要酒时,向酿酒者购买要比亲自酿造实惠;如果他是个贫穷的工人,一般说来,他向零售商零散地购买要比向酿酒者批量购买实惠得多。他如果好吃,就可能购买很多酒肉;他如果想在同伴中装出有钱的样子,就可能买很多衣服,诸如此类的买卖自由对整个工人阶层都是有利的,虽然他们可能会滥用这种自由,而且某一部分人比另一部分人更甚。此外,个人可能会因为嗜酒无度而倾家荡产,但对一个国家,似乎用不着担心会发生这样的危险。尽管每个国家都有许多人,在酒水方面的开销超出自己的支付能力,但更多的人在这方面的开支少一些。值得一提的是,经验表明,酒水廉价似乎并不是酗酒的缘由,反而却是节制的理由。一般说来,生活在产酒国家的公民是最有节制的,例如西班牙人、意大利人以及法国南部各省的人们,饮酒很少超过常量。他们很少无节制地狂饮那些跟啤酒一样便宜的白酒,来表现慷慨哥们义气。相反,在那些由于天气太热或太冷不产葡萄因而葡萄酒稀少昂贵的国家,如北方民族和热带民族(几内亚海岸的黑人),酗酒才是一种普遍的恶习。据说,法国军队从葡萄酒昂贵的北部开到葡萄酒低廉的南部后,起初士兵们看到如此物美价廉的葡萄酒,便沉溺于其中,但驻守数月之后,大部分士兵就开始和当地居民一样开始戒酒了。可以设想,如果将外国葡萄酒税、麦芽税、麦酒税、啤酒税一律取消,那么英国的中下层人们完全可能引发短暂的酗酒恶习,但不久就会出现永久、普遍的戒酒风气。如今,酗酒既不是那些时髦人群的恶习,也不是那些有能力消费昂

_{反对法国葡萄酒贸易的论证逻辑上都是荒谬的。}

expensive liquors. A gentleman drunk with ale, has scarce ever been seen among us. ① The restraints upon the wine trade in Great Britain, besides, do not so much seem calculated to hinder the people from go-ing, if I may say so, to the alehouse, as from going where they can buy the best and cheapest liquor. They favour the wine trade of Portugal, and discourage that of France. The Portuguese, it is said, indeed, are better customers for our manufactures than the French, and should therefore be encouraged in preference to them. As they give us their custom, it is pretended, we should give them ours. The sneaking arts of underling tradesmen are thus erected into political maxims for the conduct of a great empire; for it is the most underling tradesmen only who make it a rule to employ chiefly their own customers. A great trader purchases his goods always where they are cheapest and best, without regard to any little interest of this kind.

The sneaking arts of underling tradesmen have been erected into political maxims and commerce has become a source of discord instead of unity.

By such maxims as these, however, nations have been taught that their interest consisted in beggaring all their neighbours. Each nation has been made to look with an invidious eye upon the prosperity of all the nations with which it trades, and to consider their gain as its own loss. Commerce, which ought naturally to be, among nations, as among individuals, a bond of union and friendship, has become the most fertile source of discord and animosity. The capricious ambition of kings and ministers has not, during the present and the preceding century, been more fatal to the repose of Europe, than the impertinent jealousy of merchants and manufacturers. The violence and injustice of the rulers of mankind is an ancient evil, for which, I am afraid, the nature of human affairs can scarce admit of a remedy. But the mean rapacity, the monopolizing spirit of merchants and manufacturers, who neither are, nor ought to be, the rulers of mankind, though it cannot perhaps be corrected, may very easily be prevented from disturbing the tranquillity of any body but themselves.

That it was the spirit of monopoly which originally both invented and propagated this doctrine, cannot be doubted; and they who first taught it were by no means such fools as they who believed it. In every country it always is and must be the interest of the great body of

---

① [Lectures, p. 179.]

贵饮料的人们的恶习，因喝麦酒而烂醉如泥的绅士已经很少见到。[1] 此外，英国对葡萄酒贸易的限制，与其说是为了防止老百姓买葡萄酒，还不如说是为了防止他们买廉价的烈酒。那些限制对葡萄牙的葡萄酒贸易有利，对法国却不利。据说，葡萄牙人是我国的好顾客，因为他们购买我国制造的产品，但法国人就不是。所以，我们对葡萄牙予以优待，因为他们照顾了我们的生意，我们应当回报。小商人的卑鄙手段居然成为一个大帝国的政治原则。可是，只有那些小商贩们，才会用这种手段对待顾客，大商人才不会注意这些小节，他们只会到价格最低、质量最好的地方去采购货物。

小商人卑鄙的手段成为政治原则，商业往来不是促进团结，而成为相互倾轧的根源。

根据这些原则，各国都认为，周边的国家都变穷了，他们才能获利。每个国家都嫉妒与己通商的国家的繁荣，认为这些国家的赢利就是他们的损失。和个人买卖一样，国际贸易原本应该是团结与友谊的纽带，但现在却成为不和与仇恨的最大根源。在本世纪及上世纪，王公大臣们反复无常的野心对欧洲和平造成了危害，但它并不比商人和制造商们狂妄的妒忌心所造成的危害更严重。人类统治者的暴力与不公，自古以来就是祸害，由于人类的本性，它是无法根除的。至于那些商人和制造商，既不是也不会成为人类的统治者，虽然无法改变他们自私贪婪和垄断精神，但让他们不去打扰别人的安宁，却是很容易做到的。

毫无疑问，是那些想进行垄断的人最先制造并传播这种理论的，而且，他们绝不像后来信奉这种理论的人那么傻。在任何一个国家，百姓的利益总在于而且必然在于，向售价最低的商人购

① 《关于法律、警察、岁入及军备的演讲》，第179页。

<small>The sophistry of merchants inspired by the spirit of monopoly has confounded the common sense of mankind.</small>　the people to buy whatever they want of those who sell it cheapest. The proposition is so very manifest, that it seems ridiculous to take any pains to prove it; nor could it ever have been called in question, had not the interested sophistry of merchants and manufacturers confounded the common sense of mankind. Their interest is, in this respect, directly opposite to that of the great body of the people. As it is the interest of the freemen of a corporation to hinder the rest of the inhabitants from employing any workmen but themselves, so it is the interest of the merchants and manufacturers of every country to secure to themselves the monopoly of the home market. Hence in Great Britain, and in most other European countries, the extraordinary duties upon almost all goods imported by alien merchants. Hence the high duties and prohibitions upon all those foreign manufactures which can come into competition with our own. Hence too the extraordinary restraints upon the importation of almost all sorts of goods from those countries with which the balance of trade is supposed to be disadvantageous; that is, from those against whom national animosity happens to be most violently inflamed.

<small>Wealthy neighbours are an advantage to a nation as well as an individual.</small>　The wealth of a neighbouring nation, however, though dangerous in war and politics, is certainly advantageous in trade. In a state of hostility it may enable our enemies to maintain fleets and armies superior to our own; but in a state of peace and commerce it must likewise enable them to exchange with us to a greater value, and to afford a better market, either for the immediate produce of our own industry, or for whatever is purchased with that produce. As a rich man is likely to be a better customer to the industrious people in his neighbourhood, than a poor, so is likewise a rich nation. A rich man, indeed, who is himself a manufacturer, is a very dangerous neighbour to all those who deal in the same way. All the rest of the neighbourhood, however, by far the greatest number, profit by the good market which his expence affords them. They even profit by his underselling the poorer workmen who deal in the same way with him. The manufacturers of a rich nation, in the same manner, may no doubt be very dangerous rivals to those of their neighbours. This very competition, however, is advantageous to the great body of the people, who profit greatly besides by the good market which the great expence of such a nation affords them in every other way. Private people who want to make a fortune, never think of retiring to the remote and poor provinces of the country, but resort either to the capital, or to some

第四篇 第三章

买自己需要的东西。这种道理显而易见,如果还要费力气证明它是否正确,反倒很可笑。如果不是这些商人和制造商为了私利,用诡辩混淆了人们的视听,这也许不是什么问题。就利益而言,商人和制造商与百姓是对立的。就如同在各个行业中,自由职业者要阻止雇主雇佣其他人来替代自己,才能保证自己的收益,同样,商人和制造商要保住对部分国内市场的垄断权才能获利。因此,在英国以及欧洲其他大多数国家,对几乎所有的由外国商人进口的商品,都课以特别重的关税。因此,对一切进口后会与本国制造品发生竞争的外国制造品,都课以很高的关税或禁止进口。也因此,那些被认为贸易差额不利于我国的国家,或者我们对其有激烈民族仇恨的国家,它们的货物出口到我国时,我们都对其加以特别的限制。

> 人们断而起的垄断精神,已经混淆了人们的视听。商人被激辩诡辩混淆了人们的视听。

邻国的财富,尽管在战争或政治中会对我国形成威胁,但在贸易中,则确实对我国有利。在敌对状态时,敌国可以用这些财富装备起比我国更强大的舰队和陆军;和平通商时,他们又可以利用这些财富与我国进行更多价值的贸易,为我国的工业产品或其他物品提供一个更好的市场。相比穷人而言,富人对于他勤劳的邻居来说,是个更好的顾客,国家之间亦是如此。事实上,一个富裕的制造商对于其周围地区的同行来说,是一个危险的邻居,但是,对于其他的大多数邻居来说,他的花费却提供了一个市场,使他们受益。他和实力较差的同行之间进行竞争而低价抛售货物时,他们还会从中渔利。同样,一个富裕国家的制造商,无疑对邻国的同行造成极大的威胁。但二者之间的竞争却对老百姓很有利。此外,富国的巨大花费,必然能通过其他方式给百姓提供良好的市场,使他们得利。想发财的人肯定不会隐居到穷乡僻

> 人一样,对国家来说也是有利的事情。个人来富有邻居的情况,与国家有富邦的情件的情。

— 1057 —

of the great commercial towns. They know, that, where little wealth circulates, there is little to be got, but that where a great deal is in motion, some share of it may fall to them. The same maxims which would in this manner direct the common sense of one, or ten, or twenty individuals, should regulate the judgment of one, or ten, or twenty millions, and should make a whole nation regard the riches of its neighbours, as a probable cause and occasion for itself to acquire riches. A nation that would enrich itself by foreign trade, is certainly most likely to do so when its neighbours are all rich, industrious, and commercial nations. A great nation surrounded on all sides by wandering savages and poor barbarians might, no doubt, acquire riches by the cultivation of its own lands, and by its own interior commerce, but not by foreign trade. It seems to have been in this manner that the ancient Egyptians and the modern Chinese acquired their great wealth. The ancient Egyptians, it is said, neglected foreign commerce, and the modern Chinese, it is known, hold it in the utmost contempt, and scarce deign to afford it the decent protection of the laws. The modern maxims of foreign commerce, by aiming at the impoverishment of all our neighbours, so far as they are capable of producing their intended effect, tend to render that very commerce insignificant and contemptible.

The French trade, if not restrained, would be much more advantageous to Great Britain than the American.

It is in consequence of these maxims that the commerce between France and England has in both countries been subjected to so many discouragements and restraints. If those two countries, however, were to consider their real interest, without either mercantile jealousy or national animosity, the commerce of France might be more advantageous to Great Britain than that of any other country, and for the saine reason that of Great Britain to France. France is the nearest neighbour to Great Britain. In the trade between the southern coast of England and the northern and north-western coasts of France, the returns might be expected, in the same manner as in the inland trade, four, five, or six times in the year. The capital, therefore, employed in this trade, could in each of the two countries keep in motion four, five, or six times the quantity of industry, and afford employment and subsistence to four, five, or six times the number of people, which an equal capital could do in the greater part of the other branches of foreign trade. Between the parts of France and Great Britain most remote from one another, the returns might be expected, at least, once in the year, and even this trade would so far be at least equally advantageous as the greater part of the other branches of our foreign European trade. It would be, at least, three times more advantageous, than the

壤，而是到首都或商业大都市。因为他们知道，财富流通少的地方，所可获得的财富也少；财富流通多的地方，他们也可以分到一杯羹。这些常识既然能影响1个、10个、20个人，同样也能影响100万、1000万、2000万人，而且使整个国家都认为，邻国的富裕对自己来说可能就是致富的机会。想通过对外贸易致富的国家，如果其邻国都是富裕、勤劳、商业化的民族，当然就很容易达到目的。一个国家的周围如果都是一些游牧、未开化的民族以及贫穷的野蛮人，那么，耕种本国土地和经营国内商业，无疑可使国家致富，但要靠国际贸易致富，那就绝对不可能了。古代的埃及和近代中国似乎就是靠耕种本国土地、发展国内商业而致富的。据说，古代埃及忽视外国商业，近代中国对它也极端轻视，不给予国际贸易以任何正当的法律保护。近代外国通商原则就是使所有邻国陷于贫困境地，如果它能达到这一目的，那它就一定会让这种贸易变得微不足道、无足轻重。

法国和英国之间的贸易之所以会在两国都受到那么多的阻碍与限制，就是这些原则导致的后果。如果这两个国家能摒弃商业上的嫉妒和民族的仇恨来审视二者之间的利害关系，那么对双方来说，与对方进行贸易，都要比与欧洲其他任何国家进行贸易更加有利。法国是英国最近的邻居，英国南部沿海各地与法国北部及西北部沿海各地进行贸易，每年可以往返四次、五次乃至六次，就好像在国内做生意一样。两个国家这种贸易上的投资，与在其他国际贸易部门的投资相比，能够拉动四倍、五倍乃至六倍的生产，能够雇佣和养活四倍、五倍乃至六倍的人数。两国之间相距最远的地方之间的贸易，也至少可望每年往返一次。所以，这种贸易至少也和我国与欧洲其他大部分地方的贸易一样有利。

对贸易不受限制，它对英国的好处要远大于英国对法国的好处。如果法国的美国的好处。

boasted trade with our North American colonies, in which the returns were seldom made in less than three years, frequently not in less than four or five years. France, besides, is supposed to contain twenty-four millions of inhabitants. Our North American colonies were never supposed to contain more than three millions: And France is a much richer country than North America; though, on account of the more unequal distribution of riches, there is much more poverty and beggary in the one country, than in the other. France therefore could afford a market at least eight times more extensive, and, on account of the superior frequency of the returns, four and twenty times more advantageous, than that which our North American colonies ever afforded. The trade of Great Britain would be just as advantageous to France, and, in proportion to the wealth, population and proximity of the respective countries, would have the same superiority over that which France carries on with her own colonies. Such is the very great difference between that trade which the wisdom of both nations has thought proper to discourage, and that which it has favoured the most.

But the traders of France and England are jealous of each other.
But the very same circumstances which would have rendered an open and free commerce between the two countries so advantageous to both, have occasioned the principal obstructions to that commerce. Being neighbours, they are necessarily enemies, and the wealth and power of each becomes, upon that account, more formidable to the other; and what would increase the advantage of national friendship, serves only to inflame the violence of national animosity. They are both rich and industrious nations; and the merchants and manufacturers of each, dread the competition of the skill and activity of those of the other. Mercantile jealousy is excited, and both inflames, and is itself inflamed, by the violence of national animosity: And the traders of both countries have announced, with all the passionate confidence of interested falsehood, the certain ruin of each, in consequence of that unfavourable balance of trade, which, they pretend, would be the infallible effect of an unrestrained commerce with the other.

No country has ever been impoverished by an unfavourable balance, and those which have the freest trade have been the most enriched by foreign trade.
There is no commercial country in Europe of which the approaching ruin has not frequently been foretold by the pretended doctors of this system, from an unfavourable balance of trade. After all the anxiety, however, which they have excited about this, after all the vain attempts of almost all trading nations to turn that balance in their own favour and against their neighbours, it does not appear that any one nation in Europe has been in any respect impoverished by this cause. Every town and country, on the contrary, in proportion as they have opened their ports to all nations, instead of being ruined by this free trade, as the principles of the commercial system would lead us to expect, have been enriched by it. Though there are in Europe, indeed, a few towns which in some respects deserve the name of free ports,

如果同我国与北美殖民地的贸易相比,至少也赢利三倍。此外,据说法国有 2300 万居民,而我国北美殖民地居民不过 300 万人。法国又比北美洲富饶得多,尽管法国贫富不均,贫民和乞丐比北美多得多。所以,与我国北美殖民地比较,法国所能提供的市场,至少要大八倍;再加上往返更为频繁,因此利润要多 24 倍。与英国的贸易,也同样有利于法国。从两国财富、人口与邻近的程度来看,其好处大于法国与其殖民地间的贸易。这就是两国加以阻止的贸易和偏爱的贸易之间的巨大差别。

然而,恰恰就是这些可以给两国带来开放自由的、并且可以双赢的贸易机会,却成为这种贸易的主要障碍。因为是邻国,它们必定是敌对的国家,因为一方的富强,增加了另一方的恐惧,而本来可以增进国际友谊的有利因素,却成为助长激烈民族仇恨的添加剂。它们都是勤劳富裕的民族,但双方的商人和制造商,都担心会在技术与商业活动中遇到来自对方国家的商人和制造商的竞争。商业上的嫉妒,因激烈的民族仇恨而引起,激烈的民族仇恨又助长了商业上的嫉妒,两者相互助长。两个国家的商人,都信誓旦旦地谎称,不受限制的国际贸易,必然会产生不利的贸易差额,从而一定导致国家的灭亡。

<small>英法两国之间贸易,但两国的商人相互嫉妒。</small>

欧洲各商业国家无不经常受到许多装模作样的重商主义体系学者的警告:贸易逆差正在使国家走向灭亡。这让各个国家很是担忧,于是几乎各国都试图使本国对外国的贸易差额为顺差。但是,这一切过后,似乎没有一个欧洲国家因上述原因而变得贫困。相反,实行门户开放并允许自由贸易的城市与国家,非但没有因这种自由贸易而灭亡,反而却因此富强起来。事实上,欧洲今日虽然有几个称得上自由港的城市,但是却没有几个国家能称

<small>没有一个国家因贸易逆差而贫困,那些最自由贸易的国家也是因贸易而致富的国家。</small>

there is no country which does so. Holland, perhaps, approaches the nearest to this character of any, though still very remote from it; and Holland, it is acknowledged, not only derives its whole wealth, but a great part of its necessary subsistence, from foreign trade.

There is another balance, indeed, which has already been explained, [1] very different from the balance of trade, and which, according as it happens to be either favourable or unfavourable, necessarily occasions the prosperity or decay . of every nation. This is the balance of the annual produce and consumption. If the exchangeable value of the annual produce, it has already been observed, exceeds that of the annual consumption, the capital of the society must annually increase in proportion to this excess. The society in this case lives within its revenue, and what is annually saved out of its revenue, is naturally added to its capital, and employed so as to increase still further the annual produce. If the exchangeable value of the annual produce, on the contrary, fall short of the annual consumption, the capital of the society must annually decay in proportion to this deficiency. The expence of the society in this case exceeds its revenue, and necessarily encroaches upon its capital. Its capital, therefore, must necessarily decay, and, together with it, the exchangeable value of the annual produce of its industry.

This balance of produce and consumption is entirely different from, what is called, the balance of trade. It might take place in a nation which had no foreign trade, but which was entirely separated from all the world. It may take place in the whole globe of the earth, of which the wealth, population, and improvement may be either gradually increasing or gradually decaying.

The balance of produce and consumption may be constantly in favour of a nation, though what is called the balance of trade be generally against it. A nation may import to a greater value than it exports for half a century, perhaps, together; the gold and silver which comes into it during all this time may be all immediately sent out of it; its circulating coin may gradually decay, different sorts of paper money being substituted in its place, and even the debts too which it contracts in the principal nations with whom it deals, may be gradually increasing; and yet its real wealth, the exchangeable value of the annual produce of its lands and labour, may, during the same period, have been increasing in a much greater proportion. The state of our North American colonies, and of the trade which they carried on with Great Britain, before the commencement of the present disturbances, may serve as a proof that this is by no means an impossible supposition.

---

[1] [This paragraph was written in the year 1775.]

得上是自由港。或许,荷兰姑且可以算是一个,但它距离标准还很远。因为自由港不仅全部财富得对外贸易,而且大部分生活资料也得对外贸易。

还有另外一种平衡,前面已经谈到,它和贸易平衡很不相同。一国的盛衰,要看这种差额是顺差还是逆差,这就是年生产与年消费的差额。前面说过,如果年生产的交换价值大于年消费的交换价值,社会的资本每年就必然会成比例增加。在这种情况下,社会每年的收入,除了维持其生存外,从中节省下来的部分,便会自然添加到社会资本上去,并用以进一步增加年产量。反之,如果年生产的交换价值小于年消费的交换价值,社会的资本每年就必然会按比例而减少。这个时候,社会的支出超过了社会的收入,就必然会侵蚀社会的资本。资本必然会减少,从而其年产品的交换价值也会减少。

繁荣与衰败依赖于生产和消费的差额,

生产和消费平衡与所谓的贸易平衡完全不同。它主要产生在那些不与世界往来、没有国际贸易的国家。就整个地球而言,随着财富、人口与社会进步都在逐渐增加或减少,也可以出现这种差额。

生产与消费平衡跟所谓的贸易平衡完全不同,

即使一个国家一直是贸易逆差,但其生产与消费的差额却可以是顺差。即便是半个多世纪里,这个国家进口的价值都大于出口的价值,其进口的金银马上被出口,其流通铸币逐渐减少并被各种纸币所替代,甚至其对各主要通商国家所负的债务在逐渐增加,但是,这个国家的真实财富,它的土地劳动年产品的交换价值,可在这期间,仍然按照比以前大得多的比例不断增加。我国北美殖民地的情况,它们发生骚乱之前①与英国的贸易,都可证明这绝不是不可能的假设。

即使一家国贸易逆差时,生产与消费也可以是顺差。

① 这一段写于1775年。

— 1063 —

CHAPTER IV
Of Drawbacks

<small>Merchants demand and encouragements to exportation.</small> Merchants and manufacturers are not contented with the monopoly of the home market, but desire likewise the most extensive foreign sale for their goods. Their country has no jurisdiction in foreign nations, and therefore can seldom procure them any monopoly there. They are generally obliged, therefore, to content themselves with petitioning for certain encouragements to exportation.

<small>Drawbacks of duty paid on domestic produce are reasonable, as they preserve the natural distribution of labour.</small> Of these encouragements what are called Drawbacks seem to be the most reasonable. To allow the merchant to draw back upon exportation, either the whole or a part of whatever excise or inland duty is imposed upon domestic industry, can never occasion the exportation of a greater quantity of goods than what would have been exported had no duty been imposed. Such encouragements do not tend to turn towards any particular employment a greater share of the capital of the country, than what would go to that employment ① of its own accord, but only to hinder the duty from driving away any part of that share to other employments. They tend not to overturn that balance which naturally establishes itself among all the various employments of the society; but to hinder it from being overturned by the duty. They tend not to destroy, but to preserve, what it is in most cases advantageous to preserve, the natural division and distribution of labour in the society.

The same thing may be said of the drawbacks upon the re-exportation of foreign goods imported; which in Great Britain generally

---

① [Eds. 1 and 2 read 'go to it'.]

第四章　退税

商人和制造商不仅仅满足于在国内市场的垄断,还希望占领最广泛的国外销售市场,但是他们国家在外国没有管辖权,因此在那里取得垄断是不可能的。所以,通常他们只好从政府那里争取一些出口津贴政策。

> 商人要求补贴出口。

在所有的奖励政策中,所谓的退税似乎是最合理的。商人出口货物时,退还本国的国产税或国内税的全部或一部分,不会使货物的出口量比没有退税时增大。比起按照自然规律所投向的行业,①这种奖励不会使大部分资本违反自然趋势投入到特殊的行业,而且还避免了由于对某行业课税而使该行业的资本转用到其他行业。这些奖励不会打破社会各行业间自然而然建立起的平衡,但却可以阻止这种平衡被税收破坏,它们似乎没有破坏而是保护了社会劳动的自然分工与分配,在大多数情况下,这种保护是有益的。

> 国产品的退税是合理的,因为它们维持了自然的劳动分工。

进口的外国货物再出口时,也可以退税。在英国,这部分退

---

① 在版本 1 和版本 2 中为"投向它"。

<small>so are also drawbacks of duty paid on goods imported.</small> amount to by much the largest part of the duty upon importation. ① By the second of the rules, annexed to the act of parliament, ② which imposed, what is now called, the old subsidy, every merchant, whether English or alien, was allowed to draw back half that duty upon exportation; the English merchant, provided the exportation took <small>Under the old subsidy a drawback of one-half is allowed.</small> place within twelve months; the alien, provided it took place within nine months. Wines, currants, and wrought silks were the only goods which did not fall within this rule, having other and more advantageous allowances. The duties imposed by this act of parliament were, at that time, the only duties upon the importation of foreign goods. The term within which this, and all other drawbacks, could be claimed, was afterwards (by 7 Geo. I . chap. 21. sect. 10.) extended to three years. ③

<small>Of more recent duties the whole is generally allowed,</small> The duties which have been imposed since the old subsidy, are, the greater part of them, wholly drawn back upon exportation. This general rule, however, is liable to a great number of exceptions, and the doctrine of drawbacks has become a much less simple matter, than it was at their first institution.

<small>and in some cases the whole even of the old subsidy is allowed.</small> Upon the exportation of some foreign goods, of which it was expected that the importation would greatly exceed what was necessary for the home consumption, the whole duties are drawn back, without retaining even half the old subsidy. Before the revolt of our North American colonies, we had the monopoly of the tobacco of Maryland and Virginia. We imported about ninety-six thousand hogsheads, and the home consumption was not supposed to exceed fourteen thousand. To facilitate the great exportation which was necessary, in order to rid us of the rest, the whole duties were drawn back, provided the exportation took place within three years. ④

We still have, though not altogether, yet very nearly, the monopoly of the sugars of our West Indian islands. If sugars are exported within a year, therefore, all the duties upon importation are drawn

---

① [The next three pages are not in eds. 1 and 2.]

② [12 Car. II . , c. 4.]

③ [Henry Saxby, *The British Customs*, containing an Historical and Practical Account of each branch of that part of the Revenue, 1757, pp. 10、308.]

④ [Saxby, *British Customs*, p. 12.]

税约占了进口税①的绝大部分。根据旧补助税的议会法令②的附则的第二项规定,允许每个商人,不论国籍,在出口的时候退一半税。英国的商人必须在 12 个月内将货物出口,外国商人必须在九个月内出口。只有葡萄酒、小葡萄干和丝精制品,因已经享受其他更优惠的津贴,故不再适用该条例。这个议会法令所规定的关税,在当时是唯一的对外国商品所施加的进口税。后来,这种以及其他各种退税的申请期限可延长到三年(乔治一世七年法令第 21 号第 11 条)。③

> 进口的货物也可以退税。

> 根据旧补助税法,可以退一半税。

旧补助税以后所课的各种税,有大部分在出口时会全部退还。但是该通则有许多例外,所以,退税远不如最初制定的时候那么简单了。

> 更近些时候,整个税都可以退还。

有些外国商品的进口量会大大超过国内消费的需求量,这也在预料之中,所以,这些外国商品再出口时,全部的关税都予以退还,甚至连一半旧补助税都不保留。在我国美洲殖民地未曾造反以前,我们垄断了马里兰和弗吉尼亚的烟草,进口了约 96000 大桶,但国内消费据说不及 14000 大桶。为了便于这些剩余的大量烟草出口,凡是在三年内出口,④所纳关税全部予以退还。

> 在某些时候,整个旧补助金都允许退还。

我们仍然垄断(虽不是全部,但已近于全部)我国西印度群岛的砂糖。所以如果在一年内出口,那么进口时所纳的一切税,

---

① 版本 1 和版本 2 中以下三段没有。
② 查理二世十二年第 4 号法令。
③ 萨克斯贝:《不列颠关税法》,包括历史上和实际上部分税收的各个分支,1757 年,第 10、308 页。
④ 萨克斯贝:《不列颠关税法》,第 12 页。

— 1067 —

back, ① and if exported within three years, all the duties, except half the old subsidy, which still continues to be retained upon the exportation of the greater part of goods. Though the importation of sugar exceeds, a good deal, what is necessary for the home consumption, the excess is inconsiderable, in comparison of what it used to be in tobacco.

<small>In the case of some p-rohibited goods there is no drawback.</small> Some goods, the particular objects of the jealousy of our own manufacturers, are prohibited to be imported for home consumption. They may, however, upon paying certain duties, be imported and warehoused for exportation. But upon such exportation, no part of these duties are drawn back. Our manufacturers are unwilling, it seems, that even this restricted importation should be ·encouraged, and are afraid lest some part of these goods should be stolen out of the warehouse, and thus come into competition with their own. It is under these regulations only that we can import wrought silks, ② French cambrics and lawns, callicoes painted, printed, stained, or dyed, &c.

<small>French imports generally are allowed a smaller drawback on re-exportation.</small> We are unwilling even to be the carriers of French goods, and choose rather to forego a profit to ourselves, than to suffer those, whom we consider as our enemies, to make any profit by our means. Not only half the old subsidy, but the second twenty-five per cent. is retained upon the exportation of all French goods. ③

<small>Wines have been peculiarly favoured,</small> By the fourth of the rules annexed to the old subsidy, the drawback allowed upon the exportation of all wines amounted to a great deal more than half the duties which were, at that time, paid upon their importation; and it seems, at that time, to have been the object of the legislature to give somewhat more than ordinary encouragement to the carrying trade in wine. Several of the other duties too, which were imposed, either at the same time, or subsequent to the old subsidy; what is called the additional duty, the new subsidy, the one-third and two-thirds subsi-

---

① [Saxby, British Customs. , p. 11.]
② [6 Geo. Ⅲ, c. 28; 11 Geo. Ⅲ. , c. 49.]
③ [7 and 8 W. Ⅲ. , c. 20; 1 Geo. Ⅰ. , c. 12, § 3; Saxby, British Customs, p. 45; above vol. i. , p. 437. The first 25 per cent. was imposed in 1692, the second in 1696.]

都可退还;①如果在 3 年内出口,除了旧补助税的一半,其他一切税都可退还。大部分货物出口的时候,旧补助税的半数迄今依然扣留。砂糖进口量虽然大大超过国内消费量,但与烟草通常的进口剩余量比较,是微不足道的。

有些货物是我国制造商嫉妒的对象,所以被禁止进口供给国内消费。但是如果缴纳一定数额的税款,则可以进口,存放在仓库以待再出口。但它们出口时,所纳的税是完全不退还的。即使有了这些奖励政策,制造商们似乎也不愿进口,他们唯恐自己货栈的货物有一部分会被偷出来,与自己的货物竞争。在这样的限制下,我国只进口精制丝品、②法国亚麻布与上等细麻布、印花染色棉布等。

在这种情况下,某些被禁止的货物不予退税。

我们甚至不愿意作法国货物的贩运商,并且选择了宁可放弃我们自己的利润,也不愿让被认为是敌人的法国利用我们赢利。法国货物出口时,不仅旧补助税的一半不退还,而且附加的 25% 的税也不能退还。③

从法国进口的货物再出口时只退一小部分的税。

根据旧补助税附则第四条,所有葡萄酒在出口时所准许退还的税,达到进口时所纳税的一半还要多,立法者当时的目的似乎是要特别鼓励葡萄酒转口贸易。与旧补助税同时征课或稍后征课的一些其他税,如所谓附加税、新补助税、1/3 补助税及 2/3 补

葡萄酒受到特别的喜爱,

---

① 萨克斯贝:《不列颠关税法》,第 11 页。
② 乔治三世六年第 28 号法令;乔治三世二年第 49 号法令。
③ 威廉三世七年和八年第 20 号法令;乔治一世一年第 12 号法令,第三章;萨克贝斯:《不列颠税法》第 45 页;前文第 1 卷,第 437 页。第一次征收 25% 于 1692 年,第二次于 1696 年。

dies, the impost 1692, the coinage on wine, were allowed to be wholly drawn back upon exportation. ① All those duties, however, except the additional duty and impost 1692, ② being paid down in ready money, upon importation, the interest of so large a sum occasioned an expence, which made it unreasonable to expect any profitable carrying trade in this article. Only a part, therefore, of the duty called the impost on wine, ③ and no part of the twenty-five pounds the ton upon French wines, ④ or of the duties imposed in 1745, ⑤ in 1763, ⑥ and in 1778, ⑦ were allowed to be drawn back upon exportation. The two imposts of five per cent., imposed in 1779 and 1781, upon all the former duties of customs, ⑧ being allowed to be wholly drawn back upon the exportation of all other goods, were likewise allowed to be drawn back upon that of wine. The last duty that has been particularly imposed upon wine, that of 1780, ⑨ is allowed to be wholly drawn back, an indulgence, which, when so many heavy duties are retained, most probably could never occasion the exportation of a single ton of wine. These rules take place with regard to all places of lawful exportation, except the British colonies in America.

---

① [Saxby, *British Customs*, pp. 13、22、39、46. 'The additional duty' was imposed in 1703. For the 'impost 1692' and the subsidies. 'The coinage on wine' was the duty levied under 18 Car. Ⅱ., c. 5, for defraying the expenses of the mint.]

② [Saxby, *British Customs*, pp. 13, 38.]

③ [1 Jac. Ⅱ., c. 3, and continuing Acts: £ 8 a tun on French and £ 12 on other wine.]

④ [7 and 8 W. Ⅲ., c. 20, § 3; 1 Geo. Ⅰ., st. 2, c. 12, §3.]

⑤ [18 Geo. Ⅱ., c. 9; Saxby, *British Customs*, p. 64: £ 8 a tun on French and £ 4 on other wine.]

⑥ [? 1762. 3 Geo. Ⅲ., c. 12: £ 8 a tun on French and £ 4 on other wine.]

⑦ [18 Geo. Ⅲ., c. 27: £ 8 8s. on French and £ 4 4s. on other wine.]

⑧ [*I. e.*, 5 per cent., not on the value of the goods, but on the amount of the previously existing duties; 19 Geo. Ⅲ., c, 25. and 22 Geo. Ⅲ., c. 66.]

⑨ [20 Geo. Ⅲ., c. 30: £ 8 a tun on French and £ 4 on other wine.]

助税、1692年关税、葡萄酒检验税,都允许在出口①时全部退还。②但所有这些税,除了附加税与1692年关税,在进口时都需要缴纳现金;如此巨额资金的利息,是一笔不小的开支,所以在该条款下的转口贸易无赢利的希望。只有一部分葡萄酒关税,③在出口的时候予以退还,而法国葡萄酒进口每大桶所交纳的25镑的税,④即1745年、⑤1763年⑥和1778年⑦征课的关税,出口时均不给退还。1779年和1781年对于一切货物进口⑧所附加的那两种5%的关税,在所有其他货物出口时都允许全部退还。葡萄酒出口的时候全部退还。1780年⑨特别课加在葡萄酒上的最后关税,也全部退还,这在当时关税多而且重、很难促成一桶葡萄酒出口的时候,无疑是一种恩赐。这种规定,除了我国北美殖民地以外,对所有依法出口的地方都适用。

---

① 萨克贝斯:《不列颠税法》,第13、22、39、46页。"附加税"征收于1703年。1692年征收"关税"和"补助税"。"葡萄酒检验税"实施于查理二世十八年,第5号法令是为支付薄荷的费用。

② 萨克斯贝:《不列颠关税法》,第13、38页。

③ 詹姆十二世一年第3号法令,对法国酒每桶4镑、其他酒12镑。

④ 威廉三世七年和八年第20号法令第3节。乔治一世一年,第2次会议第12号法令第3节。

⑤ 乔治二世十八年第9号法令;萨克贝斯:《不列颠关税法》,第64页:法国酒每桶8镑、其他酒4镑。

⑥ 1762年,乔治三世三年第12号法令:法国酒每桶8镑,其他酒4镑。

⑦ 乔治三世十八年第27号法令,法国酒每桶8镑,其他酒4镑。

⑧ 5%,不是货物的价值,而是以前所交税的5%;乔治三世十九年,第25号法令,乔治三世二十二年,第66号法令。

⑨ 乔治三世二十年第3号法令:法国酒每桶8镑,其他酒4镑。

especially when exported to the American colonies,
The 15th Charles Ⅱ. chap. 7. called an act for the encouragement of trade, ① had given Great Britain the monopoly of supplying the colonies with all the commodities of the growth or manufacture of Europe; and consequently with wines. In a country of so extensive a coast as our North American and West Indian colonies, where our authority was always so very slender, and where the inhabitants were allowed to carry out, in their own ships, their non-enumerated commodities, at first, to all parts of Europe, and afterwards, to all parts of Europe South of Cape Finisterre, it is not very probable that this monopoly could ever be much respected; and they probably, at all times, found means of bringing back some cargo from the countries to which they were allowed to carry out one. They seem, however, to have found some difficulty in importing European wines from the places of their growth, and they could not well import them from Great Britain, where they were loaded with many heavy duties, of which a considerable part was not drawn back upon exportation. Madeira wine, not being a European commodity, ② could be imported directly into America and the West Indies, countries which, in all their non-enumerated commodities, enjoyed a free trade to the island of Madeira. These circumstances had probably introduced that general taste for Madeira wine, which our officers found established in all our colonies at the commencement of the war which began in 1755, and which they brought back with them to the mother-country, where that wine had not been much in fashion before. Upon the conclusion of that war, in 1763 (by the 4th Geo. Ⅲ. Chap. 15. Sect. 12.), all the duties, except 3*l*. 10 *s.* were allowed to be drawn back, upon the exportation to the colonies of all wines, except French wines, to the commerce and consumption of which national prejudice would allow no sort of encouragement. The period between the granting of this indulgence and the revolt of our North American colonies was probably

---

① [The colonial part of the Act is said in its particular preamble(§5)to be for the purpose of 'maintaining a greater correspondence and kindness between' the colonies and mother country, and for keeping the colonies 'in a firmer dependence'.]

② [The framers of the Act were not so sure about Madeira being non-European. They excepted wine of the Madeiras and Azores by special provision, § 7 of 15 Car, Ⅱ., c. 7, § 13.]

第四篇　第四章

查理二世十五年第 7 号法令称为贸易奖励法,①使英国有了向殖民地供应欧洲产品或制造品的垄断权,后来还包括了葡萄酒。但北美殖民地及西印度殖民地的海岸线太长了,我国对这些地方的统治不力。最初允许当地的居民用自己的船只,把未被政府禁运的商品运往欧洲各地,后来可以运往菲尼斯特雷角以南欧洲各国。这种垄断权不大可能受到人们尊重。无论什么时候,他们也许都有方法从抵达港带回一些货物。不过,他们进口欧洲的葡萄酒可能有些困难;也无法从葡萄酒课税繁重并且其大部分又不能在出口时退还的不列颠进口葡萄酒。马德拉的葡萄酒,由于不是欧洲产物,②便可直接进口到美洲与西印度群岛。这些国家与马德拉岛能够自由交换各种禁运名单以外的商品。在这种情况下,马德拉葡萄酒被引进到了国内。1755 年战争开始后,我国军官在我国各殖民地发现人们对马德拉葡萄酒情有独钟。于是这些军官把这种酒带回国内,在那之前,这种葡萄酒在国内还不大流行。战争结束以后,在 1763 年(乔治三世四年法令第 15 号第 12 条),除了法国葡萄酒,一切葡萄酒都允许在出口到殖民地的时候,除 3 镑 10 先令以外,退还其他的税,因为国民的偏见不允许奖励法国葡萄酒的贸易与消费。但是,准许那种恩赐和我国北美殖民地发生叛乱这两个事件相隔的时间似乎太短,那些国家

---

①　在这项法令的绪论中,关于殖民地的部分据说是为了"更好维持殖民地国家和祖国之间的一致性和友爱",并且使殖民地保持"更牢固的独立"。

②　这些法令对于马德拉不属于欧洲不是很确信,因此它们用特别的条款把马德拉和亚速群岛的葡萄酒排除在外。乔治二世十五年第 7 号法令,第 7、13 节。

too short to admit of any considerable change in the customs of those countries.

though the export of other foreign commodities to those colonies was discouraged,

The same act, which, in the drawback upon all wines, except French wines, thus favoured the colonies so much more than other countries; in those, upon the greater part of other commodities, favoured them much less. Upon the exportation of the greater part of commodities to other countries, half the old subsidy was drawn back. But this law enacted, that no part of that duty should be drawn back upon the exportation to the colonies of any commodities, of the growth or manufacture either of Europe or the East Indies, except wines, white callicoes and muslins.

Drawbacks were originally granted to encourage the carrying trade, which was absurd, but they are reasonable enough.

Drawbacks were, perhaps, originally granted for the encouragement of the carrying trade, which, as the freight of the ships is frequently paid by foreigners in money, was supposed to be peculiarly fitted for bringing gold and silver into the country. But though the carrying trade certainly deserves no peculiar encouragement, though the motive of the institution was, perhaps, abundantly foolish, the institution itself seems reasonable enough. Such drawbacks cannot force into this trade a greater share of the capital of the country than what would have gone to it of its own accord, had there been no duties upon importation. They only prevent its being excluded altogether by those duties. The carrying trade, though it deserves no preference, ought not to be precluded, but to be left free like all other trades. It is a necessary resource for those capitals which cannot find employment either in the agriculture or in the manufactures of the country, either in its home trade or in its foreign trade of consumption.

The revenue gains by their existence when they do not amount to the whole of the duty paid.

The revenue of the customs, instead of suffering, profits from such drawbacks, by that part of the duty which is retained. If the whole duties had been retained, the foreign goods upon which they are paid, could seldom have been exported, nor consequently imported, for want of a market. The duties, therefore, of which a part is retained, would never have been paid.

They would be justified even if they always did amount to the whole duty paid,

These reasons seem sufficiently to justify drawbacks, and would justify them, though the whole duties, whether upon the produce of domestic industry, or upon foreign goods, were always drawn back upon exportation. The revenue of excise would in this case, indeed, suffer a little, and that of the customs a good deal more; but the natural balance of industry, the natural division and distribution of labour, which is always more or less disturbed by such duties, would be more nearly re-established by such a regulation.

的风俗习惯还没有产生显著的变化。

除法国葡萄酒以外的一切葡萄酒都实行退税的这种做法,使殖民地受实惠的程度大大超过其他国家,但就其他大部分货物的退税情况而言,殖民地所受实惠的程度却要小得多。在大部分货物出口到其他各国的时候,旧补助税可以退还一半。但这项法令却规定,除葡萄酒、白棉布及细棉布以外,所有欧洲或东印度生产或制造的商品,在出口到殖民地时,旧补助税分文不得退还。

> 尽管不鼓励其他国家商品出口到这些殖民地,

设立退税制度的本意也许是为了要鼓励转口贸易,因为转口贸易中,外国人常以货币支付船舶的运费,所以它被认为是特别适合给国家带回金银收入的方法。虽然转口贸易不值得特别鼓励,虽然设立退税制度的动机非常可笑,但这种制度本身,却似乎很合理。这种退税,绝不会使现在投入贸易的资本大于没有设立进口税的时候。它们使进口税不至于完全排斥这种贸易。转口贸易虽不值得鼓励,但也不应该被阻止,而应该像其他各种行业一样自由发展。对于那些在农业以及国内和国际贸易中用不着的资本,这种贸易是一种必要的对策。

> 最初制定退税是为了鼓励转口贸易,尽管这很荒谬,但也很合理。

海关的税收,不会因为这种退税而受到损害,反而会获利。因为退税时,他们能够保留其中一部分关税。如果全部关税都被保留,那么纳税的外国商品由于缺乏市场不能出口,因而也不会进口。这样,本可以保留一部分的关税,也会没有了。

> 如果退还的税和交纳的税相等,税收会因退税而增加。

这些理由似乎足以充分证明退税的合理性。不管是对国内工业产品还是对外国产物征收的关税,即使在出口时全部退回,退税也是合理的。事实上,在这种情况下,国产税的收入会稍受损失,而海关的税收则损失;尽管劳动分工和分配的自然平衡会受到影响,但会因为这种规定而重新建立。

> 即使退还全部的税,也是合理的,

> but only to independent countries, not to those in respect of which there is a monopoly of trade.

These reasons, however, will justify drawbacks only upon exporting goods to those countries which are altogether foreign and independent, not to those in which our merchants and manufacturers enjoy a monopoly. A drawback, for example, upon the exportation of European goods to our American colonies, will not always occasion a greater exportation than what would have taken place without it. By means of the monopoly which our merchants and manufacturers enjoy there, the same quantity might frequently, perhaps, be sent thither, though the whole duties were retained. The drawback, therefore, may frequently be pure loss to the revenue of excise and customs, without altering the state of the trade, or rendering it in any respect more extensive. How far such drawbacks can be justified, as a proper encouragement to the industry of our colonies, or how far it is advantageous to the mother-country, that they should be exempted from taxes which are paid by all the rest of their fellow-subjects, will appear hereafter when I come to treat of colonies.

> They give rise to frauds.

Drawbacks, however, it must always be understood, are useful only in those cases in which the goods for the exportation of which they are given, are really exported to some foreign country; and not clandestinely re-imported into our own. That some drawbacks, particularly those upon tobacco, have frequently been abused in this manner, and have given occasion to many frauds equally hurtful both to the revenue and to the fair trader, is well known.

但这些理由仅仅说明,我们只有把货物出口到完全独立的外国,而不是出口到我国商人、制造商享有垄断权的地方的时候,退税才是合理的。例如,欧洲货物出口到我国美洲殖民地的时候,退税并不能使出口额比没有设立退税制度时的出口额大。因为我国商人、制造商在那里享有垄断权,所以,即使免除全部的税额,出口到那里的货物量还是一样。所以,这种情况下,退税常常是国产税及海关税收的纯损失,没有改变贸易的状态,也没有扩大贸易量。至于在什么程度上,这种退税可认为是对我国殖民地产业的适当奖励,或者说在什么程度上,允许他们免除本国其他人所不能免除的赋税,才有利于本国,我打算在讨论殖民地那一个章节的时候,再加以详细论述。

但必须明白,只在出口货物真正运送到国外而不再秘密运回我国的时候,退税制度才会带来益处。众所周知,有些退税,尤其是烟草的退税,就往往以上面的方式被人利用,这种欺诈行为,既有害于国民收入,又有害于公正的商人。

CHAPTER V
Of Bounties

<small>Foreigners cannot be forced to buy our goods, so it is proposed to pay them to do so.</small> Bounties upon exportation are, in Great Britain, frequently petitioned for, and sometimes granted to the produce of particular branches of domestic industry. By means of them our merchants and manufacturers, it is pretended, will be enabled to sell their goods as cheap or cheaper than their rivals in the foreign market. A greater quantity, it is said, will thus be exported, and the balance of trade consequently turned more in favour of our own country. We cannot give our workmen a monopoly in the foreign, as we have done in the home market. We cannot force foreigners to buy their goods, as we have done our own countrymen. The next best expedient, it has been thought, therefore, is to pay them for buying. It is in this manner that the mercantile system proposes to enrich the whole country, and to put money into all our pockets by means of the balance of trade.

<small>Bounties are not demanded for any but losing trades,</small> Bounties, it is allowed, ought to be given to those branches of trade only which cannot be carried on without them. But every branch of trade in which the merchant can sell his goods for a price which replaces to him, with the ordinary profits of stock, the whole capital employed in preparing and sending them to market, can be carried on without a bounty. Every such branch is evidently upon a level with all the other branches of trade which are carried on without bounties, and cannot therefore require one more than they. Those trades only require bounties in which the merchant is obliged to sell his goods for a price which does not replace to him his capital, together with the ordinary profit; or in which he is obliged to sell them for less than it really costs him to send them to market. The bounty is given in order to make up this loss, and to encourage him to continue,

第五章　津贴

在英国,某些特别的国内生产行业常常要求出口津贴,有时也可获批准。商人和制造商们装作好像有了津贴,就能在外国市场上以低廉的或者比竞争对手更为低廉的价格出售货物。据说出口量会因此而大增,贸易差额也会变得对我国有利。在国外市场上,我们不可能像在本国那样给自己的生产者争取垄断权,也不能像对待本国老百姓那样,强迫他们购买我国的产品。于是,人们想出了一个折中的办法,即付钱请外国人来购买我们的货物。商业体制正是提倡用这种方法来富国,通过贸易平衡的办法让钱流入我们的口袋。

<small>强国我们所议付他们，让他们来买。不能迫外国人买我们的东西，以提我们钱给</small>

津贴本来只应该发给那些没有津贴就无法经营的贸易行业。但无论什么贸易行业,如果商人所售价格,可以偿还制造货物和投入市场所使用的资本,并且能够保证基本利润的实现,那么即使没有津贴,该行业也能够继续经营下去。像这样的行业,与其他没有设立津贴的各行业相比,明显处在有利的地位。所以,这样的行业像其他行业一样也不需要津贴。只有商人的商品售价不足以补还其资本并无法保证基本利润的实现,或售价不足以支付货物投入市场所花的实际费用,这时候才有必要发给津贴。津贴发放的目的,在于补偿商人的损失,奖励他继续经营或开创那

<small>只有那些亏损的生意才会要求津贴。</small>

国民财富的性质与原理

or perhaps to begin, a trade of which the expence is supposed to be greater than the returns, of which every operation eats up a part of the capital employed in it, and which is of such a nature, that, if all other trades resembled it, there would soon be no capital left in the country.

and their effect is to force trade into disadvantageous channels.

The trades, it is to be observed, which are carried on by means of bounties, are the only ones which can be carried on between two nations for any considerable time together, in such a manner as that one of them shall always and regularly lose, or sell its goods for less than it really costs to send them to market. But if the bounty did not repay to the merchant what he would otherwise lose upon the price of his goods, his own interest would soon oblige him to employ his stock in another way, or to find out a trade in which the price o f the goods would replace to him, with the ordinary profit, the capital employed in sending them to market. The effect of bounties, like that of all the other expedients of the mercantile system, can only be to force the trade of a country into a channel much less advantageous than that in which it would naturally run of its own accord.

Charles Smith forgets the cost of raising the corn upon which the bounty is paid.

The ingenious and well-informed author of the tracts upon the corn-trade ① has shown very clearly, that since the bounty upon the exportation of corn was first established, the price of the corn exported, valued moderately enough, has exceeded that of the corn imported, valued very high, by a much greater sum than the amount of the whole bounties which have been paid during that period. This, he imagines, upon the true principles of the mercantile system, is a clear proof that this forced corn trade is beneficial to the nation; the value of the exportation exceeding that of the importation by a much greater sum than the whole extraordinary expence which the public has been at in order to get it exported. He does not consider that this extraordinary expence, or the bounty, is the smallest part of the expence which the exportation of corn really costs the society. The capital which the farmer employed in raising it, must likewise be taken into the account. Unless the price of the corn when sold in the foreign markets replaces, not only the bounty, but this capital, together with the ordinary profits of stock, the society is a loser by the difference, or the national stock is so much diminished. But the very reason for which it has been thought necessary to grant a bounty, is the supposed insufficiency of the price to do this.

The average price of corn, it has been said, has fallen considerably

---

① [Charles Smith (already described as 'very well-informed' above, vol. i. , p. 426), *Three Tracts on the Corn Trade and Corn Laws*, 2nd ed. , 1766, pp. 132 – 138.]

种开支大于收益的行业。也就是说,商人每经营一次,其投入的资本就要亏损一部分。假如一切其他的行业都这样亏损,那么全国的资本不久就会荡然无存了。

应该指出,依靠津贴经营的贸易,只可能这么一种情形:在相当长时期内,两个国家有贸易往来,一方总是亏损,或者货物的售价低于货物投放市场的实际费用。如果没有津贴补偿商人的损失,他从自身的利益考虑,不久就会被迫改变投资方向,寻找那种他能够以货物售价收回投入的资金并实现基本利润的行业。像重商主义体系中其他条例一样,津贴只不过是迫使一国的贸易向没有市场优势的行业发展,而不是让其顺其自然地发展。

> 结果是迫使生意转向无利润的行业。

有一位博学的作者,在其关于粮食贸易的论文集里,①很清楚地指出,自从首次设立粮食出口津贴以来,实际价值中等的出口粮食的价格,超过了实际价值较高的进口粮食的价格,超过的数额要大大高于这期间津贴的总额。他认为,按照重商主义体系原理,这是明明白白地证明,这种强制性的粮食贸易有利于国家,因为出口价值大大超过了进口价值。但是,他不明白,这种特别费用,或者说这种津贴,在社会出口粮食的实际花费中只占很小的一部分。因为农场主用来栽种粮食的资金也要考虑进去。如果粮食在外国市场上所售的价格,不够补偿津贴和这种资本以及最普通的利润,那么这个差额就是社会的损失,也就是说,国民收入减少了这么多。但也正是因为有这种差额,才认为必须发给津贴。

> 查尔斯·密斯忽略了粮食栽植的费用,这种粮食得到了津贴。

据说自从设立津贴以来,粮食的平均价格已显著下降。我曾

---

① 查理·史密斯(前文提到他非常"博学")关于粮食贸易和粮食法律的三篇论文,第二版,1766年,第132~138页。

The fall in the price of corn since the establishment of the bounty. That the average price of corn began to fall somewhat towards the end of the last century, and has continued to do so during the course of the sixty-four first years of the present, I have already endeavoured to show. But this event, supposing it to be as real as I believe it to be, must have happened in spite of the bounty, and cannot possibly have happened in consequence of it. It has happened in France, as well as in England, though in France there was, not only no bounty, but, till 1764, the exportation of corn was subjected to a general prohibition. This gradual fall in the average price of grain, it is probable, therefore, is ultimately owing neither to the one regulation nor to the other, but to that gradual and insensible rise in the real value of silver, which, in the first book of this discourse, I have endeavoured to show has taken place in the general market of Europe, during the course of the present century. It seems to be altogether impossible that the bounty could ever contribute to lower the price of grain. ①	

The fall in the price of corn since the establishment of the bounty is due to other causes.

The bounty keeps up the price both in years of plenty and of scarcity.

In years of plenty, it has already been observed, the bounty, by occasioning an extraordinary exportation, necessarily keeps up the price of corn in the home market above what it would naturally fall to. To do so was the avowed purpose of the institution. In years of scarcity, though the bounty is frequently suspended, yet the great exportation which it occasions in years of plenty, must frequently hinder more or less the plenty of one year from relieving the scarcity of another. Both in years of plenty, and in years of scarcity, therefore, the bounty necessarily tends to raise the money price of corn somewhat higher than it otherwise would be in the home market.

It has been supposed to encourage cultivation and so to lower price.

That, in the actual state of tillage, the bounty must necessarily have this tendency, will not, I apprehend, be disputed by any reasonable person. But it has been thought by many people that it tends to encourage tillage, and that in two different ways; first, by opening a more extensive foreign market to the corn of the farmer, it tends, they imagine, to increase the demand for, and consequently the production of that commodity; and secondly, by securing to him a better price than he could otherwise expect in the actual state of tillage, it tends, they suppose, to encourage tillage. This double encouragement must, they imagine, in a long period of years, occasion such an increase in

---

① [These three sentences beginning with 'It has happened in France,' appear first in Additions and Corrections and ed. 3.]

第四篇　第五章

力图说明,从上世纪末粮食平均价格就开始下跌,而且现在之前的 64 年间仍在下跌。如果真像我所猜想的那样,那么没有津贴这种情况也会发生,它不可能是津贴所产生的后果。法国没有设立津贴,而且 1764 年以前,还禁止粮食的出口,但它的粮食平均价格和英国一样,都下跌了。所以,粮食平均价格的逐步下跌,或许并不是这种条例或那种条例造成的,归根结底而是由于白银的实际价值在不知不觉逐渐上升而造成的。我曾在本书第一篇中试图说明,本世纪以来,欧洲市场上,白银的价值普遍都在逐渐上升。看来津贴对粮食价格的下跌①不可能起到任何作用。

<small>津贴来的当于别的因素。设立津贴以粮价下跌归因</small>

　　前面已经说过,由于津贴在丰年会引起额外的出口,所以它必须把国内市场上粮食的价格稳定在一定的水平。这也是制定津贴的目的。在歉岁,津贴虽大都会暂时停止发放,但它在丰年的出口,或多或少都必定会使一年的丰收不能减缓另一年的不足。所以,无论年岁丰歉,津贴必然会提高粮食的货币价格,使其略高于没有津贴的时国内市场上粮食的货币价格。

<small>在丰年和荒年,津贴使价格保持在一定水平。</small>

　　在现实耕种条件下,津贴必然会产生这种效果。我想任何有理智的人,都不会对此有异议。但许多人却认为津贴能够奖励耕种,方法是两种:(一)津贴给农场主的粮食开辟了更为广阔的海外市场,因而能够增加粮食的需求量,进而可以刺激粮食的生产;(二)津贴使农场主得到的更高的价格,比他们在没有津贴的时候(按实际耕种情况考虑)所希望的价格高,因而可以刺激他们耕种。他们认为,在一个很长的时期内,这种双重奖励必定会大大

<small>津贴被认为可以鼓励耕种因此可以降低价格。</small>

---

　　①　这三个句子是以"它发生在法国"开始的,首次出现在附录和更正中,第三版中

1083

the production of corn, as may lower its price in the home market, much more than the bounty can raise it, in the actual state which tillage may, at the end of that period, happen to be in. ①

The addition to the price of corn at home caused by the bounty is a heavy tax on the people, which restrains population and industry and in the long run tends to diminish the consumption of corn.

I answer, that whatever extension of the foreign market can be occasioned by the bounty, must, in every particular year, be altogether at the expence of the home market; as every bushel of corn which is exported by means of the bounty, and which would not have been exported without the bounty, would have remained in the home market to increase the consumption, and to lower the price of that commodity. The corn bounty, it is to be observed, as well as every other bounty upon exportation, imposes two different taxes upon the people; first, the tax which they are obliged to contribute, in order to pay the bounty; and secondly, the tax which arises from the advanced price of the commodity in the home market, and which, as the whole body of the people are purchasers of corn, must, in this particular commodity, be paid by the whole body of the people. In this particular commodity, therefore, this second tax is by much the heaviest of the two. Let us suppose that, taking one year with another, the bounty of five shillings upon the exportation of the quarter of wheat, raises the price of that commodity in the home market only sixpence the bushel, or four shillings the quarter, higher than it other ways would have been in the actual state of the crop. Even upon this very moderate supposition, ② the great body of the people, over and above contributing the tax which pays the bounty of five shillings upon every quarter of wheat exported, must pay another of four shillings upon every quarter which they themselves consume. But, according to the very well informed author of the tracts upon the corn-trade, the average proportion of the corn exported to that consumed at home, is not more than that of one to thirty-one. ③ For every five shillings, therefore, which they contribute to the payment of the first tax, they must contribute six pounds four shillings to the payment of the second.

---

① [Eds. 1 and 2 read (beginning at the third line of the paragraph) ' But it has been thought by many people, that by securing to the farmer a better price than he could otherwise expect in the actual state of tillage, it tends to encourage tillage; and that the consequent increase of corn may, in a long period of years, lower its price more than the bounty can raise it in the actual state which tillage may at the end of that period happen to be in. ' The alteration is given in Additions and Corrections. The next two paragraphs appear first in Additions and Corrections and ed. 3.]

② [It is really anything but a moderate supposition. It is not at all likely that the increase of demand caused by the offer of a bounty on exportation would raise the price of a commodity to the extent of four-fifths of the bounty.]

③ [C. Smith, *Three Tracts on the Corn Trade*, 2nd ed, p. 144.]

第四篇 第五章

增加粮食的生产量,以至于在这个时期末的实际耕种情况下,国内市场上粮价可能下降的幅度,远远大于津贴所能提高的幅度。①

我认为,津贴虽然可以引起的国外市场的扩大,但它必定是以牺牲国内市场为代价。因津贴而出口的粮食,如果没有津贴,就一定会留在国内市场上增加了消费量,从而降低粮食的价格。应该指出,和一切其他出口津贴一样,粮食津贴需要人民承担两种不同的税。首先,为了偿付津贴,老百姓必须纳税;其次,津贴使国内市场上该商品的价格提高,从而产生更多的税,老百姓必须共同缴纳,因为老百姓都需要购买粮食。所以,就该商品而言,第二种税,比第一种税要重得多。让我们假设,逐年平均计算,每出口一夸特小麦给予5先令的津贴,那么国内市场上该商品的价格,比在没有设立津贴时的价格,每蒲式耳高6便士,即每夸特高4先令。按照这个假设,②老百姓除了共同担负每夸特小麦出口津贴5先令以外,他们每消费一夸特,还须多支付4先令。但根据上述那位博学的粮食贸易论文作者的观点,粮食出口与国内消费的平均比例不超过1:31。③ 所以,如果他们所缴纳的第一种税为5先令,那么第二种税一定是6镑4先令。把这样沉重的税加

---

① 在版本1和版本2中"但是许多人认为,它给农场主提供了更好的价格,它鼓励耕种,随之产生的粮食的增产或许在相当长时期内,将降低粮食价格,在这个时期末的实际耕种情况,下降的比津贴提高的还多"。参见附录和更正。下面两段首次出现在附录和更正以及第三版中。

② 它并没有什么意思,只是一个适当的假设。因为出口津贴而引起的需求增长会引起商品价格上涨到4/5津贴的程度,是根本不可能的。

③ 查理·史密斯关于粮食贸易和粮食法律的三篇论文,第二版,第144页。

So very heavy a tax upon the first necessary of life, must either reduce the subsistence of the labouring poor, or it must occasion some augmentation in their pecuniary wages, proportionable to that in the pecuniary price of their subsistence. So far as it operates in the one way, it must reduce the ability of the labouring poor to educate and bring up their children, and must, so far, tend to restrain the population of the country. So far as it operates in the other, it must reduce the ability of the employers of the poor, to employ so great a number as they otherwise might do, and must, so far, tend to restrain the industry of the country. The extraordinary exportation of corn, therefore, occasioned by the bounty, not only, in every particular year, diminishes the home, just as much as it extends the foreign market and consumption, but, by restraining the population and industry of the country, its final tendency is to stunt and restrain the gradual extension of the home market; and thereby, in the long run, rather to diminish, than to augment, the whole market and consumption of corn.

<small>The enhancement of price would encourage production if it was an enhancement of real price, but it is not;</small> This enhancement of the money price of corn, however, it has been thought, by rendering that commodity more profitable to the farmer, must necessarily encourage its production. ①

I answer, that this might be the case if the effect of the bounty was to raise the real price of corn, or to enable the farmer, with an equal quantity of it, to maintain a greater number of labourers in the same manner, whether liberal, moderate, or scanty, that other labourers are commonly maintained in his neighbourhood. But neither the bounty, it is evident, nor any other human institution, can have any such effect. It is not the real, but the nominal price of corn, which can in any considerable degree be affected by the bounty. ② And though the tax which that institution imposes upon the whole body of the people, may be very burdensome to those who pay it, it is of very little advantage to those who receive it. ③

<small>it is only a degradation of the value of silver,</small> The real effect of the bounty is not so much to raise the real value of corn, as to degrade the real value of silver; or to make an equal quantity of it exchange for a smaller quantity, not only of corn, but

---

① [This and the preceding paragraph are not in eds. 1 and 2.]

② [It does not occur to Smith that the additional corn might require greater labour to produce it than an equal quantity of the old.]

③ [In place of this and the preceding sentence eds. 1 and 2 read only ' It is not the real but the nominal price of corn only which can be at all affected by the bounty. ' The alteration is given in Additions and Corrections.]

在生活的首要必需品上,必然会使劳苦贫民减少生活必需品,货币工资随着生活品货币价格的提高而提高。就前者而言,必然会使劳苦贫民抚养子女、教育子女的能力降低,因而会抑制国内人口的增长。就后者而言,必然会降低雇主雇佣穷人的能力,抑制国内产业的发展。这样,津贴所引起的粮食的异常出口,不仅会扩大国外市场与国外消费,同时也会按比例减少国内市场与国内消费,而且由于压制国内人口与产业的正常发展,最后必然会阻碍国内市场的扩大。所以,从长远来看,与其说它会扩大粮食的整个市场与整个消费量,还不如说它会缩小粮食的整个市场与整个消费量。

有人认为,粮食货币价格的提高,给农场主提供了能赚更多利润的商品,从而必然会刺激生产。①

我认为,如果津贴真的能够达到提高粮食真实价格的效果,或者能够使农场主能以同量粮食,按照当地人的生活方式养活更多的人,无论是宽裕、中等还是俭省,那么或许可能如上面所说的情形。但是显然,津贴不会有这种效果,任何人为制度都绝不会产生这样的效果。受津贴影响②的只是粮食的名义价格,而不是它的真正价值。这种用制度加在老百姓身上的税收,对缴纳者是沉重的负担,对收受者③则无利益可言。

津贴产生的真正效果,与其说是提高粮食的实际价值,还不如说是压低了白银的实际价值。换句话说,它使等量的白银,只

---

① 这段和下一段在版本1和版本2中没有出现。
② 史密斯没有想到,多产的粮食可能需要更多的劳动力。
③ 在版本1和版本2中,"受津贴影响的不是粮食的真实价格而是名义价格",参见附录和更正。

of all other home-made commodities: for the money price of corn regulates that of all other home-made ① commodities.

<small>for corn regulates the money price of labour,</small>　It regulates the money price of labour, which must always be such as to enable the labourer to purchase a quantity of corn sufficient to maintain him and his family either in the liberal, moderate, or scanty manner in which the advancing, stationary or declining circumstances of the society oblige his employers to maintain him.

<small>of all rude produce,</small>　It regulates the money price of all the other parts of the rude produce of land, which, in every period of improvement, must bear a certain proportion to that of corn, though this proportion is different in different periods. It regulates, for example, the money price of grass and hay, of butcher's meat, of horses, and the maintenance of horses, of land carriage consequently, or of the greater part of the inland commerce of the country.

<small>and of almost all manufactures.</small>　By regulating the money price of all the other parts of the rude produce of land, it regulates that of the materials of almost all manufactures. By regulating the money price of labour, it regulates that of manufacturing art and industry. And by regulating both, it regulates that of the complete manufacture. The money price of labour, and of every thing that is the produce either of land or labour, must necessarily either rise or fall in proportion to the money price of corn.

<small>So farmers and landlords are not benefited by the increased price due to the bounty.</small>　Though in consequence of the bounty, therefore, the farmer should be enabled to sell his corn for four shillings the bushel instead of three and sixpence, and to pay his landlord a money rent proportionable to this rise in the money price of his produce; yet if, in consequence of this rise in the price of corn, four shillings will purchase no more home-made goods of any other kind than three and sixpence would have done before, neither the circumstances of the farmer, nor

---

①　['Home-made' here and in the line above is not in eds. 1 and 2.]

能换回较少量的粮食或其他一切国产①商品,因为粮食的货币价格支配着其他一切商品的货币价格。

粮食的货币价格支配着劳动的货币价格。劳动的货币价格,必须能使劳动者经常有能力购买一定数量的粮食,维持自己及家庭的生活,不管生活得是宽裕、中等还是俭省。社会的进步、退步或停滞等情况,使劳动者的雇主们也不得不按照同样的方式来维持劳动者的生活。因为粮食价值决定着劳动价值,

粮食的货币价格,支配一切其他未加工的土地生产物的货币价格。在改良的任何阶段中,这些产物的货币价格,一定会和粮食的货币价格保持一定的比例。虽然这种比例,在改良的不同阶段会有所不同。牧草、干草、家畜肉、马、马粮、内陆运输以及大部分国内行业,其货币价格都受粮食货币价格的支配。决定着所有未加工产品的价值,

粮食的货币价格,支配了所有其他土地未加工生产物的货币价格,便支配了几乎所有制造业原料的货币价格;支配了劳动的货币价格,便支配了制造技术和工业的货币价格。由于它有这两个支配作用,所以它便支配着所有制造产品的货币价格。劳动的货币价格,一切土地生产物或劳动生产物的货币价格,都必然根据粮食货币价格的升降而按比例而升降。决定着所有几乎所有制造产品的价值。

尽管津贴的结果是,农场主可以把粮食卖到每蒲式耳 4 先令,而不是 3 先令 6 便士,并向地主缴纳货币租金,这些租金与已经上升的生产物货币价格是成一定比例的。但粮食价格上涨的结果是,现在用四先令购得的任何一种国产。商品不过和以前用 3 先令 6 便士可购得的商品一样多,而农场主与地主的生活状况,因津贴而上涨的价格并未使农场主和地方受益。

---

① 这里的"国产"没有出现在版本 1 和版本 2 中。

those of the landlord, will be much mended by this change. The farmer will not be able to cultivate much better; the landlord will not be able to live much better. In the purchase of foreign commodities this enhancement in the price of corn may give them some little advantage. In that of home-made commodities it can give them none at all. And almost the whole expence of the farmer, and the far greater part even of that of the landlord, is in home-made commodities. ①

<small>A worldwide degradation of the value of silver is of little consequence,</small>
That degradation in the value of silver which is the effect of the fertility of the mines, and which operates equally, or very near equally, through the greater part of the commercial world, is a matter of very little consequence to any particular country. The consequent rise of all money prices, though it does not make those who receive them really richer, does not make them really poorer. A service of plate becomes really cheaper, and every thing else remains precisely of the same real value as before.

<small>but degradation confined to one country discourages the industry of that country.</small>
But that degradation in the value of silver which, being the effect either of the peculiar situation, or of the political institutions of a particular country, takes place only in that country, is a matter of very great consequence, which, far from tending to make any body really richer, tends to make every body really poorer. The rise in the money price of all commodities, which is in this case peculiar to that country, tends to discourage more or less every sort of industry which is carried on within it, and to enable foreign nations, by furnishing almost all sorts of goods for a smaller quantity of silver than its own workmen can afford to do, to undersell them, not only in the foreign, but even in the home market.

<small>In Spain and Portugal gold and silver are naturally cheaper than in the rest of Europe,</small>
It is the peculiar situation of Spain and Portugal as proprietors of the mines, to be the distributors of gold and silver to all the other countries of Europe. Those metals ought naturally, therefore, to be somewhat cheaper in Spain and Portugal than in any other part of Europe. The difference, however, should be no more than the amount of the freight and insurance; and, on account of the great value and small bulk of those metals, their freight is no great matter, and their insurance is the same as that of any other goods of equal value. Spain and Portugal, therefore, could suffer very little from their peculiar situation,

---

① [This and the two preceding sentences from 'in the purchase' appear first in Additions and Corrections and ed. 3.]

都不能由于这种价格的变更而改善很多。农场主的耕种,不会有很大的进步;地主的生活,不会变得更好。这样上涨的粮食价格,虽然使他们购买外国商品时,获得一些微利,但购买国产商品时,一点便宜也占不到。农场主的全部花费、地主的大部分花费,都用在国产商品①上。

矿山资源丰富而引起白银价格下跌,可能对大部分商业领域会产生相同或几乎相同的影响,但对个别国家来说,则无关紧要。随之产生的一切货币价格的上升,既不会使收受者更富裕,也不会使收受者更贫穷。金银器皿的价格比从前便宜了,但其他物品的实际价值,却和从前完全一样。世界范围内的银价下跌影响不大,

如果个别国家的白银价格由于受到特殊情况或政治制度的影响而下跌,即使仅仅发生在一个国家,却也会成为举足轻重的事情。因为这种事情不会使任何人变得更富裕,却会使所有人变得更贫穷。商品货币价格的上升,虽然只是该国的特殊情况,但多少会阻抑国内各种产业的发展,从而使外国降价出售货物,以便该国的工人能够承受得起。这不仅仅是国外市场,国内商场也是如此。但是仅限于某个国家的银价下跌,会阻碍国家的产业。

西班牙和葡萄牙盛产金银,所以能够给欧洲其他国家提供金银。这两种金属的价格,在西班牙和葡萄牙自然要比在欧洲其他各国略为便宜,但差价不应大于运输费和保险费之和。由于金银体积小价值大,运输费不是大问题;至于保险费,也与任何其他等值货物的保险费相同。所以,如果这两国的政治维持不变,那么在西班牙和葡萄牙,金银自然比欧洲其他国家便宜,

---

① 这个和"用于购买"之前的两个句子首次出现在附录和更正以及第三版中。

国民财富的性质与原理

if they did not aggravate its disadvantages by their political institutions.

but by the hindrances to exportation they are made still cheaper, and agriculture and manufactures are thereby discouraged.

Spain by taxing, and Portugal by prohibiting the exportation of gold and silver, load that exportation with the expence of smuggling, and raise the value of those metals in other countries so much more above what it is in their own, by the whole amount of this expence. ① When you dam up a stream of water, as soon as the dam is full, as much water must run over the dam-head as if there was no dam at all. The prohibition of exportation cannot detain a greater quantity of gold and silver in Spain and Portugal than what they can afford to employ, than what the annual produce of their land and labour will allow them to employ, in coin, plate, gilding, and other ornaments of gold and silver. When they have got this quantity the dam is full, and the whole stream which flows in afterwards must run over. The annual exportation of gold and silver from Spain and Portugal accordingly is, by all accounts, notwithstanding these restraints, very near equal to the whole annual importation. As the water, however, must always be deeper behind the dam-head than before it, so the quantity of gold and silver which these restraints detain in Spain and Portugal must, in proportion to the annual produce of their land and labour, be greater than what is to be found in other countries. The higher and stronger the dam-head, the greater must be the difference in the depth of water behind and before it. The higher the tax, the higher the penalties with which the prohibition is guarded, the more vigilant and severe the police which looks after the execution of the law, the greater must be the difference in the proportion of gold and silver to the annual produce of the land and labour of Spain and Portugal, and to that of other countries. It is said accordingly to be very considerable, and that you frequently find there a profusion of plate in houses, where there is nothing else which would, in other countries, be thought suitable or correspondent to this sort of magnificence. The cheapness of gold and silver, or what is the same thing, the dearness of all commodities, which is the necessary effect of this redundancy of the precious metals, discourages both the agriculture and manufactures of Spain and Portugal, and enables foreign nations to supply them with many sorts of rude, and with almost all sorts of manufactured produce, for a smaller quantity of gold and silver than what they themselves can either raise or make them for at home. The tax and prohibition operate

---

① [Spain's prohibition of exportation of gold and silver had only been abolished at a recent period. The tax was 3 per cent. till 1768, then 4 per cent.]

它们会因为白银价格低廉而吃亏。

对于金银的出口,西班牙课以赋税,葡萄牙予以禁止。走私便使得金银在别国的价值高于西、葡二国,高出部分便等于走私的全部费用。① 这样就好比修筑堤坝,坝内蓄满了水,水就会要越过坝头朝外流,就如堤坝形不存在。禁止金银出口,也会产生同样的后果,并不能使该国保留其未消耗掉的金银量。一国土地和劳动的年产物,制约了该国在铸币、金银器皿、镀金以及在金银装饰品上所使用的金银量。如果金银的数量饱和了,就如同坝内蓄满了水,必然会向外溢出。这样,西、葡两国虽然限制金银的出口,但每年从两国出口的金银,几乎等于其每年的进口额。但是,正如坝内的水肯定要比坝外的水要深,由于限制而保留在西、葡两国内的金银量和国家的土地和劳动的年产物成正比,因此必然高于其他各国的金银量。坝头越高越牢固,坝内外的水深差别必然越大。所以,税收越高,禁令所立的刑罚越严峻,警察执法越严厉,西、葡两国金银与土地和劳动的年产物的比例,与其他各国类似比例相比,差别也就越悬殊。据说这种差别很大,在西、葡两国,人们常常可以看到家家户户有许许多多的金银器皿,而在其他国家则看不到。这正是贵金属过剩的必然结果,即导致金银的贬值,或者说导致所有其他商品的升值,这就阻碍了西、葡两国的农业与制造业的发展,这就使得外国能供给它们各种未加工生产物以及几乎所有种类的制造品,而且比它们自己国内生产或制造所花费的金银量更少。课税及禁运,可以起到两个方面的作用。

禁出它然宜农制因
止口,仍业到
它,便和
们此造此受
尽管业
止口,
出它
们便

---

① 西班牙禁止金银出口仅仅在近期才废除。税收一直是 3%,直到 1768 年才是 4%。

in two different ways. They not only lower very much the value of the precious metals in Spain and Portugal, but by detaining there a certain quantity of those metals which would otherwise flow over other countries, they keep up their value in those other countries somewhat above what it otherwise would be, and thereby give those countries a double advantage in their commerce with Spain and Portugal. Open the flood-gates, and there will presently be less water above, and more below, the dam-head, and it will soon come to a level in both places. Remove the tax and the prohibition, and as the quantity of gold and silver will diminish considerably in Spain and Portugal, so it will increase somewhat in other countries, and the value of those metals, their proportion to the annual produce of land and labour, will soon come to a level, or very near to a level, in all. The loss which Spain and Portugal could sustain by this exportation of their gold and silver would be altogether nominal and imaginary. The nominal value of their goods, and of the annual produce of their land and labour, would fall, and would be expressed or represented by a smaller quantity of silver than before: but their real value would be the same as before, and would be sufficient to maintain, command, and employ, the same quantity of labour. As the nominal value of their goods would fall, the real value of what remained of their gold and silver would rise, and a smaller quantity of those metals would answer all the same purposes of commerce and circulation which had employed a greater quantity before. The gold and silver which would go abroad would not go abroad for nothing, but would bring back an equal value of goods of some kind or another. Those goods too would not be all matters of mere luxury and expence, to be consumed by idle people who produce nothing in return for their consumption. As the real wealth and revenue of idle people would not be augmented by this extraordinary exportation of gold and silver, so neither would their consumption be much augmented by it. Those goods would, probably, the greater part of them, and certainly some part of them, consist in materials, tools, and provisions, for the employment and maintenance of industrious people, who would reproduce, with a profit, the full value of their consumption. A part of the dead stock of the society would thus be turned into active stock, and would put into motion a greater quantity of industry than had been employed before. The annual produce of their land and labour would immediately be augmented a little, and in a few years would, probably, be augmented a great deal; their industry being thus relieved from one of the most oppressive burdens which it at present labours under.

The bounty upon the exportation of corn necessarily operates exactly in the same way as this absurd policy of Spain and Portugal.

它们不仅大大降低西、葡二国贵金属的价值,而且限制了多余数量的金银流入到国外,从而使其他各国贵金属的价格比其本身实际价值略高,使其他各国与西、葡二国通商时能够享受双重利益。要是水闸打开,那么坝内的水会立刻减少,坝外的水立刻增多,坝内外的水位不久就会相等。同样,如果撤销这种关税与禁令,那么西、葡两国的金银量就会减少,其他各国的金银量就会增多,这些金属的价值,它们与土地劳动年产物的比例,不久就会在所有国家之间相同或几乎相同。西、葡二国,认为出口金银而可能遭受损失,完全是名义上的、想象上的。它们货物的名义价值,即土地和劳动年产物的名义价值将下降,或者说用比以前小的金银量来表示或替代,但其实际价值和从前相同,其所能维持、支配和雇佣的劳动量,也将和从前相同。货物的名义价值下跌,而剩余金银的实际价值上升,往日为通商流通而使用较多的金银量,现在使用较少的数量就能达到目的。流向外国的金银,不会白白地流往外国,它们必然会交换回同等价值的各种货物。这些货物并不全部是奢侈品和消费品,让那些不从事生产的游手好闲者消费的。游手好闲者的真实财富与收入,不会由于这种异常的金银出口而增加,其消费也不会由此而增加。所以,这些货物的大部分,或者说至少也有一部分是材料、工具、食品,用于雇佣劳动人民并维持他们的生活。他们能再生产出他们所要消费的全部价值,并且创造利润。这样,社会的一部分呆滞资产就可以成为流动资产,从而增加产业的生产量。土地和劳动的年产品,也会马上随之略有增加,再过几年,会大量增加,从而产业目前所承受的一个沉重负担便解除了。

粮食出口津贴同西、葡二国对金银出口实行的不合理政策所

国民财富的性质与原理

<small>The corn bounty acts in the same way;</small> Whatever be the actual state of tillage, it renders our corn somewhat dearer in the home market than it otherwise would be in that state, and somewhat cheaper in the foreign; and as the average money price of corn regulates more or less that of all other commodities, it lowers the value of silver considerably in the one, and tends to raise it a little in the other. It enables foreigners, the Dutch in particular, not only to eat our corn cheaper than they otherwise could do, but sometimes to eat it cheaper than even our own people can do upon the same occasions; as we are assured by an excellent authority, that of Sir Matthew Decker. ① It hinders our own workmen from furnishing their goods for so small a quantity of silver as they otherwise might do; and enables the Dutch to furnish their's for a smaller. It tends to render our manufactures somewhat dearer in every market, and their's somewhat cheaper than they otherwise would be, and consequently to give their industry a double advantage over our own.

<small>it discourages manufactures without much benefiting farmers and country gentlemen.</small> The bounty, as it raises in the home market, not so much the real, as the nominal price of our corn, as it augments, not the quantity of labour which a certain quantity of corn can maintain and employ, but only the quantity of silver which it will exchange for, it discourages our manufactures, without rendering any considerable service either to our farmers or country gentlemen. It puts, indeed, a little more money into the pockets of both, and it will perhaps be somewhat difficult to persuade the greater part of them that this is not rendering them a very considerable service. But if this money sinks in its value, in the quantity of labour, provisions, and home-made commodities of all different kinds which it is capable of purchasing, as much as it rises in its quantity, the service will be little more than nominal and imaginary.

<small>It is essentially serviceable only to the corn merchants.</small> There is, perhaps, but one set of men in the whole commonwealth to whom the bounty either was or could be essentially serviceable. These were the corn merchants, the exporters and importers of corn. In years of plenty the bounty necessarily occasioned a greater exportation than would otherwise have taken place; and by hindering the plenty of one year from relieving the scarcity of another, it occasioned

---

① [*Essay on the Causes of the Decline of the Foreign Trade*, *consequently of the Value of the Lands of Britain*, *and on the means to restore both*, and ed. , 1750, pp. 55、171.]

起的作用一样荒唐。不论耕种的实际情况怎么样,比起没有设立津贴,粮食出口津贴总会使国内市场上的粮食价格略高,使外国市场上的粮食价格略低。因为粮食的平均货币价格,或多或少支配一切其他商品的平均货币价格。所以,这种津贴会大大减低国内白银的价值,并稍稍提高外国白银的价值。这种津贴,使外国人,尤其是荷兰人,不但能吃到便宜的粮食,而且甚至有时吃到的粮食的价格比我们国内的价格还便宜;一位卓越的权威作者马太·德克尔先生,①曾明确指出这一点。这种津贴,阻碍了我们的工人以少量的白银提供货物,却使荷兰人能以更少的白银提供货物。津贴使得我国的制造品,无论在哪里,都要比荷兰人的昂贵一些。因而,与我们的产业相比,他们的产业能享受双重的利益。

粮食津贴起着同样的作用;

　　这种津贴,在国内市场上所提高的,不是我国粮食的真实价格,而是粮食的名义价格。它所增加的,不是一定量粮食所能维持和雇佣的劳动量,而是一定量粮食所能交换的白银量。所以,这必然阻碍我国制造业的发展,不能给我国农场主或乡绅带来任何帮助。的确,这两者都会因此而多增加了一点货币收入,所以,要使他们大部分人相信津贴对他们并无多大帮助,或许有点困难;但是,如果货币贬值了,所能购买的劳动量、食物量和各种国产商品量都减少了,这种好处也不过是名义上、想象上的了。

它阻碍了制造业,没有给农场主和乡绅多益处。

　　津贴对其有或者可能有实质上的帮助的,在整个国家,也许只有一种人,即粮食商人或粮食出口商和粮食进口商。津贴必然使丰年粮食出口量增加,而且,由于丰年的收成不能减缓歉岁的

实质上,它只对粮食商人有利。

---

① 关于国际贸易减少,不列颠土地价值降低的原因以及恢复二者的方法的论文,第二版,1750 年,第 55、171 页。

in years of scarcity a greater importation than would otherwise have been necessary. It increased the business of the corn merchant in both; and in years of scarcity, it not only enabled him to import a greater quantity, but to sell it for a better price, and consequently with a greater profit than he could otherwise have made, if the plenty of one year had not been more or less hindered from relieving the scarcity of another. It is in this set of men, accordingly, that I have observed the greatest zeal for the continuance or renewal of the bounty.

The country gentlemen established the duties on the importation of corn, and the bounty, in imitation of the manufacturers,

Our country gentlemen, when they imposed the high duties upon the importation of foreign corn, which in times of moderate plenty amount to a prohibition, and when they established the bounty, seem to have imitated the conduct of our manufacturers. By the one institution, they secured to themselves the monopoly of the home market, and by the other they endeavoured to prevent that market from ever being overstocked with their commodity. By both they endeavoured to raise its real value, in the same manner as our manufacturers had, by the like institutions, raised the real value of many different sorts of manufactured goods. They did not perhaps attend to the great and essential difference which nature has established between corn and almost every other sort of goods. When, either by the monopoly of the home market, or by a bounty upon exportation, you enable our woollen

without attending to the essential difference between corn and other goods.

or linen manufacturers to sell their goods for somewhat a better price than they otherwise could get for them, you raise, not only the nominal, but the real price of those goods. You render them equivalent to a greater quantity of labour and subsistence, you increase not only the nominal, but the real profit, the real wealth and revenue of those manufacturers, and you enable them either to live better themselves, or to employ a greater quantity of labour in those particular manufactures. You really encourage those manufactures, and direct towards them a greater quantity of the industry of the country, than what would probably go to them of its own accord. But when by the like institutions you raise the nominal or money-price of corn, you do not raise its real value. You do not increase the real wealth, the real revenue either of our farmers or country gentlemen. You do not encourage the growth of corn, because you do not enable them to maintain and employ more labourers in raising it. The nature of things has stamped upon corn a real value which cannot be altered by merely altering its money price. No bounty upon exportation, no monopoly of the home market, can raise that value. The freest competition cannot lower it. Through the world in general that value

不足,它必然使歉岁粮食进口量增大。所以,无论是丰年还是歉岁,它都增加了粮食商人的生意。在歉岁,这种津贴不但使他能进口更多粮食,而且能以较好的价格出售粮食,从而能获得较大的利润。所以,我认为,最拥护继续发给这种津贴的,就是这种人。

我国的乡绅,在对外国粮食的进口课以重税(在丰年便禁止进口),和对本国粮食的出口给予津贴时,似乎是在效仿制造商的行为。用前一种方式,他们保护了国内市场的垄断权;用后一种方式,他们企图防止国内市场上粮食积压过剩。总之,他们试图使用这两种方式提高商品的实际价值。这与制造商所采取的方式是一样的。但他们也许没注意到,粮食和其他各种货物间存在着巨大、本质的差别。以垄断国内市场或奖励出口的办法,可以使羊毛或者亚麻布制造商以更好的价格出售他们的货物。因为这些办法,不但提高了这些货物的名义价格,而且提高了这些货物的真实价格,使这些货物等同于更多的劳动量与消费品量。这样,不仅增加了这些制造商的名义利润、名义财富与名义收入,而且增加了他们的实际利润、实际财富与实际收入,他们就能够生活得更好,并在制造业中雇佣较多的劳动力。这实际上就是鼓励这些制造商投入更多更大的产业。但这种制度提高的只是粮食的名义价值,而不是粮食的实际价值,它并不能增加农场主和乡绅的实际财富或实际收入,也不会鼓励粮食的耕种,不能使同等量的粮食养活和雇佣更多的耕种粮食的劳动者。从本质上讲,粮食的实际价值不能随货币价格的改变而改变。出口津贴和国内市场垄断,都不能提高粮食的实际价值。同样,最自由的竞争也不能降低它的实际价值。在世界任何地方,粮食的实际价值都是

乡绅们制造商设立了出口津贴,有效仿制造商却没认识到粮食与其他货物本质区别。

is equal to the quantity of labour which it can maintain, and in every particular place it is equal to the quantity of labour which it can maintain in the way, whether liberal, moderate, or scanty, in which labour is commonly maintained in that place. Woollen or linen cloth are not the regulating commodities by which the real value of all other commodities must be finally measured and determined; corn is. The real value of every other commodity is finally measured and determined by the proportion which its average money price bears to the average money price of corn. The real value of corn does not vary with those variations in its average money price, which sometimes occur from one century to another. It is the real value of silver which varies with them.

All the expedients of the mercantile system force industry into less advantageous channels: bounties on exports force it into actually disadvantageous channels: the bounty on corn does not encourage its production.

Bounties upon the exportation of any home-made commodity are liable, first, to that general objection which may be made to all the different expedients of the mercantile system ; the objection of forcing some part of the industry of the country into a channel less advantageous than that in which it would run of its own accord: and, secondly, to the particular objection of forcing it, not only into a channel that is less advantageous, but into one that is actually disadvantageous; the trade which cannot be carried on but by means of a bounty being necessarily a losing trade. The bounty upon the exportation of corn is liable to this further objection, that it can in no respect promote the raising of that particular commodity of which it was meant to encourage the production. When our country gentlemen, therefore, demanded the establishment of the bounty, though they acted in imitation of our merchants and manufacturers, they did not act with that complete comprehension of their own interest which commonly directs the conduct of those two other orders of people. They loaded the public revenue with a very considerable expence; they imposed a very heavy tax upon the whole body of the people; but they did not, in any sensible degree, increase ①the real value of their own commodity; and by lowering somewhat the real value of silver, they discouraged, in some degree, the general industry of the country, and, instead of advancing, retarded more or less the improvement of their own lands, which necessarily depends upon the general industry of the country.

---

① [Eds. 1 and 2 read ' They loaded the public revenue with a very considerable expence, but they did not in any respect increase. ' The alteration is given in Additions and Corrections.]

等于它所能维持的劳动量;就个别地方而言,粮食的实际价值就等于粮食按照当地维持劳动者生活的一般方式所能维持的劳动量,无论是宽裕、省俭还是适中。羊毛和亚麻布不是占支配地位的商品,一切其他商品的实际价值,并非由羊毛和亚麻布的价值来衡量决定。虽然粮食的平均货币价格在不同时期有时会有所不同,但其真实价值却不随这种变化而变化,变化的只是白银的实际价值。

给任何国产商品发放出口津贴,都不可避免地遭到人们的反对。首先,重商主义体系的这种权宜之计,一般都可能遭到反对,因为这会迫使国内部分产业的资金转向利润较少的行业,而不是让它们顺其自然地发展。其次,国产商品出口津贴特别会遭到人们的反对,因为它迫使国内一部分产业的资金流向利润较少甚至没有优势的行业。无津贴就不能经营的行业,必然是一种亏损行业。粮食出口津贴遭到人们的反对,原因还有:无论从哪一点说,它都不能促进它所要促进的那种商品的生产。乡绅们效仿商人和制造商,要求设置这种津贴,但商人和造商知道指导自身行动的利益所在,他们却不完全理解。他们使国家的税收负担了一笔极大的开支,给百姓增添了沉重的赋税,但他们没有显著增加[①]自己商品的实际价值。白银的实际价值也因此稍微贬低,在一定程度上,他们阻碍了国家一般产业的发展,而土地改良有赖于国家一般产业的发展,所以,他们不但没有促进,反而或多或少地妨碍了土地的改良。

[①] 版本1和版本2中,"他们使公民税收负担了非常可观的花费,但他们没有任何程度地增加",这种改变见附录和更正。

国民财富的性质与原理

<small>A bounty on production would be more effectual than one on exportation and would lower the price of the commodity, but such bounties have been rare, owing to the interest of merchants and manufacturers.</small>

To encourage the production of any commodity, a bounty upon production, one should imagine, would have a more direct operation, than one upon exportation. It would, besides, impose only one tax upon the people, that which they must contribute in order to pay the bounty. Instead of raising, it would tend to lower the price of the commodity in the home market; and thereby, instead of imposing a second tax upon the people, it might, at least in part, repay them for what they had contributed to the first. Bounties upon production, however, have been very rarely granted. The prejudices established by the commercial system have taught us to believe, that national wealth arises more immediately from exportation than from production. It has been more favoured accordingly, as the more immediate means of bringing money into the country. Bounties upon production, it has been said too, have been found by experience more liable to frauds than those upon exportation. How far this is true, I know not. That bounties upon exportation have been abused to many fraudulent purposes, is very well known. But it is not the interest of merchants and manufacturers, the great inventors of all these expedients, that the home market should be overstocked with their goods, an event which a bounty upon production might sometimes occasion. A bounty upon exportation, by enabling them to send abroad the surplus part, and to keep up the price of what remains in the home market, effectually prevents this. Of all the expedients of the mercantile system, accordingly, it is the one of which they are the fondest. I have known the different undertakers of some particular works agree privately among themselves to give a bounty out of their own pockets upon the exportation of a certain proportion of the goods which they dealt in. This expedient succeeded so well, that it more than doubled the price of their goods in the home market, notwithstanding a very considerable increase in the produce. The operation of the bounty upon corn must have been wonderfully different, if it has lowered the money price of that commodity.

<small>The herring and whale fishery bounties are in part given on production.</small>

Something like a bounty upon production, however, has been granted upon some particular occasions. The tonnage bounties given to the white-herring and whale-fisheries may, perhaps, be considered as somewhat of this nature. ① They tend directly, it may be supposed, to

---

① [The whale fishery bounty under 11 Geo. Ⅲ. , c. 38, was 40s. per ton for the first five years, 30e. for the second five years, and 20s. for the third.]

— 1102 —

有人认为,如果要鼓励一种商品的生产,发放生产津贴比发放出口津贴具有更直接的效果。而且,它只给百姓增加了一种税收,也就是说,百姓只需缴纳用以支付津贴的税。生产津贴不会提高,而是减低该商品在国内市场上的价格。所以,他们不必再缴纳第二种税,所缴纳的第一种税,也至少可得到一部分的偿还。但是,生产津贴发放得非常稀少。重商主义体系所形成的偏见使人们相信,国民财富来自于生产的慢,来自于出口的快。出口津贴被看作是能够更直接地带回货币的方法,因此更受欢迎。又有人说,根据经验,生产津贴比出口津贴更容易产生欺诈行为。我不知道这种说法的真实性有多大,但出口津贴,常常被滥用来做许多欺诈骗人的勾当,是众所周知的事。商人、制造商以及这一切方法的发明者的本质利益在于,他们的货物不能在国内市场上积压,而生产津贴有时会引起这种情况的发生。但出口津贴可使过剩的产品销往外国,这样可以保证国内货物的售价,从而能切实防止过剩情况的发生。因此,各种策略中,出口津贴便成为最受他们欢迎的一种了。据我所知,某些特别行业的经营者,甚至愿意自己掏钱设立津贴以鼓励部分货物的出口。这种策略非常成功,虽然大大增加了商品的产量,但在国内市场上货物的价格仍然涨了一倍以上。但是,粮食津贴要是真的降低了粮食的货币价格,其作用可真是太不一般了。

但是,在某些特殊情况下,曾出现了类似生产津贴的津贴。按吨数发放给白鲱鱼渔业的津贴,①就可看作是这种性质的津

---

① 根据乔治三世十一年第 38 号法令,发放给捕鲸业的津贴第一个五年为每吨 40 先令,第二个五年为每吨 30 个先令,到第三个五年为 20 先令。

国民财富的性质与原理

render the goods cheaper in the home market than they otherwise would be. In other respects their effects, it must be acknowledged, are the same as those of bounties upon exportation. By means of them a part of the capital of the country is employed in bringing goods to market, of which the price does not repay the cost, together with the ordinary profits of stock.

<small>They are supposed to augment the number of sailors and ships.</small>

But though the tonnage bounties to those fisheries do not contribute to the opulence of the nation, it may perhaps be thought that they contribute to its defence, ① by augmenting the number of its sailors and shipping. This, it may be alleged, may sometimes be done by means of such bounties at a much smaller expence, than by keeping up a great standing navy, if I may use such an expression, in the same way as a standing army. ②

<small>In granting the herring bounties Parliament has been imposed on, since (1) the herring buss bounty is too large,</small>

Notwithstanding these favourable allegations, however, the following considerations dispose me to believe, that in granting at least one of these bounties, the legislature has been very grossly imposed upon.

First, the herring buss bounty seems too large.

From the commencement of the winter fishing 1771 to the end of the winter fishing 1781, the tonnage bounty upon the herring buss fishery has been at thirty shillings the ton. During these eleven years the whole number of barrels caught by the herring buss fishery of Scotland amounted to 378, 347. The herrings caught and cured at sea, are called sea sticks. In order to render them what are called merchantable herrings, it is necessary to repack them with an additional

---

① [Eds. 1 and 2 read 'they may perhaps be defended as conducing to its defence'.]

② [The next four pages, to page 24 line 10, are not in eds. 1 and 2, which read in place of them: 'Some other bounties may be vindicated perhaps upon the same principle. It is of importance that the kingdom should depend as little as possible upon its neighbours for the manufactures necessary for its defence; and if these cannot otherwise be maintained at home, it is reasonable that all other branches of industry should be taxed in order to support them. The bounties upon the importation of naval stores from America, upon British made sail-cloth, and upon British made gunpowder, may perhaps all three be vindicated upon this principle. The first is a bounty upon the production of America, for the use of Great Britain. The two others are bounties upon exportation.' The new paragraphs, with the two preceding paragraphs as amended, are given in Additions and Corrections.]

贴。这或许意味着,它直接使该商品在国内市场上的价格,比没有津贴时低廉。从其他方面来看,必须得承认,其效果与出口津贴的效果相同。有了这种津贴,国内一部分资本就用来给市场供货,但其价格以及投资所创造的基本利润还不足以补偿其费用。

这种按照吨数发放渔业的津贴,虽然对国民财富的增长起不到什么作用,但是由于可增加船舶及水手数目,所以,就被认为有助于国防。① 或许可以断言,有时候这么做,与维持常备陆军所花的费用相比,如果我可以这样表达的话,用这种津贴来巩固国防,来维持庞大的常备海军,费用也许要小得多。②

<small>它们被认为可以增加水手和船舶的数量。</small>

在这种辩护下,以下几个方面却使我相信,在立法者制定的各种津贴中,至少有一种是因为他们被欺骗了而制定的。

<small>在给鲱鱼业津贴时国会受了欺骗,因为</small>

第一,鲱鱼业渔船的津贴似乎太大了。

从1771年冬季鱼汛开始直到1781年冬季鱼汛结束,鲱鱼业渔船的津贴为每吨30先令。在这11年内,苏格兰渔船捕捞的鲱鱼总量为378347桶,在海上捕获即行腌存的鲱鱼称为海条,为了到市场销售,须再用一定数量的盐来腌制并加以包装,成为商

<small>(1)鲱鱼渔船津贴太大了。</small>

---

① 在版本1和版本2中为"它们或许因为有助于国防而被保护"。

② 在版本1和版本2中没有以下四页文字,而是"或许可以用同一原则来维护其他别的津贴。对于国防必须的制造品,国家应当尽可能少地依靠邻国。如果这些东西在国内不能维持生产,那么对其他产业征税以支持它们,也是合情合理的。从美国进口的海军军需品,英国制造的帆篷布,英国制造的枪支,加在这些东西上的三种津贴或许都可用这种原则来维护。第一种津贴是给美国的产品,因为它是被大不列颠使用的。其他两种是出口津贴",这些新的段落,以及之前的段落都修正过了。参见附录和更正。

quantity of salt; and in this case, it is reckoned, that three barrels of sea sticks, are usually repacked into two barrels of merchantable herrings. The number of barrels of merchantable herrings, therefore, caught during these eleven years, will amount only, according to this account, to 252, 231 $\frac{1}{3}$. During these eleven years the tonnage bounties paid amounted to 155, 463l. 11 s. or to 8 s. 2 $\frac{1}{4}$ d. upon every barrel of sea sticks, and to 12 s. 3 $\frac{3}{4}$ d. upon every barrel of merchantable herrings.

The salt with which these herrings are cured, is sometimes Scotch, and sometimes foreign salt; both which are delivered free of all excise duty to the fish-curers. The excise duty upon Scotch salt is at present 1 s. 6 d. that upon foreign salt 10 s. the bushel. A barrel of herrings is supposed to require about one bushel and one- fourth of a bushel foreign salt. Two bushels are the supposed average of Scotch salt. If the herrings are entered for exportation, no part of this duty is paid up; if entered for home consumption, whether the herrings were cured with foreign or with Scotch salt, only one shilling the barrel is paid up. It was the old Scotch duty upon a bushel of salt, the quantity which, at a low estimation, had been supposed necessary for curing a barrel of herrings. In Scotland, foreign salt is very little used for any other purpose but the curing of fish. But from the 5th April 1771, to the 5th April 1782, the quantity of foreign salt imported amounted to 936, 974 bushels, at eighty-four pounds the bushel: the quantity of Scotch salt delivered from the works to the fish-curers, to no more than 168, 226, at fifty-six pounds the bushel only. It would appear, therefore, that it is principally foreign salt that is used in the fisheries. Upon every barrel of herrings exported there is, besides, a bounty of 2s. 8d. and more than two-thirds of the buss caught herrings are exported. Put all these things together, and you will find that, during these eleven years, every barrel of buss caught herrings, cured with Scotch salt when exported, has cost government 17 s. 11 $\frac{3}{4}$$d$. ; and when entered for home consumption 14 s. 3 $\frac{3}{4}$ d. : and that every barrel cured with foreign salt, when exported, has cost government 1 l. 7 s. 5 $\frac{3}{4}$ d. ; and when entered for home consumption 1l. 3 s. 9 $\frac{3}{4}$ d. The price of a barrel of good merchantable herrings runs from seventeen and eighteen to four and five and twenty shillings; about a

用鲱鱼。通常情况下,三桶海条可以重新包装为两桶商用鲱鱼。所以,在这11年间,所获商用鲱鱼,计有252231又1/3桶。在这11年间,按吨数支付的津贴,总计为155463镑11先令,即每桶海条得8先令2便士又1/4便士,商用鲱鱼每桶得12先令3便士又3/4便士。

腌鲱鱼所用的盐,有时是苏格兰产的,有时是外国产的,但都可免纳一切国产税。每蒲式耳苏格兰盐,现在须缴纳国产税1先令6便士,每蒲式耳外国盐须缴纳10先令。据说,每桶鲱鱼须用大约1便士又1/4蒲式耳的外国盐。若用苏格兰盐,平均须用两蒲式耳。如果鲱鱼是供出口用的,盐税就可以全免。如果是供国内消费的,无论用的是外国盐还是苏格兰盐,每桶要缴纳1先令的税金,这就是苏格兰过去对每蒲式耳盐所课的税。根据最低的估计,一桶鲱鱼所需用的盐,要1蒲式耳。我们知道,在苏格兰,外国盐通常只用于腌鱼。从1771年4月5日到1782年4月5日,进口的外国盐,共计936974蒲式耳,每蒲式耳重84磅。苏格兰所供给腌鱼业盐的数量,却不超过168226蒲式耳,每蒲式耳仅56磅。由此可见,鲱鱼所用的盐,大部分是外国盐。此外,每桶鲱鱼出口可领取2先令8便士的津贴。渔船捕获的鲱鱼,2/3以上用于出口。所以,把所有这些进行综合计算,就会知道,在这11年间,渔船每捕获鲱鱼一桶,若用苏格兰盐腌存,出口时要花费政府17先令11便士又3/4便士。如果供国内消费,需花费政府的14先令3便士又3/4便士。如果用外国盐腌存,出口时则需花费政府1镑7先令5便士又3/4便士,如果供国内消费则需耗费政府1镑3先令9便士又3/4便士。品质良好的鲱鱼每桶的价格,最低为17先令或19先令,最高为24先令或25先令,平均价格约

guinea at an average.

(2) the bounty is not proportioned to the fish caught.　　Secondly, the bounty to the white herring fishery is a tonnage bounty; and is proportioned to the burden of the ship, not to her diligence or success in the fishery; and it has, I am afraid, been too common for vessels to fit out for the sole purpose of catching, not the fish, but the bounty. In the year 1759, when the bounty was at fifty shillings the ton, the whole buss fishery of Scotland brought in only four barrels of sea sticks. In that year each barrel of sea sticks cost government in bounties alone 113*l*. 15*s*. ; each barrel of merchantable herrings 159*l*. 7*s*. 6*d*.

(3) the bounty is given to busses, whereas the fishery ought to be carried on by boats.　　Thirdly, the mode of fishing for which this tonnage bounty in the white herring fishery has been given (by busses or decked vessels from twenty to eighty tons burthen), seems not so well adapted to the situation of Scotland as to that of Holland; from the practice of which country it appears to have been borrowed. Holland lies at a great distance from the seas to which herrings are known principally to resort; and can, therefore, carry on that fishery only in decked vessels, which can carry water and provisions sufficient for a voyage to a distant sea. But the Hebrides or western islands, the islands of Shetland, and the northern and north-western coasts of Scotland, the countries in whose neighbourhood the herring fishery is principally carried on, are everywhere intersected by arms of the sea, which run up a considerable way into the land, and which, in the language of the country, are called sea-lochs. It is to these sea-lochs that the herrings principally resort during the seasons in which they visit those seas; for the visits of this, and, I am assured, of many other sorts of fish, are not quite regular and constant. A boat fishery, therefore, seems to be the mode of fishing best adapted to the peculiar situation of Scotland: the fishers carrying the herrings on shore, as fast as they are taken, to be either cured or consumed fresh. But the great encouragement which a bounty of thirty shillings the ton gives to the buss fishery, is necessarily a discouragement to the boat fishery; which, having no such bounty, cannot bring its cured fish to market upon the same terms as the buss fishery. The boat fishery, accordingly, which, before the establishment of the buss bounty, was very considerable, and is said to have employed a number of seamen, not inferior to what the buss fishery employs at present, is now gone almost entirely to decay. Of the former extent, however, of this now ruined and abandoned fishery, I must acknowledge, that I cannot pretend to speak with much precision. As no bounty was paid upon the outfit of the boat-fishery, no account was taken of it by the officers of the customs or salt duties.

　　Fourthly, in many parts of Scotland, during certain seasons of the year, herrings make no inconsiderable part of the food of the common people. A bounty, which tended to lower their price

为 1 几尼。

第二，鲱鱼的津贴按照吨位计算，按照捕鱼船的载重量来予以发放，并不是按照勤惰表现与成败结果来发放。恐怕许多渔船出海的真正目的不是捕鱼，而是捞取津贴。1759 年，津贴为每吨 50 先令，但苏格兰全部渔船所获，却不过 4 桶海条。单就津贴一项而言，每桶海条就耗费政府 113 镑 15 先令，而每桶商用鲱鱼的耗费为 150 镑 7 先令 6 便士。

（2）津贴与捕获的鱼量不成比例。

第三，按吨数计算津贴的鲱鱼渔业，往往用载重 20 吨至 80 吨的大渔船或甲板船作业。这种捕鱼法也许是从荷兰学来的，但它适用于荷兰而不太适用于苏格兰。荷兰的陆地与大批鲱鱼经常出没的海域相距很远，所以非得使用甲板船不可，因为甲板船可携带充足的水与食物，以备远航之用。但苏格兰的赫布里迪兹群岛或西部群岛，塞得兰群岛以及北部与西北部海岸，都是鲱鱼迁徙群居的地方。鲱鱼（我相信，还有许多种其他各类的鱼）出没的时间很不一定，所以小舟渔业看来最适宜于苏格兰的特殊情况。渔夫一旦捕得鲱鱼，就可以马上运上岸来进行腌存或生食。每吨 30 先令津贴，虽然可以给予大船渔业很大的奖励，但必然会阻碍小舟渔业的发展。小舟渔业没有得到这种津贴就不能与大船渔业在同样条件下，给市场提供腌鱼。在大船渔业出现以前，小舟渔业的规模相当可观，据说从前曾雇佣了不少海员，但现在却衰落了。至于这种在今天已经十分凋零而且无人问津的小舟渔业，以前究竟达到什么规模，我必须承认，我也说不确切。由于小舟渔业没有得到什么津贴，所以关税和盐税官吏都不曾做过记录。

（3）津贴按渔船来计算，但应该按渔舟来计算。

第四，苏格兰有许多地方，在每年某个季节里，鲱鱼成为普通百姓生活中相当重要的一部分食品。津贴可以使国内市场上鲱

(4) the bounty has raised, or at any rate not lowered, the price of herrings.

Profits in the business have not been high.

in the home market, might contribute a good deal to the relief of a great number of our fellow-subjects, whose circumstances are by no means affluent. But the herring buss bounty contributes to no such good purpose. It has ruined the boat fishery, which is, by far, the best adapted for the supply of the home market, and the additional bounty of 2 s. 8 d. the barrel upon exportation, carries the greater part, more than two thirds, of the produce of the buss fishery abroad. Between thirty and forty years ago, before the establishment of the buss bounty, sixteen shillings the barrel, I have been assured, was the common price of white herrings. Between ten and fifteen years ago, before the boat fishery was entirely ruined, the price is said to have run from seventeen to twenty shillings the barrel. For these last five years, it has, at an average, been at twenty-five shillings the barrel. This high price, however, may have been owing to the real scarcity of the herrings upon the coast of Scotland. I must observe too, that the cask or barrel, which is usually sold with the herrings, and of which the price is included in all the foregoing prices, has, since the commencement of the American war, risen to about double its former price, or from about three shillings to about six shillings. I must likewise observe, that the accounts I have received of the prices of former times, have been by no means quite uniform and consistent; and an old man of great accuracy and experience has assured me, that more than fifty years ago, a guinea was the usual price of a barrel of good merchantable herrings; and this, I imagine, may still be looked upon as the average price. All accounts, however, I think, agree, that the price has not been lowered in the home market, in consequence of the buss bounty.

When the undertakers of fisheries, after such liberal bounties have been bestowed upon them, continue to sell their commodity at the same, or even at a higher price than they were accustomed to do before, it might be expected that their profits should be very great; and it is not improbable that those of some individuals may have been So. In general, however, I have every reason to believe, they have been quite otherwise. The usual effect of such bounties is to encourage rash undertakers to adventure in a business which they do not understand, and what they lose by their own negligence and ignorance, more than compensates all that they can gain by the utmost liberality of government. In 1750, by the same act which first gave the bounty of thirty shillings the ton for the encouragement of the white herring fishery (the 23 Geo. II. chap. 24.), a joint stock company was erected, with a capital of five hundred thousand pounds, to which the subscribers (over and above all other encouragements, the tonnage bounty just now mentioned, the exportation bounty of two shillings and eight pence the barrel, the delivery of both British and foreign salt duty free) were, during the space of fourteen years, for every

鱼价格下跌,对于生活不太优裕的大多数同胞来说,这也许是一个很大的救济。但鲱鱼业大渔船津贴,不可能收到这样好的效果。因为最适宜于供应国内市场的小舟渔业,遭到了它的破坏;而每桶两先令8便士的附加出口津贴,使大渔船所捕的鲱鱼,有2/3以上出口到外国去。在三四十年之前,大渔船津贴尚未设立时,每桶的普通价格为16先令。10~15年之前,小舟渔业尚未完全衰落,据说那时每桶鲱鱼的普通价格为17先令至20先令,在最近五年里平均每桶为25先令。价格之所以这样高,也许因为苏格兰沿海各地实际上缺少鲱鱼。此外,我必须指出,连同与鲱鱼一起卖掉的桶的价格(那种桶价计算在上述各种价格内),自从美洲战事开始以来,已经涨了约一倍,即大约由3先令涨至6先令。必须指出,这与我所收录的以往价格的记载,是完全一致的。有一位很精明、富有经验的老人曾对我说,五十多年以前,优种商用鲱鱼每桶的普通价格为一几尼。我认为,直到现在也可以把那看作是平均的价格。但我相信,这一切记载都说明,国内市场上鲱鱼的价格下降并不是因为大渔船津贴的发放。

(4) 津贴提高了或者至少没有降低鲱鱼的价格。

这些渔民领到如此丰厚的津贴以后,如果仍以平时的价格或更高一些的价格出售他们的商品,他们就可获得很大的利润。就某些人而言,情况可能是这样,但一般说来,我却有理由相信,情况绝非如此。这种津贴的效果是,鼓励了轻率的企业家去冒险经营他们所不了解的业务,但他们由于怠惰无知而遭受损失。1750年,根据第一次以每吨30先令的标准来奖励鲱鱼渔业的法令(乔治二世二十三年第24号法令),成立了一个合股公司。资本55镑,纳资人除了享受其他各种津贴外,如上述的吨数津贴,如每桶2先令6便士的出口津贴,还一律免纳盐税,在14年间,每纳税

这种行业的利润不高。

国民财富的性质与原理

hundred pounds which they subscribed and paid into the stock of the society, entitled to three pounds a year, to be paid by the receiver-general of the customs in equal half-yearly payments. Besides this great company, the residence of whose governor and directors was to be in London, it was declared lawful to erect different fishing-chambers in all the different out-ports of the kingdom, provided a sum not less than ten thousand pounds was subscribed into the capital of each, to be managed at its own risk, and for its own profit and loss. The same annuity, and the same encouragements of all kinds, were given to the trade of those inferior chambers, as to that of the great company. The subscription of the great company was soon filled up, and several different fishing-chambers were erected in the different out-ports of the kingdom. In spite of all these encouragements, almost all those different companies, both great and small, lost either the whole, or the greater part of their capitals; scarce a vestige now remains of any of them, and the white herring fishery is now entirely, or almost entirely, carried on by private adventurers.

<small>Bounties for manufactures necessary for the defence of the country are not unreasonable.</small>

If any particular manufacture was necessary, indeed, for the defence of the society, it might not always be prudent to depend upon our neighbours for the supply; and if such manufacture could not otherwise be supported at home, it might not be unreasonable that all the other branches of industry should be taxed in order to support it. The bounties upon the exportation of British-made sail-cloth, and British-made gun-powder, may, perhaps, both be vindicated upon this principle.

<small>It is less absurd to give bounties in times of prosperity than in times of distress.</small>

But though it can very seldom be reasonable to tax the industry of the great body of the People, in order to support that of some particular class of manufacturers; yet in the wantonness of great prosperity, when the public enjoys a greater revenue than it knows well what to do with, to give such bounties to favourite manufactures, may, perhaps, be as natural, as to incur any other idle expence. In public, as well as in private expences, great wealth may, perhaps, frequently be admitted as an apology for great folly. But there must surely be something more than ordinary absurdity, in continuing such profusion in times of general difficulty and distress.

<small>Some allowances called bounties are, properly speaking, drawbacks.</small>

What is called a bounty is sometimes no more than a drawback, and consequently is not liable to the same objections as what is properly a bounty. The bounty, for example, upon refined sugar exported, may be considered as a drawback of the duties upon the brown and muscovado sugars from which it is made. The bounty upon wrought silk exported, a drawback of the duties upon raw and thrown silk imported. The bounty upon gunpowder exported, a drawback of the duties upon brimstone and saltpetre imported. In the language of the customs those allowances only are called drawbacks, which are given upon goods exported in the same form in which they are imported. When that form has been so altered by manufacture of any kind,

— 1112 —

100磅，每年可收取3磅，并由关税征收官每半年支付半额。这家大公司的经理及理事都住在伦敦。他们认为，投资不少于1万英镑，且自主经营、自负盈亏的小渔业公司是合法的。这些比较小的渔业公司同样可取得同一的年金以及各种津贴。大公司的资本不久就满额了，而在国内各海港，也设立了好几家渔业分公司。可是，虽然有这一系列津贴措施，但所有这些公司，无论大小，几乎将他们资本的全部或大部分都赔进去了，到了现在，我们根本就看不到这些公司的痕迹了。鲱鱼渔业现今几乎全部由私人经营。

如果某一种制造业确是国防所需，那么依靠邻国供应这种制造品，未必是明智的办法。如果这一制造业没有津贴就不能在国内生存，那么对其他一切产业课税以维持这种制造业，未必就是不合理的。对于英国制造的帆布及火药的出口津贴，也许都可以用这个原理来辩护。

> 那些国防御必需制造业发放津贴是合理的。对家来说，造业放并不合。

对整个产业课税来支持个别制造业，很难说是合理的，但在百姓都有很丰厚的收入，并且不知道怎样用钱的那种繁荣时期，对于所重视的制造业，发放这样的津贴也就像做另一种无谓的花费一样，不足为怪。不论是公家的还是私人的，有钱的人花了冤枉钱也容易被人原谅。但在普遍困难与穷困时期，还继续这样浪费，就太荒唐了。

> 穷困时期，起比繁荣时期发津贴还算太荒谬。

所谓津贴，有时就是指退税，因此不能与真正的津贴一概而论。例如，出口精砂糖的津贴，可以看成是对赤砂糖、黑砂糖所纳赋税的退还。出口精丝制品的津贴，可以看成是对硫黄砂石进口税的退还。如果商品进口以后，还以同样的形态出口，这时发给的补助称为退税；如果商品进口以后，其形态被某种制造业改变，

> 有些津贴准确地应该叫做退税。

as to come under a new denomination, they are called bounties.

Prizea to successful artists and manufacturers do not divert industry to less advantageous channels, but encourage perfection.

Premiums given by the public to artists and manufacturers who excel in their particular occupations, are not liable to the same objections as bounties. By encouraging extraordinary dexterity and ingenuity, they serve to keep up the emulation of the workmen actually employed in those respective occupations, and are not considerable enough to turn towards any one of them a greater share of the capital of the country than what would go to it of its own accord. Their tendency is not to overturn the natural balance of employments, but to render the work which is done in each as perfect and complete as possible. The expence of premiums, besides, is very trifling; that of bounties very great. The bounty upon corn alone has sometimes cost the public in one year more than three hundred thousand Pounds.

Bounties are sometimes called premiums, as drawbacks are sometimes called bounties. But we must in all cases attend to the nature of the thing. without paying any regard to the word.

Digression concerning the Corn Trade and Corn Laws

The corn bounty and corn laws are undeserving of praise.

I cannot conclude this chapter concerning bounties, without observing that the praises which have been bestowed upon the law which establishes the bounty upon the exportation of corn, and upon that system of regulations which is connected with it, are altogether unmerited. A particular examination of the nature of the corn trade, and of the principal British laws which relate to it, will sufficiently demonstrate the truth of this assertion. The great importance of this subject must justify the length of the digression.

There are four branches of the corn trade:

I. The Inland Dealer, whose interest is the same as that of the people, viz. , that the consumption should be proportioned to the supply available.

The trade of the corn merchant is composed of four different branches, which, though they may sometimes be all carried on by the same person, are in their own nature four separate and distinct trades. These are, first, the trade of the inland dealer; secondly, that of the merchant importer for home consumption; thirdly, that of the merchant exporter of home produce for foreign consumption; and, fourthly, that of the merchant carrier, or of the importer of corn in order to export it again.

I. The interest of the inland dealer, and that of the great body of the people, how opposite soever they may at first sight appear, are, even in years of the greatest scarcity, exactly the same. It is his interest to raise the price of his corn as high as the real scarcity of the season requires, and it can never be his interest to raise it higher.

以至于名称发生改变,变成新的名目,那么所发给的补助叫做津贴。

社会给予有业务专长的技术家与制造商的奖金,也不能一概称为津贴,它们虽然可奖励高超的技巧与技能,从而提高各行业中现有工人的竞争力,但不会使国家的资本违反自然规律,以过大的比例流向任何一个行业。这种奖金不会破坏各行业间的均衡,却能使各行业的产品尽可能达到完善。另外,奖金的花费极小,而津贴的花费极大。单就粮食津贴而言,社会每年所花费有时达30万镑以上。

津贴有时称为奖金,正如退税有时称为津贴。但我们必须在所有情况下注意到事情的实质情况,不必考虑词语本身。

谈谈粮食贸易及粮食法律的其他题外内容:

粮食出口津贴的法律以及与相关的一系列规定,都受到赞赏。我要说明这种赞赏都是不对的。在没有说明以前,我还不能结束津贴这一章的内容。对粮食贸易的性质及与粮食贸易有关的英国主要法律的专门研究,可充分证明我的论点是正确的。这个论题太重要了,所以有必要做一些论述。

粮食商人的贸易,包含四个不同部门,这四个部门虽然有时全由一人经营,但按其性质,实际是四种不同的独立的贸易:(一)内地商人的贸易;(二)为国内进口消费品的商人的贸易;(三)供国外消费的国内生产物出口商人的贸易;(四)转口贸易,即进口粮食以待出口的贸易。

第一,从表面看起来,内地商人的利益与大多数百姓的利益相抵触,但实际上,甚至在歉岁也是完全一致的。商人的利益在于,把粮食价格提高到实际歉收所要求的程度,但再高了就对他

By raising the price he discourages the consumption, and puts every body more or less, but particularly the inferior ranks of people, upon thrift and good management. If, by raising it too high, he discourages the consumption so much that the supply of the season is likely to go beyond the consumption of the season, and to last for some time after the next crop begins to come in, he runs the hazard, not only of losing a considerable part of his corn by natural causes, but of being obliged to sell what remains of it for much less than what he might have had for it several months before. If by not raising the price high enough he discourages the consumption so little, that the supply of the season is likely to fall short of the consumption of the season, he not only loses a part of the profit which he might otherwise have made, but he exposes the people to suffer before the end of the season, instead of the hardships of a dearth, the dreadful horrors of a famine. It is the interest of the people that their daily, weekly, and monthly consumption, should be proportioned as exactly as possible to the supply of the season. The interest of the inland corn dealer is the same. By supplying them, as nearly as he can judge, in this proportion, he is likely to sell all his corn for the highest price, and with the greatest profit; and his knowledge of the state of the crop, and of his daily, weekly, and monthly sales, enable ① him to judge, with more or less accuracy, how far they really are supplied in this manner. Without intending the interest of the people, he is necessarily led, by a regard to his own interest, to treat them, even in years of scarcity, pretty much in the same manner as the prudent master of a vessel is sometimes obliged to treat his crew. When he foresees that provisions are likely to run short, he puts them upon short allowance. Though from excess of caution he should sometimes do this without any real necessity, yet all the inconveniencies which his crew can thereby suffer are inconsiderable, in comparison of the danger, misery, and ruin, to which they might sometimes be exposed by a less provident conduct. Though from excess of avarice, in the same manner, the inland corn merchant should sometimes raise the price of his corn somewhat higher than the scarcity of the season requires, yet all the inconveniencies which the people can suffer from this conduct, which effectually secures them from a famine in the end of the season, are inconsiderable, in comparison of what they might have been exposed to by a more liberal way of dealing in the beginning of it. The corn merchant himself is likely to suffer the most by this excess of avarice; not only from the indignation which it generally excites against him, but, though he should escape the effects of this indignation, from the quantity of corn which it necessarily leaves upon his hands in the end

---

① [There are two knowledges, one of the state of the crop and the other of the daily sales.]

不利。价格的提高将阻碍消费,使一切人尤其使下层老百姓或多或少地变得节约并合理安排。假若价格提得太高,就会在很大程度上阻碍消费,致使供大于求,直到新收成的粮食上市,这时他有危险了,之前剩下的粮食有相当一部分不仅会由于自然原因损失大部分,而且此时所售价格将会比数月前低得多。但如果价格提高得不够多,就不会阻碍消费,结果是供不应求,这时他不仅会损失一部分应得的利润,而且将使百姓在一个季节结束之前,面临饥荒的可怕威胁。百姓的利益在于,他们每天、每星期、每月的消费应尽可能按比例供给。内地商人的利益也一样,即按比例向老百姓供给粮食。这样他的粮食才能卖出最好的价钱,所得利润才可能最大。收成怎么样,每日、每星期和每月售价怎么样,他都了解,这样多少能够使①他正确地判断粮食的实际销售量。假若他不顾百姓的利益,而是出于他自身的利益,在粮食紧缺时,按照谨慎的船长有时对待船员的办法来对待老百姓,即在他预见到粮食快要缺乏时,就让他们节省粮食。当然,有时船长顾虑太多,实际上没有必要的时候也让他们这样做会使他们感到困难,但这种困难和有时因船长行为不谨慎而遭受的危险和死亡比较起来,就不算什么了。同样,内地粮食商人由于过分贪婪,有时把粮食价格提高到超过粮食紧缺时所应有的程度,这种可有效地使百姓避免季节末挨饿的做法所带来的困难,和因商人在季初廉售而产生的饥荒的威胁比较起来,也不算什么。而且,粮食商人自己也将因为这种过分贪婪而深受其害;因为它会激发人们对他产生愤恨,而且他即使能够避免这种愤恨的影响,但是,到了季末,他手上必

---

① 这里包含两层意思,一种是粮食,一种是日常销售。

of the season, and which, if the next season happens to prove favourable, he must always sell for a much lower price than he might otherwise have had.

<small>The interest of a monopoly might perhaps be to destroy a portion of the crop, but corn cannot be monopolised where the trade is free.</small>
Were it possible, indeed, for one great company of merchants to possess themselves of the whole crop of an extensive country, it might, perhaps, be their interest to deal with it as the Dutch are said to do with the spiceries of the Moluccas, to destroy or throw away a considerable part of it, in order to keep up the price of the rest. But it is scarce possible, even by the violence of law, to establish such an extensive monopoly with regard to corn; and, wherever the law leaves the trade free, it is of all commodities the least liable to be engrossed or monopolized by the force of a few large capitals, which buy up the greater part of it. Not only its value far exceeds what the capitals of a few private men are capable of purchasing, but supposing they were capable of purchasing it, the manner in which it is produced renders this purchase altogether impracticable. As in every civilized country it is the commodity of which the annual consumption is the greatest, so a greater quantity of industry is annually employed in producing corn than in producing any other commodity. When it first comes from the ground too, it is necessarily divided among a greater number of owners than any other commodity; and these owners can never be collected into one place like a number of independent manufacturers, but are necessarily scattered through all the different corners of the country. These first owners either immediately supply the consumers in their own neighbourhood, or they supply other inland dealers who supply those consumers. The inland dealers in corn, therefore, including both the farmer and the baker, are necessarily more numerous than the dealers in any other commodity, and their dispersed situation renders it altogether impossible for them to enter into any general combination. If in a year of scarcity therefore, any of them should find that he had a good deal more corn upon hand than, at the current price, he could hope to dispose of before the end of the season, he would never think of keeping up this price to his own loss, and to the sole benefit of his rivals and competitors, but would immediately lower it, in order to get rid of his corn before the new crop began to come in. The same motives, the same interests, which would thus regulate the conduct of any one dealer, would regulate that of every other, and oblige them all in general to sell their corn at the price which, according to the best of their judgment, was most suitable to the scarcity or plenty of the season.

Whoever examines, with attention, the history of the dearths and famines which have afflicted any part of Europe, during either the course of the present or that of the two preceding centuries, of several

定会剩余一定量的粮食,如果下一个年成丰收了,那么他必须以比他此前可能售卖的价格低得多的价格来抛售这些粮食。

如果一个大商业集团垄断了国家的全部粮食,那么他们为了自身利益,或许会像荷兰人处理马鲁古群岛的香料那样,为了提高存货的价格,把存货的大部分毁坏或扔掉。但要建立这样广泛的粮食垄断,即使凭借法律的威力,也几乎不可能;而且,在法律准许自由贸易的地方,最不易被少数大资本势力所垄断、所独占的商品要算粮食。这不仅仅是因为它们的价值远远超出了少数私人资本的购买能力;而且即使有购买能力,其生产方式也会使购买不能实现。在任何文明国家,粮食都是年消费量最多的商品。所以,生产粮食的产业部门要比生产任何其他商品的部门多。当粮食刚刚从土地上收获以后,与其他产品相比,它所分配给的所有者必然要多得多。这些所有者绝不可能像独立制造商一样,集中居住在一个地方,他们必然是散居在国内各地。这种最早的所有者,要么立即直接供给邻近地域的消费者,或供给其他内地商人,由他们再间接供给消费者。因此,内地粮食商人,包括农场主和面包师,其人数必然多于经营任何其他商品的商人,而且散居各地,不会结成任何团体。因此,在歉岁,如果有商人发觉手中有许多粮食不能按时价在季末脱手,他就不会还卖这个价格,使竞争者得利自己受损,而会立即减低价格,希望在下一季的粮食出来之前,把手中的余粮售出去。同样的动机和利益也将支配其他所有的商人,迫使他们普遍都根据自己判断,按照对季节丰歉最为适宜的价格,出售他们的粮食。

我相信,不管是谁,只要细心研究本世纪以及过去两个世纪欧洲各地出现的粮食紧缺或饥荒,这些情况有相当准确的记载,

> 垄断的可能会一部粮食,但易毁坏利益,贸易自由的地方,是不能垄断粮食,在自由贸易地方,粮食不会被垄断的。

> Dearths are never occasioned by combination, but always by scarcity, and famines are always caused by the supposed remedies for dearths applied by government.

of which we have pretty exact accounts, will find, I believe, that a dearth never has arisen from any combination among the inland dealers in corn, nor from any other cause but a real scarcity, occasioned sometimes, perhaps, and in some particular places, by the waste of war, but in by far the greatest number of cases, by the fault of the seasons; and that a famine has never arisen from any other cause but the violence of government attempting, by improper means, to remedy the inconveniencies of a dearth.

In an extensive corn country, between all the different parts of which there is a free commerce and communication, the scarcity occasioned by the most unfavourable seasons can never be so great as to produce a famine; and the scantiest crop, if managed with frugality and œconomy, will maintain, through the year, the same number of people that are commonly fed in a more affluent manner by one of moderate plenty. The seasons most unfavourable to the crop are those of excessive drought or excessive rain. But, as corn grows equally upon high and low lands, upon grounds that are disposed to be too wet, and upon those that are disposed to be too dry, either the drought or the rain which is hurtful to one part of the country is favourable to an‐

> Scarcities are never great enough to cause famine.

other; and though both in the wet and in the dry season the crop is a good deal less than in one more properly tempered, yet in both what is lost in one part of the country is in some measure compensated by what is gained in the other. In rice countries, where the crop not only requires a very moist soil, but where in a certain period of its growing it must be laid under water, the effects of a drought are much more dismal. Even in such countries, however, the drought is, perhaps, scarce ever so universal, as necessarily to occasion a famine, if the government would allow a free trade. The drought in Bengal, a few years ago, might probably have occasioned a very great dearth. Some improper regulations, some injudicious restraints imposed by the servants of the East India Company upon the rice trade, contributed, perhaps, to turn that dearth into a famine.

> Governments cause famines by ordering corn to be sold at a reasonable price.

When the government, in order to remedy the inconveniencies of a dearth, orders all the dealers to sell their corn at what it supposes a reasonable price, it either hinders them from bringing it to market, which may sometimes produce a famine even in the beginning of the season; or if they bring it thither, it enables the people, and thereby encourages them to consume it so fast, as must necessarily produce a

第四篇 第五章

就一定能够发现,粮食紧缺既不是因为内地粮食商人的联合,也不是因为别的,而是因为粮食的确缺乏。这种紧缺有时起因于战争的消耗,但大多数情况下,却起因于收成不好。饥荒发生的原因还有些是因为政府以不适当的粗暴手段来克服粮食紧缺所造成的。

在贸易自由和交通自由的产粮大国,由于天气原因而造成的收成最差的年月,也不会产生严重的粮食紧缺,以至于引起饥荒。不够多的粮食,如果设法节约,虽然比一般丰收年度略为紧缩,但也可维持同样人数一年的生活。对粮食来说,最不好的年成莫过于干旱和水涝。但小麦可栽种在高原上,也可以栽种在洼地上,既可栽于潮湿土地,亦可栽于干燥土地,所以,有害于洼地的淫雨,则有利于高原,有害于高原的干燥,则有利于洼地。虽然,在干旱与多雨的季节,收成都比风调雨顺的季节少得多;但无论是干旱或是多雨,国内某一地方的损失,都可在一定程度上由另一地方的所得来补偿。在产稻国家,作物不仅需要极润湿的土壤,而且在稻子的某段生长期内,还须浸在水里,所以,干旱的影响要可怕得多。但即使在这样的国家,干旱也不会那么普遍以至于会引起饥荒。而且只要政府允许自由贸易,饥荒就可以避免。数年前,孟加拉的干旱可能只是引起了极大的粮食紧缺,但也许是因为东印度公司人员采用了不适当的条例,很不明智地限制稻米的贸易,最终导致了饥荒。

如果政府为了解决饥荒,命令一切商人以它认为合理的价格售卖粮食,只会产生两种结果:要么使他们不给市场提供粮食,以致在季初就发生饥荒;要么愿意给市场提供粮食,这样实际上是鼓励人民迅速消费,以致季末时无法避免饥荒。无限制无拘束的

— 1121 —

国民财富的性质与原理

famine before the end of the season. The unlimited, unrestrained freedom of the corn trade, as it is the only effectual preventative of the miseries of a famine, so it is the best palliative of the inconveniencies of a dearth; for the inconveniencies of a real scarcity cannot be remedied; they can only be palliated. No trade deserves more the full protection of the law, and no trade requires it so much; because no trade is so much exposed to popular odium.

<small>The corn merchant is odious to the populace, and this deters respectable people from entering the trade.</small>

In years of scarcity the inferior ranks of people impute their distress to the avarice of the corn merchant, who becomes the object of their hatred and indignation. Instead of making profit upon such occasions, therefore, he is often in danger of being utterly ruined, and of having his magazines plundered and destroyed by their violence. It is in years of scarcity, however, when prices are high, that the corn merchant expects to make his principal profit. He is generally in contract with some farmers to furnish him for a certain number of years with a certain quantity of corn at a certain price. This contract price is settled according to what is supposed to be the moderate and reasonable, that is, the ordinary or average price, which, before the late years of scarcity, was commonly about eight-and-twenty shillings for the quarter of wheat, and for that of other grain in proportion. In years of scarcity, therefore, the corn merchant buys a great part of his corn for the ordinary price, and sells it for a much higher. That this extraordinary profit, however, is no more than sufficient to put his trade upon a fair level with other trades, and to compensate the many losses which he sustains upon other occasions, both from the perishable nature of the commodity itself, and from the frequent and unforeseen fluctuations of its price, seems evident enough, from this single circumstance, that great fortunes are as seldom made in this as in any other trade. The popular odium, however, which attends it in years of scarcity, the only years in which it can be very profitable, renders people of character and fortune averse to enter into it. It is abandoned to an inferior set of dealers; and millers, bakers, mealmen, and meal factors, together with a number of wretched hucksters, are almost the only middle people that, in the home market, come between the grower and the consumer.

The ancient policy of Europe, instead of discountenancing this popular odium against a trade so beneficial to the public, seems, on the contrary, to have authorised and encouraged it.

粮食贸易自由是防止饥荒的唯一有效办法,所以亦是减轻粮食紧缺的最好方法。因为真正的粮食紧缺,是不能除去而只能减缓的。没有一种商业比粮食贸易更值得法律的充分保护,也没有一种商业比粮食贸易更需要这种保护,因为没有一种商业,比粮食贸易更容易引起人们的公愤。

饥荒时期,下层老百姓往往把他们的困苦归咎于粮食商人的贪婪,于是,粮食商人成为他们憎恶和愤恨的目标。这个时候粮食商人不但赚不到钱,而且,常常会处在彻底破产或者粮仓随时可能遭到民众暴力抢夺或破坏的危险之中。但粮食商人牟取丰厚利润的时候,也就是粮食价格昂贵的歉岁。他通常与某些农场主订约,在一定年限内,按一定价格收购一定数量的粮食。这个契约价格是按照被认为适中的合理的价格,即按照普通或平均价格而制定的。在上次歉收年份以前,普通价格约为小麦每夸特 28 先令;其他各种粮食价格以此为基准。所以,歉岁到来时,粮食商人把以前用普通价格购买的大量粮食以高得多的价格售卖。这是一种非常的利润,但这种非常的利润只是仅使他的行业得以与其他行业处在同一水平上,只够补偿因商品本身易腐损或者因频繁、无法预知的价格变动而造成的各种各样的损失。这点是很明显的,因为粮食生意不像在其他生意中有那么多人发大财。他只是在歉岁牟取丰厚利润,但因此也引起人们的公愤。稍有品格及财产的人,大都不愿涉足这个行业。该行业于是都丢给下层商人去经营;在国内市场上,夹在生产者及消费者中间的人,便几乎只有磨坊主、面包房主、制粉商、面粉经售人以及若干困苦的小贩了。

_{粮食商人受到大众的憎恶,阻止了有身份的人从事这种生意。}

欧洲往日的政策不但不去消除人们对那些有利于社会行业

国民财富的性质与原理

<small>This popular odium was encouraged by legislation.</small>　　By the 5th and 6th of Edward VI. cap. 14. it was enacted, That whoever should buy any corn or grain ① with intent to sell it again, should be reputed an unlawful engrosser, and should, for the first fault suffer two months imprisonment, and forfeit the value of the corn; for the second, suffer six months imprisonment, and forfeit double the value; and for the third, be set in the pillory, suffer imprisonment during the king's pleasure, and forfeit all his goods and chattels. The ancient policy of most other parts of Europe was no better than that of England.

<small>Many restraints were imposed on traders.</small>　　Our ancestors seem to have imagined that the people would buy their corn cheaper of the farmer than of the corn merchant, who, they were afraid, would require, over and above the price which he paid to the farmer, an exorbitant profit to himself. They endeavoured, therefore, to annihilate his trade altogether. They even endeavoured to hinder as much as possible any middle man of any kind from coming in between the grower and the consumer; and this was the meaning of the many restraints which they imposed upon the trade of those whom they called kidders or carriers of corn, a trade which nobody was allowed to exercise without a licence ascertaining his qualifications as a man of probity and fair dealing. ② The authority of three justices of the peace was, by the statute of Edward VI. necessary, in order to grant this licence. But even this restraint was afterwards thought insufficient, and by a statute of Elizabeth, ③ the privilege of granting it was confined to the quarter-sessions.

---

① ['Any corn growing in the fields, or any other corn or grain, butter, cheese, fish or other dead victuals whatsoever'. But grain was exempted when below certain prices, e. g. , wheat, 6s 8d. the quarter.]

② [This and the preceding sentence are misleading. The effect of the provisions quoted in the preceding paragraph would have been to 'annihilate altogether' the trade of the corn merchant if they had been left unqualified. To avoid this consequence 5 and 6 Ed. VI. , c. 14, § 7, provides that badgers, laders, kidders or carriers may be licensed to buy corn with the intent to sell it again in certain circumstances. So that the licensing of kidders was a considerable alleviation, not, as the text suggests, an aggravation.]

③ [5 Eliz. , c. 12, § 4.]

的憎恶,反而似乎认为此种憎恶是正当的而加以鼓励。

> 这种偏见受到立法者的鼓励。

爱德华六世五年及六年第 14 号法令规定,凡购买小麦和谷物①想投倒卖的人,均为犯法的垄断者。初犯,处以两个月监禁和等于粮食价值的罚款;再犯,处以六个月监禁,和等于粮食价值两倍的罚款;三犯,处以头手枷刑,刑期长短由国王决定,没收其他不动产。欧洲其他大部分地方以往的政策,和英国过去的政府制定的政策基本一样。

我们的前辈们以为,老百姓向农场主购买粮食要比向粮食商人购买便宜一些,他们担心粮食商人除了收取他付给农场主的价钱外,还会索取高额的利润,所以他们想完全消灭这种行业。他们甚至企图尽可能防止生产者与消费者间有任何中间环节,对于所谓粮食商或粮食贩运商经营的行业所加的种种限制,其用意就在于此。那时,没有许可证证明经营者诚实公正,②他就不许经营这种行当。依据爱德华六世的法令,颁发这种许可证一定要有三位治安推事认可。但是,人们认为这样的限制还不够。到了伊丽莎白③时代,她颁布的一个法令中规定,只有一年召开四次会议的法庭才有权颁发这种许可证。

> 许多限制被强加于贸易。

---

① "任何生长在田地中的谷类,或者其他小麦或谷物,黄油,奶酪,鱼类和其他任何无生命的食品"。但是当谷类低于某个价格时可以免税,如小麦每夸特为 6 先令 8 便士。

② 在前面段落中引用的那些条款的产生的效果是"一起消灭"粮食商人的贸易,如果他们是个公正的。为避免这种结果,爱德华六世五年和六年第 14 号法令第 7 章,证明小商贩、贩运商、搬运工等可以得到购买粮食在某一范围内出售的许可,所以,这种许可是一种缓和,而不是像下文说的恶化。

③ 伊丽莎白五年第 12 号法令第 4 节。

国民财富的性质与原理

Endeavours were made to force the farmers to be retailers, though manufacturers were forbidden to be so.

The ancient policy of Europe endeavoured in this manner to regulate agriculture, the great trade of the country, by maxims quite different from those which it established with regard to manufactures, the great trade of the towns. By leaving the farmer no other customers but either the consumers or their immediate factors, ① the kidders and carriers of corn, it endeavoured to force him to exercise the trade, not only of a farmer, but of a corn merchant or corn retailer. On the contrary, it in many cases prohibited the manufacturer from exercising the trade of a shopkeeper, or from selling his own goods by retail. It meant by the one law to promote the general interest of the country, or to render corn cheap, without, perhaps, its being well understood how this was to be done. By the other it meant to promote that of a particular order of men, the shopkeepers, who would be so much undersold by the manufacturer, it was supposed, that their trade would be ruined if he was allowed to retail at all.

The manufacturer, however, though he had been allowed to keep a shop, and to sell his own goods by retail, could not have undersold the common shopkeeper. Whatever part of his capital he might have placed in his shop, he must have withdrawn it from his manufacture. In order to carry on his business on a level with that of other people, as he must have had the profit of a manufacturer on the one part, so he must have had that of a shopkeeper upon the other. Let us suppose, for example, that in the particular town where he lived, ten per cent. was the ordinary profit both of manufacturing and shopkeeping stock; he must in this case have charged upon every piece of his own goods which he sold in his shop, a profit of twenty per cent. When he carried them from his workhouse to his shop, he must have valued them at the price for which he could have sold them to a dealer or shopkeeper, who would have bought them by wholesale. If he valued them lower, he lost a part of the profit of his manufacturing capital.

---

① [Ed. 1 reads 'the consumer or his immediate factors'. It should be noticed that under 5 and 6 Edward Ⅵ. , c. 14, § 7, the kidder might sell in 'open fair or market' as we ll as to consumers privately.]

欧洲古代的政策，都试图用这种方式来管理国家中最大的贸易行业即农业，但这种政策与城市中最大的贸易行业即制造业的政策完全不同。这种政策，使农场主没有别的客户，只有消费者或他们粮食的直接经售者、①粮食销售商及粮食贩运商，因而强迫他们不但要扮演农场主的角色，而且还要扮演粮食批发商及零售商的角色。相反，在制造业方面，政策在很多情况下禁止制造商兼营开店的生意，不许他们零售自己的商品。前一种政策的用意，是要保护全体百姓的利益，或者说，使粮食保持便宜的价格，尽管人们并不清楚应该怎样做。后一种政策要保护的是另外一种人，即商店老板。有人认为，如果制造商低价销售其产品，那么这些商店老板的生意就会全部破产。

（旁注：力图强迫农场主成为零售商，尽管不允许制造商这样。）

虽然当时允许制造商开设店铺零售货物，但是制造商绝不会把货物卖得比一般店铺老板还便宜。不管投在店铺内的这一部分资本是多是少，它必定是从制造业中抽取出来的。为了使自己的生意与他人的处在相同水平上，他这一部分资本必须获取与其他商店老板一样的利润，正如他那一部分资本必须取得制造商的利润一样。例如，假设在他所居住的城市里，制造业资本及商业销售资本的普通利润都是10%，那么制造商自行开店零售，他在店铺中每售出一件货物，即须获得20%的利润。当他把货物搬运到店铺时，他对货物定下的价格，很可能是他向零售店老板所能索取的批发价格。如果比这低，他便失去了一部分制造业资本的

---

① 在版本1中为"消费者或他的直接经售者"，应当知道，在爱德华六世的五年和六年第14号法令第7章规定，粮食销售商或许在"公平开放的市场"上卖，也可以私下卖给消费者。

When again he sold them from his shop, unless he got the same price at which a shopkeeper would have sold them, he lost a part of the profit of his shopkeeping capital. Though he might appear, therefore, to make a double profit upon the same piece of goods, yet as these goods made successively a part of two distinct capitals, he made but a single profit upon the whole capital employed about them; and if he made less than this profit, he was a loser, or did not employ his whole capital with the same advantage as the greater part of his neighbours.

What the manufacturer was prohibited to do, the farmer was in some measure enjoined to do; to divide his capital between two different employments; to keep one part of it in his granaries and stack yard, for supplying the occasional demands of the market; and to employ the other in the cultivation of his land. But as he could not afford to employ the latter for less than the ordinary profits of farming stock, so he could as little afford to employ the former for less than the ordinary profits of mercantile stock. Whether the stock which really carried on the business of the corn merchant belonged to the person who was called a farmer, or to the person who was called a corn merchant, an equal profit was in both cases requisite, in order to indemnify its owner for employing it in this manner; in order to put his business upon a level with other trades, and in order to hinder him from having an interest to change it as soon as possible for some other. The farmer, therefore, who was thus forced to exercise the trade of a corn merchant, could not afford to sell his corn cheaper than any other corn merchant would have been obliged to do in the case of a free competition.

<small>The dealer confined to one branch of business can sell cheaper.</small>   The dealer who can employ his whole stock in one single branch of business, has an advantage of the same kind with the workman who can employ his whole labour in one single operation. As the latter acquires a dexterity which enables him, with the same two hands, to perform a much greater quantity of work; so the former acquires so easy and ready a method of transacting his business, of buying and disposing of his goods, that with the same capital he can transact a much greater quantity of business. As the one can commonly afford his work a good deal cheaper, so the other can commonly afford his goods somewhat cheaper than if his stock and attention were both employed about a greater variety of objects. The greater part of manufacturers could not afford to retail their own goods so cheap as a vigilant and active shopkeeper, whose sole business

利润。当在他自己店铺内出售货物时,如果价格低于其他店铺,那他的销售资本的利润,也失去了一部分。在这种情况下,对于同一件货物,他虽然好像取得了双倍的利润,但因这种货物曾先后充作两种不同资本的一部分,所以,就投入的整体资本来说,他所取得的,其实只是单一的利润。如果所得利润比这少,那他就亏损了,也就是说,他所投下的全部资本,未取得与其他大部分商铺相同的利润。

不允许制造商做的事,在一定程度上却允许农场主做,也就是说,他可以把他的资本分别投入于两种不同用途,即把一部分投入谷仓及干草场上,以供应市场上不时的需要,而把其余部分投入土地耕种。但他投于后一部分所得利润,不能低于农业资本的普通利润,而他投于前一部分所得利润,亦不能低于商业资本的普通利润。实际用来经营粮食生意的资本,无论是属于农场主还是属于粮食商人,都要有相同的利润,来补偿投资者,并使他的职业能与其他职业处于同等地位,使他不致见异思迁。因此,在自由竞争中,粮食商人不得不贱卖,而被迫兼营粮食商业的农场主,绝不能把他的粮食卖得比这个价格还要便宜。

把全部资本集中投在某一行业的商人和把全部劳动用在某一工作的劳动者一样,都会得到好处。后者从此学得一种技艺,同样都是两只手,他完成的工作就是比别人多得多。同样,前者也从此掌握了简便实用的生意方法,用同量的资本,他的生意要比别人多得多。通常情况下,比起把资金和精力分散投在多个方面,劳动者能因此以便宜得多的价格,为别人工作;而商人也能因此以更低廉的价格,卖出他们的货物。因此大部分制造商,不能像灵活的商人那样,以低廉的价格零售货物,因为商人唯一的工

_{一意人得宜 做生意卖 只种的会便些。}

it was to buy them by wholesale, and to retail them again. The greater part of farmers could still less afford to retail their own corn, to supply the inhabitants of a town, at perhaps four or five miles distance from the greater part of them, so cheap as a vigilant and active corn merchant, whose sole business it was to purchase corn by wholesale, to collect it into a great magazine, and to retail it again.

<small>Laws preventing the manufacturer from being a shopkeeper and compelling the farmer to be a corn merchant were both impolitic and unjust, but the latter was the most pernicious,</small>

The law which prohibited the manufacturer from exercising the trade of a shopkeeper, endeavoured to force this division in the employment of stock to go on faster than it might otherwise have done. The law which obliged the farmer to exercise the trade of a corn merchant, endeavoured to hinder it from going on so fast. Both laws were evident violations of natural liberty, and therefore unjust; and they were both too as impolitic as they were unjust. It is the interest of every society, that things of this kind should never either be forced or obstructed. The man who employs either his labour or his stock in a greater variety of ways than his situation renders necessary, can never hurt his neighbour by underselling him. He may hurt himself, and he generally does so. Jack of all trades will never be rich, says the proverb. But the law ought always to trust people with the care of their own interest, as in their local situations they must generally be able to judge better of it than the legislator can do. The law, however, which obliged the farmer to exercise the trade of a corn merchant, was by far the most pernicious of the two.

<small>by obstructing the improvement of land.</small>

It obstructed not only that division in the employment of stock which is so advantageous to every society, but it obstructed likewise the improvement and cultivation of the land. By obliging the farmer to carry on two trades instead of one, it forced him to divide his capital into two parts, of which one only could be employed in cultivation. But if he had been at liberty to sell his whole crop to a corn merchant as fast as he could thresh it out, his whole capital might have returned immediately to the land, and have been employed in buying more cattle, and hiring more servants, in order to improve and cultivate it better. But by being obliged to sell his corn by retail, he was obliged to keep a great part of his capital in his granaries and stack yard through the year, and could not, therefore, cultivate so well as with the same capital he might otherwise have done. This law, therefore, necessarily obstructed the improvement of the land, and, instead of tending to render corn cheaper, must have tended to render it scarcer, and therefore dearer, than it would otherwise have been.

After the business of the farmer, that of the corn merchant is in reality the trade which, if properly protected and encouraged,

作就是批发买进、零售卖出。大部分农场主,更不能像那些灵活的粮食商人那样,以那么低廉的价格,把粮食零售给离他们四五里的城镇居民,因为粮食商唯一的业务就是批量购进,囤积货物,然后再零卖出去。

禁止制造商兼营销售的法律,试图促使资本用途的划分进行得更快些。强迫农场主兼营粮食商业的法律,却妨碍这种划分的进行。这两种法律,显然都违反了自然规律,所以都是不正当的;因为不正当,所以都是失策的。社会的利益在于,这一类事情不应该被强制或妨碍。那些劳动或资本投入范围太大而超出其自身实际情况的人,低价销售并不会伤害其邻人,只会伤害他自己,一般都是这种情形。俗话说,什么都做的人永远发不了财。法律应该相信百姓自己能照顾好自己的利益。百姓是当事人,肯定比立法者更能了解自己的利益。强迫农场主充当粮食销售商的法律是这两种法律当中最有害的。

禁止制造商兼营销售的法律和强迫农场主兼营粮食商业的法律都是不正当的,但后者处害最大;

这项法律,不仅妨碍了非常有利于社会的资本用途的划分,而且妨碍了土地的改良与耕种。强迫农场主从事两种贸易而不是一种,即强迫他们把资本一分为二,只有一部分资金用于耕种。如果他们的全部农作物,一收获就可自由卖给粮食商人,他们的资本便可以立即收回再投到土地上,购买更多的耕牛,雇佣更多的佣工,更好地改良和耕种土地。如果强迫他们零售自己的粮食,他们就不得不挪用一大部分资本,投入到他们的粮仓及草场上,再不能像没有建立这种法律以前那样,把全部资本用于耕种土地。所以,这种法律必然妨碍土地的改良,不但不能使谷价低廉,反而会引起粮食的减产,继而抬高粮食的价格。

妨碍了土地改良。

除了农场主的生意,粮食商人的贸易如果能够得到适当保护

国民财富的性质与原理

Corn merchants support the farmers just as wholesale dealers support the manufacturers.would contribute the most to the raising of corn. It would support the trade of the farmer, in the same manner as the trade of the wholesale dealer supports that of the manufacturer.

The wholesale dealer, by affording a ready market to the manufacturer, by taking his goods off his hand as fast as he can make them, and by sometimes even advancing their price to him before he has made them, enables him to keep his whole capital, and sometimes even more than his whole capital, constantly employed in manufacturing, and consequently to manufacture a much greater quantity of

Wholesale dealers allow manufacturers to devote their whole capital to manufacturing.goods than if he was obliged to dispose of them himself to the immediate consumers, or even to the retailers. As the capital of the wholesale merchant too is generally sufficient to replace that of many manufacturers, this intercourse between him and them interests the owner of a large capital to support the owners of a great number of small ones, and to assist them in those losses and misfortunes which might otherwise prove ruinous to them.

An intercourse of the same kind universally established between the farmers and the corn merchants, would be attended with effects equally beneficial to the farmers. They would be enabled to keep their

So corn merchants should allow farmers to devote their whole capital to cultivation.whole capitals, and even more than their whole capitals, constantly employed in cultivation. In case of any of those accidents, to which no trade is more liable than theirs, they would find in their ordinary customer, the wealthy corn merchant, a person who had both an interest to support them, and the ability to do it, and they would not, as at present, be entirely dependent upon the forbearance of their landlord, or the mercy of his steward. Were it possible, as perhaps it is not, to establish this intercourse universally, and all at once, were it possible to turn all at once the whole farming stock of the kingdom to its proper business, the cultivation of land, withdrawing it from ev-

Accordingly the statute of Edward Ⅵ. endeavoured to annihilate a trade which is the best palliative and preventative of a dearth.ery other employment into which any part of it may be at present diverted, and were it possible, in order to support and assist upon occasion the operations of this great stock, to provide all at once another stock almost equally great, it is not perhaps very easy to imagine how great, how extensive, and how sudden would be the improvement which this change of circumstances would alone produce upon the whole face of the country.

The statute of Edward Ⅵ. , therefore, by prohibiting as much as possible any middle man from coming in between the grower and the consumer, endeavoured to annihilate a trade, of which the free exercise is not only the best palliative of the inconveniencies of a dearth, but the best preventative of that calamity: after the trade of the farmer,

及津贴,它对粮食增产的贡献最大,这就像批发商人的贸易会支持制造商的贸易一样。

批发商给制造商提供了现成的市场,货物一生产出来即被他们买去,甚至有时货物尚未生产出来以前,批发商就预付货款。这样制造商能够把他们所有的资本,甚至更多的资本不断地投入到制造业上,产量要比他们自己直接把货物卖给消费者及零售商人的时候要高得多。此外,批发商人的资本,一般是足够补偿许多制造商的资本的,所以他们间的这种来往,使得大资本家,愿意支持许多小资本家,并在他们亏损与不幸时给予他们援助,从而避免破产的危险。

农场主和粮食商人之间也可以普遍建立起这样的关系,结果会同样有利于农场主。农场主因此能把全部资本甚至更多的资本投在耕种上。业其实比其他任何行业都更容易遭受各种意外。但如果建立了这种关系,无论发生什么意外,他们都会发现,他们的老顾客,即富裕的粮食商人,有兴趣也有能力支持他们。这样,他们就不必像现在那样,只能依赖于地主的宽容和管家的慈悲。如果能(恐怕是不可能的)迅速把这种关系普遍地建立起来;如果能立即把全部农业资本,从其他一切不适合的用途撤回来,并投入到合适的用途;即土地耕种上,如果在必要时,为支持扶助这个大资本的运作,再提供一个几乎同样大的资本,那么,仅仅这种事态的变更,就会给国内全部土地产生巨大、广泛的影响,我们难以想象出它会给国家带来多么大的改观。

爱德华六世的法令,禁止生产者与消费者之间存在任何中间人,试图消灭这种有利的贸易。这种贸易自由进行时,不仅是减轻粮食供应不足的最佳方法,而且是预防灾难的最佳方案。除了

国民财富的性质与原理

no trade contributing so much to the growing of corn as that of the corn merchant.

Its provisions were moderated by later statutes down to 15 Car. Ⅱ., c. 7.
The rigour of this law was afterwards softened by several subsequent statutes, which successively permitted the engrossing of corn when the price of wheat should not exceed twenty, twenty-four, thirty-two, and forty shillings the quarter. ① At last, by the 15th of Charles Ⅱ. c. 7. the engrossing or buying of corn in order to sell it again, as long as the price of wheat did not exceed forty-eight shillings the quarter, and that of other grain in proportion, was declared lawful to all persons not being forestallers, that is, not selling again in the same market within three months. ② All the freedom which the trade of the inland corn dealer has ever yet enjoyed, was bestowed upon it by this statute. The statute of the twelfth of the present king, which repeals almost all the other ancient laws against engrossers and forestallers, does not repeal the restrictions of this particular statute, which therefore still continue in force. ③

which is absurd, as it supposes,
This statute, however, authorises in some measure two very absurd popular prejudices.

(1) that engrossing is likely to be hurtful after a certain price has been reached,
First, it supposes that when the price of wheat has risen so high as forty-eight shillings the quarter, and that of other grain in proportion, corn is likely to be so engrossed as to hurt the people. But from what has been already said, it seems evident enough that corn can at no price be so engrossed by the inland dealers as to hurt the people; and forty-eight shillings the quarter besides, though it may be considered as a very high price, yet in years of scarcity it is a price which frequently takes place immediately after harvest, when scarce any part of the new crop can be sold off, and when it is impossible even for ignorance to

---

① [Diligent search has hitherto failed to discover these statutes.]

② [§ 4 incorrectly quoted. The words are 'not forestalling nor selling the same in the same market within three months '. Under 5 and 6 Ed. Ⅵ., c. 14.]

③ [12 Geo. Ⅲ., c. 71, repeals 5 and 6 Ed. Ⅵ., c. 14, but does not mention 15 Car. Ⅱ., c. 7, which is purely permissive. If 15 Car. Ⅱ., c. 7, remained of any force in this respect it must have been merely in consequence of the common law being unfavourable to forestalling.]

农场主的生意,最有利于粮食生产的,便是粮食商人的生意了。

该法律非常严厉,但之后的几项法规则缓和了一些。这些法律规定,只要小麦价格不超过 1 夸特 20 先令、24 先令、32 先令或 40 先令,①大量收买粮食是合法的。最后,查理二世 15 年第 7 号法令规定,在小麦价格不超过 48 先令 1 夸特的条件下(其他粮食价格以此为准),只要购买者不是垄断者,即不是购买粮食后在三个月内②在同一市场售卖的人,大量购买或囤积粮食以待售卖,都是合法的。内地粮商曾经享受过的贸易自由,总算由这项法令失而复得了。乔治三世十二年的法令,几乎废止了其他一切取缔囤积及垄断的古代法令,但查理二世十五年法令所设的限制,未曾撤废,因此继续有效。③

查理二世十五年的法令,在一定程度上认可了两种极不合理的世俗偏见。

第一,这个法令认为,小麦价格涨至 1 夸特 48 先令,其他各种粮食亦相应涨价时,囤积粮食很可能损伤老百姓的利益。但据我们上面所说,似乎很明显,价格无论怎样,内地粮商囤积都不会伤害老百姓。而且,48 先令虽是很高的价格,但在歉岁,这是在刚刚收获以后常有的价格。如果粮食短缺,新收割的粮食会马上给卖掉。那么在这个时候就是最愚蠢的人也不会认为,还会有粮食

---

① 到目前为止,虽经过辛苦的搜索但没有找到这号法令。
② 第四章引用得不正确。原话是"不能大量购买,不能在三个月之内在同一市场出售"。爱德华六世五年和六年第 14 号法令。
③ 乔治二世十二年第 71 号法令取消了爱德华六世五年、六年第 14 号法令,但没有提及乔治二世 15 年第 7 号法令,表示准许后者。如果查理二世十五年第 7 号法令仍然有效,那一定只是由于习惯法对垄断行为是不赞成的。

suppose that any part of it can be so engrossed as to hurt the people.

(2) that forestalling is likely to be hurtful after a certain price has been reached.

Secondly, it supposes that there is a certain price at which corn is likely to be forestalled, that is, bought up in order to be sold again soon after in the same market, so as to hurt the people. But if a merchant ever buys up corn, either going to a particular market or in a particular market, in order to sell it again soon after in the same market, it must be because he judges that the market cannot be so liberally supplied through the whole season as upon that particular occasion, and that the price, therefore, must soon rise. If he judges wrong in this, and if the price does not rise, he not only loses the whole profit of the stock which he employs in this manner, but a part of the stock itself, by the expence and loss which necessarily attend the storing and keeping of corn. He hurts himself, therefore, much more essentially than he can hurt even the particular people whom he may hinder from supplying themselves upon that particular market day, because they may afterwards supply themselves just as cheap upon any other market day. If he judges right, instead of hurting the great body of the people, he renders them a most important service. By making them feel the inconveniencies of a dearth somewhat earlier than they otherwise might do, he prevents their feeling them afterwards so severely as they certainly would do, if the cheapness of price encouraged them to consume faster than suited the real scarcity of the season. When the scarcity is real, the best thing that can be done for the people is to divide the inconveniencies of it as equally as possible through all the different months, and weeks, and days of the year. The interest of the corn merchant makes him study to do this as exactly as he can: and as no other person can have either the same interest, or the same knowledge, or the same abilities to do it so exactly as he, this most important operation of commerce ought to be trusted entirely to him; or, in other words, the corn trade, so far at least as concerns the supply of the home market, ought to be left perfectly free.

The fear of engrossing and forestalling is as groundless as that of witchcraft.

The popular fear of engrossing and forestalling may be compared to the popular terrors and suspicions of witchcraft. The unfortunate wretches accused of this latter crime were not more innocent of the misfortunes imputed to them, than those who have been accused of the former. The law which put an end to all prosecutions against witchcraft, which put it out of any man's power to gratify his own malice by accusing his neighbour of that imaginary crime, seems effectually to have put an end to those fears and suspicions,

被囤积起来以伤害人民。

　　第二,这个法令认为,在一定价格下,粮食最易为人所囤积垄断,也就是说,买了以后不久又在同一市场内出售,以致伤害老百姓。但是,如果商人到某一市场或在某一市场尽可能地多地收购粮食,为了不久以后在同一市场内再出售,那一定是因为他判断出,市场上的粮食供应不可能每个季节都充足,不久粮食即将涨价。如果他判断错了,价格没有上涨,那他不但赚不到利润,而且因为储藏粮食需要费用,反而必然要亏本。这样,他自己所受的伤害,比起个别百姓所遭受的伤害要大得多。虽然由于他的囤积,在某一时期个别百姓可能买不到粮食,但在此后的任何时期,他们却能以和其他时期同样低廉的价格买得到。反之,如果他的判断是对的,那他就不但无害于人民大众,反而给他们提供了很大的帮助,使他们早些感到粮食紧缺,就不至于后来猛然地感到粮食紧缺的痛苦。要是目前价格低廉,百姓在粮食紧缺时期里还消费太快,到后来一定会猛然地感到粮食紧缺的痛苦。如果真的出现粮食紧缺,从百姓的角度考虑,最好把这种痛苦尽可能分摊到每个月、每个星期、每一天。从粮商自身的利益考虑,需要认真研究并尽可能对市场变化做出准确的判断。其他任何人都不会有这种兴趣,也没有这种知识,更没有这种能力来研究市场。所以,这种最重要的商业活动,应当全部委托给他。换言之,至少在国内市场的供应上,粮食贸易应当完全自由。

　　百姓对大量收买与囤积垄断的恐惧,可以比作是对妖术的恐惧与疑惑。因妖术而被问罪的可怜人和因囤积而被问罪的人一样,都是无罪的。法律对人们出于恶意平白无故地以想象上的罪名控告邻人使用妖术的行为予以了禁止。这似乎有效地消除了

(2) 价格达到一定水平后,囤积垄断很可能有害。

对囤积垄断的忧虑,就像对妖术的忧虑一样,是无根据的。

by taking away the great cause which encouraged and supported them. The law which should restore entire freedom to the inland trade of corn, would probably prove as effectual to put an end to the popular fears of engrossing and forestalling.

The 15th of Charles Ⅱ. c. 7. however, with all its imperfections, has perhaps contributed more both to the plentiful supply of the home market, and to the increase of tillage, than any other law in the statute book. It is from this law that the inland corn trade has derived all the liberty and protection which it has ever yet enjoyed; and both the supply of the home market, and the interest of tillage, are much more effectually promoted by the inland, than either by the importation or exportation trade.

The proportion of the average quantity of all sorts of grain imported into Great Britain to that of all sorts of grain consumed, it has been computed by the author of the tracts upon the corn trade, does not exceed that of one to five hundred and seventy. For supplying the home market, therefore, the importance of the inland trade must be to that of the importation trade as five hundred and seventy to one. ①

The average quantity of all sorts of grain exported from Great Britain does not, according to the same author, exceed the one-and-thirtieth part of the annual produce. ② For the encouragement of tillage, therefore, by providing a market for the home produce, the importance of the inland trade must be to that of the exportation trade as thirty to one.

I have no great faith in political arithmetic, and I mean not to warrant the exactness of either of these computations. I mention them only in order to show of how much less consequence, in the opinion of the most judicious and experienced persons, the foreign trade of corn is than the home trade. The great cheapness of corn in the years immediately preceding the establishment of the bounty, may perhaps, with reason, be ascribed in some measure to the operation of this statute of Charles Ⅱ. , which had been enacted about five-and twenty years before, and which had therefore full time to produce its effect.

A very few words will sufficiently explain all that I have to say concerning the other three branches of the corn trade.

---

① [Charles Smith, *Three Tracts on the Corn Trade and Corn Laws*, 2nd ed. , 1766, p. 145. The figures have been already quoted above.]

② ['The export is bare one thirty-second part of the consumption, one thirty-third part of the growth exclusive of seed, one thirty-sixth part of the growth including the seed. ' *Ibid.* , p. 144.]

引起恐惧与猜疑的主要起源,从而有效地消灭了这种恐惧与猜疑。恢复内地粮食贸易自由的法律,可能也会有效地消灭百姓对囤积与垄断的恐惧。

查理二世十五年第 7 号法令虽然有各种不足之处,但比起法典中其他任何法律,它对丰富国内市场和增加耕种所起的贡献要更大。通过这项法令,内地粮食贸易获得了自由与保护,与进出口贸易相比,国内贸易更有效地促进了国内市场以及耕种业的发展。

> 查理二世十五年第 7 号法令仍然是最好的法律,因为它给予国内粮食贸易所能拥有的一切自由。

根据那位论述粮食贸易作者的计算,英国平均每年进口与消费的各种粮食之间的比例,不超过 1:570。所以,在国内市场的供应上,内地贸易的重要性是进口贸易的 570 倍。①

> 国内贸易比国际贸易重要得多。

根据该作者的计算,英国每年平均出口的各种粮食量,不过占年产额的 1/30。② 所以,在给本国产物提供市场、奖励耕种方面,内地贸易比出口贸易要重要 30 倍。

我不相信政治算术,也不想证明以上两种计算的正确性。我提及它们仅仅是为了说明,根据这位考虑最周全最有经验的人的观点,粮食的对外贸易与国内贸易比较,是多么的微不足道。津贴设立之前粮价低廉,或许有理由在一定程度上归因于查理二世那项法令的作用。该法令大约颁布于 25 年前,它有足够的时间产生这种结果。

关于其他三种粮食贸易部门,只要几句话就足以解释我所说

---

① 查理·史密斯,关于粮食贸易和粮食供应法律的二篇论义,第二版,1766 年,第 145 页。这些数字在前文引述过。

② "出口仅为消费量的 1/32,为除种子外生产量的 1/33,包括种子在内的生产量的 1/36。"同上书,第 144 页。

| 国民财富的性质与原理

II. The Importer, whose trade benefits the people and does not really hurt the farmers and country gentlemen.

Ⅱ. The trade of the merchant importer of foreign corn for home consumption, evidently contributes to the immediate supply of the home market, and must so far be immediately beneficial to the great body of the people. It tends, indeed, to lower somewhat the average money price of corn, but not to diminish its real value, or the quantity of labour which it is capable of maintaining. If importation was at all times free, our farmers and country gentlemen would, probably, one year with another, get less money for their corn than they do at present, when importation is at most times in effect prohibited; but the money which they got would be of more value, would buy more goods of all other kinds, and would employ more labour. Their real wealth, their real revenue, therefore, would be the same as at present, though it might be expressed by a smaller quantity of silver; and they would neither be disabled nor discouraged from cultivating corn as much as they do at present. On the contrary, as the rise in the real value of silver, in consequence of lowering the money price of corn, lowers somewhat the money price of all other commodities, it gives the industry of the country, where it takes place, some advantage in all foreign markets, and thereby tends to encourage and increase that industry. But the extent of the home market for corn must be in proportion to the general industry of the country where it grows, or to the number of those who produce something else, and therefore have something else, or what comes to the same thing, the price of something else, to give in exchange for corn. But in every country the home market, as it is the nearest and most convenient, so is it likewise the greatest and most important market for corn. That rise in the real value of silver, therefore, which is the effect of lowering the average money price of corn, tends to enlarge the greatest and most important market for corn, and thereby to encourage, instead of discouraging, its growth.

The Act of 2 Car. Ⅱ., c. 13, imposed very high duties on importation

By the 22d of Charles Ⅱ. c. 13. the importation of wheat, whenever the price in the home market did not exceed fifty-three shillings and four pence the quarter, was subjected to a duty of sixteen

的内容了。

第二，商人进口外国粮食以供国内消费的贸易，显然对国内市场的直接供给起到了作用，因而给大多数百姓带来了直接的利益。诚然，它会稍微减低粮食的平均货币价格，但不会减低粮食的实际价值，不会减少粮食所能维持的劳动量。如果进口随时都是自由的，我国农场主和乡绅每年出售粮食所得的货币，要比禁止进口时得到的少。但他们所得的货币，将有更高的价值，将可购买更多的其他物品，雇佣更多的劳动。他们的真实财富与真实收入，虽表现为较少的银量，但和现在一样；他们既不会丧失财力，积极性也不会受到打击，也仍和现在一样。反之，由于粮食的货币价格跌落而引起的白银实际价值的上涨，会稍微减低一切其他商品的货币价格，使该国的产业在外国市场上获得一定的优势，从而能鼓励并促进该国产业的发展。但国内粮食市场的规模，必须与国内的普通产业保持一定的比例，或者说，必须与生产可用于与粮食交换，或者手上有其他有价值的物品可用于交换粮食人数保持一定的比例。但在所有的国家里，国内市场都是粮食最近和最方便的市场，所以也是最大和最重要的市场。粮食平均货币价格下跌而使银的实际价值上升，有助于扩大粮食最大和最重要的市场，会促进粮食生产，而不会阻碍粮食生产。

查理二世二十二年第13号法令规定，在国内市场上，小麦价格不超过1夸特53先令4便士时，小麦的进口，每夸特须纳税16先令；在国内市场上，小麦价格不超过1夸特4镑时，小麦的进

shillings the quarter; and to a duty of eight shillings whenever the price did not exceed four pounds. ① The former of these two prices has, for more than a century past, taken place only in times of very great scarcity; and the latter has, so far as I know, not taken place at all. Yet, till wheat had risen above this latter price, it was by this statute subjected to a very high duty; and, till it had risen above the former, to a duty which amounted to a prohibition. The importation of other sorts of grain was restrained at rates, and by duties, in proportion to the value of the grain, almost equally high. ② Subsequent laws

---

① [This was not the first law of its kind. 3 Ed. IV. , c. 2, was enacted because 'the labourers and occupiers of husbandry within this realm of England be daily grievously endamaged by bringing of corn out of other lands and parts into this realm of England when corn of the growing of this realm is at a low price, ' and forbids importation of wheat when not over 6s. 8d. , rye when not over 4s. and barley when not over 3s. the quarter. This Act was repealed by 21 Jac. I. , c. 28, and 15 Car. II. , c. 7, imposed a duty of 5s. 4d. on imported wheat, 4s. on rye, 2s. 8d. on barley, 2s. on buckwheat, 1s. 4d. on oats and 4s. on pease and beans, when the prices at the port of importation did not exceed for wheat, 48s. ; barley and buckwheat, 28s. ; oats, 13s. 4d. ; rye, pease and beans, 32s. per quarter.]

② Before the 13th of the present king, the following were the duties payable upon the importation of the different sorts of grain:

Grain.	Duties.		Duties.	Duties.
Beans to 28s. per qr.	19s. 10d. after	till 40s.	- 16s. 8d.	then 12d.
Barley to 28s.	19s. 10d.	32s.	- 16s.	12d.

Malt is prohibited by the annual Malt-tax Bill.

Oats to 16s.	5s. 10d. after		$9\frac{1}{2}$d.
Pease to 40s.	16s. 0d. after		$9\frac{3}{4}$d.
Rye to 36s.	19s. 10d. till	40s.	- 16s. 8d. then 12d.
Wheat to 44s.	21s. 9d. till	53s. 4d.	-17s. then 8s.

till 41. and after that about 1s. 4d.
Buck wheat to 32s. per qr. to pay 16s.

口,每夸特须纳税 8 先令。① 前一种价格,只在一世纪以前粮食非常紧缺的时候发生过;后一种价格,则据我所知,从未发生过。可是,根据这号法令,小麦在未涨至后一种价格以前,要交纳很高的税;等小麦的价格涨得超过前一种价格的时候要缴纳的税,就等于禁止其进口。至于限制其他各种粮食进口的税率与关税,和其价格相比,也几乎同样的沉重。② 而且,以后的法令,还继续加重

① 这不是这类法律中的第一个。爱德华四世三年第 2 号法令规定,国内市场上每夸特小麦不超过 6 先令 8 便士,黑麦不超过 4 先令,大麦不超过 3 先令时,禁止进口,这项法律被詹姆士一世二十一年第 28 号法令废止,查理二世十五年第 7 号法令规定进口税小麦 5 先令 4 便士,黑麦 4 先令,大麦 2 先令 8 便士,荞麦 2 先令,燕麦 1 先令 4 便士,豌豆和蚕豆 2 先令,其条件是,进口港的价格每夸特不超过小麦 48 先令,大麦和乔麦 28 先令,燕麦 13 先令 4 便士,黑麦、豌豆和蚕豆 32 先令。

② 谷类(每夸特价格)　　　　　税
　蚕豆　28 先令以下　　　　　19 先令 10 便士
　　　　40 先令以下　　　　　16 先令 8 便士
　　　　40 先令以上　　　　　12 便士
　　　　大麦 28 先令以上　　　19 先令 10 便士
　　　　32 先令以下　　　　　16 先令
　　　　32 先令以上　　　　　12 便士
根据每年抽税一次的麦芽税法案,麦芽是禁止输入的。
　燕麦　16 先令以下　　　　　5 先令 10 便士
　　　　16 先令以下　　　　　9 便士
　　　　豌豆 40 先令 F.IT　　 16 先令
　　　　40 先令以上　　　　　9 便士
　黑麦　36 先令以下　　　　　19 先令 10 便士
　　　　40 先令以下　　　　　16 先令 8 便士
　　　　40 先令以上　　　　　12 便士
　小麦　44 先令以下　　　　　21 先令 9 便士
　　　　53 先令 4 便士　　　　17 先令
　　　　4 镑以下　　　　　　　8 先令
　　　　4 镑以上　　　　　　　约 1 先令 4 便士
　荞麦　32 先令以下　　　　　16 先令

still further increased those duties.

<small>but its operation was generally suspended in years of scarcity.</small>　The distress which, in years of scarcity, the strict execution of those laws might have brought ①upon the people, would probably have been very great. But, upon such occasions, its execution was generally suspended by temporary statutes, ②which permitted, for a limited time, the importation of foreign corn. The necessity of these temporary statutes sufficiently demonstrates the impropriety of this general one.

<small>Restraint was necessary on account of the bounty.</small>　These restraints upon importation, though prior to the establishment of the bounty, were dictated by the same spirit, by the same principles, which afterwards enacted that regulation. How hurtful soever in themselves, these or some other restraints upon importation became necessary in consequence of that regulation. If, when wheat was either below forty-eight shillings the quarter, or not much above it, foreign corn could have been imported either duty free, or upon paying only a small duty, it might have been exported again, with the benefit of the bounty, to the great loss of the public revenue, and to the entire perversion of the institution, of which the object was to extend the market for the home growth, not that for the growth of foreign countries.

<small>Ⅲ. The Exporter, whose trade indirectly contributes to the plentiful supply of the home market.</small>　Ⅲ. The trade of the merchant exporter of corn for foreign consumption, certainly does not contribute directly to the plentiful supply of the home market. It does so, however, indirectly. From whatever source this supply may be usually drawn, whether from home growth or from foreign importation, unless more corn is either usually grown, or usually imported into the country, than what is usually consumed in it, the supply of the home market can never be very plentiful. But unless the surplus can, in all ordinary cases, be exported, the growers will be careful never to grow more, and the importers never to import more, than what the bare consumption of the home market requires. That market will very seldom be overstocked; but it will generally be understocked, the people, whose business it is to supply it, being generally afraid lest their goods should be left upon their hands. The prohibition of exportation limits the improvement and cultivation of the country to what the supply of its own inhabitants requires. The

---

　　① [Eds. 1 and 2 do not contain ' subsequent laws still further increased those duties,' and read ' the distress which in years of scarcity the strict execution of this statute might have brought'.]

　　② [These do not seem to have been numerous. There were cases in 1757 and 1766. See the table in Charles Smith, *Three Tracts upon the Corn Trade and Corn Laws*, 2nd ed. , pp. 44﹐45.]

了这种赋税。

在歉收岁份,严格执行这种法律而使百姓遭受的困苦,①也许是很大的。但在这个时候,这种法律往往由于颁发了临时条例②而停止实施,这些条例允许外国粮食在一定时期内进口。需要实施这种暂行条例,就充分说明了法律的不适用性。

<small>但在饥荒之年,它通常暂停执行。</small>

尽管限制进口的种种条款先于津贴的设立,但它制定时的精神与原则,则与后来制定津贴条例的精神与原则是一样的。但在设立津贴制度以后,这种或那种进口限制政策,无论本身是怎样有害,也变得很有必要了。倘若在1夸特小麦不及48先令或略微高出这个价格时,外国粮食则可以自由进口,或出口时仅缴纳小额的关税,那也许就有人为了津贴,把粮食再出口,不但国家的收入会有很大的损失,而且以推广本国产物市场而不是为了扩大国外市场的制度也会被推翻。

<small>因为津贴种种限制是必须的。</small>

第三,供给外国消费的粮食出口贸易,对丰富国内市场没有直接的贡献,但有间接的贡献。无论粮食来自什么地方,不管是本国生产还是从国外进口,除非这些粮食多于所消费的粮食,否则国内市场的供给绝不会充足。但是通常情况下,如果剩余部分不能出口,那么生产者和进口商将根据国内市场消费需要而生产或进口,不会多了以至于超出实际需要。因为供货担心货物会全部积压在自己手中,所以市场存货很少过剩,常年是存货不足。禁止出口把国内土地的改良与耕种限制了本国居民的需

<small>第三,商人间作出口对丰富国内市场起按作用。</small>

---

① 在版本1和版本2中没有"在随后的法律中仍然增加了那些税收",参见"在歉收年份严厉执行这项法令所带来的困苦"。

② 这种情况不是很多。在1757年和1766年出现过,可参见查理·史密斯的论文,关于粮食贸易和粮食法律的三篇论文,第二版,第44、45页。

freedom of exportation enables it to extend cultivation for the supply of foreign nations.

Liberty of exportation was made complete in 1700.

By the 12th of Charles II. c. 4. the exportation of corn was permitted whenever the price of wheat did not exceed forty shillings the quarter, and that of other grain in proportion. ① By the 15th of the same prince, ② this liberty was extended till the price of wheat exceeded forty-eight shillings the quarter; and by the 22d, ③ to all higher prices. A poundage, indeed, was to be paid to the king upon such exportation. But all grain was rated so low in the book of rates, that this poundage amounted only upon wheat to a shilling, upon oats to four pence, and upon all other grain to six pence the quarter. ④ By the lst of William and Mary, ⑤ the act which established the bounty, this small duty was virtually taken off whenever the price of wheat did not exceed fortyeight shillings the quarter; and by the 11th and 12th of William III. c. 20. it was expressly taken off at all higher prices.

though the interest of the exporter sometimes differs from that of the people of his country.

The trade of the merchant exporter was, in this manner, not only encouraged by a bounty, but rendered much more free than that of the inland dealer. By the last of these statutes, corn could be engrossed at any price for exportation; but it could not be engrossed for inland sale, except when the price did not exceed forty-eight shillings the quarter. ⑥The interest of the inland dealer, however, it has already been shown, can never be opposite to that of the great body of the people. That of the merchant exporter may, and in fact sometimes is. If, while his own country labours under a dearth, a neighbouring country should be afflicted with a famine, it might be his interest to

---

① [Earlier statutes are 15 Hen. VI. , c. 2; 20 Hen. VI. , c. 6; 23 Hen. VI. , c. 6; 1 and 2 P. and M. , c. 5; 5 Eliz. , c. 5, §26; 13 Eliz. , c. 13; and 1 Jac. , c. 25, §§ 26, 27.]

② [C. 7.]

③ [C. 13.]

④ [The 'Book of Rates' rated wheat for export at 20s. , oats at 6s. 8d. , and other grain at 10s. the quarter, and the duty was a shilling in the pound on these values.]

⑤ [1 W. and M. , c. 12.]

⑥ [Because as to inland sale 15 Car. II. , c. 7 , remained in force.]

要。自由出口可以扩大国内耕种事业,以供给外国市场。

查理二世十二年第 4 号法令规定,在 1 夸特小麦价格不超过 40 先令,其他各种粮食的价格与该价格成比例,允许粮食出口。①查理二世十五年又规定,小麦价格不超过每夸特 48 先令,可以自由出口;②到了二十二年,③无论价格多高,都允许自由出口。当然,出口时,必须向国王缴纳港口税。由于一切粮食在关税表中的税率都很低,所以就港口税而言,小麦仅为 1 夸特 1 先令,燕麦 1 夸特 4 便士,其他各种粮食 6 便士。④ 威廉和玛利⑤一年制定津贴法令以后,在实际执行中,如果 1 夸特小麦不超过 48 先令,这个小额的税不需要缴纳。在威廉三世二十年第 20 号法令里,这个小额的税干脆给取消了。（在1700年出口才完全自由,）

出口商的贸易不仅受津贴的鼓励,而且比内地商人的贸易自由得多。根据上述最后一个法令,无论价格怎样,粮食都可囤积以待出口;但除非 1 夸特价格不超过 48 先令,⑥否则是不允许的。上面说过,国内商人的利益绝不会和百姓的利益对立。但出口商人的利益,则可能和百姓的利益对立,事实上有时的确是这样。在国家正处于饥荒之时,邻国也闹饥荒,出口商出于自身的（尽管出口商的利益有时与国内百姓的利益不同。）

---

① 较早的法令有亨利六世十五年第 2 号;亨利六世二十年第 6 号;亨利二十三年第 6 号;威廉和玛利一年、二年第 5 号;伊丽莎白五年 5 号第 26 条;伊丽莎白十三年第 13 号和詹姆士一年第 25 号第 26、27 条。
② 第 7 号法令。
③ 第 13 号法令。
④ "税率表",估值每夸特出口小麦 20 先令,燕麦 6 先令 8 便士,其他谷物 10 先令;税额按这些价值为每镑 1 先令。
⑤ 威廉和玛利第 1 年第 12 号法令。
⑥ 因为国内贸易法令查理二世十五年第 7 号法令仍然生效。

carry corn to the latter country in such quantities as might very much aggravate the calamities of the dearth. The plentiful supply of the home market was not the direct object of those statutes; but, under the pretence of encouraging agriculture, to raise the money price of corn as high as possible, and thereby to occasion, as much as possible, a constant dearth in the home market. By the discouragement of importation, the supply of that market, even in times of great scarcity, was confined to the home growth; and by the encouragement of exportation, when the price was so high as forty-eight shillings the quarter, that market was not, even in times of considerable scarcity, allowed to enjoy the whole of that growth. The temporary laws, prohibiting for a limited time the exportation of corn, and taking off for a limited time the duties upon its importation, expedients to which Great Britain has been obliged so frequently to have recourse, ① sufficiently demonstrate the impropriety of her general system. Had that system been good, she would not so frequently have been reduced to the necessity of departing from it.

The bad policy of some great countries may sometimes render it necessary for small countries to restrain exportation.

Were all nations to follow the liberal system of free exportation and free importation, the different states into which a great continent was divided would so far resemble the different provinces of a great empire. As among the different provinces of a great empire the freedom of the inland trade appears, both from reason and experience, not only the best palliative of a dearth, but the most effectual preventative of a famine; so would the freedom of the exportation and importation trade be among the different states into which a great continent was divided. The larger the continent, the easier the communication through all the different parts of it, both by land and by water, the less would any one particular part of it ever be exposed to either of these calamities, the scarcity of any one country being more likely to be relieved by the plenty of some other. But very few countries have entirely adopted this liberal system. The freedom of the corn trade is almost every where more or less restrained, and, in many countries, is confined by such absurd regulations, as frequently aggravate the unavoidable misfortune of a dearth, into the dreadful calamity of a famine. The demand of such countries for corn may frequently become so great and so urgent, that a small state in their neighbourhood, which happened at the same time to be labouring under some degree of dearth, could not venture to supply them without exposing itself to the like dreadful calamity. The very bad policy of one country may

---

① [The Acts prohibiting exportation were much more numerous than the others.]

利益,可能把大量粮食运往邻国,大大加重本国粮食紧缺的灾难。这种法令的直接目的,不是使国内市场供应充足,而是在奖励农业的幌子下,尽量提高粮食的货币价格,使国内市场上经常出现紧缺。阻碍进口的结果,甚至在粮食严重紧缺时,国内市场也只能依赖于本国的粮食生产。在价格已高至1夸特48先令时还奖励出口的结果,是在粮食严重紧缺期间,国内粮食也不能全部供应国内市场。在有限期间禁止粮食出口,并在有限期间内免除粮食进口税的暂行法律,英国不得不常常采用,①这在事实上充分说明了它的法律的不适用性。如果一般法律是适用的,那么就没有必要停止施行了。

假设一切国家都采用进出口自由制度,大陆内的各个国家,就会像国内的各个省份一样。从道理和经验上讲,大国国内各省间的贸易自由,不仅是缓和粮食紧缺的最好方法,而且也是防止饥荒的最好方法;大陆内各国间的进出口贸易自由,也具有同样的作用,大陆越广大,大陆内各地之间水运陆运交通越便利,其中任何地区遭受这两种灾难的可能性便越小。一国的紧缺,很容易由另一国的丰足缓和。但几乎没有一个国家完全采取这种自由制度,粮食贸易的自由,几乎在所有地方都多少受到限制;许多国家的限制粮食贸易的不合理法律,往往加重缺粮所带来的不幸,导致发展成为可怕的饥荒灾难。这种国家对粮食的需要,是那么巨大、那么迫切,邻近小国会觉得,自己粮食不足的情况下还要供给它们,恐怕自己也会陷入同样可怕的灾难。因此,如果一个国家采用了这种最坏的政策,往往会使别的国家认

许多大国有时采取的政策,不当使小国有必要制限出口。

---

① 禁止出口的法律比其他种类的法律要多得多。

thus render it in some measure dangerous and imprudent to establish what would otherwise be the best policy in another. The unlimited freedom of exportation, however, would be much less dangerous in great states, in which the growth being much greater, the supply could seldom be much affected by any quantity of corn that was likely to be exported. In a Swiss canton, or in some of the little states of Italy, it may, perhaps, sometimes be necessary to restrain the exportation of corn. In such great countries as France or England it scarce ever can. To hinder, besides, the farmer from sending his goods at all times to the best market, is evidently to sacrifice the ordinary laws of justice to an idea of public utility, to a sort of reasons of state; an act of legislative authority which ought to be exercised only, which can be pardoned only in cases of the most urgent necessity. The price at which the exportation of corn is prohibited, if it is ever to be prohibited, ought always to be a very high price.

The corn laws are like the laws on religion. The laws concerning corn may every where be compared to the laws concerning religion. The people feel themselves so much interested in what relates either to their subsistence in this life, or to their happiness in a life to come, that government must yield to their prejudices, and, in order to preserve the public tranquillity, establish that system which they approve of. It is upon this account, perhaps, that we so seldom find a reasonable system established with regard to either of those two capital objects.

IV. The Merchant Carrier, whose trade contributes to the plentiful supply of the home market. IV. The trade of the merchant carrier, or of the importer of foreign corn in order to export it again, contributes to the plentiful supply of the home market. It is not indeed the direct purpose of his trade to sell his corn there. But he will generally be willing to do so, and even for a good deal less money than he might expect in a foreign market; because he saves in this manner the expence of loading and unloading, of freight and insurance. The inhabitants of the country which, by means of the carrying trade, becomes the magazine and storehouse for the supply of other countries, can very seldom be in want themselves. Though the carrying trade might thus contribute to reduce the average money price of corn in the home market, it would not thereby lower its real value. It would only raise somewhat the real value of silver.

British law in effect prohibited the carrying trade in corn. The carrying trade was in effect prohibited in Great Britain, upon all ordinary occasions, by the high duties upon the importation of foreign corn, of the greater part of which there was no drawback ; and upon extraordinary occasions, when a scarcity made it necessary to

为,采用原来最好的政策,在一定程度上,是危险的、不慎重的行为。但是,无限制的出口自由,对大国来说,危险性就小得多,因为大国的生产量大,无论粮食出口量如何,国内供应都不会太受影响。在瑞士或意大利两小国内,也许有时还需要限制粮食出口。但英国和法国那样的大国,却不见得有这样的必要。而且,不让农场主及时把货物运到最好的市场,显然是处于功利的观念,或以国家为理由,不顾正义和公正。立法者这种行为,除了在紧急必须的场合,是不应该有的,是不能原谅的。如果真要禁止,也只有在粮食的价格非常高的时候,才能采取这种措施。

有关粮食的法律,无论从哪方面讲,都可以与有关宗教的法律相类比。人们觉得它们与自己的生活息息相关,与自己来世的幸福也有密切的关系。因此,为了确保社会的安定,政府必须倾听民众的意见,建立民众能够接受的制度。也许正是这个原因,我们很少发现能顾及到这两个主要目的、合理的制度建立起来。

第四,贩运商的贸易,或者进口外国粮食再出口的贸易商进行的贸易,对丰富国内市场起到了相当大的作用。在国内销售粮食的确不是他贸易的直接目的,但他愿意这样做,哪怕是比他所期望的在国外市场上的价格低得多,因为这样他可以省去货物的装卸费以及运输保险费等。一个国家由于转口贸易而变成了为他国供应谷物的仓库,该国家的居民一般不会缺乏粮食。尽管转口贸易可能减低国内市场上粮食的平均货币价格,但不会因此减少粮食的实际价值,它只会略微提高白银的实际价值。

转口贸易在英国实际上是禁止的。因为一般情况下,进口外国粮食须缴纳高额税款,大部分税款也不能退还;但在一些特殊情况下,当粮食不足时,不得不制定临时法律停止征收关税,

suspend those duties by temporary statutes, exportation was always prohibited. By this system of laws, therefore, the carrying trade was in effect prohibited upon all occasions.

<small>The prosperity of Great Britain is not due to the corn bounty, but to the security of enjoying the fruits of labour.</small>

That system of laws, therefore, which is connected with the establishment of the bounty, seems to deserve no part of the praise which has been bestowed upon it. The improvement and prosperity of Great Britain, which has been so often ascribed to those laws, may very easily be accounted for by other causes. That security which the laws in Great Britain give to every man that he shall enjoy the fruits of his own labour, is alone sufficient to make any country flourish, notwithstanding these and twenty other absurd regulations of commerce; and this security was perfected by the revolution, much about the same time that the bounty was established. The natural effort of every individual to better his own condition, when suffered to exert itself with freedom and security, is so powerful a principle, that it is alone, and without any assistance, not only capable of carrying on the society to wealth and prosperity, but of surmounting a hundred impertinent obstructions with which the folly of human laws too often incumbers its operations; though the effect of these obstructions is always more or less either to encroach upon its freedom, or to diminish its security. In Great Britain industry is perfectly secure; and though it is far from being perfectly free, it is as free or freer than in any other part of Europe.

<small>That the greatest prosperity has been subsequent proves nothing.</small>

Though the period of the greatest prosperity and improvement of Great Britain, has been posterior to that system of laws which is connected with the bounty, we must not upon that account impute it to those laws. It has been posterior likewise to the national debt. But the national debt has most assuredly not been the cause of it.

<small>Spain and Portugal are poorer than Great Britain because their bad policy is more effectual, and not counteracted by general liberty and security.</small>

Though the system of laws which is connected with the bounty, has exactly the same tendency with the police of Spain and Portugal; to lower somewhat the value of the precious metals in the country where it takes place; yet Great Britain is certainly one of the richest countries in Europe, while Spain and Portugal are perhaps among the most beggarly. This difference of situation, however, may easily be accounted for from two different causes. First, the tax in Spain, the prohibition in Portugal of exporting gold and silver, and the vigilant police which watches over the execution of those laws, must, in two very poor countries, which between them import annually upwards of six millions sterling, operate, not only more directly, but much more forcibly in reducing the value of those metals there, than the corn laws can do in Great Britain. And, secondly, this bad policy is not in those countries counter-balanced by the general liberty and security of

终止出口。这样,转口贸易实际上在任何时候都是禁止的。

所以,与津贴制度有关的法律,虽然历来受人称赞,但实际上它根本不值得,英国的改良与繁荣,常被错误地当成是这些法律的功劳,但其实很容易用其他原因来解释。尽管存在上述以及其他20条不合理的商业条例,但英国法律提供的保障,即所有人都能够享有自己的劳动果实,就足以使任何国家繁荣。而且,这种保障会随着津贴的改革而进一步完善。人类受到自由和安全的危险时,会不断改善自己的状况、不断努力,尽管孤独,得不到任何帮助,但这种精神不但可以使社会走向富裕、走向繁荣,而且还能克服无数愚蠢的法律所设置的人为障碍,虽然这些障碍侵害了人们这种努力的自由,或者说降低了人们的安全感。在英国,工业是很有保障的;虽然不能说是完全自由的,但与欧洲其他各国比较,英国的工业还是一样自由或者说更加自由一些。

> 英国繁荣不是因为粮食津贴,而是由劳动果实享有权的保障。

英国最繁荣最进步的时期,是在那些与津贴有关的法律实施以后才出现的,但我们绝不能因此而断定,英国的繁荣与进步就是那些法律带来的。这种繁荣与进步同时也是在发行国债以后出现的,但我们肯定不会把发行国债当成是不列颠繁荣与进步的原因。

> 繁荣是后来发生的,但并不能证明什么。

虽然与津贴有关的法制,就如同西班牙与葡萄牙的警察一样,使国内贵金属略微贬值。但是,西班牙和葡萄牙也许是欧洲贫乏的国家;而英国却无疑是欧洲最富有的国家。这种差异很容易由上述两个原因说明。首先,对金银的出口,西班牙须纳税,葡萄牙受禁止,还有执法严厉的警察,这些因素,在这两个每年进口600万镑以上金银的国家,对降低金银价值所产生的影响,比起英国粮食法律所产生的影响,不仅更直接,而且更严重。其次,这种不良政策没有受到民众的自由权利和保障权利的抵

> 西班牙和葡萄牙比英国更贫穷,因为它们的政策产生了强效,也没有遭到自由权和保障权利的抵抗。

国民财富的性质与原理

the people. Industry is there neither free nor secure, and the civil and ecclesiastical governments of both Spain and Portugal, are such as would alone be sufficient to perpetuate their present state of poverty, even though their regulations of commerce were as wise as the greater part of them are absurd and foolish.

<small>The 13 Geo. Ⅲ., c. 43,</small>

The 13th of the present king, c. 43. seems to have established a new system with regard to the corn laws, in many respects better than the ancient one, but in one or two respects perhaps not quite so good.

<small>opens the home market at lower prices,</small>

By this statute the high duties upon importation for home consumption are taken off so soon as the price of middling wheat rises to forty-eight shillings the quarter; that of middling rye, pease or beans, to thirty-two shillings; that of barley to twenty-four shillings; and that of oats to sixteen shillings; and instead ① of them a small duty is imposed of only six-pence upon the quarter of wheat, and upon that of other grain in proportion. With regard to all these different sorts of grain, but particularly with regard to wheat, the home market is thus opened to foreign supplies at prices considerably lower than before. ②

<small>stops the bounty earlier,</small>

By the same statute the old bounty of five shillings upon the exportation of wheat ceases so soon as the price rises to forty-four shillings the quarter, instead of forty-eight, the price at which it ceased before; that of two shillings and six-pence upon the exportation of barley ceases so soon as the price rises to twenty-two shillings, instead of twenty-four, the price at which it ceased before; that of two shillings and six-pence upon the exportation of oatmeal ceases so soon as the price rises to fourteen shillings, instead of fifteen, the price at which it ceased before. The bounty upon rye is reduced from three shillings and six-pence to three shillings, and it ceases so soon as the price rises to twenty-eight shillings, instead of thirty-two, the price at which it ceased before. ③ If bounties are as improper as I have endeavoured

---

① [Ed. 1 reads only 'By this statute the high duties upon importation for home consumption are taken off as soon as the price of wheat is so high as forty-eight shillings the quarter, and instead.']

② [In place of this sentence ed. 1 reads 'The home market is in this manner not so totally excluded from foreign supplies as it was before.']

③ [Ed. 1 reads By the same statute the old bounty of five shillings upon the quarter of wheat ceases when the price rises so high as forty-four shillings, and upon that of other grain in proportion. The bounties too upon the coarser sorts of grain are reduced somewhat lower than they were before, even at the prices at which they take place.]

— 1154 —

触。在那里,产业既不自由也不安全,西班牙和葡萄牙两国文明和基督教会的政府足以使它们的贫穷状态持久存在,尽管它们的通商条例是贤明的,可大部分其他条例是愚谬愚蠢的。

关于粮食的条例,乔治三世十三年第 43 号法令似乎建立了一种新的制度,在许多方面都比旧的条例好,但有那么一两处,却还不如旧的好。 <small>乔治三世十三年43号法令,</small>

根据这号法令,只要中等小麦价格涨至 1 夸特 48 先令,中等黑麦、豌豆或蚕豆涨至 32 先令,大麦涨至 24 先令,燕麦涨至 16 先令,供应国内消费的进口贸易所纳的高额关税都可免除,或者只需交小额的税。① 对 1 夸特小麦课税 6 便士,其他谷物以此为准。这样,就各种不同的谷物尤其是小麦来说,国内市场向外国货品敞开,而且价格比从前低得多。② <small>以更低的价格打开国内市场,</small>

根据同一法令,小麦价格涨至 1 夸特 40 先令(先前是 48 先令)时,小麦出口时 5 先令的旧津贴马上停止发放;大麦价格涨到每夸特 22 先令(先前是 24 先令)时,2 先令 6 便士的津贴即停止发放;燕麦粉价格涨至 1 夸特 14 先令(先前是 15 先令)时,2 先令 6 便士的津贴即停止发给。黑麦的津贴由 3 先令 6 便士降到了 3 先令;而且其价格涨至 28 先令(先前是 32 先令)时,津贴即停止发放。③ 我试图证明津贴不适当,如果真是这样,那么津贴停发 <small>早一些停发津贴,</small>

---

① 在版本 1 中为"根据这号法令,小麦价格一到 48 先令每夸特,供应国内消费的进口津贴就取消。"

② 在版本 1 中为"用这种方式,国内市场就不会像以前那样完全排斥国外供应品。"

③ 在版本 1 中,根据同一法令,小麦价格涨至 44 先令时,出口时 5 先令的旧津贴马上停止发放,其他粮食以此为比例;粗粮价格一旦比以前的低,也取消津贴。

| 国民财富的性质与原理 |

to prove them to be, the sooner they cease, and the lower they are, so much the better.

and admits corn for reexport duty free, The same statute permits, at the lowest prices, the importation of corn, in order to be exported again, duty free, provided it is in the meantime lodged in a warehouse under the joint locks of the king and the importer. ① This liberty, indeed, extends to no more than twenty-five of the different ports of Great Britain. They are, however, the principal ones, and there may not, perhaps, be warehouses proper for this purpose in the greater part of the others.

which are improvements, So far this law seems evidently an improvement upon the ancient system.

but it gives a bounty on the export of oats, But by the same law a bounty of two shillings the quarter is given for the exportation of oats whenever the price does not exceed fourteen shillings. No bounty had ever been given before for the exportation of this grain, no more than for that of peas or beans.

and prohibits exportation of grain at prices much too low. By the same law too, the exportation of wheat is prohibited so soon as the price rises to forty-four shillings the quarter; that of rye so soon as it rises to twenty-eight shillings; that of barley so soon as it rises to twenty-two shillings; and that of oats so soon as they rise to fourteen shillings. Those several prices seem all of them a good deal too low, and there seems to be an impropriety, besides, in prohibiting exportation altogether at those precise prices at which that bounty, which was given in order to force it, is withdrawn. ② The bounty ought certainly either to have been withdrawn at a much lower price, or exportation ought to have been allowed at a much higher.

It is as good a law as can be expected at present. So far, therefore, this law seems to be inferior to the ancient system. With all its imperfections, however, we may perhaps say of it what was said of the laws of Solon, that, though not the best in itself, it is the best which the interests, prejudices, and temper of the times would admit of. It may perhaps in due time prepare the way for a better.

---

① [Ed. 1 reads 'The same statute permits at all prices the importation of corn in order to be exported again, duty free; provided it is in the meantime lodged in the king's warehouse. ']

② [Ed. 1 reads (from the beginning of the paragraph) 'But by the same law exportation is prohibited as soon as the price of wheat rises to forty-four shillings the quarter, and that of other grain in proportion. The price seems to be a good deal too low, and there seems to be an impropriety besides in stopping exportation altogether at the very same price at which that bounty which was given in order to force it is withdrawn. ']

得越早,数目越小,就越好。

这项法令允许粮食(这些粮食是为了再出口的)在其价格达到最低的时候可以进口,而且免税,条件是必须放在国王与进口商共同掌管的仓库中。① 事实上,这种自由也仅仅扩大到不列颠 25 个不同海港,不过,那些都是主要的海港,其余大部分海港之所以没有这种自由也许是因为它们没有合适的仓库。

<small>允许再出口的粮食免税的改良措施</small>

就此看来,这项法令似乎明显比旧法令有所改进。

但这项法令又规定,燕麦价格不超过 14 先令时,每夸特给予 2 先令津贴。这种粮食的出口以前从来没有津贴,豌豆或蚕豆也没有。

<small>但又给燕麦出口发放津贴</small>

还是这项法令,规定小麦价格涨至每夸特 44 先令,黑麦价格涨至每夸特 28 先令,大麦价格涨至每夸特 22 先令,燕麦涨至每夸特 14 先令,即禁止出口。这几种价格似乎都太低了,在刚涨到这个宝贵的价格水平时,撤销津贴并禁止出口不太妥当。② 要么就在更低的价格时撤销津贴,要么就在价格更高时允许出口。

<small>禁止以太低的价格出口小麦</small>

所以,到现在为止,这项法令似乎还不如以前。它有许多不完善的地方,但是我们可引用前人对梭伦的法律所作的评价,也即,就它本身而言,尽管不是最好的,但它是在当时的利益、偏见和时代特征下所允许产生的最好制度。它或许会在适当的时候为更好的法律铺垫道路。

<small>它是目前所能期待的最好的法律</small>

---

① 在版本 1 中为"同一法令规定,已进口粮食再出口时,不管是什么价格,都免税,条件是必须放在国王与进口商共同掌管的仓库中"。

② 在版本 1 中为(这一段开始)"但是根据同一法律,小麦价格一升到每夸特 44 先令就禁止出口,其他粮食以此为比例。这个价格似乎太低了,而且在刚涨到同一价格水平时就禁止出口和撤销津贴不太妥当。"

CHAPTER VI
Of Treaties Of Commerce

Treaties of commerce are advantageous to the favoured, When a nation binds itself by treaty either to permit the entry of certain goods from one foreign country which it prohibits from all others, or to exempt the goods of one country from duties to which it subjects those of all others, the country, or at least the merchants and manufacturers of the country, whose commerce is so favoured, must necessarily derive great advantage from the treaty. Those merchants and manufacturers enjoy a sort of monopoly in the country which is so indulgent to them. That country becomes a market both more extensive and more advantageous for their goods: more extensive, because the goods of other nations being either excluded or subjected to heavier duties, it takes off a greater quantity of theirs: more advantageous, because the merchants of the favoured country, enjoying a sort of monopoly there, will often sell their goods for a better price than if exposed to the free competition of all other nations.

but disadvantageous to the favouring country. Such treaties, however, though they may be advantageous to the merchants and manufacturers of the favoured, are necessarily disadvantageous to those of the favouring country. A monopoly is thus granted against them to a foreign nation; and they must frequently buy the foreign goods they have occasion for, dearer than if the free competition of other nations was admitted. That part of its own produce with which such a nation purchases foreign goods, must consequently be sold cheaper, because when two things are exchanged for one another, the cheapness of the one is a necessary consequence, or rather is the same thing with the dearness of the other. The exchangeable value of its annual produce, therefore, is likely to be diminished by every

— 1158 —

第六章 论通商条约

当一个国家用条约束缚自己,只允许某一国的某种货物进入而禁止其他国家该货物的进入,或者免除某一国货物的关税而对其他国家的货物征税,那么这个在商业上受惠的国家,或至少是其商人和制造业者,必然会从条约中获得巨大的利益。这些商人和制造业者在一个对待他们相当照顾的国家中享有一种垄断权。而这个国家也就变成了一个对于他们的货物来说更为广阔、更为有利的市场。更为广阔,是因为其他国家的货物要么无法进入要么被征以更重的税,那么这个国家就容纳了更多的本国货物;更为有利,是因为受惠国的商人在该国享受了一种垄断权,往往能够以更好的价钱出售他们的货物,而这个价钱比和其他国家自由竞争时要低。 <small>通商条约对受惠国有利。</small>

尽管这些条约可能对受惠国的商人和制造业者有利,但对施惠国却必然是不利的。当把有害于自己的垄断权赋予某一外国时,他们常常必须在准许其他国家自由竞争的条件下以更高的价格购买外国货物。这个国家用以购买外国货物的那一部分本国产品因而必须以更低廉的价格出售,因为当两个物品相互交换时,一物的低价必然是另一物昂贵的结果,或者和它是一回事。因此,一国年产物的交换价值就可能被每一个这样的条约所削 <small>但是对施惠国不利。</small>

such treaty. This diminution, however, can scarce amount to any positive loss, but only to a lessening of the gain which it might otherwise make. Though it sells its goods cheaper than it otherwise might do, it will not probably sell them for less than they cost; nor, as in the case of bounties, for a price which will not replace the capital employed in bringing them to market, together with the ordinary profits of stock. The trade could not go on long if it did. Even the favouring country, therefore, may still gain by the trade, though less than if there was a free competition.

<small>Treaties have been concluded with the object of obtaining a favourable balance of trade, e. g., the Methuen treaty,</small>

Some treaties of commerce, however, have been supposed advantageous upon principles very different from these; and a commercial country has sometimes granted a monopoly of this kind against itself to certain goods of a foreign nation, because it expected that in the whole commerce between them, it would annually sell more than it would buy, and that a balance in gold and silver would be annually returned to it. It is upon this principle that the treaty of commerce between England and Portugal, concluded in 1703, by Mr. Methuen, has been so much commended. ① The following is a literal translation② of that treaty, which consists of three articles only.

ART. I

His sacred royal majesty of Portugal promises, both in his own name, and that of his successors, to admit, for ever hereafter, into Portugal, the woollen cloths, and the rest of the woollen manufactures of the British, as was accustomed, till they were prohibited by the law; nevertheless upon this condition:

ART. II

That is to say, that her sacred royal majesty of Great Britain shall, in her own name, and that of her successors, be obliged, for ever hereafter, to admit the wines of the growth of Portugal into Britain: so that at no time, whether there shall be peace or war between the

---

① [*E. g.* , in the *British Merchant*, 1721, Dedication to vol. iii.]

② [With three small exceptions, 'British' for 'Britons' and 'law' for 'laws' in art 1, and 'for' instead of 'from' before 'the like quantity or measure of French wine, ' the translation is identical with that given in *A Collection of all the Treaties of Peace, Alliance and Commerce between Great Britain and other Powers from the Revolution in* 1688 *to the Present Time*, 1772, vol. i. , pp. 61、62.]

减。然而,这种削减不可能导致绝对的损失,只是说会减少本来可以得到的利益。尽管一国出售货物的价格低于没有条约时的货物价格,但是它可能不会低于成本价出售,也不会在没有津贴的情况下,出售价格不能补偿将货物投放市场所需的资本以及提供普通的利润。否则这种贸易就不会长久。所以,即使是施惠国也还是可以通过贸易获利,尽管这个利益不如自由竞争条件下大。

可是,一些通商条约即使根据与此非常不同的原理仍被认为有利。有时,商业国给予某一外国的某种货物有害于本国的垄断权,是因为它期望在它们的全部商业贸易中,它能每年卖出的货物比买入的多,每年有金银差额流入本国。基于这个原理,英国和葡萄牙在 1703 年有梅休因先生订立的商业条约相当受推崇。①以下是该条约的直译,只有三条:②

第一条葡萄牙国王陛下以他自己和他继承人的名义约定,从今以后允许英国的呢绒和其他毛织品像以往一样进入葡萄牙,除非有法律禁止此贸易,但有以下条件:

第二条即英国国王陛下以她自己和她继承人的名义,从今以后永远准许葡萄牙生产的葡萄酒输入英国,无论英法两国是和是战,无论是用 105 加仑桶还是 52.5 加仑桶或者其他木桶将葡萄酒

---

① 例如,在《不列颠商人》中,1721 年,第 3 卷献词。
② 有三处小的异议,第一条中 British 代替了 Britons,law 代替了 laws,还有在"the like quantity or measure of French wine"之前 for 代替了 from。翻译在这本书中是一样的:《自 1688 年革命以来大不列颠和其他强国签订的所有和平条约、联合条约和通商条约汇编》,1772 年,第 1 卷,第 61、62 页。

kingdoms of Britain and France, any thing more shall be demanded for these wines by the name of custom or duty, or by whatsoever other title, directly or indirectly, whether they shall be imported into Great Britain in pipes or hogsheads, or other casks, than what shall be demanded for the like quantity or measure of French wine, deducting or abating a third part of the custom or duty. But if at any time this deduction or abatement of customs, which is to be made as aforesaid, shall in any manner be attempted and prejudiced, it shall be just and lawful for his sacred royal majesty of Portugal, again to prohibit the woollen cloths, and the rest of the British woollen manufactures.

ART. III

The most excellent lords the plenipotentiaries promise and take upon themselves that their above-named masters shall ratify this treaty; and within the space of two months the ratifications shall be exchanged.

which is evidently advantageous to Portugal and disadvantageous to Great Britain.

By this treaty the crown of Portugal becomes bound to admit the English woollens upon the same footing as before the prohibition; that is, not to raise the duties which had been paid before that time. But it does not become bound to admit them upon any better terms than those of any other nation, of France or Holland for example. The crown of Great Britain, on the contrary, becomes bound to admit the wines of Portugal, upon paying only two-thirds of the duty, which is paid for those of France, the wines most likely to come into competition with them. So far this treaty, therefore, is evidently advantageous to Portugal, and disadvantageous to Great Britain.

Portugal sends much gold to England;

It has been celebrated, however, as a masterpiece of the commercial policy of England. Portugal receives annually from the Brazils a greater quantity of gold than can be employed in its domestic commerce, whether in the shape of coin or of plate. The surplus is too valuable to be allowed to lie idle and locked up in coffers, and as it can find no advantageous market at home, it must, notwithstanding any prohibition, be sent abroad, and exchanged for something for which there is a more advantageous market at home. A large share of it comes annually to England, in return either for English goods, or for those of other European nations that receive their returns through England. Mr. Baretti was informed that the weekly packet-boat from Lisbon brings, one week with another, more than fifty thousand pounds in gold to England. ① The sum had probably

---

① [Joseph Baretti, *Journey from London to Genoa, through England, Portugal, Spain and France*, 3rd ed., 1770, vol. i., pp. 95,96, but the amount stated is not so large as in the text above: it is 'often' from thirty to fifty and even sixty thousand pounds, 'and not' one week with another 'but ' almost every week '. The gold all came in the packet boat because it, as a war vessel, was exempt from search. —Raynal, *Histoire philosophique*, Amsterdam ed. 1773, tom. iii., pp. 413,414.]

输入英国,都不得以关税、税收或者其他名义,直接或间接地征收比同量法国葡萄酒更多的税,同时,关税必须削减 1/3。如果在任何时候上述关税的削减在任何形式上被侵害,葡萄牙国王陛下重新禁止英国的呢绒和其他毛织品输入将是正当而合法的。

第三条 两国特命全权大使应负责烦请各自的国王批准条约,并在两个月之内交换批准的条约。

根据这项条约,葡萄牙国王有义务允许英国的毛织品以禁令以前的条件进口,即不能提高禁止以前支付的税额。但他没有义务以比其他任何国家(如法国或者荷兰)更好的条件进口英国的毛织品。而大不列颠国王却有义务让葡萄牙的葡萄酒以法国葡萄酒进入需支付的 2/3 的税额进口,后者是最有可能和前者竞争的。因此,这个条约就很明显对葡萄牙有利而对大不列颠不利。这显然有利于葡萄牙而不利于大不列颠。

然而,这么一项条约却被认为是英国商业政策上的杰作。葡萄牙每年从巴西获得大量黄金,比其以硬币或镀金器皿形式用于国内贸易的还多。剩余的黄金太有价值,闲置在金柜中不用太可惜,既然国内找不到有利的市场,所以尽管有禁止出口的禁令,它也必须被运往国外以交换在国内市场更为有利的物品。其中大部分每年流往英国,用来交换英国货物或者将货物运到英国做生意的其他欧洲国家的货物。巴勒特先生听说来自里斯木的定期邮船每周给英国带来平均 50000 磅以上的黄金①。这个数目可葡萄牙输送了不少黄金到英国;

---

① 约瑟夫·巴勒特:《从伦敦经英格兰、葡萄牙、西班牙和法国到热那亚的旅行》,第 3 版,1770 年,第 1 卷,第 95、96 页,但是数目没有文章中说的那么大:"常常"是从"三万到五万甚至六万磅",不是"每周"而是"几乎每周"。黄金全部用邮船运输,因为作为战舰,它可以免受检查。见雷纳尔:《哲学史》,阿姆斯特丹,1773 年,第 3 卷,第 413、414 页。

国民财富的性质与原理

been exaggerated. It would amount to more than two millions six hundred thousand pounds a year, which is more than the Brazils are supposed to afford. ①

Our merchants were some years ago out of humour with the crown of Portugal. Some privileges which had been granted them, not by treaty, but by the free grace of that crown, at the solicitation, indeed, it is probable, and in return for much greater favours, defence and protection, from the crown of Great Britain, had been either infringed or revoked. The people, therefore, usually most interested in celebrating the Portugal trade, were then rather disposed to represent it as less advantageous than it had commonly been imagined. The far greater part, almost the whole, they pretended, of this annual importation of gold, was not on account of Great Britain, but of other European nations; the fruits and wines of Portugal annually imported into Great Britain nearly compensating the value of the British goods sent thither.

Let us suppose, however, that the whole was on account of Great Britain, and that it amounted to a still greater sum than Mr. Baretti seems to imagine: this trade would not, upon that account, be more advantageous than any other in which, for the same value sent out, we received an equal value of consumable goods in return.

It is but a very small part of this importation which, it can be supposed, is employed as an annual addition either to the plate or to the coin of the kingdom. The rest must all be sent abroad and exchanged for consumable goods of some kind or other. But if those consumable goods were purchased directly with the produce of English industry, it would be more for the advantage of England, than first to purchase with that produce the gold of Portugal, and afterwards to purchase with that gold those consumable goods. A direct foreign trade of consumption is always more advantageous than a round-about one; and to bring the same value of foreign goods to the home market, requires a much smaller capital in the one way than in the other. If a smaller share of its industry, therefore, had been employed in producing goods fit for the Portugal market, and a greater in producing those fit for the other markets, where those consumable goods for which there is a demand in Great Britain are to be had, it would have been more for the advantage of England. To procure both the gold, which it wants for its own use, and the consumable goods, would, in this way, employ a much smaller capital than at present.

① [Raynal, Histoire Philosophique, vol. i, pp. 208, 209.]

能有些言过其实,否则一年总额会达到 260 万磅,这远远超过了巴西所能供给的量①。

几年前我国商人就对葡萄牙国王失去了好感。过去葡萄牙国王不是根据条约给予他们的特权要么被侵犯要么被取消。虽然这些特权由葡萄牙国王恩赐,或者的确是由商人要求的,但是葡萄牙却也得到了英国国王更多的恩惠、防卫和保护。因此,通常对赞美葡萄牙贸易最感兴趣的人们也觉得贸易的有利程度不及想象中的那么大。他们认为每年进口黄金中的大部分,甚至几乎是全部,并不有利于英国,而是惠及其他欧洲国家;每年输入英国的水果和葡萄酒几乎抵消了运往该国的英国货物的价值。

(边注:听说几乎全部的进口黄金都是为了他欧洲国家的利益,曾经是其中的。)

然而,让我们假设,全部黄金都是为了英国的利益,而且数额比巴勒特设想的似乎还要大,这种贸易也不能说是比出口货物价值和进口货物价值相等的贸易有利。

(边注:即便如此,这种贸易也不会比其他贸易更有价值。)

可以想象,这种进口只有极小一部分是用来增加每年国内镀金器皿和硬币的。其余的必定要被送往国外去交换某些消费品。但是如果这些消费品是直接用英国的本国产品来交换,而不是首先用英国产品购买葡萄牙黄金,然后用黄金来购买这种消费品,那就对英国更有利了。直接的消费品外贸总比迂回的消费品外贸更有利;而且把同样价值的外国货物引入国内市场所需的资本要少很多。因此,如果国内产业仅用小部分去生产葡萄牙市场需要的货物,而用大部分去生产适合其他市场的货物,而英国能从市场中得到它所需要的消费品,那这对英国来说是更为有利的。这样,英国为了得到自己所需的黄金和消费品所使用的资本比现

(边注:大部分黄金被送往国外交换货物,本国直接购买先在葡萄牙购买黄金更好。)

---

① 雷纳尔:《哲学史》,第 1 卷,第 208、209 页。

There would be a spare capital, therefore, to be employed for other purposes, in exciting an additional quantity of industry, and in raising a greater annual produce.

<small>Britain would find little difficulty in procuring gold even if excluded from trade with Portugal.</small>

Though Britain were entirely excluded from the Portugal trade, it could find very little difficulty in procuring all the annual supplies of gold which it wants, either for the purposes of plate, or of coin, or of foreign trade. Gold, like every other commodity, is always somewhere or another to be got for its value by those who have that value to give for it. The annual surplus of gold in Portugal, besides, would still be sent abroad, and though not carried away by Great Britain, would be carried away by some other nation, which would be glad to sell it again for its price, in the same manner as Great Britain does at present. In buying gold of Portugal, indeed, we buy it at the first hand; whereas, in buying it of any other nation, except Spain, we should buy it at the second, and might pay somewhat dearer. This difference, however, would surely be too insignificant to deserve the public attention.

<small>It is said that all our gold comes from Portugal, but if it did not come from Portugal it would come from other countries.</small>

Almost all our gold, it is said, comes from Portugal. With other nations the balance of trade is either against us, or not much in our favour. But we should remember, that the more gold we import from one country, the less we must necessarily import from all others. The effectual demand for gold, like that for every other commodity, is in every country limited to a certain quantity. If nine-tenths of this quantity are imported from one country, there remains a tenth only to be imported from all others. The more gold besides that is annually imported from some particular countries, over and above what is requisite for plate and for coin, the more must necessarily be exported to some others; and the more that most insignificant object of modern policy, the balance of trade, appears to be in our favour with some particular countries, the more it must necessarily appear to be against us with many others.

It was upon this silly notion, however, that England could not subsist without the Portugal trade, that, towards the end of the late war, France and Spain, without pretending either offence or provocation, required the king of Portugal to exclude all British ships from his ports, and for the security of this exclusion, to receive into them French or Spanish garrisons. Had the king of Portugal submitted to

今要少得多。于是,英国就会有多余的资本用于其他的方面,用来推进更多的产业和生产更多的产品。

即使英国完全不与葡萄牙通商,它也不难得到自己每年所需的用于制造镀金器皿、铸造硬币或对外贸易的所有黄金供应。黄金,像其他商品一样,对于有价值可以用来交换它的价值的人来说,总是能在这里或那里获得。葡萄牙每年多余的黄金仍然要运往国外,即使英国不买,其他国家也会去买。而这个国家又会像今天英国这样出售黄金获取价值。诚然,购买葡萄牙的黄金,我们是第一手购买;购买其他国家的黄金,除了西班牙的,我们是第二手购买,花的钱要多点。然而,这个差别太过微小,不值得政府注意。

据说,我们的黄金全部来自葡萄牙。与其他国家的贸易差额要么对我国不利,要么利益不大。但是我们应该记住,我们从一个国家进口黄金越多,从别国进口黄金就必然会越少。对黄金的有效需求,就像对其他商品的有效需求一样,在任何国家都有一定的数额限制。如果我国从一国进口该需求的9/10,那么从其他国家就只能进口1/10。每年从某些国家进口的黄金超过在镀金器皿和硬币上所需分量越多,向其他国家出口的黄金就越多;现行政策最无意义的目标——贸易差额,在某些国家看来越是对我们有利,那么在其他国家看来越是对我们不利。

然而,正是基于没有葡萄牙就没有英国贸易这种愚蠢的想法,在最近这次战争结束时,法国和西班牙没有借口受到侮辱或挑衅,就要求葡萄牙国王驱逐一切在葡萄牙港口的英国船只,并且为了阻止英国船只再次入港,他们要求葡萄牙接受法国或西班牙守备队进入港口。假如葡萄牙国王接受了其姻兄西班牙国王

| 国民财富的性质与原理

<small>If the attempt of France and Spain to exclude British ships from Portuguese ports had been successful, it would have been an advantage to England.</small> those ignominious terms which his brother-in-law the king of Spain proposed to him, Britain would have been freed from a much greater inconveniency than the loss of the Portugal trade, the burden of supporting a very weak ally, so unprovided of every thing for his own defence, that the whole power of England, had it been directed to that single purpose, could searce perhaps have defended him for another campaign. The loss of the Portugal trade would, no doubt, have occasioned a considerable embarrassment to the merchants at that time engaged in it, who might not, perhaps, have found out, for a year or two, any other equally advantageous method of employing their capitals; and in this would probably have consisted all the inconveniency which England could have suffered from this notable piece of commercial policy.

<small>The great importation of gold and silver is for foreign trade.</small> The great annual importation of gold and silver is neither for the purpose of plate nor of coin, but of foreign trade. A round-about foreign trade of consumption can be carried on more advantageously by means of these metals than of almost any other goods. As they are the universal instruments of commerce, they are more readily received in return for all commodities than any other goods; and on account of their small bulk and great value, it costs less to transport them backward and forward from one place to another than almost any other sort of merchandize, and they lose less of their value by being so transported. Of all the commodities, therefore, which are bought in one foreign country, for no other purpose but to be sold or exchanged again for some other goods in another, there are none so convenient as gold and silver. In facilitating all the different round-about foreign trades of consumption which are carried on in Great Britain, consists the principal advantage of the Portugal trade; and though it is not a capital advantage, it is, no doubt, a considerable one.

<small>Very little is required for plate and coin.</small> That any annual addition which, it can reasonably be supposed, is made either to the plate or to the coin of the kingdom, could require but a very small annual importation of gold and silver, seems evident enough; and though we had no direct trade with Portugal, this small quantity could always, somewhere or another, be very easily got.

<small>New gold plate is mostly made from old.</small> Though the goldsmiths trade be very considerable in Great Britain, the far greater part of the new plate which they annually sell, is made from other old plate melted down; so that the addition annually made to the whole plate of the kingdom cannot be very great, and could require but a very small annual importation.

It is the same case with the coin. Nobody imagines, I believe, that even the greater part of the annual coinage, amounting, for ten years together, before the late reformation of the gold coin, to upwards of eight hundred thousand pounds a year in gold,

所提出的这些侮辱性的条件,英国就可以从比失去与葡萄牙的贸易大得多的困境中解放出来,即支持一个在国防上毫无准备的弱小盟国,以至在一次战争中,英国即使倾尽全力恐怕也不能做有效的保卫。丧失葡萄牙贸易毫无疑问会给当时从事这种贸易的商人带来巨大的困难,使他们一两年内可能无法找到其他有利的支配资本的方法,这也许就是英国在这个引人注目的商业政策中所遭受的所有困难。

> 如果西班牙和法国将船只驱逐葡萄牙港口的企图得以成功,那将会对英国有利。

每年大量的金银进口既不是为了制造镀金器皿也不是为了铸造硬币,而是为了进行国外贸易。迂回的消费品外贸用这种金属比用几乎任何其他货物能更加有利地进行。金银是普遍的商业手段,相对于其他商品来说更容易被人们接受从而换取商品,因为它们体积小价值大,比其他商品来回地从一地运到另一地花费要少,而且在运输过程中损失的价值也少。因此,所有的商品中,如果要在某一外国购买而在其他外国销售以换取其他商品,金银是最为便利的了。葡萄牙贸易的主要好处是促进英国进行的各种迂回的消费品外贸。尽管这不是一种最重要的利益,但这无疑是一个相当大的利益。

> 对外贸易大量进口黄金。

据合理假定,每年为增加国内的镀金器皿和硬币仅需少量的金银进口,这似乎很明显;尽管我们和葡萄牙没有直接贸易,这少量的金银总是能很轻易地从其他地方得到。

> 镀金器皿和硬币需要的金银非常少。

虽然金匠行业在英国非常大,但是每年出售的大部分的新镀金器皿都是由旧器皿熔化制成的。所以全国每年增加的器皿数量不是很大,只需要很少量的黄金进口。

> 新的镀金器皿大部分是用旧器皿改铸的。

硬币的情况也是一样。我相信,没有人会想到,最近金币改铸以前的10年间,每年铸造的80万磅金币的大部分是对以前国

国民财富的性质与原理

New coin is mostly made from old, as there is a profit on melting good coin. was an annual addition to the money before current in the kingdom. In a country where the expence of the coinage is defrayed by the government, the value of the coin, even when it contains its full standard weight of gold and silver, can never be much greater than that of an equal quantity of those metals uncoined; because it requires only the trouble of going to the mint, and the delay perhaps of a few weeks, to procure for any quantity of uncoined gold and silver an equal quantity of those metals in coin. But, in every country, the greater part of the current coin is almost always more or less worn, or otherwise degenerated from its standard. In Great Britain it was, before the late reformation, a good deal so, the gold being more than two per cent. and the silver more than eight per cent. below its standard weight. But if forty-four guineas and a half, containing their full standard weight, a pound weight of gold, could purchase very little more than a pound weight of uncoined gold, forty-four guineas and a half wanting a part of their weight could not purchase a pound weight, and something was to be added in order to make up the deficiency. The current price of gold bullion at market, therefore, instead of being the same with the mint price, or 46*l*. 14*s*. 6*d*. was then about 47*l*. 14*s*. and sometimes about forty-eight pounds. When the greater part of the coin, however, was in this degenerate condition, forty-four guineas and a half, fresh from the mint, would purchase no more goods in the market than any other ordinary guineas, because when they came into the coffers of the merchant, being confounded with other money, they could not afterwards be distinguished without more trouble than the difference was worth. Like other guineas they were worth no more than 46 *l*. 14 *s*. 6 *d*. If thrown into the melting pot, however, they produced, without any sensible loss, a pound weight of standard gold, which could be sold at any time for between 47 *l*. 14*s*. and 48 *l*. either in gold or silver, as fit for all the purposes of coin as that which had been melted down. There was an evident profit, therefore, in melting down new coined money, and it was done so instantaneously, that no precaution of government could prevent it. The operations of the mint were, upon this account, somewhat like the web of Penelope; the work that was done in the day was undone in the night. The mint was employed, not so much in making daily additions to the coin, as in replacing the very best part of it which was daily melted down.

Were the private people, who carry their gold and silver to the mint, to pay themselves for the coinage, it would add to the value of those metals in the same manner as the fashion does to that of plate.

内流通的货币的增加额。在铸币费用由政府负担的国家,即使硬币包含了充分的标准重量的金银,其价值也不会比等量的未铸成硬币的金属的价值大多少。因为任何数量的未铸造的金银,只需不怕麻烦到造币厂去一下,等上几个星期,就能得到等量的金银硬币。不过每个国家的大部分的流通硬币都或多或少有些磨损,或由于其他原因而低于它的标准。英国在最近的改铸以前就是这样,金币低于标准重量的程度达2%以上,而银币则达8%以上。但是如果足够标准重量的44几尼半(即1磅金)只能购买比1磅多一点的未铸硬币,那么,重量低于1磅重的44几尼半就买不到1磅重的未铸黄金,因而必须增加一些来补足差额。所以,市场上的金币流通价格不是和造币厂的46镑14先令6便士一样,而是47镑14先令,有时大约是48镑。然而,当大部分硬币处于这种低标准状态时,从造币厂新铸的44几尼半的金币在市场上不会买到比普通几尼能购买的更多的货物;因为当它们在商人金柜中和其他货币混在一起后,就难以辨认,即使辨认,所费也多于所值。就像其他几尼一样,新铸几尼只值46镑14先令6便士。但是,如果将它们投入熔炉中,就能产生1磅重的标准金,几乎没有什么损失,在任何时候都能换得金币或银币47镑14先令或48镑,像被熔化的硬币一样用于各种用途。熔化新铸造的硬币显然有利可图,人们纷纷立即这样做,政府的任何防范措施均为无效。基于这一点,造币厂的工作有些像传说中的潘内洛普网,白天做的晚上就予以拆除。造币厂与其说是逐日增加硬币,不如说是替换每天熔化的硬币的最好的部分。

　　如果将他们的金银送往铸币厂的私人自己出铸币的费用,那么这就会增加金银的价值,如同加工费会增加镀金器皿的价值一

新硬币大部分旧硬币是改铸的,因为熔化良币有利可图。

| 国民财富的性质与原理

A seignorage raises the value of coin above that of bullion of equal weight,

Coined gold and silver would be more valuable than uncoined. The seignorage, if it was not exorbitant, would add to the bullion the whole value of the duty; because, the government having every where the exclusive privilege of coining, no coin can come to market cheaper than they think proper to afford it. If the duty was exorbitant indeed, that is, if it was very much above the real value of the labour and expence requisite for coinage, false coiners, both at home and abroad, might be encouraged, by the great difference between the value of bullion and that of coin, to pour in so great a quantity of counterfeit money as might reduce the value of the government money. In France, however, though the seignorage is eight per cent. no sensible inconveniency of this kind is found to arise from it. The dangers to which a false coiner is every where exposed, if he lives in the country of which he counterfeits the coin, and to which his agents or correspondents are exposed if he lives in a foreign country, are by far too great to be incurred for the sake of a profit of six or seven per cent.

as in France

The seignorage in France raises the value of the coin higher than in proportion to the quantity of pure gold which it contains. Thus by the edict of January 1726, the ① mint price of fine gold of twenty-four carats was fixed at seven hundred and forty livres nine sous and one denier one-eleventh, the mark of eight Paris ounces. The gold coin of France, making an allowance for the remedy of the mint, contains twenty-one carats and three-fourths of fine gold, and two carats one-fourth of alloy. The mark of standard gold, therefore, is worth no more than about six hundred and seventy-one livres ten deniers. But in France this mark of standard gold is coined into thirty Louisd'ors of twenty-four livres each, or into seven hundred and twenty livres. The coinage, therefore, increases the value of a mark of standard gold bullion, by the difference between six hundred and seventy-one livres ten deniers, and seven hundred and twenty livres; or by forty-eight livres nineteen sous and two deniers.

---

① See *Dictionaire des Monnoies*, tom ii. article Seigneurage, p. 489. par M. Abot de Bazinghen, Conseiller-Commissaire en la Cour des Monnoies à. Paris. Garnier, in his edition of the *Wealth of Nations*, vol. v. , p. 234, says the book 'n' est guére qu'une compilation faite sans soin et sans discernement, ' and explains that the mint price mentioned above remained in force a very short time. It having failed to bring bullion to the mint, much higher prices were successively offered, and when the *Wealth of Nations* was published the seignorage only amounted to about 3 per cent. On the silver coin it was then about 2 per cent. , in place of the 6 per cent.]

样。经过铸造成为货币的金银会比未经铸造的金银价值更高。铸币税要是不太重,会以其全部价值加入金银的价值之内。因为,政府在任何地方都享有铸币的特权,没有硬币能够以比此更低的价值进入市场。如果税费收太高,也就是说,收的税如果大于铸币所需劳动和花销的实际价值,那么国内国外的伪造货币者会受金银和硬币之间巨大的价值差的鼓励,把大量的伪币注入国内市场,从而可能降低政府货币的价值。可是,在法国,尽管铸币税是8%,但从未发现有任何明显的不便。住在国内进行伪造的伪造货币者以及其在国外的代理人或通信人危机四伏,仅仅为了6%或7%的利润去冒险未免不值。

法国的铸币税使硬币价值在比例上高于它所含纯金量。因此,根据法国政府1726年1月令,24克拉纯金的铸币厂价格是740里弗9苏1$\frac{1}{11}$迪尼厄,合巴黎的8盎司的1马克①。扣除铸币厂的公差,法国金币包含21.75克拉纯金和2.25卡拉合金。所以,标准金1马克价值不会超过671里弗零10迪尼厄。但在法国,标准金1马克被铸成30个金路易,每个24里弗,总共720里弗。可见,铸币税增加了标准金1马克的价值,即671里弗零10迪尼厄与720里弗之间的差额,也就是增加了48里弗19苏2迪尼厄的价值。

---

① 参见《货币辞典》,第2卷,铸币税条款,第489页,M.阿博·得·加尼尔(法语Garnier),在他的《国民财富的性质与原理》,第5卷,第234页提到(法语),并解释说上述提到的造币厂价格在非常短的时间内仍将大规模地保持。它没能将金银送入造币厂,却提供了更高的价格。当《国民财富的性质与原理》出版时,铸币税只有大约3%,银币只有大约2%,不是6%。

| 国民财富的性质与原理

It diminishes or destroys the profit obtained by melting coin.

A seignorage will, in many cases, take away altogether, and will, in all cases, diminish the profit of melting down the new coin. This profit always arises from the difference between the quantity of bullion which the common currency ought to contain, and that which it actually does contain. If this difference is less than the seignorage, there will be loss instead of profit. If it is equal to the seignorage, there will neither be profit nor loss. If it is greater than the seignorage, there will indeed be some profit, but less than if there was no seignorage. If, before the late reformation of the gold coin, for example, there had been a seignorage of five per cent. upon the coinage, there would have been a loss of three per cent. upon the melting down of the gold coin. If the seignorage had been two per cent. there would have been neither profit nor loss. If the seignorage had been one per cent. there would have been a profit, but of one per cent. only instead of two per cent. Wherever money is received by tale, therefore, and not by weight, a seignorage is the most effectual preventative of the melting down of the coin, and, for the same reason, of its exportation, It is the best and heaviest pieces that are commonly either melted down or exported; because it is upon such that the largest profits are made.

The abolition of seignorage in England was probably due to the bank of England,

The law for the encouragement of the coinage, by rendering it dutyfree, was first enacted, during the reign of Charles Ⅱ. for a limited time; and afterwards continued, by different prolongations, till 1769, when it was rendered perpetual. The bank of England, in order to replenish their coffers with money, are frequently obliged to carry bullion to the mint; and it was more for their interest, they probably imagined, that the coinage should be at the expence of the government, than at their own. It was, probably, out of complaisance to this great company that the government agreed to render this law perpetual. Should the custom of weighing gold, however, come to be disused, as it is very likely to be on account of its inconveniency;

but the bank would have lost nothing by a seignorage whether it equalled the depreciation,

should the gold coin of England come to be received by tale, as it was before the late recoinage, this great company may, perhaps, find that they have upon this, as upon some other occasions, mistaken their own interest not a little.

Before the late recoinage, when the gold currency of England was two per cent. below its standard weight, as there was no seignorage, it was two per cent. below the value of that quantity of standard gold bullion which it ought to have contained. When this great company, therefore, bought gold bullion in order to have it coined, they were obliged to pay for it two per cent. more than it was worth after

— 1174 —

铸币税在很多情况下会完全消除熔铸新硬币获得的利润,在所有的情况下会减少这种利润。这种利润通常来源于普通货币应当含有的金银数量和实际含有的数量之间的差。如果这个差小于铸币税,那么熔铸新硬币就既不存在利润也不存在损失。如果这个差大于铸币税,的确会有一些利润,但是会比没有征收铸币税时少。例如,如果在最近一次改铸之前铸币税税率为5%,那么在熔化过程中就有3%的损失。若铸币税税率为2%,那么就会没有利润或损失。如果铸币税税率是1%,那么就只会有1%的利润而不会是2%。因此,当货币以个数而不是重量接受时,铸币税就是防止熔解硬币和硬币出口最有效的办法。通常被熔解或被出口的硬币是最好最重的硬币,因为只有用它们才能获得最大的利润。

> 铸币税减少或消除了熔铸硬币的利润。

用免税鼓励铸币的法律,是在查理二世统治时制定的,但只在一段时间内有效。以后经过了不同时间的延长,到1769年才成为永久法律。英国银行为了向金柜补充货币,不得不经常将金银送到铸币厂;它们或许认为,由政府支付铸币费用而不是由它们自己支付会更能获益。可能是出于尊重这个公司的要求,政府同意此法律永久化。然而,如果废除称量黄金的习惯(因为称量不方便所以很有可能实现),如果英国金币以个数接受(就像最近一次改铸以前那样),这家大公司或许会发现,它们这次和其他几次一样,大大错误估计了它们的自身利益了。

> 英国取消铸币税可能是由于银行的缘故。

在最近一次改铸以前,由于没有铸币税,英国金币低于标准重量2%,它的价值也比它应该含有的标准金银量价值低2%。因此,当这个大公司为了铸币购买金银时,它必须要付出比铸造后的硬币价值还多2%的价值。但是如果对铸币征收一个2%的

> 采用铸币税,银行会遭任何损失,无论其是否与贬值相等。

the coinage. But if there had been a seignorage of two per cent. upon the coinage, the common gold currency, though two per cent. below its standard weight, would notwithstanding have been equal in value to the quantity of standard gold which it ought to have contained; the value of the fashion compensating in this case the diminution of the weight. They would indeed have had the seignorage to pay, which being two per cent. their loss upon the whole transaction would have been two per cent. exactly the same, but no greater than it actually was.

<small>exceeded it,</small>
If the seignorage had be en five per cent and the gold currency only two per cent. below its standard weight, the bank would in this case have gained three per cent. upon the price of the bullion; but as they would have had a seignorage of five per cent. to pay upon the coinage, their loss upon the whole transaction would, in the same manner, have been exactly two per cent.

<small>or fell short of it.</small>
If the seignorage had been only one per cent and the gold currency two per cent. below its standard weight, the bank would in this case have lost only one per cent. upon the price of the bullion; but as they would likewise have had a seignorage of one per cent. to pay, their loss upon the whole transaction would have been exactly two per cent. in the same manner as in all other cases.

<small>Nor would it lose if there were no depreciation,</small>
If there was a reasonable seignorage, while at the same time the coin contained its full standard weight, as it has done very nearly since the late re-coinage, whatever the bank might lose by the seignorage, they would gain upon the price of the bullion; and whatever they might gain upon the price of the bullion, they would lose by the seignorage. They would neither lose nor gain, therefore, upon the whole transaction, and they would in this, as in all the foregoing cases, be exactly in the same situation as if there was no seignorage.

<small>A seignorage is paid by no one,</small>
When the tax upon a commodity is so moderate as not to encourage smuggling, the merchant who deals in it, though he advances, does not properly pay the tax, as he gets it back in the price of the commodity. The tax is finally paid by the last purchaser or consumer. But money is a commodity with regard to which every man is a merchant. Nobody buys it but in order to sell it again; and with regard to it there is in ordinary cases no last purchaser or consumer. When the tax upon coinage, therefore, is so moderate as not to encourage false coining, though every body advances the tax, nobody finally pays it; because every body gets it back in the advanced value of the coin.

铸币税，那么普通金币尽管比标准重量低2%却有着和应含的标准金量相等的价值；在这里，铸造的价值抵消了重量的不足。的确，它们应该支付这2%的铸币税，但是它们在整个业务中损失的也正好是2%，不比实际中的损失大。

如果铸币税是5%，金币只低于其标准重量2%，这种情况下，银行会在金银上赚3%，但由于它们在铸币时会付5%的铸币税，所以它们在整个业务中正好同样要损失掉2%。_{铸币税超过贬值，}

如果铸币税只有1%，金币低于其标准重量2%，这种情况下，银行会在金银价上损失1%，但由于它们在铸币时会付5%的铸币税，所以它们在整个业务中损失的跟其他情况下一样也是2%。_{铸币税不及贬值。}

如果铸币税合理，同时硬币含有十足的标准重量，就像它在最近改铸以来含金量十足那样，那么不管银行因为铸币税损失多少，它在金银价格上就会得到多少；不管它在金银价格上得到多少，它在铸币税上就会损失多少。因此，它们在整个业务中既没有损失也没有利益，它们会像在所有其他情况下一样，就好像没有铸币税那样。_{没有贬值，银行也不会损失。}

当一种商品被征收的税相当适度而没有引发走私时，经营这种商品的商人虽然预付了此种税，但他也能在商品价格中将它了回来。这个税最终会由最后的购买者或者消费者来支付。但是货币是一种商品，在这个情况下，每个人都是商人。没有人不是为了再次出售而购买商品，在一般情况下货币是不会有最后的购买者或消费者。因此，当一种商品被征收的税相当适度而没有引发造假币时，虽然每一个人预付了这种赋税，但是也没有人最后支付它，因为每个人都从硬币增加的价值上寻回了。_{铸币税没有人支付，}

and could not have augmented the expense of the bank.	A moderate seignorage, therefore, would not in any case augment the expence of the bank, or of any other private persons who carry their bullion to the mint in order to be coined, and the want of a moderate seignorage does not in any case diminish it. Whether there is or is not a seignorage, if the currency contains its full standard weight, the coinage costs nothing to any body, and if it is short of that weight, the coinage must always cost the difference between the quantity of bullion which ought to be contained in it, and that which actually is contained in it.
The government loses and nobody gains by the absence of seignorage.	The government, therefore, when it defrays the expence of coinage, not only incurs some small expence, but loses some small revenue which it might get by a proper duty; and neither the bank nor any other private persons are in the smallest degree benefited by this useless piece of public generosity. The directors of the bank, however, would probably be unwilling to agree to the imposition of a seignorage upon the authority of a speculation which promises them no gain, but only pretends to insure them from any loss. In the present state of the gold coin, and as long as it
Supposing the coin should again become depreciated, a seignorage would preserve the bank from considerable loss.	continues to be received by weight, they certainly would gain nothing by such a change. But if the custom of weighing the gold coin should ever go into disuse, as it is very likely to do, and if the gold coin should ever fall into the same state of degradation in which it was before the late recoinage, the gain, or more properly the savings of the bank, in consequence of the imposition of a seignorage, would probably be very considerable. The bank of England is the only company which sends any considerable quantity of bullion to the mint, and the burden of the annual coinage falls entirely, or almost entirely, upon it. If this annual coinage had nothing to do but to repair the unavoidable losses and necessary wear and tear of the coin, it could seldom exceed fifty thousand or at most a hundred thousand pounds. But when the coin is degraded below its standard weight, the annual coinage must, besides this, fill up the large vacuities which exportation and the melting pot are continually making in the current coin. It was upon this account that during the ten or twelve years immediately preceding the late reformation of the gold coin, the annual coinage amounted at an average to more than eight hundred and fifty thousand pounds. But if there had been a seignorage of four or five per cent. upon the gold coin, it would probably, even in the state in which things then were, have put an effectual stop to the business both of exportation and of the melting pot. The bank, instead of losing every year about two and a half per cent. upon the bullion which was to be coined into more than eight hundred and fifty thousand pounds, or incurring an annual loss of more than twenty-one thousand two hundred and fifty pounds, would not probably have incurred the tenth part of that loss.

第四篇 第六章

可见,适度的铸币税不会增加银行的费用,也不会增加将金银送往铸币厂去铸造硬币的任何私人开支。不管有没有铸币税,如果通货中含有足够的标准重量,铸造不会花任何人的钱;如果重量不足,铸造费就是铸币应该含有的金银和实际含有金银之差。

> 它不会增加银行的开支。

当政府支付铸造费用时,它不仅承担小额的费用,还损失了通过适当的税收得到的小额的收入;银行和任何个人都没有从这种徒劳的慷慨中得到任何好处。

> 铸造政府有损失,但不交税政府有损失,也没有人得利。

然而,银行的董事们可能不愿意仅仅根据这一推测就同意征收铸币税,这一推测不能承诺兑现他们的利润,而只能保证他们免于损失。以金币目前的状况看,只要继续按秤量被接受,他们肯定没法从这样一个改变中得到利益。但是,如果秤量金币的习惯一旦被废除(这是很可能被废除的),如果金币的质量又降低到最近一次改铸前的水平,那么银行通过征收铸币税的所得,或者更确切地说是银行的储蓄,可能会相当大。英国银行是把大量金银送往铸币厂,每年铸币的费用全部或基本上全部由它负担的唯一一家公司。如果每年铸币只是为了弥补不可避免的损失和必要的硬币磨损,那费用就极少会超过五万镑,最多也不超过 10 万镑。但是如果硬币重量低于标准重量,每年铸币要弥补除了这个以外由于不断出口和熔化而连续不断地产生的硬币缺口。由于这个原因,在最近金币改铸前的 10 到 20 年间,每年铸造的金币平均 85 万镑。但是如果对金币征收 4% 或 5% 的铸造税,那么即使在当时的情况下,还是有可能有效阻止硬币出口和熔铸的。银行每年不会为了把金银熔铸成 85 万镑以上金币而损失大约 2.5%,或者说不会损失 21250 镑以上,它的损失可能还不到这个数字

> 假设硬币重新变得贬值了,铸造税会让银行避免重大损失。

| 国民财富的性质与原理

The saving to the government may be regarded as too trifling, but that of the bank is worth consideration.

The revenue allotted by parliament for defraying the expence of the coinage is but fourteen thousand pounds a year, ① and the real expence which it costs the government, or the fees of the officers of the mint, do not upon ordinary occasions, I am assured, exceed the half of that sum. The saving of so very small a sum, or even the gaining of another which could not well be much larger, are objects too inconsiderable, it may be thought, to deserve the serious attention of government. But the saving of eighteen or twenty thousand pounds a year in case of an event which is not improbable, which has frequently happened before, and which is very likely to happen again, is surely an object which well deserves the serious attention even of so great a company as the bank of England.

Some of the foregoing reasonings and observations might perhaps have been more properly placed in those chapters of the first book which treat of the origin and use of money, and of the difference between the real and the nominal price of commodities. But as the law for the encouragement of coinage derives its origin from those vulgar prejudices which have been introduced by the mercantile system; I judged it more proper to reserve them for this chapter. Nothing could be more agreeable to the spirit of that system than a sort of bounty upon the production of money, the very thing which, it supposes, constitutes the wealth of every nation. It is one of its many admirable expedients for enriching the country.

---

① [Under 19 Geo. II., c. 14, §2, a maximum of £ 15,000 is prescribed.]

— 1180 —

的 10%。

　　由议会分配下来用来支付铸币的费用每年只有 14000 镑[①]，而政府的实际开支，或铸币厂职员的费用，我确定通常不会超过该数目的一半。可能有人会认为，节省如此小的数目，甚至是得到比这大不了多少的另一批钱，太不值得政府认真重视了。但是一年 18000 英镑或 20000 英镑的节省并非不可能，过去常常发生过，将来也有可能再次发生，这对于英国银行如此大的公司来说显然是一件值得认真考虑的事情。

　　上述论证和观察，有些更适合于放在第一部分中的章节，它们讲的是论货币起源及其用途，以及论商品真实价格与名义价格的区别。但是，由于鼓励铸币的法律起源于重商主义体系的庸俗偏见，所以我认为放在本章更适合。没有什么比给予货币生产奖励更符合那个体系的精神的了，货币是构成国家财富的东西。奖励货币生产是重商主义体系下使国家富裕的一条最好的政策。

> 政府的储蓄可能会很少，但是银行的储蓄值得考虑。

[①] 根据乔治二世十九年第 14 号法律第 2 条，最高为 15000 镑。

CHAPTER VII
Of Colonies

Part First   Of The Motives For Establishing New Colonies

The interest which occasioned the first settlement of the different European colonies in America and the West Indies, was not altogether so plain and distinct as that which directed the establishment of those of ancient Greece and Rome.

<small>Greek colonies were sent out when the population grew too great at home. The mother city claimed no authority.</small> All the different states of ancient Greece possessed, each of them, but a very small territory, and when the people in any one of them multiplied beyond what that territory could easily maintain, a part of them were sent in quest of a new habitation in some remote and distant part of the world; the warlike neighbours who surrounded them on all sides, rendering it difficult for any of them to enlarge very much its territory at home. The colonies of the Dorians resorted chiefly to Italy and Sicily, which, in the times preceding the foundation of Rome, were inhabited by barbarous and uncivilized nations: those of the Ionians and Eolians, the two other great tribes of the Greeks, to Asia Minor and the islands of the Egean Sea, of which the inhabitants seem at that time to have been pretty much in the same state as those of Sicily and Italy. The mother city, though she considered the colony as a child, at all times entitled to great favour and assistance, and owing in return much gratitude and respect, yet considered it as an emancipated child, over whom she pretended to claim no direct authority or jurisdiction. The colony settled its own form of government, enacted its own laws, elected its own magistrates, and made peace or war with its neighbours as an independent state, which had no occasion to wait for the approbation or consent of the mother city. Nothing can be more plain and distinct than the interest which directed every such establishment.

第七章　论殖民地

第一部分　论建立新殖民地的动机

使欧洲人在美洲和西印度建立第一批殖民地的利益,不如在古希腊和罗马建立殖民地的利益那么明显。

每个古希腊城邦只有非常小的领地,当一城邦的人口数增加到本国领土不能轻易承受的状态时,他们中的一部分人会被送出去,到世界上一些遥远的地方寻找新的住所。围绕在他们周围好战的邻邦使他们难以在本国扩大自己的领土。多里安人的殖民地主要在意大利和西西里,这两地在罗马建国之前均为野蛮和未开化民族的居住地。伊沃尼亚人和伊沃利亚人(希腊另外两大部落)的殖民地在小亚细亚和爱琴海各岛,当时这两个地方居民的状态似乎和西西里与意大利的极为相似。母市虽然把殖民地当作孩子,随时给予巨大的恩惠和帮助,并且受到他的很大的感恩和尊敬,但依然把他当作是一个被解放的孩子,不对他拥有任何主权或管辖权。殖民地建立自己的政府形式,采用自己的法律,选举自己的官员,作为一个独立的国家对邻国宣战或媾和,不用等待母市的批准或同意。没有什么事情比建立每一个这样的殖民地的动机更明显。

国内增多希腊殖民地建立。母市不行使权力。当人口太多时殖民地得以建立。

| 国民财富的性质与原理

Roman colonies were sent out to satisfy the demand for lands and to establish garrisons in conquered territories; they were entirely subject to the mother city.
Rome, like most of the other ancient republics, was originally founded upon an Agrarian law, which divided the public territory in a certain proportion among the different citizens who composed the state. The course of human affairs, by marriage, by succession, and by alienation, necessarily deranged this original division, and frequently threw the lands, which had been allotted for the maintenance of many different families into the possession of a single person. To remedy this disorder, for such it was supposed to be, a law was made, restricting the quantity of land which any citizen could possess to five hundred jugera, about three hundred and fifty English acres. This law, however, though we read of its having been executed upon one or two occasions, was either neglected or evaded, and the inequality of fortunes went on continually increasing. The greater part of the citizens had no land, and without it the manners and customs of those times rendered it difficult for a freeman to maintain his independency. In the present times, though a poor man has no land of his own, if he has a little stock, he may either farm the lands of another, or he may carry on some little retail trade; and if he has no stock, he may find employment either as a country labourer, or as an artificer. But, among the ancient Romans, the lands of the rich were all cultivated by slaves, who wrought under an overseer, who was likewise a slave; so that a poor freeman had little chance of being employed either as a farmer or as a labourer. All trades and manufactures too, even the retail trade, were carried on by the slaves of the rich for the benefit of their masters, whose wealth, authority, and protection made it difficult for a poor freeman to maintain the competition against them. The citizens, therefore, who had no land, had scarce any other means of subsistence but the bounties of the candidates at the annual elections. The tribunes, when they had a mind to animate the people against the rich and the great, put them in mind of the ancient division of lands, and represented that law which restricted this sort of private property as the fundamental law of the republic. The people became clamorous to get land, and the rich and the great, we may believe, were perfectly determined not to give them any part of theirs. To satisfy them in some measure, therefore, they frequently proposed to send out a new colony. But conquering Rome was,

罗马也像大多数其他的古代共和国一样，最初建立在一种土地分配法的基础上。这种分配法是在组成国家的不同公民之间按照一定的比例来划分公共领土。人类事务的变化，如结婚、继承、转让，必然打乱这种最初的分配格局，常常使那些分配给许多不同家庭用以维持生计的土地集中到一个人的手中。为了修复这种混乱，当时人们就是认为这是混乱，一部法律得以制定，严格限制土地的拥有量，法律规定每个公民能拥有的土地为500朱格拉，合350英亩。然而，尽管我们了解这部法律在一两个场合被执行过，却要么被忽略要么被回避，因而财富不均呈继续扩大化趋势。大部分的公民没有土地，而在当时的风俗习惯下，没有土地就使得一个自由人难以维持他的独立性。现在，虽然穷人没有自己的土地，但是如果他有一点点资本，他就可以耕种其他人的土地或者做一点零售买卖；如果他没有资本，他也可以找到工作，要么当农村的劳动者要么做工匠。但是，在古罗马，富人的土地全部由奴隶耕种，奴隶们在监工监视下工作，而监工自己也是奴隶；因此贫穷的自由人几乎没有机会被雇为农场主或者劳动者。所有的商业和制造业，甚至是零售贸易，也是富人的奴隶为了他们主人的利益而经营的，而主人的财富、权力和保护使得贫穷的自由人难以同他们竞争。所以，没有土地的公民，除了在每年的选举中得到候选人的赠金外，几乎没有其他的手段来谋生。当护民官想要激起民愤来反对富人时，他们就回想起古代的土地分配，并指出这一限制私人财产的法律是共和国的基本法。人们变得吵吵嚷嚷，要求得到土地，而我们可以相信，富人们绝对不会分给他们任何土地。因此，为了某种程度上满足他们，富人们常常提出到外面建立新的殖民地。但是，作为征服者的罗马，在这样的场合

罗马殖民地是为了满足需要对土地的服征服部领他土建们备完母全市属于队立的和领守土

even upon such occasions, under no necessity of turning out her citizens to seek their fortune, if one may say so, through the wide world, without knowing where they were to settle. She assigned them lands generally in the conquered provinces of Italy, where, being within the dominions of the republic, they could never form any independent state; but were at best but a sort of corporation, which, though it had the power of enacting byelaws for its own government, was at all times subject to the correction, jurisdiction, and legislative authority of the mother city. The sending out a colony of this kind, not only gave some satisfaction to the people, but often established a sort of garrison too in a newly conquered province, of which the obedience might otherwise have been doubtful. A Roman colony, therefore, whether we consider the nature of the establishment itself, or the motives for making it, was altogether different from a Greek one. The words accordingly, which in the original languages denote those different establishments, have very different meanings. The Latin word (*Colonia*) signifies simply a plantation. The Greek word (αποικια), on the contrary, signifies a separation of dwelling, a departure from home, a going out of the house. But, though the Roman colonies were in many respects different from the Greek ones, the interest which prompted to establish them was equally plain and distinct. Both institutions derived their origin either from irresistible necessity, or from clear and evident utility.

The utility of the American colonies is not so evident.
The establishment of the European colonies in America and the West Indies arose from no necessity: and though the utility which has resulted from them has been very great, it is not altogether so clear and evident. It was not understood at their first establishment, and was not the motive either of that establishment or of the discoveries which gave occasion to it; and the nature, extent, and limits of that utility are not, perhaps, well understood at this day.

The Venetians had a profitable trade in East India goods,
The Venetians, during the fourteenth and fifteenth centuries, carried on a very advantageous commerce in spiceries, and other East India goods, which they distributed among the other nations of Europe. They purchased them chiefly in Egypt, at that time under the dominion of the Mammeluks, the enemies of the Turks, of whom the Venetians were the enemies; and this union of interest, assisted by the money of Venice, formed such a connection as gave the Venetians almost a monopoly of the trade.

The great profits of the Venetians tempted the avidity of the Portu-

下,也没有必要把它的公民送到外面去寻找财富,因为它不清楚他们会在什么地方定居。它一般给予他们被征服的意大利省份的土地,这些土地在共和国的统治范围内,因而他们就不会建立任何的独立城邦,最多形成一种自治团体。这种团体尽管有制定地方法律的权力,却还是受母市的修正、管辖和立法管理。建立这样的殖民地,不仅给予人们一定的满足感,而且也在新征服的地区建立了一种守备部队,因为该地的服从程度还是令人怀疑的。所以,不管我们是考虑它的性质还是建立的动机,罗马的殖民地都是和希腊的不一样。相应的,最初表示这些不同建制的文字也具有非常不同的意义。拉丁语 Colonia 表示殖民,而希腊语 apoikia 则表示离家、离乡、出门。虽然罗马殖民地在很多方面与希腊殖民地有着区别,但是促使他们建立殖民地的利益却是很明显的。这两种制度都来源于无法抗拒的需要或明显的功利。

欧洲人在美洲和西印度建立殖民地不是出于什么必要性,尽管能从中获取的利益是非常大的,但它却不是那么明显。在最初建立殖民地的时候这种利益并不为人所知,也肯定不是建立和发现殖民地的动机。可能到了今天,这种利益的性质、范围和限制还不为人们所了解。建立美洲殖民地的并不是那么明显的具有利色彩。

14～15世纪间,威尼斯人经营着一种极为有利的贸易,他们把东印度的香料和其他货物卖给其他的欧洲国家。他们主要从被高加索军人控制的埃及购入,高加索军人是土耳其的敌人,威尼斯人也是土耳其人的敌人。这种利益的一致,加上威尼斯的资金支持,形成了一种联合,这儿乎给予了威尼斯人一种贸易上的垄断权。威尼斯人在东印度货物的贸易上是获利的,

威尼斯人的巨大利润诱发了葡萄牙人的贪欲。他们在15世

| 国民财富的性质与原理

<small>which was envied by the Portuguese and led them to discover the Cape of Good Hope passage,</small> guese. They had been endeavouring, during the course of the fifteenth century, to find out by sea a way to the countries from which the Moors brought them ivory and gold dust across the Desert. They discovered the Madeiras, the Canaries, the Azores, the Cape de Verd islands, the coast of Guinea, that of Loango, Congo, Angola, and Benguela, and finally, the Cape of Good Hope. They had long wished to share in the profitable traffic of the Venetians, and this last discovery opened to them a probable prospect of doing so. In 1497, Vasco de Gama sailed from the port of Lisbon with a fleet of four ships, and, after a navigation of eleven months, arrived upon the coast of Indostan, and thus completed a course of discoveries which had been pursued with great steadiness, and with very little interruption, for near a century together.

<small>while Columbus endeavoured to reach the East Indies by sailing westwards.</small> Some years before this, while the expectations of Europe were in suspense about the projects of the Portuguese, of which the success appeared yet to be doubtful, a Genoese pilot formed the yet more daring project of sailing to the East Indies by the West. The situation of those countries was at that time very imperfectly known in Europe. The few European travellers who had been there had magnified the distance; perhaps through simplicity and ignorance, what was really very great, appearing almost infinite to those who could not measure it; or, perhaps, in order to increase somewhat more the marvellous of their own adventures in visiting regions so immensely remote from Europe. The longer the way was by the East, Columbus very justly concluded, the shorter it would be by the West. He proposed, therefore, to take that way, as both the shortest and the surest,

纪的时候努力寻找一条海上通道,以抵达莫尔人经过沙漠给他们带来象牙和金砂的那些国家。他们发现了马德拉群岛、加那利群岛、亚速尔群岛、佛得角群岛、几内亚海岸、洛安各、刚果、安哥拉、本格拉海岸,最后发现了好望角[1]。他们早就希望分享威尼斯人从事的有利贸易,而这一最后发现地使他们的梦想可能成为现实。1497 年,瓦斯克·达·伽马[2]从里斯本港口出发,带领四艘船的队伍,经过 11 个月的航行,到达了印度斯坦海岸,因此完成了将近一个世纪的用持之以恒的努力、且较少被中断地追求的发现过程。

> 葡萄牙人嫉妒,并导致他们发现了好望角通道,这使葡萄牙产生

在此以前的若干年里,当欧洲人对葡萄牙计划能否成功实施还心存怀疑时,一个热内亚的水手提出了一个更为大胆的计划,向西航行抵达东印度。那些国家的情况在当时的欧洲还非常不为人所知。少数到过那些国家的欧洲旅行家把距离说的很远,可能是由于单纯和无知,实际上比较大的东西,对那些无法测量的人来说,就几乎是无限大的。或者是旅行家为了夸耀他们冒险访问离欧洲相当遥远的地方的了不起。哥伦布非常正确地得出结论说,从东边去的路越远,从西方去的路就越近。因此,他提出向西走,因为这条路最短而且最有把握;他有幸说服了卡斯蒂利亚

> 哥伦布试图通过向西航行到达东印度。同时

---

〔1〕 亚速尔群岛:北大西洋中的一组火山岛,在葡萄牙大陆以西 1448 公里(900 英里)它们有几个行政区。渔业、畜牧业和旅游业对其经济十分重要。

〔2〕 瓦斯克·达·伽马(1460? ~1524),葡萄牙探险家和殖民地行政官员。第一个航行到印度的欧洲人(1497~1498),他为葡萄牙在东方的贸易和拓殖开启了富饶之门。

— 1189 —

and he had the good fortune to convince Isabella of Castile of the probability of his project. He sailed from the port of Palos in August 1492, near five years before the expedition of Vasco de Gama set out from Portugal, and, after a voyage of between two and three months, discovered first some of the small Bahama or Lucayan islands, and afterwards the great island of St. Domingo.

<small>Columbus mistook the countries he found for the Indies.</small>

But the countries which Columbus discovered, either in this or in any of his subsequent voyages, had no resemblance to those which he had gone in quest of. Instead of the wealth, cultivation and populousness of China and Indostan, he found, in St. Domingo, and in all the other parts of the new world which he ever visited, nothing but a country quite covered with wood, uncultivated, and inhabited only by some tribes of naked and miserable savages. He was not very willing, however, to believe that they were not the same with some of the countries described by Marco Polo, the first European who had visited, or at least had left behind him any description of China or the East Indies; and a very slight resemblance, such as that which he found between the name of Cibao, a mountain in St. Domingo, and that of Cipango, mentioned by Marco Polo, was frequently sufficient to make him return to this favourite prepossession, though contrary to the clearest evidence. ① In his letters to Ferdinand and Isabella he called the countries which he had discovered, the Indies. He entertained no doubt but that they were the extremity of those which had

---

① [P. F. X. de Charlevoix, *Histoire de l'Isle Espagnole ou de S. Domingue*, 1730, tom. i., p. 99.]

的伊莎贝拉[1],使他相信他计划的可行性。他 1492 年 8 月从帕洛斯港出发,几乎比瓦斯克·达·伽马从葡萄牙出发早五年,经过两到三个月的航行,首先发现了小巴哈马群岛,或卢克圆群岛,然后发现了圣多明各大岛[2]。

但是哥伦布发现的国家,包括他这次以及以后几次发现的,都不是他想要找的那些国家。没有找到中国和印度的财富、庄稼和众多的人口,他在圣多明各以及他到访的新世界的其他地方什么都没发现,除了一个被森林覆盖、尚未开垦、仅有裸体的可怜的野蛮部落居住的地方。然而,他不太愿意相信这些国家和马可·波罗描述的一些国家相差那么大。马可·波罗是到过,或者说至少留下过有关中国和东印度记述的欧洲第一人。哥伦布在发现圣多明各有一座叫西巴奥(Cibao)的山名字和马可·波罗提到的西潘哥[3]有些相似,便足以使他以为那就是心中喜爱的地方,尽管有最明显的证据表明那并不是①。在他写给费迪南和伊莎贝拉的信中,他把他发现的地方叫做印度。他毫不怀疑那是马可·

哥伦布误以为他发现的那些国家是东印度各国。

---

① P. F. X. 得·夏勒瓦:《圣多明各埃诺尔岛史》,1730 年,第 1 卷,第 99 页

[1] 卡斯蒂利亚(Castile),西班牙中部和北部一个地区和旧日的王国。从 10 世纪开始自治,1479 年伊莎贝拉和费尔德结婚后该地并入埃瑞根,由此组成了现代西班牙的核心。阿拉贡(Aragon),西班牙东北部的一个地域和前王国。1479 年它与卡斯蒂利亚合并形成了现代西班牙的核心。

[2] 巴哈马:大西洋沿岸的一个岛国,位于佛罗里达和古巴东部,大约包含 700 个岛屿和小岛以及大量的珊瑚礁。这个国家丁 1973 年从英国统治中独立出来。

[3] 日本国(Cipango),马可波罗所用诗中的日本国名,源出《马可·波罗游记》。

国民财富的性质与原理

been described by Marco Polo, and that they were not very distant from the Ganges, or from the countries which had been conquered by Alexander. Even when at last convinced that they were different, he still flattered himself that those rich countries were at no great distance, and in a subsequent voyage, accordingly, went in quest of them along the coast of Terra Firms, and towards the isthmus of Darien.

<small>Hence the names East and West Indies.</small>   In consequence of this mistake of Columbus, the name of the Indies has stuck to those unfortunate countries ever since; and when it was at last clearly discovered that the new were altogether different from the old Indies, the former were called the West, in contradistinction to the latter, which were called the East Indies.

<small>The countries discovered were not rich</small>   It was of importance to Columbus, however, that the countries which he had discovered, whatever they were, should be represented to the court of Spain as of very great consequence; and, in what constitutes the real riches of every country, the animal and vegetable productions of the soil, there was at that time nothing which could well justify such a representation of them.

<small>in animals</small>   The Cori, something between a rat and a rabbit, and supposed by Mr. Buffon ① to be the same with the Aperea of Brazil, was the largest viviparous quadruped in St. Domingo. This species seems never to have been very numerous, and the dogs and cats of the Spaniards are said to have long ago almost entirely extirpated it, as well as some other tribes of a still smaller size. ② These, however, together with a pretty large lizard, called the Ivana or Iguana, ③ constituted the principal part of the animal food which the land afforded.

<small>or vegetables,</small>   The vegetable food of the inhabitants, though from their want of industry not very abundant, was not altogether so scanty. It consisted in Indian corn, yams, potatoes, bananes, &c. plants

---

① [*Histoire Naturelle*, tom. xv. (1750), pp. 160, 162.]
② [Charlevoix, *Histoire de l' Isle Espagnole*, tom. i. , pp. 35,36.]
③ [*Ibid*. , p. 27.]

— 1192 —

波罗描述的国家的最边缘地区,离恒河或者离亚历山大征服的国家不远。即使最后被证明那是两个不同的地方,他仍然认为那些富裕的国家并不遥远,所以在后来的一次航行中他还沿着火地岛海岸,朝着达里安海峡航行,找寻那些国家。

由于哥伦布的这个错误,印度这个名称就固定在了那些不幸的国家头上;当最后清楚地发现新印度与老印度完全不同,才把前者叫做西印度,以跟后者相区别,后者就被叫做东印度。因此有了东、西印度的称呼

然而,对哥伦布来说重要的是,他发现的地方,无论是什么,对西班牙宫廷来说都应当是非常重要的,而从当时各国的财富以及动物和土壤的植物产品来说,那里没有什么东西可以证明他的发现是非常重要的。发现的国家并不富裕

科里是介于老鼠和兔子之间,被布丰先生①认为是和巴西的阿帕里亚同类的动物,是圣多明各最大的胎生四足兽。这种动物的数量似乎从来就不是太大,据说西班牙人的狗和猫早已将它们和其他一些更小的动物完全消灭②然而,这些动物和被叫做伊文诺(Ivana)或伊关诺(Iguana)③的一种特别大的蜥蜴组成了那个岛上能够提供的动物类食物的主要来源。动物方面

当地居民的植物类食物,虽然由于他们农业欠发达而不是非常丰富,但也不是完全没有。植物包括玉米、芋、薯、香蕉等,这些或植物方面,

---

① 《自然史》,第15卷,1750年,第160、162页。布丰·乔治斯·路易斯·勒克莱尔·德(1707~1788)法国博物学家,他的经典著作《自然史》(第36卷,1749~1788);另外8卷由助手完成,1804年出版以后的植物学、动物学和比较解剖学的研究奠定了基础。
② 夏勒瓦:《埃帕诺尔岛史》,第1卷,第35、36页。
③ 同上书,第27页。

which were then altogether unknown in Europe, and which have never since been very much esteemed in it, or supposed to yield a sustenance equal to what is drawn from the common sorts of grain and pulse, which have been cultivated in this part of the world time out of mind.

<small>cotton being not then considered of great consequence.</small>   The cotton plant indeed afforded the material of a very important manufacture, and was at that time to Europeans undoubtedly the most valuable of all the vegetable productions of those islands. But though in the end of the fifteenth century the muslins and other cotton goods of the East Indies were much esteemed in every part of Europe, the cotton manufacture itself was not cultivated in any part of it. Even this production, therefore, could not at that time appear in the eyes of Europeans to be of very great consequence.

<small>So Columbus relied on the minerals.</small>   Finding nothing either in the animals or vegetables of the newly discovered countries, which could justify a very advantageous representation of them, Columbus turned his view towards their minerals; and in the richness of the productions of this third kingdom, he flattered himself, he had found a full compensation for the insignificancy of those of the other two. The little bits of gold with which the inhabitants ornamented their dress, and which, he was informed, they frequently found in the rivulets and torrents that fell from the mountains, were sufficient to satisfy him that those mountains abounded with the richest gold mines. St. Domingo, therefore, was represented as a country abounding with gold, and, upon that account (according to the prejudices not only of the present times, but of those times), an inexhaustible source of real wealth to the crown and kingdom of Spain. When Columbus, upon his return from his first voyage, was introduced with a sort of triumphal honours to the sovereigns of Castile and Arragon, the principal productions of the countries which he had discovered were carried in solemn procession before him. The only valuable part of them consisted in some little fillets, bracelets, and other ornaments of gold, and in some bales of cotton. The rest were mere objects of vulgar wonder and curiosity; some reeds of an extraordinary size, some birds of a very beautiful plumage, and some stuffed skins of the huge alligator and manati; all of which were preceded by six or seven of the wretched natives, whose singular colour and appearance added greatly to the novelty of the shew.

In consequence of the representations of Columbus, the council of Castile determined to take possession of countries of which the inhabitants were plainly incapable of defending themselves. The pious purpose of converting them to Christianity sanctified the injustice of

在欧洲不为人所知,而后在欧洲也不受重视,或者被认为是能与欧洲自古以来种植的普通谷物和豆类一样提供同量的维持生命的食物。

棉花的确为最重要的制造业提供原料,而且当时被欧洲人毫无疑问地认为是岛上的植物类产品中最有价值的。但是尽管在 15 世纪末期东印度的软棉布和其他的棉花类产品都很受欧洲各国重视,但是棉纺业本身在欧洲各地并未得到发展。因此,即使这个产品当时也没有在欧洲人眼中显得非常重要。棉花当时不被认为是很重要的。

看到新发现的土地上生长的动植物都不能证明这些地方的重要性,哥伦布将眼光投向了当地的矿产;他暗自庆幸,他从第三国的丰富物产中找到了对前两个国家物产匮乏的补偿。看到当地居民用来装饰在衣服上的小金片,并听说这些是他们从山上流下来的溪水和急流中找到的,哥伦布非常满意地相信,山里一定有最富饶的金矿。因此,圣多明各被认为是一个充满黄金的国家,基于此(根据现在的偏见也根据当时的偏见),也被认为是西班牙国王和国家取之不尽的真正财富的源泉。当哥伦布第一次远航回来时,他被用凯旋仪式引见给卡斯蒂利亚和阿拉贡国王,当时发现的各国主要的产品在他前面被隆重的仪仗队抬着。其中有价值的东西只是一些饰带、手镯、其他金制饰品和几捆棉花。其他的就只是一些俗气的猎奇物品,比如,一些奇大无比的芦苇,几只有着漂亮羽毛的小鸟,几张内部装有填充物的鳄鱼和海牛皮;走在最前面的是六七个皮肤颜色和长相奇怪的土著人,这大大增加了游行的奇异色彩。因此哥伦布依靠矿物。

在哥伦布的展示之后,卡斯蒂利亚的枢密院决定占领这些国民无抵抗之力的国家。让他们信仰基督教这个幌子使得这项非

国民财富的性质与原理

<small>The Council of Castile was attracted by the gold, Columbus proposing that the government should have half the gold and silver discovered.</small> the project. But the hope of finding treasures of gold there, was the sole motive which prompted to undertake it; and to give this motive the greater weight, it was proposed by Columbus that the half of all the gold and silver that should be found there should belong to the crown. This proposal was approved of by the council.

As long as the whole or the far greater part of the gold, which the first adventurers imported into Europe, was got by so very easy a method as the plundering of the defenceless natives, it was not perhaps very difficult to pay even this heavy tax. But when the natives were once fairly stript of all that they had, which, in St. Domingo, and in all the other countries discovered by Columbus, was done completely in six or eight years, and when in order to find more it had become necessary to dig for it in the mines, there was no longer any possibility of paying this tax. The rigorous exaction of it, accordingly, <small>This was at impossible tax and was soon reduced.</small> first occasioned, it is said, the total abandonment of the mines of St. Domingo, which have never been wrought since. It was soon reduced therefore to a third; then to a fifth; afterwards to a tenth; and at last to a twentieth part of the gross produce of the gold mines. The tax upon silver continued for a long time to be a fifth of the gross produce. It was reduced to a tenth only in the course of the present century. ① But the first adventurers do not appear to have been much interested about silver. Nothing less precious than gold seemed worthy of their attention.

<small>The subsequent Spanish enterprises were all prompted by the same motive.</small> All the other enterprises of the Spaniards in the new world, subsequent to those of Columbus, seem to have been prompted by the same motive. It was the sacred thirst of gold that carried Oieda, Nicuessa, and Vasco Nugnes de Balboa, to the isthmus of Darien, that carried Cortez to Mexico, and Almagro and Pizzarro to Chili and Peru. When those adventurers arrived upon any unknown coast, their first enquiry was always if there was any gold to be found there;

---

① [Ed. 1 (in place of these two sentences) reads, 'The tax upon silver, indeed, still continues to be a fifth of the gross produce. ']

正义的计划变得神圣。但是想要在那里找到金银财宝才是促使其强取豪夺的唯一动机;为了给予这一动机更大的重量,哥伦布提议,在那里找到的半数金银属于国王。该提议也得以在枢密院通过。

> 卡斯蒂利亚枢密院被吸引,哥伦布提议发现的金银归政府一半。

只要第一批冒险者输入欧洲的全部或绝大部分黄金是通过掠夺毫无抵抗力的土著人轻易得来的,即使缴纳很重的赋税可能也不是很困难。但是当在圣多明各和哥伦布发现的其他国家的土著人被剥夺了他们所有的黄金之后(这在不到六年或八年的时间内已实现),当要取得更多的黄金必须去山里挖的时候,支付这种赋税就不再有可能性了。因此,这种赋税的严格征收,据说首先导致了圣多明各矿山被全部放弃,而且自那以后也没有再被开采过。所以金矿总产量马上降到1/3,接着1/5,之后是1/10,最后到了1/20。对银征收的税在很长时间内都是总产量的1/50。直到本世纪才降到1/10①。但是早期的冒险家似乎对银子不太感兴趣。似乎只有像金这样贵重的东西才能吸引他们的注意。

> 这是不能缴纳的税,不久就被减少了。

在哥伦布之后,西班牙冒险家在新世界的全部其他计划似乎都是出于同一个动机。由于对黄金的神圣的渴求,奥伊达、尼克萨、瓦斯克·努涅斯德·巴尔沃亚[1]来到达里安地峡,科特兹来到墨西哥,业尔马格罗和皮查罗来到智利和秘鲁。当那些冒险家到达任何不知名的海岸,他们的第一个想法就是这里能不能找到

> 后来的西班牙的计划全部都出于一个动机。

---

① 第1版中这两句是:"对银征收的税的确在很长时间内还是总产量的1/5。"

[1] 瓦斯克·努涅斯德·巴尔沃亚(1475~1517):西班牙探险家和殖民地总督,他于1513年发现太平洋,并宣称其为西班牙所有。

国民财富的性质与原理

and according to the information which they received concerning this particular, they determined either to quit the country or to settle in it.

<small>A prudent law-giver would not wish to encourage gold and silver mining,</small>   Of all those expensive and uncertain projects, however, which bring bankruptcy upon the greater part of the people who engage in them, there is none perhaps more perfectly ruinous than the search after new silver and gold mines. It is perhaps the most disadvantageous lottery in the world, or the one in which the gain of those who draw the prizes bears the least proportion to the loss of those who draw the blanks: for though the prizes are few and the blanks many, the common price of a ticket is the whole fortune of a very rich man. Projects of mining, instead of replacing the capital employed in them, together with the ordinary profits of stock, commonly absorb both capital and profit. They are the projects, therefore, to which of all others a prudent law-giver, who desired to increase the capital of his nation, would least chuse to give any extraordinary encouragement, or to turn towards them a greater share of that capital than what would go to them of its own accord. Such in reality is the absurd confidence which almost all men have in their own good fortune, that wherever there is the least probability of success, too great a share of it is apt to go to then of its own accord.

<small>but people have always believed in an Eldorado.</small>   But though the judgment of sober reason and experience concerning such projects has always been extremely unfavourable, that of human avidity has commonly been quite otherwise. The same passion which has suggested to so many people the absurd idea of the philosopher's stone, has suggested to others the equally absurd one of immense rich mines of gold and silver. They did not consider that the value of those metals has, in all ages and nations, arisen chiefly from their scarcity, and that their scarcity has arisen from the very small quantities of them which nature has any where deposited in one place, from the hard and intractable substances with which she has almost every where surrounded those small quantities, and consequently from the labour and expence which are every where necessary in order to penetrate to and get at them. They flattered themselves that veins of those metals might in many places be found as large and as abundant as those which are commonly found of lead, or copper, or tin, or iron. The dream of Sir Walter Raleigh concerning the golden city and country of Eldorado, ① may satisfy us, that even wise men are not

---

① ['That mighty, rich and beautiful empire of Guiana, and . . . that great and golden city which the Spaniards call El Dorado.'—Ralegh's *Works*, ed. Thomas Birch. 1751, VOL. ii . , p. 141.]

黄金,然后他们根据得到的这方面的信息来决定是放弃这个国家还是在这里定居。

但是,在所有的那些花费巨大而且不太确定,常常让参与其中的人破产的计划中,可能没有比探索新的金银矿山更容易使人遭受毁灭性打击了。这可能是世界上最不利的彩票,中奖人的利得只能补偿极小部分落奖人的损失。尽管中奖的彩票少而不中的彩票多,但是一张彩票的普通价格却是一个非常富裕的人的全部财产。挖矿的计划不仅不能补偿投入的资本并且带来普通的资本利润,而且通常把资本和利润全部吞噬掉。因此,所有谨慎的、想要增加国家财富的立法者,都不会对这个计划给予特别的鼓励,或者投入比自行流入该计划的资本更多的资本。实际上,所有的人对他们自己的财产都有着一种荒谬的自信,认为只要有一丝成功的可能大量的资本就会自行流入这种用途。

谨慎的立法者不愿意鼓励金银开采,

但是,人们对这个计划清醒的和经验上的判断往往是特别不利的,而从人类贪欲来判断则是完全相反的。同样的狂热,它曾向许多人提出过点石成金这一荒谬想法,也使其他人对丰富的金银矿山产生遐想。他们没有考虑到,在所有的时代和国家中,这些金属的价值主要在于它们的稀缺性,而它们的稀缺又是由于很少数量的它们被自然藏在了一个地方,被坚硬的和不可摧毁的物质包围,因而要挖掘并得到这种金属需要大量劳动力和费用。他们妄以为,这种金属的矿脉能够在许多地方被找到,巨大而且丰富,就像铅、铜、锡、铁的矿脉那样。沃尔特·罗利夫爵士所作的有关厄尔多拉多①

但是人们通常相信黄金国。

---

① 罗利夫:《著作》,托马斯·伯奇编,1751年,第2卷,第141页:"那个强大、富饶、美丽的圭业那帝国……那个西班牙人称为厄尔多拉多的黄金城。"

| 国民财富的性质与原理

always exempt from such strange delusions. More than a hundred years after the death of that great man, the Jesuit Gumila was still convinced of the reality of that wonderful country, and expressed with great warmth, and I dare to say, with great sincerity, how happy he should be to carry the light of the gospel to a people who could so well reward the pious labours of their missionary. ①

<small>In this case expections were to some extent realized, so far as the Spaniards were concerned,</small>
　　In the countries first discovered by the Spaniards, no gold or silver mines are at present known which are supposed to be worth the working. The quantities of those metals which the first adventurers are said to have found there, had probably been very much magnified, as well as the fertility of the mines which were wrought immediately after the first discovery. What those adventurers were reported to have found, however, was sufficient to inflame the avidity of all their countrymen. Every Spaniard who sailed to America expected to find an Eldorado. Fortune too did upon this what she has done upon very few other occasions. She realized in some measure the extravagant hopes of her votaries, and in the discovery and conquest of Mexico and Peru (of which the one happened about thirty, the other about forty years after the first expedition of Columbus), she presented them with something not very unlike that profusion of the precious metals which they sought for.

　　A project of commerce to the East Indies, therefore, gave occasion to the first discovery of the West. A project of conquest gave occasion to all the establishments of the Spaniards in those newly discovered countries. The motive which excited them to this conquest was a project of gold and silver mines; and a course of accidents, which no human wisdom could foresee, rendered this project much more successful than the undertakers had any reasonable grounds for expecting.

<small>but the other nations were not so successful.</small>
　　The first adventurers of all the other nations of Europe, who attempted to make settlements in America, were animated by the like chimerical views; but they were not equally successful. It was more than a hundred years after the first settlement of the Brazils,

---

　　① [P. Jos. Gumilla, *Histoire naturelle civile et géographique de l' Orénoque, etc.* , traduite par M. Eidous, 1758, tom. ii. , pp. 46、117、131、132、137、138.]

的黄金城和黄金国的梦,充分证明了,即使是聪明人也不免有此种奇异的幻想。在那位伟人死后一百多年,耶稣会会员古米拉仍然相信那个奇妙的国家的真实性,并用极大的热情,我敢说是带着极大的真诚表示,将福音之光带给那些给予传教士的虔诚工作以很大奖赏的人民他感到非常快乐①。

在西班牙人首先发现的国家中,现在看来,没有任何金银矿被认为是值得开采的。据说首批冒险家在那里找到的这些金属的数量,以及在第一次发现之后马上开采的矿山的产量,都被大大夸大了。然而,那些冒险家被报道时声称找到的东西足以唤起他们国民的贪欲。每个航行去美洲的西班牙人都期望找到黄金国。命运之神这个时候就像在其他少数场合一样,使她的忠实信徒们的奢侈希望得以实现,在墨西哥和秘鲁的发现与征服过程中(前者发生在哥伦布首次远征后大约30年,后者发生在之后的大约40年),命运之神赠予他们与他们需求的珍贵金属价值上不相上下的东西。

因此,与东印度的通商计划导致了西印度的发现。征服计划导致了西班牙人在那些新发现的土地上建立了殖民地。促使他们征服的动机是金银矿的计划,一系列人类智慧不能预见的偶然因素,使得这个计划获得了比经营者有任何合理理由期望的更大的成功。

所有其他欧洲国家的尝试在美洲定居的第一批冒险家,受同样动机驱使,但是他们却不是同样成功。巴西自第一次殖民以

---

① P. Jos·古米拉:《奥里诺科河的自然文化史与地理》,1758年,第2卷,第46、117、131、132、137、138页。

before any silver, gold, or diamond mines were discovered there. In the English, French, Dutch, and Danish colonies, none have ever yet been discovered; at least none that are at present supposed to be worth the working. The first English settlers in North America, however, offered a fifth of all the gold and silver which should be found there to the king, as a motive for granting them their patents. In the patents to Sir Walter Raleigh, to the London and Plymouth companies, to the council of Plymouth, &c. this fifth was accordingly reserved to the crown. To the expectation of finding gold and silver mines, those first settlers too joined that of discovering a north-west passage to the East Indies. They have hitherto been disappointed in both.

Part Second Causes Of The Prosperity Of New Colonies

The colony of a civilized nation which takes possession either of a waste country, or of one so thinly inhabited, that the natives easily give place to the new settlers, advances more rapidly to wealth and greatness than any other human society.

<small>Colonists take out knowledge and regular government, land is plentiful and cheap, wages are high, and children are taken care of and are profitable.</small> The colonists carry out with them a knowledge of agriculture and of other useful arts, superior to what can grow up of its own accord in the course of many centuries among savage and barbarous nations. They carry out with them too the habit of subordination, some notion of the regular government which takes place in their own country, of the system of laws which supports it, and of a regular administration of justice; and they naturally establish something of the same kind in the new settlement. But among savage and barbarous nations, the natural progress of law and government is still slower than the natural progress of arts, after law and government have been so far established, as is necessary for their protection. Every colonist gets more land than he can possibly cultivate. He has no rent, and scarce any taxes to pay. No landlord shares with him in its produce, and the share of the sovereign is commonly but a trifle. He has every motive to render as great as possible a produce, which is thus to be almost entirely his own. But his land is commonly so extensive,

来,经过百余年,才发现一些银、金或钻石矿山。在英国、法国、荷兰、丹麦等国的殖民地中,至今还没有发现过贵重金属矿山,至少是没有现在认为值得开采的矿山。然而,在北美的第一批英国殖民者把发现的1/5金银献给国王,作为给予他们许可证的动力。沃尔特·罗利夫爵士的许可证,伦敦公司及普利茅斯公司的许可证,普利茅斯参议会的许可证等等,都把所得的五分之一献给王国作为条件。这些早期的殖民者,既希望找到金银矿山,又希望找到去东印度的西北方向通道,但他们均未成功。

第二部分 新殖民地繁荣的原因

一个文明国家占有一个荒废的国度,或者是一个鲜有人们居住、而且当地居民容易向新殖民者屈服的国家,那么在这基础上建立的殖民地能比任何其他人类社会更快地发展从而走向富裕和强大。

殖民者带去了农业知识和其他有用的技术,比野蛮的未开化民族数百年来自己发展积累的知识要更为优越。他们也带去了服从的习惯、他们自己国家正规政府的一些管理模式支持政府的法律制度以及正规的司法制度;他们自然地在新殖民地建立了一些与国内同样的东西。但是在野蛮的未开化民族里,在保护自身所必要的法律和政府建立之后,法律和政府的自然进步仍要慢于技术的自然进步。每个殖民者得到的土地多于他能耕种的。他不用交地租,也很少需要支付什么税。他的产出没有地主会来分享,国王收取的那一份也很少。他可以尽量提高物品产量,因为所有的产物都归他所有。但是,他的土地通常是如此广阔,即使

that with all his own industry, and with all the industry of other people whom he can get to employ, he can seldom make it produce the tenth part of what it is capable of producing. He is eager, therefore, to collect labourers from all quarters, and to reward them with the most liberal wages. But those liberal wages, joined to the plenty and cheapness of land, soon make those labourers leave him, in order to become landlords themselves, and to reward, with equal liberality, other labourers, who soon leave them for the same reason that they left their first master. The liberal reward of labour encourages marriage. The children, during the tender years of infancy, are well fed and properly taken care of, and when they are grown up, the value of their labour greatly overpays their maintenance. When arrived at maturity, the high price of labour, and the low price of land, enable them to establish themselves in the same manner as their fathers did before them.

<small>Population and improvement, which mean wealth and greatness, are encouraged.</small>
In other countries, rent and profit eat up wages, and the two superior orders of people oppress the inferior one. But in new colonies, the interest of the two superior orders obliges them to treat the inferior one with more generosity and humanity; at least, where that inferior one is not in a state of slavery. Waste lands of the greatest natural fertility, are to be had for a trifle. The increase of revenue which the proprietor, who is always the undertaker, expects from their improvement constitutes his profit; which in these circumstances is commonly very great. But this great profit cannot be made without employing the labour of other people in clearing and cultivating the land; and the disproportion between the great extent of the land and the small number of the people, which commonly takes place in new colonies, makes it difficult for him to get this labour. He does not, therefore, dispute about wages, but is willing to employ labour at any price. The high wages of labour encourage population. The cheapness and plenty of good land encourage improvement, and enable the proprietor to pay those high wages. In those wages consists almost the whole price of the land; and though they are high, considered as the wages of labour, they are low, considered as the price of what is so very valuable. What encourages the progress of population and improvement, encourages that of real wealth and greatness.

The progress of many of the ancient Greek colonies towards wealth and greatness, seems accordingly to have been very rapid.

他一个人用尽全部劳动力以及他能够雇佣到的其他人的全部劳动,也很少能获得土地 1/10 的产出。因此,他急于从各地招集劳动力并给予他们最优厚的工资。但这些优厚的工资,加上土地的丰富和廉价,使得这些劳动力马上离开了他,以便于自己成为地主用同样优厚的工资支付其他的劳动者;这些其他的劳动者不久又选择离开,这和他们离开第一个雇主的原因是一样的。劳动的优厚报酬鼓励人们去结婚。他们的孩子在幼年期吃得非常好,也被细心照顾,当他们长大之后,他们的劳动价值大大地超过了他们的抚养费。成年以后,劳动的高价,土地的低廉促使他们像他们的父亲那样自立起来。

在其他国家,地租和利润吃掉了工资,两个上层阶级压迫着下层阶级。但在新殖民地里,两个上层阶级的利益使他们对待下层阶级时多了更多的宽宏和人道,至少下层阶级不是处于奴隶状态。极其肥沃的荒地只需付出很小的代价就能得到。地主总是经营者,他期望的从改良土地增加收入就构成他的利润;这种情况下的利润一般是很大的。但是不雇佣其他劳动者开垦和耕种土地,就无法取得巨大的利润;而土地的面积之大和人口之少这一在新殖民地上经常发生的不平衡现象,使他很难获取劳动力。因此,他不计较工资,愿意用任何价钱雇佣劳动者。劳动力的高工资刺激了人口增长。好土地的廉价和众多则鼓励了耕种改进,使地主付得起高工资。工资里几乎包含了土地的全部价格。作为劳动的工资,它们不低,但是作为如此有价值的物品的价格,它们算是低的了。刺激了人口增长和土地改善的因素也刺激了实际财富的增长和国家强大。

> 受到鼓励的是人口和改进,这意味着财富和强大。

因此,许多希腊的殖民地在财富和强大方面的增长速度似乎

| 国民财富的性质与原理

The progress of the Greek colonies was very rapid.
In the course of a century or two, several of them appear to have rivalled, and even to have surpassed their mother cities. Syracuse and Agrigentum in Sicily, Tarentum and Locri in Italy, Ephesus and Miletus in Lesser Asia, appear by all accounts to have been at least equal to any of the cities of ancient Greece. Though posterior in their establishment, yet all the arts of refinement, philosophy, poetry, and eloquence, seem to have been cultivated as early, and to have been improved as highly in them, as in any part of the mother country. The schools of the two oldest Greek philosophers, those of Thales and Pythagoras, were established, it is remarkable, not in ancient Greece, but the one in an Asiatic, the other in an Italian colony. ① All those colonies had established themselves in countries inhabited by savage and barbarous nations, who easily gave place to the new settlers. They had plenty of good land, and as they were altogether independent of the mother city, they were at liberty to manage their own affairs in the way that they judged was most suitable to their own interest.

That of the Roman colonies much less so.
The history of the Roman colonies is by no means so brilliant. Some of them, indeed, such as Florence, have in the course of many ages, and after the fall of the mother city, grown up to be considerable states. But the progress of no one of them seems ever to have been very rapid. They were all established in conquered provinces, which in most cases had been fully inhabited before. The quantity of land assigned to each colonist was seldom very considerable, and as the colony was not independent, they were not always at liberty to manage their own affairs in the way that they judged was most suitable to their own interest.

In the plenty of good land, the European colonies established in

---

① [Miletus and Crotona.]

是非常迅速的。在一两百年间,很多殖民地似乎可以和母市抗衡,甚至是超过母市了。西西里岛的锡拉库扎及阿格里琴托,意大利的塔伦图及洛克里斯,小亚细亚的以弗所和密里图斯[1],无论从哪一点来说,都至少可与古希腊的任何一城市相抗衡。尽管建立的时间较晚,但是所有的学艺、哲学、诗歌及修辞学似乎和母市的任何一个部分发展得同样早,进步得同样快。值得关注的是,两大最古老的希腊哲学流派,即达理士学派和毕太哥拉学派,并不是建在古希腊,而是一个建在亚细亚殖民地,另一个建在意大利殖民地①。所有这些殖民地都建立在野蛮的未开化民族居住的地方,那里,新殖民者很容易取得土地。他们有很多优良的土地,但是由于他们都独立于母市,所以他们能用一种最大限度满足自己利益的方式自由管理自己的事务。

> 希腊殖民地的进步是很快的。

罗马殖民地的历史绝不是那么辉煌的。的确有一些殖民地,比如佛洛伦斯,经历了许多年,在母市衰败之后,成长为一个大国。但是没有哪个殖民地的进步似乎是非常迅速的。他们都建立在被征服的城邦之上,大多数情况下人口已经稠密。分配给每个殖民者的土地数量不会很大,由于殖民地没有独立,它们不是总可以按照它们认为有利于自己的方式自由地处理自己的事务。

> 罗马殖民地的进步要慢得多。

在好的土地的丰富方面,欧洲人建立在美洲和西印度的殖民

---

① 米列达斯和克罗托拉。

[1] 锡拉库扎(Syracuse),意大利西西里岛东南部一城市,位于卡塔尼亚东南偏南,爱奥尼亚海沿岸。公元前8世纪由科林斯殖民者创建,5世纪其国力达到巅峰,但于212年落于罗马人之手。以弗所(Ephesus),位于小亚细亚今土耳其西部的希腊古城。其阿耳忒弥斯(罗马时期称为狄安娜)神庙为世界七大奇迹之一,圣保罗在其传教过程中曾造访此城。

国民财富的性质与原理

The American colonies had plenty of land and not very much interference from their mother countries.
America and the West Indies resemble, and even greatly surpass, those of ancient Greece. In their dependency upon the mother state, they resemble those of ancient Rome; but their great distance from Europe has in all of them alleviated more or less the effects of this dependency. Their situation has placed them less in the view and less in the power of their mother country. In pursuing their interest their own way, their conduct has, upon many occasions, been overlooked, either because not known or not understood in Europe; and upon some occasions it has been fairly suffered and submitted to, because their distance rendered it difficult to restrain it. Even the violent and arbitrary government of Spain has, upon many occasions, been obliged to recall or soften the orders which had been given for the government of her colonies, for fear of a general insurrection. The progress of all the European colonies in wealth, population, and improvement, has accordingly been very great.

The progress of the Spanish colonies, Mexico and Peru, has been very considerable.
The crown of Spain, by its share of the gold and silver, derived some revenue from its colonies, from the moment of their first establishment. It was a revenue too, of a nature to excite in human avidity the most extravagant expectations of still greater riches. The Spanish colonies, therefore, from the moment of their first establishment, attracted very much the attention of their mother country; while those of the other European nations were for a long time in a great measure neglected. The former did not, perhaps, thrive the better in consequence of this attention; nor the latter the worse in consequence of this neglect. In proportion to the extent of the country which they in some measure possess, the Spanish colonies are considered as less populous and thriving than those of almost any other European nation. The progress even of the Spanish colonies, however, in population and improvement, has certainly been very rapid and very great. The city of Lima, founded since the conquest, is represented by Ulloa, as containing fifty thousand inhabitants near thirty years ago. Quito, which had been but a miserable hamlet of Indians, is represented by the same author as in his time equally populous, ① Gemelli Carreri, a

---

① [Juan and Ulloa, *Voyage historique*, tom. i., p. 229.]

地很像,甚至远超过了古希腊的殖民地。在对母市的依赖方面,它们很像古罗马的殖民地;但是它们远离欧洲使它们或多或少地减轻了依赖的程度。它们的状况使它们比较少地置于母市的监督和权力影响之下。在按照自己的方式追求利益时,它们的所作所为,由于不被欧洲所知晓,或者不被欧洲理解,在很多场合下被忽视。有时,欧洲相当容忍,而且对它屈从,因为距离使得管束相当困难。即使是强暴专横的西班牙政府,在很多场合下,也不得不撤回或修改给它的殖民地政府定下的命令,因为它怕引起一场普遍的叛乱。因此,所有欧洲殖民地在财富、人口、土地改良方面的进步相当大。

> 美洲殖民地有大量土地没有受到母市的干扰。

西班牙国王,由于分享金银,从殖民地刚建立起就从它的殖民地获得了一些收入。这种收入的性质,也是在人类贪欲中激发对更大财富的更为奢侈的期望。因此,西班牙殖民地从最初建立时起,就引起了母市的非常大的注意;而其他欧洲国家的殖民地则在很长时间内很大程度上被忽视了。可能前者不因为受到关注而更加繁荣,后者不因为被忽视而更加落后。按照国家土地大小的比例,西班牙殖民地某种程度上不如欧洲其他国家的殖民地人口和繁荣状态。然而,即使是西班牙的殖民地,在人口和土地改良方面的进步也是非常迅速和巨大的。在征服后建立的城市利马,据乌洛阿所说它的居民大约30年以前就已达五万[1]。基多,原为印第安的一个小的可怜的村庄,同一作者说那个时候也有同样多的人口①。克麦利·卡勒里,据说是个冒牌的旅行家,

> 西班牙殖民地墨西哥和秘鲁进步非常大。

---

① 胡安和乌洛阿:《航行史》,第1卷,第229页。
[1] 同上书,第203页。

pretended traveller, it is said, indeed, but who seems every where to have written upon extreme good information, represents the city of Mexico as containing a hundred thousand inhabitants; ① a number which, in spite of all the exaggerations of the Spanish writers, is, probably, more than five times greater than what it contained in the time of Montezuma. These numbers exceed greatly those of Boston, New York, and Philadelphia, the three greatest cities of the English colonies. Before the conquest of the Spaniards there were no cattle fit for draught either in Mexico or Peru. The lama was their only beast of burden, and its strength seems to have been a good deal inferior to that of a common ass. The plough was unknown among them. They were ignorant of the use of iron. They had no coined money, nor any established instrument of commerce of any kind. Their commerce was carried on by barter. A sort of wooden spade was their principal instrument of agriculture. Sharp stones served them for knives and hatchets to cut with; fish bones and the hard sinews of certain animals served them for needles to sew with; and these seem to have been their principal instruments of trade. In this state of things, it seems impossible, that either of those empires could have been so much improved or so well cultivated as at present, when they are plentifully furnished with all sorts of European cattle, and when the use of iron, of the plough, and of many of the arts of Europe, has been introduced among them. But the populousness of every country must be in proportion to the degree of its improvement and cultivation. In spite of the cruel destruction of the natives which followed the conquest, these two great empires are, probably, more populous now than they ever were before: and the people are surely very different; for we must acknowledge, I apprehend, that the Spanish creoles are in many respects superior to the ancient Indians.

The Portuguese colony of Brazil is very populous. After the settlements of the Spaniards, that of the Portugueze in Brazil is the oldest of any European nation in America. But as for a long time after the first discovery, neither gold nor silver mines were found in it, and as it afforded, upon that account, little or no revenue to the crown, it was for a long time in a great measure neglected;

---

① [In Awnsham and John Churchill's *Collection of Voyages and Travels*, 1704, vol. iv., p. 508.]

但他在各处的写作似乎都是根据极端可靠的消息写的,他说墨西哥城有10万居民①;这个数字,无论西班牙作家如何夸大,可能都要比蒙特祖玛时代的居民多五倍以上。这些数字大大超过了三大英国殖民地城市波士顿、纽约和费城的人口数。在西班牙人征服之前,墨西哥和秘鲁没有适合在旱地劳动的牛。无峰驼是他们唯一的用以负重的兽类,它们的体力大大低于普通的驴子。他们不知道什么叫耕犁,他们不知如何使用铁。他们没有铸币,也没有任何通商媒介。他们的商业靠物物交换,一种木制的锄头就是他们的主要农具。尖石是他们切割的刀斧。鱼骨和某些动物的硬腱成了他们缝衣服的针。所有这些似乎就是他们的主要生产工具了。在这种状态下,两个帝国似乎不可能像现在那样把土地改良或者耕种得那么好,因为现在它们有了各种欧洲牲畜,铁、犁和许多欧洲技术的使用已经引进。但是每个国家的人口数必须和它的土地改良和耕种成比例。尽管有征服后对土著人的残忍灭绝,这两个帝国现在的人口大概比以前还要多。人也肯定是非常不同了,因为我认为我们必须承认,西班牙后裔的克里奥尔人在许多方面比古印第安人强。

在西班牙人殖民美洲之后,葡萄牙人在巴西的殖民成了其他欧洲国家在美洲殖民最早的一个。但是在第一次被发现之后的很长时间,此处都没有发现金银矿,因此,它也只能贡献一点甚至不能贡献收入给国王,于是它很长时间里很大程度上被忽视了,

<small>葡萄牙人的巴西殖民地人口非常多。</small>

---

① 昂沙姆和约翰·丘吉尔:《航行记和旅游记大全》,1704年,第4卷,第508页。

and during this state of neglect, it grew up to be a great and powerful colony. While Portugal was under the dominion of Spain, Brazil was attacked by the Dutch, who got possession of seven of the fourteen provinces into which it is divided. They expected soon to conquer the other seven, when Portugal recovered its independency by the elevation of the family of Braganza to the throne. The Dutch then, as enemies to the Spaniards, became friends to the Portugueze, who were likewise the enemies of the Spaniards. They agreed, therefore, to leave that part of Brazil, which they had not conquered, to the king of Portugal, who agreed to leave that part which they had conquered to them, as a matter not worth disputing about with such good allies. But the Dutch Government soon began to oppress the Portugueze colonists, who, instead of amusing themselves with complaints, took arms against their new masters, and by their own valour and resolution, with the connivance, indeed, but without any avowed assistance from the mother country, drove them out of Brazil. The Dutch, therefore, finding it impossible to keep any part of the country to themselves, were contented that it should be entirely restored to the crown of Portugal. ① In this colony there are said to be more than six hundred thousand people, ② either Portugueze or descended from Portugueze, creoles, mulattoes, and a mixed race between Portugueze and Brazilians. No one colony in America is supposed to contain so great a number of people of European extraction.

When Spain declined, various countries obtained a footing in America.

Towards the end of the fifteenth, and during the greater part of the sixteenth century, Spain and Portugal were the two great naval powers upon the ocean: for though the commerce of Venice extended to every part of Europe, its fleets had scarce ever sailed beyond the Mediterranean. The Spaniards, in virtue of the first discovery, claimed all America as their own; and though they could not hinder so great a naval power as that of Portugal from settling in Brazil, such was, at that time, the terror of their name,

---

① [Raynal, *Histoire philosophique*, Amsterdam ed. , 1773, tom. iii. , pp. 347—352.]

② [*Ibid.* , tom. iii. , p. 424.]

而在这段被忽视的时间内,它成长为一个强大的殖民地。在葡萄牙还受西班牙统治的时候,荷兰侵占了巴西,占领了巴西划分为 14 个省份中的七个。当葡萄牙恢复了独立,布拉甘查王朝登上王位,他们期望很快征服其他七个省。作为西班牙人敌人的荷兰那时变成了葡萄牙人的朋友,葡萄牙也是西班牙的敌人。因此,荷兰人同意将他们没有征服的巴西的部分领土留给葡萄牙的国王,而国王也同意把荷兰征服的土地保留给他们,因为作为关系如此良好的同盟为这个而争论不值得。但是荷兰政府不久就开始镇压葡萄牙殖民者,殖民者不是靠抱怨来发泄,而是拿起武器来反抗他们的新主人。虽未得到母市的公开帮助,但在母市默许之下,依靠自己的勇气和决心,把荷兰赶出了巴西。因此,荷兰人发现自己保留那个国家的任何部分已不可能时,便同意葡萄牙国王完全拥有巴西。① 这个殖民地据说有超过 60 万的人口,②包括葡萄牙人及其后裔、克里奥尔人、西印度人还有葡萄牙和巴西的混血种族。没有哪个在美洲的殖民地被认为拥有如此大数目的有欧洲血统的人。

15 世纪末和 16 世纪的大部分时间里,西班牙和葡萄牙是两大海上军事强国。尽管威尼斯的贸易延伸到欧洲任何地方,但是它从来没有走出过地中海。西班牙人第一个发现美洲,因此它使整个美洲归它所有,尽管它不能阻碍葡萄牙如此强大的海军强国在巴西殖民。但当时听到这两个名字就觉得可怕,以至于欧洲大

<hr />

① 雷纳尔:《哲学史》,阿姆斯特丹版,1773 年,第 3 卷,第 347~352 页。
② 同上书,第 424 页。

国民财富的性质与原理

that the greater part of the other nations of Europe were afraid to establish themselves in any other part of that great continent. The French, who attempted to settle in Florida, were all murdered by the Spaniards. ① But the declension of the naval power of this latter nation, in consequence of the defeat or miscarriage of, what they called, their Invincible Armada, which happened towards the end of the sixteenth century, put it out of their power to obstruct any longer the settlements of the other European nations. In the course of the seventeenth century, therefore, the English, French, Dutch, Danes, and Swedes, all the great nations who had any ports upon the ocean, attempted to make some settlements in the new world.

The Swedish colony of New Jersey was prospering when swallowed up by New York.

The Swedes established themselves in New Jersey; and the number of Swedish families still to be found there, sufficiently demonstrates, that this colony was very likely to prosper, had it been protected by the mother country. But being neglected by Sweden it was soon swallowed up by the Dutch colony of New York, which again, in 1674, fell under the dominion of the English.

The Danish colonies of St. Thomas and Santa Cruz have been very prosperous since the exclusive company was dissolved.

The small islands of St. Thomas and Santa Cruz are the only countries in the new world that have ever been possessed by the Danes. These little settlements too were under the government of an exclusive company, which had the sole right, both of purchasing the surplus produce of the colonists, and of supplying them with such goods of other countries as they wanted, and which, therefore, both in its purchases and sales, had not only the power of oppressing them, but the greatest temptation to do so. The government of an exclusive company of merchants is, perhaps, the worst of all governments for any country whatever. It was not, however, able to stop altogether the progress of these colonies, though it rendered it more slow and languid. The late king of Denmark dissolved this company, and since that time the prosperity of these colonies has been very great.

The Dutch colony of Surinam is prosperous though still under an exclusive company.

The Dutch settlements in the West, as well as those in the East Indies, were originally put under the government of an exclusive company. The progress of some of them, therefore, though it has been considerable, in comparison with that of almost any country that has been long peopled and established, has been languid and slow in comparison with that of the greater part of new colonies. The colony of Surinam, though very considerable, is still inferior to the greater part of the sugar colonies of the other European nations. The colony of Nova Belgia, now divided into the two provinces of New York and New

---

① [Raynal, *Histoire philosophique*, tom. vi. , p. 8.]

部分其他的国家不敢在那个大陆建立自己的殖民地。想要在佛罗里达建立殖民地的法国被西班牙人全部消灭。① 自16世纪末所谓的无敌舰队被打败或失算,西班牙的海军实力开始衰落,再也无力阻挡其他欧洲国家在那里殖民。因此,17世纪时,英国、法国、荷兰、丹麦、瑞典等所有有港口的大国,都想在新世界建立他们的殖民地。

瑞典在新泽西建立了他们的殖民地;至今还能找到不少瑞典人的家族,这足以证明,如果受到母市的保护,这个殖民地很可能会繁荣起来。但是由于瑞典的忽视,该殖民地很快就被荷兰殖民地纽约侵吞了,而纽约在1674年则落入了英国的统治之下。

<small>瑞典的殖民地新泽西被吞并后慢慢繁荣。</small>

圣托马斯和圣克罗斯两个小岛是丹麦在新世界曾经拥有的唯一的两片国土。这两个小的殖民地也在一个专营公司的统治之下,它有权购买殖民者的剩余产品,并向他们提供他们所需要的其他国家的产品,因此,在买和卖两方面不但有权压迫他们,而且有最大的诱惑去这样做。专营商业公司的统治或许对任何国家来说都是最差的政府。然而,它无法完全阻挡这些殖民地的进步,尽管它使得这个进步更加缓慢。丹麦前国王解散了这家公司,自那时候起,这些殖民地就开始大大繁荣起来。

<small>圣克罗斯和圣托马斯殖民地自公司解散以来非常繁荣。</small>

荷兰在西部以及东印度的殖民地开始也是在一个专营公司统治之下。因此,尽管有些殖民地与老殖民地比起来进步非常大,但是与一些新殖民地比较,进步就很缓慢。苏里南殖民地,虽然进步不小,但仍然比不上其他欧洲国家的大部分蔗田殖民地。诺瓦·伯尔基业殖民地,现在划分成纽约和新泽西,即使仍然在

<small>荷兰殖民地苏里南很繁荣,尽管仍由专营公司统治。</small>

---

① 雷纳尔:《哲学史》,第6卷,第8页。

国民财富的性质与原理

Jersey, would probably have soon become considerable too, even though it had remained under the government of the Dutch. The plenty and cheapness of good land are such powerful causes of prosperity, that the very worst government is scarce capable of checking altogether the efficacy of their operation. The great distance too from the mother country would enable the colonists to evade more or less, by smuggling, the monopoly which the company enjoyed against them. At present the company allows all Dutch ships to trade to Surinam upon paying two and a half per cent. upon the value of their cargo for a licence; and only reserves to itself exclusively the direct trade from Africa to America, which consists almost entirely in the slave trade. This relaxation in the exclusive privileges of the company, is probably the principal cause of that degree of prosperity which that colony at present enjoys. Curaçoa and Eustatia, the two principal islands belonging to the Dutch, are free ports open to the ships of all nations; and this freedom, in the midst of better colonies whose ports are open to those of one nation only, has been the great cause of the prosperity of those two barren islands.

The French colony of Canada has shown rapid progress since the dissolution of the exclusive company.
The French colony of Canada was, during the greater part of the last century, and some part of the present, under the government of an exclusive company. Under so unfavourable an administration its progress was necessarily very slow in comparison with that of other new colonies; but it became much more rapid when this company was dissolved after the fall of what is called the Mississippi scheme. When the English got possession of this country, they found in it near double the number of inhabitants which father Charlevoix had assigned to it between twenty and thirty years before. ① That jesuit had travelled over the whole country, and had no inclination to represent it as less considerable than it really was.

The French colony of St. Domingo was established by pirates and free-booters, who, for a long time, neither required the protection, nor acknowledged the authority of France; and when that race of banditti became so far citizens as to acknowledge this authority, it was for a long time necessary to exercise it with very great gentleness.

---

① [p. F. X. de Charlevoix, *Histoire et description générale de la Nouvelle France, avec le journal historique d' un voyage dans l' Amérique Septentrionnale*, 1744, ton. ii. , p. 390, speaks of a population of 20000 to 25000 in 1713. Raynal says in 1753 and 1758 the population, excluding troops and Indians, was 91000. *Histoire philosophique*, Amsterdam ed. , 1773, tom. vi. , p. 137.]

荷兰统治下,可能不久就会很繁荣。良好土地的丰富和低廉是造成如此繁荣、如此强大的原因,以至于最差的政府也不能完全阻止这种因素的有效作用。与母市距离太大,这里的人通过走私,多少可以回避这种公司享有的垄断。现在,这家公司允许所有荷兰船只通过缴纳他们货物价值2.5%的税获得许可证来与苏里南做贸易,而自己只保留非洲至美洲的直接贸易的垄断权,那几乎都是奴隶买卖。公司特权的放松可能是这个殖民地现在享有繁荣程度的主要原因。属于荷兰的两个主要岛屿库拉索亚和尤斯特沙是对所有船只开放的港口;这种自由,在港口只对一个国家船只开放的好一点的殖民地中间,是这两个不毛之地繁荣的巨大原因。

法国的加拿大殖民地,在上个世纪大部分时间和现在的一些时间里,都是由一个专营公司统治。在如此不利的政府管理下,与其他新殖民地相比,它的进步必然非常缓慢;但是当这个公司在所谓的密西西比计划失败被解散后,它的进步就迅速多了。当英国人占有这片领土时,他们发现这里的人口数目比夏勒瓦神父20到30年前所说的要多一倍①。这个耶稣会会员游遍全国,没有必要少报实际的人数。

法国殖民地圣多明各是由海盗们建立的。很长时间以来,他们既不寻求保护,也不承认法国的政权;后来,那批海盗被招安承认了法国的政权,但在一段长时期内仍受到非常优越的待遇。这

———

① P.F.X.得·夏勒瓦:《新法兰西的历史和概况,附北美航行历史志》,1744年,第2卷,第390页,说1713年的居民数为20000人到25000人。雷纳尔说在1753年和1758年除了军队和印第安的人口数为91000。《哲学史》,阿姆斯特丹版,1773年,第6卷,第137页。

| 国民财富的性质与原理

St. Domingo, in spite of various obstacles, and the other French sugar colonies, are very thriving.

During this period the population and improvement of this colony increased very fast. Even the oppression of the exclusive company, to which it was for some time subjected, with all the other colonies of France, though it no doubt retarded, had not been able to stop its progress altogether. The course of its prosperity returned as soon as it was relieved from that oppression. It is now the most important of the sugar colonies of the West Indies, and its produce is said to be greater than that of all the English sugar colonies put together. The other sugar colonies of France are in general all very thriving.

But the progress of the English colonies has been the most rapid.

But there are no colonies of which the progress has been more rapid than that of the English in North America.

Plenty of good land, and liberty to manage their own affairs their own way, seem to be the two great causes of the prosperity of all new colonies.

They have not so much good land as the Spanish and Portugueze, but their institutions are more favour. able to its improvement.

In the plenty of good land the English colonies of North America, though, no doubt, very abundantly provided, are, however, inferior to those of the Spaniards and Portugueze, and not superior to some of those possessed by the French before the late war. But the political institutions of the English colonies have been more favourable to the improvement and cultivation of this land, than those of any of the other three nations.

(1) The engrossing of uncultivated land has been more restrained.

First, the engrossing of uncultivated land, though it has by no means been prevented altogether, has been more restrained in the English colonies than in any other. The colony law which imposes upon every proprietor the obligation of improving and cultivating, within a limited time, a certain proportion of his lands, and which, in case of failure, declares those neglected lands grantable to any other person; though it has not, perhaps, been very strictly executed, has, however, had some effect.

(2) Primogeniture and entails are less prevalent and alienation more frequent.

Secondly, in Pennsylvania there is no right of primogeniture, and lands, like moveables, are divided equally among all the children of the family. In three of the provinces of New England the oldest has only a double share, as in the Mosaical law. Though in those provinces, therefore, too great a quantity of land should sometimes be engrossed by a particular individual, it is likely, in the course of a generation or two, to be sufficiently divided again. In the other English

段时间内，该殖民地的人口数和土地改良的增长非常快。虽然有一个时期像所有其他的法国殖民地一样受一个专营公司的压迫，尽管这种压迫阻碍了其进步，但是进步却并没有因此而停止。它一从压迫中解放出来就进入了繁荣时期。它现在是西印度最重要的蔗田殖民地，它的产量据说比所有英国蔗田殖民地的产量加在一起还要大。其他法国蔗田殖民地总体上来说也非常繁荣。

尽管有不同的阻碍，圣多明各和其他法国蔗田殖民地都非常繁荣。

但是没有哪个殖民地的进步比英国在北美的殖民地的进步更迅速。

但是英国殖民地的进步最快。

大量肥沃的土地和按照自己的方式管理自己事务的自由，似乎是所有新殖民地繁荣的两大原因。

在肥沃的土地方面，英国在北美的殖民地，尽管毫无疑问有丰富的肥沃土地，不如那些西班牙人和葡萄牙人的殖民地，也不比上次战争以前法国人拥有的殖民地。但是英国殖民地的政治制度与其他任何第三国的制度相比，都更有利于土地的改良和耕种。

他们没有西班牙和葡萄牙的殖民地拥有的那么多好地，但是他们的制度对土地改良更有利。

第一，未耕种的土地的垄断，尽管在英国殖民地未被完全阻止，却比在其他任何殖民地受到更大的限制。殖民地法律规定，每个地主有义务在有限的时间内改良和耕种一定比例的土地，如果没能履行义务，那么没有耕种的土地就被给予别人。这一规定可能并没有被严格执行，但却有一定的成效。

（1）未耕种的土地受到更多的限制。

第二，在宾夕法尼亚，没有长子继承权，土地像动产一样，平均分配给家庭当中的每一个子女。在新英格兰的三个省份中，长子只能得到双份，就像摩西法律一样。因此，在这些省份中，有时某个人可能占有大量的土地，但是经过一代或者两代，就可能被充分地重新划分。在其他英国殖民地中，长子继承权的确存在，

（2）长子继承和限定继承不那么流行，土地转让比较常见。

colonies, indeed, the right of primogeniture takes place, as in the law of England. But in all the English colonies the tenure of the lands, which are all held by free socage, facilitates alienation, and the grantee of any extensive tract of land, generally finds it for his interest to alienate, as fast as he can, the greater part of it, reserving only a small quitrent. In the Spanish and Portugueze colonies, what is called the right of Majorazzo takes place in the succession of all those great estates to which any title of honour is annexed. Such estates go all to one person, and are in effect entailed and unalienable. The French colonies, indeed, are subject to the custom of Paris, which, in the inheritance of land, is much more favourable to the younger children than the law of England. But, in the French colonies, if any part of an estate, held by the noble tenure of chivalry and homage, is alienated, it is, for a limited time, subject to the right of redemption, either by the heir of the superior or by the heir of the family; and all the largest estates of the country are held by such noble tenures, which necessarily embarrass alienation. But, in a new colony, a great uncultivated estate is likely to be much more speedily divided by alienation than by succession. The plenty and cheapness of good land, it has already been observed, are the principal causes of the rapid prosperity of new colonies. The engrossing of land, in effect, destroys this plenty and cheapness. The engrossing of uncultivated land, besides, is the greatest obstruction to its improvement. But the labour that is employed in the improvement and cultivation of land affords the greatest and most valuable produce to the society. The produce of labour, in this case, pays not only its own wages, and the profit of the stock which employs it, but the rent of the land too upon which it is employed. The labour of the English colonists, therefore, being more employed in the improvement and cultivation of land, is likely to afford a greater and more valuable produce, than that of any of the other three nations, which, by the engrossing of land, is more or less diverted towards other employments.

(3) Taxes are more moderate.

Thirdly, the labour of the English colonists is not only likely to afford a greater and more valuable produce, but, in consequence of the moderation of their taxes, a greater proportion of this produce belongs to themselves, which they may store up and employ in putting into motion a still greater quantity of labour. The English colonists have never yet contributed any thing towards the defence of the mother

就像英国法律中规定的一样。但是在所有的英国殖民地中,土地占用全都是根据自由租佃制,这使得土地易于割让,得到大片土地的人会觉得将大部分让出,自己只保留一小部分缴纳免役地租的土地,对自己是有利的。在西班牙和葡萄牙的殖民地上,所有附有勋爵称号的大地产的继承都实行所谓的长子继承。这些地产全部由一个人继承,实际上是限定继承,不可割让的。法国殖民地的确都遵守巴黎的习惯,在土地继承上,跟英国的法律相比,对年纪更小的孩子要有利得多。但是在法国殖民地,有骑士称号和领地称号的贵族占有地,如果有任何部分被割让,那么在有限的期间内,按照赎买权,得由领地继承人或家族继承人赎回。如果这个国家所有的大地产都被贵族把持,那么这显然会阻碍转让。但是在新殖民地,大片未耕种的地产通过转让比通过继承能更快地被分割。已经说过,良好土地的丰富和廉价是新殖民地快速繁荣的主要原因。土地垄断在效果上会破坏这种丰富和廉价。同时,未耕种土地的垄断是对它进行改良最大的障碍。但是在土地改良和耕种时,雇佣的劳动可以生产出利润最大和最有价值的产品。在这种情况下,劳动的产物不仅支付了它自己的工资和雇佣劳动的资本的利润,而且支付用劳动耕种的土地的地租。因此,英国殖民者的劳动,在土地改良和耕种时被更多地雇佣,可能会比其他任何第三国有更大更有价值的产出。而第三国的劳动由于土地的垄断,或多或少地转向其他用途。

第三,英国殖民者的劳动不仅可能提供更大更有价值的产出,而且由于他们税收的比例适中,很大一部分这种产出属于他们自己,他们可以将其储存,可以用它来雇佣更多的劳动力。英国殖民者从未给他们的母国防御贡献任何东西,也没有对其内政(3)税更加适中。

country, or towards the support of its civil government. They themselves, on the contrary, have hitherto been defended almost entirely at the expence of the mother country. But the expence of fleets and armies is out of all proportion greater than the necessary expence of civil government. The expence of their own civil government has always been very moderate. It has generally been confined to what was necessary for paying competent salaries to the governor, to the Judges, and to some other officers of police, and for maintaining a few of the most useful public works. The expence of the civil establishment of Massachusett's Bay, before the commencement of the present disturbances, used to be but about 18, 000*l.* a year. That of New Hampshire and Rhode Island 3, 500 *l.* each. That of Connecticut 4, 000*l.* That of New York and Pennsylvania 4, 500 *l.* each. That of New Jersey 1, 200*l.* That of Virginia and South Carolina 8, 000 *l.* each. The civil establishments of Nova Scotia and Georgia are partly supported by an annual grant of parliament. But Nova Scotia pays, besides, about 7, 000 *l.* a year towards the public expences of the colony; and Georgia about 2,500l. a year. All the different civil establishments in North America, in short, exclusive of those of Maryland and North Carolina, of which no exact account has been got, did not, before the commencement of the present disturbances, cost the inhabitants above 64, 700 l. a year; an ever-memorable example at how small an expence three millions of people may not only be governed, but well governed. The most important part of the expence of government, indeed, that of defence and protection, has constantly fallen upon the mother country. The ceremonial too of the civil government in the colonies, upon the reception of a new governor, upon the opening of a new assembly, &c. though sufficiently decent, is not accompanied with any expensive pomp or parade. Their ecclesiastical government is conducted upon a plan equally frugal. Tithes are unknown among them; and their clergy, who are far from being numerous, are maintained either by moderate stipends, or by the voluntary contributions of the people. The power of Spain and Portugal, on the contrary, derives some support from the taxes levied upon their colonies. France, indeed, has never drawn any considerable revenue from its colonies, the taxes which it levies upon them being generally spent among them. But the colony government of all these three nations is conducted upon a much more expensive plan, and is accompanied with a much more expensive ceremonial. The sums spent upon the reception of a new viceroy of Peru, for example, have frequently been enormous. [1] Such

---

① [Juan and Ulloa, *Voyage historique*, tom. i. , pp. 437 - 441, give a lurid account of the magnificence of the ceremonial.]

给予任何支持。相反,他们自己的防御至今还是靠母国的开支。但是海陆军费用比例不当,大大超过了必要的行政开支。他们自己的行政开支通常都非常适中。一般来说,这些费用包括必须支付给总督、法官和一些其他警务人员的适当的工资。在当前混乱发生之前,马塞诸塞湾每年的行政设施费大约是 18000 镑;新汉普郡和罗得岛的行政设施费,分别都是 3500 镑;康涅狄格 4000 镑;纽约和宾夕法尼亚各 4500 镑;新泽西 1200 镑;弗吉尼亚和南卡罗来纳各 8000 镑;诺瓦斯克夏及佐治亚的行政费,一部分由议会每年拨款支持。但同时诺瓦斯克夏每年支付 7000 镑的殖民地行政费用,佐治亚每年仅出大约 2500 镑。总之,在北美,所有不同的行政设施费,除了马里兰及北卡罗利纳这两州无确切记载可查外,在当前混乱发生之前,居民每年需付的费用不过 647000 镑。这么少的开支不仅统治了 300 万人,而且统治得这么好,这真是一个值得牢记的例子。诚然,政府开支最主要部分是防卫和保护开支,而且经常落到母国的头上。在欢迎新总督到任及新议会开幕之际,殖民地政府的仪式,虽十分隆重,但并不铺张浪费。他们教会的开支同样节俭。这里的人们不知道什一税,他们人数不多的牧师,靠适中的俸禄和人们的自愿捐助来维持生活。相反,西班牙和葡萄牙的政权从殖民地保证的税收中得到了一些支持。的确,法国从来没有从他的殖民地中取得任何大量的收入,从殖民地征收的税也是通常又花在了殖民地人们的身上。但是这三个国家的殖民地政府的开支都相当巨大,并且有花费更为巨大的仪式相伴随。例如,迎接一位秘鲁新总督到任的开支就通常非常巨大[①]。

[①] 胡安和乌洛阿:《航行史》,第 1 卷,第 437~441 页,对仪式的隆重作了惊人的描述。

ceremonials are not only real taxes paid by the rich colonists upon those particular occasions, but they serve to introduce among them the habit of vanity and expence upon all other occasions. They are not only very grievous occasional taxes, but they contribute to establish perpetual taxes of the same kind still more grievous; the ruinous taxes of private luxury and extravagance. In the colonies of all those three nations too, the ecclesiastical government is extremely oppressive. Tithes take place in all of them, and are levied with the utmost rigour in those of Spain and Portugal. All of them besides are oppressed with a numerous race of mendicant friars, whose beggary being not only licensed, but consecrated by religion, is a most grievous tax upon the poor people, who are most carefully taught that it is a duty to give, and a very great sin to refuse them their charity. Over and above all this, the clergy are, in all of them, the greatest engrossers of land.

(4) The trade monopoly of the mother country has been less oppressive, Fourthly, in the disposal of their surplus produce, or of what is over and above their own consumption, the English colonies have been more favoured, and have been allowed a more extensive market, than those of any other European nation. Every European nation has endeavoured more or less to monopolize to itself the commerce of its colonies, and, upon that account, has prohibited the ships of foreign nations from trading to them, and has prohibited them from importing European goods from any foreign nation. But the manner in which this monopoly has been exercised in different nations has been very different.

since there has been no exclusive company with its interest to buy the produce of the colonies as cheap as possible, Some nations have given up the whole commerce of their colonies to an exclusive company, of whom the colonies were obliged to buy all such European goods as they wanted, and to whom they were obliged to sell the whole of their own surplus produce. It was the interest of the company, therefore, not only to sell the former as dear, and to buy the latter as cheap as possible, but to buy no more of the latter, even at this low price, than what they could dispose of for a very high price in Europe. It was their interest, not only to degrade in all cases the value of the surplus produce of the colony, but in many cases to discourage and keep down the natural increase of its quantity. Of all the expedients that can well be contrived to stunt the natural growth of a new

这些仪式的开支不仅使富裕的殖民者在一些特殊的场合支付实际税款,而且让他们在所有的场合下都养成了一种虚荣和奢侈的习惯。它们不仅是偶然的令人非常痛苦的税,而且是帮助建立一种同样的更加令人痛苦的永久的税,即,使人倾家荡产的奢侈消费习惯。这三个国家的殖民地中,教会也具有极端的压迫性。三国殖民地全部都征收什一税,在西班牙和葡萄牙两地的殖民地中征收最为严厉。同时,三国殖民地也受到一帮数量众多的行乞和尚的压迫,他们的行乞不仅合法,而且由宗教予以神圣化,这是压在贫穷人民头上的最令人痛苦的税。穷人们被告知给予是一种责任,拒绝施舍是一种非常大的罪过。除了这个,在三国殖民地内和尚是最大的土地垄断者。

第四,在处理他们的剩余产品或者是超过自己消费能力的生产物时,英国殖民地比其他任何欧洲国家的殖民地受到的照顾更多,拥有的市场更广阔。每个欧洲国家都或多或少企图垄断本国殖民地的商业,基于这个原因,禁止外国船只与其进行贸易,也禁止他们进口其他国家的欧洲货物。但是这种垄断在不同的国家被操作的方式是非常不同的。（4）母国的贸易垄断不那么压迫了,

一些国家把他们殖民地的整个商业交给一个专营公司打理,殖民地必须向公司购买他们需要的欧洲货物,他们也要把他们的剩余产品全部卖给这个公司。因此,公司的利益是,尽可能贵地出售前者,尽可能便宜地购买后者,但是即使是非常低的价格,也不会购进后者太多,而超过在欧洲以非常高的价格能够处理的量。他们的利益不仅是在所有的情况下降低殖民地剩余产品的价值,而且在许多情况下抑制和降低殖民地剩余产品的自然增长。在所有的能用来阻止新殖民地自然增长的一切办法中,专营因为没有专营公司了,殖民地利可以便宜购买欧货产品,

colony, that of an exclusive company is undoubtedly the most effectual. This, however, has been the policy of Holland, though their company, in the course of the present century, has given up in many respects the exertion of their exclusive privilege. This too was the policy of Denmark till the reign of the late king. It has occasionally been the policy of France, and of late, since 1755, after it had been abandoned by all other nations, on account of its absurdity, it has become the policy of Portugal with regard at least to two of the principal provinces of Brazil, Fernambuco and Marannon. ①

nor any restriction of commerce to a particular port and to particular licensed ships,

Other nations, without establishing an exclusive company, have confined the whole commerce of their colonies to a particular port of the mother country, from whence no ship was allowed to sail, but either in a fleet and at a particular season, or, if single, in consequence of a particular licence, which in most cases was very well paid for. This policy opened, indeed, the trade of the colonies to all the natives of the mother country, provided they traded from the proper port, at the proper season, and in the proper vessels. But as all the different merchants, who joined their stocks in order to fit out those licensed vessels, would find it for their interest to act in concert, the trade which was carried on in this manner would necessarily be conducted very nearly upon the same principles as that of an exclusive company. The profit of those merchants would be almost equally exorbitant and oppressive. The colonies would be ill supplied, and would be obliged both to buy very dear, and to sell very cheap. This, however, till within these few years, had always been the policy of Spain, and the price of all European goods, accordingly, is said to have been enormous in the Spanish West Indies. At Quito, we are told by Ulloa, a pound of iron sold for about four and six-pence, and a pound of steel for about six and nine-pence sterling. ② But it is chiefly in order to purchase European goods, that the colonies part with their own produce. The more, therefore, they pay for the one, the less they really get for the other, and the dearness of the one is the same thing with the cheapness of the other. The policy of Portugal is in this respect

---

① [Maranon in 1755 and Fernambuco four years later. Raynal, *Histoire philosophique*, Amsterdam ed. , 1773, tom. iii. , p. 402.]

② [Iron sometimes at 100 écus the quintal and steel at 150. Juan and Ulloa, *Voyage historique*, tom. i. , p. 252.]

公司毫无疑问是最有效的。可是这是荷兰的政策,尽管在本世纪中他们的公司在许多方面放弃了他们的特权。这也是丹麦的政策,直到前一任国王为止。法国的政策偶尔也是如此;近来,自 1755 年以来,由于其荒谬,该政策被其他的国家摒弃,但是葡萄牙仍在巴西的两个主要省份弗纳姆布克和马拉隆①推行这个政策。

其他没有建立专营公司的国家,将其殖民地的商业固定于母国的一个特别港口,只有成队的船在特别的季节,或者在大多数情况下通过支付大量费用而取得特殊执照的单独船只,才能被允许出航。诚然,这个政策打开了殖民地与所有母国居民的贸易的通道,只要他们在合适的港口合适的季节通过特定的船只进行贸易。但是,由于那些将资本联合为了使用这种特定船只的不同的商人会觉得,采取一致行动比较符合自己的利益。通过这种方式进行贸易必然要遵循与专营公司同样的原则。这些商人的利润和专营公司的利润几乎同样是高得离谱的。殖民地不能得到良好的供给,被逼迫以高价买进低价卖出。然而,直到最近这些年之前,西班牙奉行的还是这个政策。因此,所有欧洲货物的价格在西属西印度都很高。乌洛阿告诉我们,在基多,1 磅铁售价大约是 4 先令 6 便士,1 磅钢售价大约是 6 先令 9 便士②。但是殖民地出售自己的产品,主要是为了购买欧洲货物。因此,他们为一种产品付出越多,实际上从另一种产品得到的越少,一物的昂贵和另一物的廉价是同一个概念。就这一点说,葡萄牙对于弗纳

---

① 马拉隆在 1755 年,弗纳姆布克在 4 年后。雷纳尔:《哲学史》,阿姆斯特丹版,1773 年,第 3 卷,第 402 页。

② 铁有时是每昆特尔 100 厄科,钢 150 厄科。胡安和乌洛阿:《航行史》,第 1 卷,第 252 页。

the same as the ancient policy of Spain, with regard to all its colonies, except Fernambuco and Marannon, and with regard to these it has lately adopted a still worse.

but freedom for every subject to trade with every port in the mother country,
Other nations leave the trade of their colonies free to all their subjects, who may carry it on from all the different ports of the mother country, and who have occasion for no other licence than the common dispatches of the customhouse. In this case the number and dispersed situation of the different traders renders it impossible for them to enter into any general combination, and their competition is sufficient to hinder them from making very exorbitant profits. Under so liberal a policy the colonies are enabled both to sell their own produce and to buy the goods of Europe at a reasonable price. But since the dissolution of the Plymouth company, when our colonies were but in their infancy, this has always been the policy of England. It has generally too been that of France, and has been uniformly so since the dissolution of what, in England, is commonly called their Mississippi company. The profits of the trade, therefore, which France and England carry on with their colonies, though no doubt somewhat higher than if the competition was free to all other nations, are, however, by no means exorbitant; and the price of European goods accordingly is not extravagantly high in the greater part of the colonies of either of those nations.

and freedom to export everything but the enumerated commodities to other places besides the mother country.
In the exportation of their own surplus produce too, it is only with regard to certain commodities that the colonies of Great Britain are confined to the market of the mother country. These commodities having been enumerated in the act of navigation and in some other subsequent acts, have upon that account been called *enumerated commodities*. ① The rest are called *non-enumerated*; and may be exported directly to other countries, provided it is in British or Plantati on ships, of which the owners and three-fourths of the mariners are British subjects.

Some most important productions are not enumerated,
Among the non-enumerated commodities are some of the most important productions of America and the West Indies; grain of all sorts, lumber, salt provisions, fish, sugar, and rum.

---

① [The commodities originally enumerated in 12 Car. II. , c. 18, § 18, were sugar, tobaccocotton-wool, indigo, ginger, fustic and other dyeing woods.]

姆布克和马拉隆二省以外的殖民地采取的政策和西班牙过去的政策完全一样,而对这两个省最近采取了更差的政策。

其他国家允许它们的臣民与它们的殖民地自由地进行贸易。他们能从母国所有不同的港口运出货物,除了海关的普通证件,其他的特许证是不需要的。在这种情况下,商人的人数众多和居住分散使他们不可能形成普遍的结合,他们彼此之间的竞争已经足够阻止他们获取非常高额的利润。在这样自由的政策下,殖民地能够以一个合理的价格出售自己的产品和购买欧洲的货物。但是自从普利茅斯公司解散以来,当时我们的殖民地还处于幼年时期,英国的政策就一直是这样。这也是法国推行的政策,而且自从通常被英国人称为密西西比公司解散以来,法国的政策就一直如此。因此,法国和英国在它们的殖民地经营的贸易的利润,尽管毫无疑问高于所有其他国家自由竞争时的利润,但是绝不是过度的高;因此,欧洲货物的价格在两国的大部分殖民地并不是特别高。^{每民由国一口贸易,但是个有和母每个港行}

在出口他们的剩余产品方面,英国殖民地只对某些商品做出限定要求运到母国市场。这些商品被航海法和一些此后颁布的其他法律所列举,所以被叫做"列举商品"①。其他的叫做非列举商品,只要是装在英国或者殖民地船只上,可以直接被出口到其他国家,但是其中船主和3/4的船员必须是英国国民。

在非列举商品中有美洲和西印度的一些最重要的产品,包括各种谷物、木材、腌制食品、鱼、糖和甜酒。

---

① 查理二世十二年第18号法律第18条,最初列举的商品是糖、烟草、棉花、羊毛、靛青、生姜、佛提树染料和其他染色用木料。

as grain,   Grain is naturally the first and principal object of the culture of all new colonies. By allowing them a very extensive market for it, the law encourages them to extend this culture much beyond the consumption of a thinly inhabited country, and thus to provide beforehand an ample subsistence for a continually increasing population.

timber,   In a country quite covered with wood, where timber consequently is of little or no value, the expence of clearing the ground is the principal obstacle to improvement. By allowing the colonies a very extensive market for their lumber, the law endeavours to facilitate improvement by raising the price of a commodity which would otherwise be of little value, and thereby enabling them to make some profit of what would otherwise be mere expence.

cattle,   In a country neither half-peopled nor half cultivated, cattle naturally multiply beyond the consumption of the inhabitants, and are often upon that account of little or no value. But it is necessary, it has already been shewn, that the price of cattle should bear a certain proportion to that of corn before the greater part of the lands of any country can be improved. By allowing to American cattle, in all shapes, dead and alive, a very extensive market, the law endeavours to raise the value of a commodity of which the high price is so very essential to improvement. The good effects of this liberty, however, must be somewhat diminished by the 4th of George III. c. 15. which puts hides and skins among the enumerated commodities, and thereby tends to reduce the value of American cattle.

fish,   To increase the shipping and naval power of Great Britain, by the extension of the fisheries of our colonies, is an object which the legislature seems to have had almost constantly in view. Those fisheries, upon this account, have had all the encouragement which freedom can give them, and they have flourished accordingly. The New England fishery in particular was, before the late disturbances, one of the most important, perhaps, in the world. The whale-fishery which, notwithstanding an extravagant bounty, is in Great Britain carried on to so little purpose, that in the opinion of many people (which I do not, however, pretend to warrant) the whole produce does not much exceed the value of the bounties which are annually paid for it, is in New England carried on without any bounty to a very great extent.

谷物自然而然是所有新殖民地最初和最主要的生产对象。比如谷物，法律通过允许殖民地有非常广阔的谷物市场，鼓励他们扩大这种作物种植以超过人口较少的国家的消费需要，从而为持续增长的人口提前提供足够的生活资料。

在一个森林覆盖的国家，木材因此会很少或者几乎没有价木材，值，清理土地的费用是改良土地的主要障碍。法律通过允许殖民地拥有非常广阔的木材市场，而提高没什么价值的商品的价格来促进土地改良，因而使殖民地能获取一些利润，否则只能是纯粹的开支。

在一个国家，一半的地方无人居住，土地也只开发了一半，牲牲畜，畜自然地增长超过了居民的消费，因此通常价值非常小或者没有价值。但是，已经说过，在任何国家的大片土地能够被改良之前，牲畜价格应当和玉米价格成一定比例。法律通过允许殖民地拥有非常广阔的各种形式的美国牲畜的市场，不管是活的还是死的，来提高该商品的价值，该商品的高价对土地改良来说是非常重要的。然而，这一自由的良好效果必然由于乔治三世四年第15号法律而受到减弱，这一法律把皮革和毛皮当作列举商品，因此就减少了美国牲畜的价值。

通过扩大我们殖民地的渔业来增加英国的航运业和海军实鱼，力，似乎是议会孜孜以求的目标。因此，该渔业受到了自由制度所能给予的一切鼓励，因而大大繁荣起来。在最近的骚乱之前，特别是新英格兰的渔业，可能也算是世界上最重要的渔业之一。捕鲸业，虽然有不少的津贴，但成绩不大，许多人认为（然而我不想为此做保证）整个的产出并没有大大超过每年所支付的津贴的价值，在新英格兰虽然没有津贴，却以很大的规模在经营。鱼是

Fish is one of the principal articles with which the North Americans trade to Spain, Portugal, and the Mediterranean.

<small>sugar,</small> Sugar was originally an enumerated commodity which could be exported only to Great Britain. But in 1731, upon a representation of the sugar-planters, its exportation was permitted to all parts of the world. ① The restrictions, however, with which this liberty was granted, joined to the high price of sugar in Great Britain, have rendered it, in a great measure, ineffectual. Great Britain and her colonies still continue to be almost the sole market for all the sugar produced in the British plantations. Their consumption increases so fast, that, though in consequence of the increasing improvement of Jamaica, as well as of the Ceded Islands, ② the importation of sugar has increased very greatly within these twenty years, the exportation to foreign countries is said to be not much greater than before.

<small>and rum.</small> Rum is a very important article in the trade which the Americans carry on to the coast of Africa, from which they bring back negroe slaves in return.

<small>Grain, meat and fish would have competed too strongly with British produce if forced into the British market.</small> If the whole surplus produce of America in grain of all sorts, in salt provisions, and in fish, had been put into the enumeration, and thereby forced into the market of Great Britain, it would have interfered too much with the produce of the industry of our own people. It was probably not so much from any regard to the interest of America, as from a jealousy of this interference, that those important commodities have not only been kept out of the enumeration, but that the importation into Great Britain of all grain, except rice, and of salt provisions, has, in the ordinary state of the law, been prohibited.

The non-enumerated commodities could originally be exported to all parts of the world. Lumber and rice, having been once put into the enumerati on, when theywere after wards taken out of it,

---

① [There seems to be some mistake here. The true date is apparently 1739, under the Act 12 Geo. Ⅱ., c. 30.]

② [Garnier, in his note to this passage, tom. iii., p. 323, points out that the islands ceded by the peace of Paris in 1763 were only Grenada and the Grenadines, but that the term here includes the other islands won during the war, St. Vincent, Dominica and Tobago.]

北美与西班牙、葡萄牙和地中海地区进行贸易的主要商品之一。

糖一开始是只能被运往英国的列举商品。但是在1731年，在甘蔗种植者的呼吁下，它被允许运往世界各地①。然而，在给予自由的同时施加的限制措施，加上在英国糖的价格很高，在很大程度上不起作用。英国和她的殖民地依然几乎是在英国蔗糖殖民地生产的糖的唯一市场。他们的消费增长如此迅速，以至于虽然牙买加和被割让的各岛②的土地改良加快，糖的进口在这20年中增长非常迅速，但是出口到国外的据说并不比以前多多少。

甜酒是美洲和非洲沿岸进行贸易的非常重要的商品，从那里他们带回了黑奴。

如果美洲把各种谷物、腌制食品和鱼的剩余产品均划分为列举商品，从而被迫进入英国市场，那么就会过多地干预我们自己国民的生产产品。可能不是那么多地考虑美洲的利益，而只是对这种干涉的嫉妒，这些重要的商品不仅没有被列入列举商品之内，而且，除了大米以外的所有的谷物以及腌制食品，在法律的普通状态下，被禁止输入英国。

非列举商品一开始可以被运往世界各地。木材和大米，曾经被列入列举商品名单，当它们后来成为非列举商品后，只能出口

---

① 这里似乎有错误。根据乔治二世十二年第30号法律，真实的年份显然是1739年。

② 加尼尔在他给这段话（第3卷，第323页）加的注释中指出，1763年巴黎和约割让地岛只有格林纳达和格林纳丁斯群岛，但是这个词这里包含了在战争中取胜得到的其他岛屿，圣文森特、多米尼加和多巴哥。

国民财富的性质与原理

Originally nonenumerated commoditites could be exported to any part of the world. Recently they have been confined to countries south of Cape Finisterre.

were confined, as to the European market, to the countries that lie south of Cape Finisterre. ① By the 6th of George Ⅲ. c. 52. all non-enumerated commodities were subjected to the like restriction. The parts of Europe which lie south of Cape Finisterre, are not manufacturing countries, and we were less jealous of the colony ships carrying home from them any manufactures which could interfere with our own.

The enumerated commodities are of two sorts: first, such as are either the peculiar produce of America, or as cannot be produced, or at least are not produced, in the mother country. Of this kind are, melasses, coffee, cacao-nuts, tobacco, pimento, ginger, whale-fins, raw silk, cotton-wool, beaver, and other peltry of America, indigo, fustic, and other dying woods: secondly, such as are not the peculiar produce of America, but which are and may be produced in the mother country, though not in such quantities as to supply the greater part of her demand, which is principally supplied from foreign countries. Of this kind are all naval stores, masts, yards, and bowsprits, tar, pitch, and turpentine, pig and bar iron, copper ore, hides and skins, pot and pearl ashes.

The enumerated commodities are (1) commodities not produced at all in the mother country, and (2) commodities of which only a small part of the supply is produced in the mother country.

The largest importation of commodities of the first kind could not discourage the growth or interfere with the sale of any part of the produce of the mother country. By confining them to the home market, our merchants, it was expected, would not only be enabled to buy them cheaper in the Plantations, and consequently to sell them with a better profit at home, but to establish between the Plantations and foreign countries an advantageous carrying trade, of which Great Britain was necessarily to be the center or emporium, as the European country into which those commodities were first to be imported. The importation of commodities of the second kind might be so managed too, it was supposed, as to interfere, not with the sale of those of the same kind which were produced at home, but with that of those which were imported from foreign countries; because, by means of proper duties, they might be rendered always somewhat dearer than the former, and yet a good deal cheaper than the latter. By confining such commodities to the home market, therefore, it was proposed to discourage the produce, not of Great Britain, but of some foreign countries with which the balance of trade was believed to be unfavourable to Great Britain.

---

① [Rice was put in by 3 and 4 Ann, c. 5, and taken out by 3 Geo. Ⅱ. , c. 28; timber was taken out by 5 Geo. Ⅲ, c. 45.]

到欧洲市场,限于菲尼斯特雷角以南的地方①。根据乔治三世6年第52号法律,所有非列举商品都受到同样的限制。菲尼斯特雷角以南的欧洲国家都不是制造业国,所以我们不太嫉妒殖民地的船只会从它们那里运回任何能干涉我们自己生产的商品。

列举商品有两类:第一类是美洲的特殊产品,或者是不能在母国生产的产品或至少是母国不生产的产品。属于这一类的有:蜜糖、咖啡、椰子果、烟草、红胡椒、生姜、鲸须、生丝、棉花、海狸皮和美洲其他毛皮、靛青、黄佛提树及其他各种染色树木。第二类是非美洲的特殊产品,可以在母国生产,但其产量不能满足其需求,主要靠从外国进口的。属于这一类的有所有海军用品、船桅、帆桁、牙樯、松脂、柏油、松香油、生铁、铜矿、生皮、皮革、锅罐、珍珠灰。第一类商品的最大限量的进口不会阻碍母国任何产品的增长或者干涉其销售。我们的商人,通过限制它们只能输入本国市场,期望不仅在殖民地以更低的价格购入,而且在殖民地和外国之间建立一种有利的转口贸易,英国必然成为这种贸易的中心或总市场,因为它是那些商品输入欧洲进入的第一个国家。通常认为第二类商品的进口也可以如此经营;不是去干涉这些在国内生产的同样产品的销售,而是那些从外国进口的产品的销售,因为,通过合适的关税,那些产品可能常常比前者要贵,而比后者要便宜很多。因此,通过限制这些商品只能输入国内市场,不是想阻碍英国的产品生产,而是阻碍那些贸易差额会对英国不利的外

---

① 大米由安妮女王三年、四年第5号法律列入名单,由乔治二世三年第28号法律从名单中抽出,木材由乔治三世五年第45号法律从名单中抽出。

| 国民财富的性质与原理

On the importation of naval stores to Great Britain a bounty was given.

The prohibition of exporting from the colonies, to any other country but Great Britain, masts, yards, and bowsprits, tar, pitch, and turpentine, naturally tended to lower the price of timber in the colonies, and consequently to increase the expence of clearing their lands, the principal obstacle to their improvement. But about the beginning of the present century, in 1703, the pitch and tar company of Sweden endeavoured to raise the price of their commodities to Great Britain, by prohibiting their exportation, except in their own ships, at their own price, and in such quantities as they thought proper. ① In order to counteract this notable piece of mercantile policy, and to render herself as much as possible independent, not only of Sweden, but of all the other northern powers, Great Britain gave a bounty upon the importation of naval stores from America and the effect of this bounty was to raise the price of timber in America, much more than the confinement to the home market could lower it; and as both regulations were enacted at the same time, their joint effect was rather to encourage than to discourage the clearing of land in America.

American pig iron is exempt from duty.

Though pig and bar iron too have been put among the enumerated commodities, yet as, when imported from America, they are exempted from considerable duties to which they are subject when imported from any other country, ② the one part of the regulation contributes more to encourage the erection of furnaces in America, than the other to discourage it. There is no manufacture which occasions so great a consumption of wood as a furnace, or which can contribute so much to the clearing of a country over-grown with it.

These regulations have raised the value of timber and thus helped to clear the country.

The tendency of some of these regulations to raise the value of timber in America, and thereby to facilitate the clearing of the land, was neither, perhaps, intended nor understood by the legislature. Though their beneficial effects, however, have been in this respect accidental, they have not upon that account been less real.

① [Anderson, *Commerce*, A. D. 1703.]
② [23 Geo. II., c. 29.]

国的商品生产。

  禁止从殖民地将船桅、帆桁、牙樯、松脂、柏油、松香油运往英国以外的其他国家,自然会降低木材在殖民地的价格,因此增加清理它们土地的费用,而这是土地改良的主要障碍。但是大约在本世纪初,1703年的时候,瑞典柏油松脂公司试图提高它们进口英国商品的价格,它们禁止其出口,除非是用它们自己的船,按照它们自己的价格,以及它们认为合适的数量出口①。为了对抗这个引人注目的商业政策,并使自己尽可能地独立于瑞典和其他北方强国,英国对从美洲进口的海军用品发放奖金,而这一奖金的效果就是提高美洲木材的价格,使之大大超过限制只能输入国内市场而被压低的程度。由于两个规定同时颁布,它们的综合效果不是阻碍而是鼓励美洲土地的清理。

<small>对进口到英国商品发放奖金。海军用品</small>

  尽管生铁和铁条也被放进列举商品之列,但是从美洲进口它们则免去了从任何其他国家进口时需要缴纳的相当多的关税②,规定中的一部分内容鼓励在美洲建设造铁厂的行为,要大于另外一些内容阻碍此行为。没有一种制造业消费木材能够像熔铁炉那样大,或者说能对一个树木茂盛的国家的土地清理做出巨大贡献。

<small>美洲生铁是免税的。</small>

  有些规定想要提高美洲木材价值,以及由此方便土地清理的倾向,可能既不是立法者的本意也无法被他们理解。然而,尽管它们的有利影响从这方面来说是偶然的,但是并不会因为这点而显得不真实。

<small>这些规定增加了木材价值,帮助此国家进行了清理。</small>

---

① 安德森:《商业》,1703年。
② 乔治二世二十三年第29号法律。

| 国民财富的性质与原理

Freedom of trade prevails between the British American colonies and the British West Indies.

The most perfect freedom of trade is permitted between the British colonies of America and the West Indies, both in the enumerated and in the non-enumerated commodities. Those colonies are now become so populous and thriving, that each of them finds in some of the others a great and extensive market for every part of its produce. All of them taken together, they make a great internal market for the produce of one another.

British liberality does not extend to refined manufactures.

The liberality of England, however, towards the trade of her colonies has been confined chiefly to what concerns the market for their produce, either in its rude state, or in what may be called the very first stage of manufacture. The more advanced or more refined manufactures even of the colony produce, the merchants and manufacturers of Great Britain chuse to reserve to themselves, and have prevailed upon the legislature to prevent their establishment in the colonies, sometimes by high duties, and sometimes by absolute prohibitions.

Manufactured sugar is subject to heavy duty.

While, for example, Muskovado sugars from the British plantations, pay upon importation only 6 s. 4 d. the hundred weight; white sugars pay 1 l. 1 s. 1 d. ; and refined, either double or single, in loaves 4 l. 2 s. 5 d. $\frac{8}{20}$. When those high duties were imposed, Great Britain was the sole, and she still continues to be the principal market to which the sugars of the British colonies could be exported. They amounted, therefore, to a prohibition, at first of claying or refining sugar for any foreign market, and at present of claying or refining it for the market, which takes off, perhaps, more than nine-tenths of the whole produce. The manufacture of claying or refining sugar accordingly, though it has flourished in all the sugar colonies of France, has been little cultivated in any of those of England, except for the market of the colonies themselves. While Grenada was in the hands of the French, there was a refinery of sugar, by claying at least, upon almost every plantation. Since it fell into those of the English, almost all works of this kind have been given up, and there are at present, October 1773, I am assured, not above two or three remaining in the island. At present, however, by an indulgence of the custom-house,

Steel furnaces and slit-mills may not be erected in the colonies,

clayed or refined sugar, if reduced from loaves into powder, is commonly imported as Muskovado.

While Great Britain encourages in America the manufactures of pig and bar iron, by exempting them from duties to which the like commodities are subject when imported from any other country, she imposes an absolute prohibition upon the erection of steel furnaces and

— 1238 —

英国的美洲殖民地和西印度之间的贸易,在列举商品和非列举商品方面,被给予了最大限度的自由。那些殖民地现在变得人口众多、繁荣旺盛,每个殖民地都在其他殖民地给其产品找到了一个巨大和广阔的市场。如果把它们合成一个整体来看,它们成了各种产品巨大的国内市场。

美洲英国殖民地与西印度国之间的贸易十分自由。

然而,英国对于其殖民地贸易的宽大政策,主要限于它们的原料和初级产品的市场。对于殖民地更先进的或者更精密的制造品,英国商人和制造商选择将其留给自己,并让议会有时通过高关税,有时通过绝对的禁止阻止殖民地制造品的贸易。

英国的宽大政策没有扩展到精密制造业。

例如,从英国殖民地进口粗制砂糖,每英担仅交税 6 先令 4 便士,白糖交税 1 镑 1 先令 1 便士,单制或复制的精制砂糖交税 4 镑 2 先令 5 $\frac{8}{20}$ 便士。当被征收这么重的税时,英国是英属殖民地的食糖出口的唯一市场,现在仍然是其主要的市场。因此,这么高的税,开始是禁止白糖或者精制砂糖供应外国市场,现在是禁止制造白糖或者精制砂糖去供应或许可能销售全部产品 9/10 以上的市场。因此,尽管白糖或者精制砂糖的制造在法国蔗糖殖民地十分发达,而在英国殖民地上除了供应本身需要外,很少发展。当格伦纳达在法国人手中时,几乎每个殖民地都有一个炼糖厂,至少是漂白。自落入英国人之手,所有的这类砂糖厂就被放弃,到现在,1773 年 10 月,我确信,岛上剩下的厂不会超过两到三家。然而,目前由于海关的纵容,白糖或者精制砂糖如果从块变成粉,通常被当作混糖进口。

砂糖被征重税。精制糖被收税。

炼钢厂和铁厂不允许在殖民地建立。

英国鼓励在美洲生产生铁和铁条,并对其免征从其他国家进口同类产品所需交纳的关税,但是它绝对禁止在它的美洲殖民地

— 1239 —

slit-mills in any of her American plantations. ① She will not suffer her colonists to work in those more refined manufactures even for their own consumption; but insists upon their purchasing of her merchants and manufacturers all goods of this kind which they have occasion for.

<small>Hats, wools and woollen goods produced in America may not be carried in bulk from province to province.</small>

She prohibits the exportation from one province to another by water, and even the carriage by land upon horseback or in a cart, of hats, of wools and woollen goods, of the produce of America; a regulation which effectually prevents the establishment of any manufacture of such commodities for distant sale, and confines the industry of her colonists in this way to such coarse and household manufactures, as a private family commonly makes for its own use, or for that of some of its neighbours in the same province.

To prohibit a great people, however, from making all that they can of every part of their own produce, or from employing their stock and industry in the way that they judge most advantageous to themselves, is a manifest violation of the most sacred rights of mankind.

<small>Such prohibitions, though a violation of sacred rights, have not as yet been very hurtful.</small>

Unjust, however, as such prohibitions may be, they have not hitherto been very hurtful to the colonies. Land is still so cheap, and, consequently, labour so dear among them, that they can import from the mother country, almost all the more refined or more advanced manufactures cheaper than they could make them for themselves. Though they had not, therefore, been prohibited from establishing such manufactures, yet in their present state of improvement, a regard to their own interest would, probably, have prevented them from doing so. In their present state of improvement, those prohibitions, perhaps, without cramping their industry, or restraining it from any employment to which it would have gone of its own accord, are only impertinent badges of slavery imposed upon them, without any sufficient reason, by the groundless jealousy of the merchants and manufacturers of the mother country. In a more advanced state they might be really oppressive and insupportable.

Great Britain too, as she confines to her own market some of the most important productions of the colonies, so in compensation she gives to some of them an advantage in that market; sometimes

---

① [23 Geo. Ⅱ., c. 29. Anderson, *Commerce*, A. D. 1750.]

上建立炼钢厂和铁工厂①。它不会允许自己的殖民者从事这些比较精密的制造业,即使是为了他们自己的消费;它们坚持从英国商人和制造业者那里购买所有它们需要的所有货物。

它禁止通过水路甚至是在陆上用马驮或者用马车将美洲生产的帽子、羊毛和毛织品从一个省运到另一个省;这个规定有效地阻止了这种商品的制造业的建立来供远距离销售,将其殖民地的工业限制在粗糙的和家庭制造,因为一户私人家庭通常出于自己的使用或者同省邻人的需要而制造。

> 美洲生产的帽子、羊毛和毛织品不能从一省运往另一省。

然而,禁止一个伟大的民族制造他们能自己制造的产品的任何一部分,或禁止按照他们认为最有利于自己的方式去使用资本和劳动,都是对最神圣的人类权力的明显侵犯。不过,尽管这种禁令可能是不公正的,但是到现在为止还没有对殖民地造成很大的伤害。土地还是这么廉价,因此劳动在它们当中是那么昂贵,他们能从母国进口比他们自己制造要更便宜的,几乎所有的精密或者更先进的制造品。因此,尽管他们没有被禁止建立这样的制造业,但是按照他们现在的改良状况,他们考虑自己的利益可能会阻止他们这样去做。按照他们现在的改良状况,这些禁令可能没有约束他们的产业,或者阻止他们产业的本来会自行进行的改进。不过这是母国商人和制造者,由于无根据的嫉妒毫无理由地加在他们身上的无理的奴役的标记。在一个比较进步的情况下,这些禁令很可能是不能容忍的真正压迫。

> 禁令虽犯了神圣的权利,但没有造成大害。这种侵犯神权的禁令……

英国将它殖民地的一些最重要的产物限制输入自己的市场,所以为了补偿,它让一些产品在那个市场享有优势:有时是从其

---

① 乔治二世二十三年第 29 号法律。安德森:《商业》,1750 年。

The importation into Great Britain of various colonial productions is encouraged either by abatement of duties or by bounties. by imposing higher duties upon the like productions when imported from other countries, and sometimes by giving bounties upon their importation from the colonies. In the first way she gives an advantage in the home-market to the sugar, tobacco, and iron of her own colonies, and in the second to their raw silk, to their hemp and flax, to their indigo, to their naval-stores, and to their building-timber. This second way of encouraging the colony produce by bounties upon importation, is, so far as I have been able to learn, peculiar to Great Britain. The first is not. Portugal does not content herself with imposing higher duties upon the importation of tobacco from any other country, but prohibits it under the severest penalties.

In regard to imports from Europe the British colonies have had more liberal treatment than those of other countries, With regard to the importation of goods from Europe, England has likewise dealt more liberally with her colonies than any other nation.

Great Britain allows a part, almost always the half, generally a larger portion, and sometimes the whole of the duty which is paid upon the importation of foreign goods, to be drawn back upon their exportation to any foreign country. No independent foreign country, it was easy to foresee, would receive them if they came to it loaded with the heavy duties to which almost all foreign goods are subjected on their importation into Great Britain. Unless, therefore, some part of those duties was drawn back upon exportation, there was an end of the carrying trade; a trade so much favoured by the mercantile system.

drawbacks being allowed, Our colonies, however, are by no means independent foreign countries; and Great Britain having assumed to herself the exclusive right of supplying them with all goods from Europe, might have forced them (in the same manner as other countries have done their colonies) to receive such goods, loaded with all the same duties which they paid in the mother country. But, on the contrary, till 1763, the same drawbacks were paid upon the exportation of the greater part of foreign goods to our colonies as to any independent foreign country. In 1763, indeed, by the 4th of Geo. III. c. 15. this indulgence was a good deal abated, and it was enacted, "That no part of the duty called" the old subsidy should be drawn back for any goods of the growth, "production, or manufacture of Europe or the East Indies, which" should be exported from this kingdom to any British colony or

他国家进口同类产品时对它们征收高额税款,有时是对从殖民地进口的产品给予奖金。通过第一种方法,它在国内市场给予殖民地的糖、烟草和铁给予优惠,用第二种方法在国内市场给予殖民地的生丝、大麻、亚麻、靛青、海军用品和建筑木材优惠。第二种通过给予奖金来鼓励殖民地产品进口的方法,据我所知,目前只有英国在采用。第一种方法则不只是英国在用。葡萄牙并不满足对从任何其他国家的烟草进口征收重税,而是采取最严厉的措施来禁止。

英国各殖民地产品税减或者奖金予以鼓励

至于从欧洲进口的货物,英国对自己的殖民地比对任何其他国家处理上要更加宽大。

在从欧洲进口上,英国殖民地受到他比其他国家更自由的对待,

英国允许将外国货物进口时缴纳的税当中的一部分,几乎通常是一半,一般是较大的一部分,有时是全部,在这些货物出口到其他国家后退还给他们。很容易预见,如果外国货物进入英国要缴纳很重的税,任何独立国家都不会接受这种货物进口。因此,除非重税的某一部分在出口时被退回,否则转口贸易就会中止;而转口贸易是重商主义体系提倡的贸易。

但是,我们的殖民地绝不是独立的国家,英国取得了给殖民地提供所有欧洲货物的垄断权,就像其他国家对待殖民地一样,英国强迫其殖民地接受这些在进入母国前就被征收重税的货物。但是正好相反,直到1763年以前,像出口到任何独立的外国一样,出口到我们殖民地很大部分的外国货物也有退税。的确,1763年,根据乔治三世四年第15号法律,这种宽松政策被大大取消,法律规定:"欧洲或东印度生长、生产或制造的产品,从本王国运往任何英属殖民地或在美洲的殖民地时,称为旧补助税的那一

允许退税,

"plantation in America; wines, white callicoes and muslins excepted." Before this law, many different sorts of foreign goods might have been bought cheaper in the plantations than in the mother country; and some may still.

<small>owing to the advice of interested merchants.</small> Of the greater part of the regulations concerning the colony trade, the merchants who carry it on, it must be observed, have been the principal advisers. We must not wonder, therefore, if, in the greater part of them, their interest has been more considered than either that of the colonies or that of the mother country. In their exclusive privilege of supplying the colonies with all the goods which they wanted from Europe, and of purchasing all such parts of their surplus produce as could not interfere with any of the trades which they themselves carried on at home, the interest of the colonies was sacrificed to the interest of those merchants. In allowing the same drawbacks upon the re-exportation of the greater part of European and East India goods to the colonies, as upon their re-exportation to any independent country, the interest of the mother country was sacrificed to it, even according to the mercantile ideas of that interest. It was for the interest of the merchants to pay as little as possible for the foreign goods which they sent to the colonies, and consequently, to get back as much as possible of the duties which they advanced upon their importation into Great Britain. They might thereby be enabled to sell in the colonies, either the same quantity of goods with a greater profit, or a greater quantity with the same profit, and, consequently, to gain something either in the one way or the other. It was, likewise, for the interest of the colonies to get all such goods as cheap and in as great abundance as possible. But this might not always be for the interest of the mother country. She might frequently suffer both in her revenue, by giving back a great part of the duties which had been paid upon the importation of such goods; and in her manufactures, by being undersold in the colony market, in consequence of the easy terms upon which foreign manufactures could be carried thither by means of those drawbacks. The progress of the linen manufacture of Great Britain, it is commonly said, has been a good deal retarded by the drawbacks upon the re-exportation of German linen to the American colonies.

种赋税的任何部分均不退还;葡萄酒、白洋布和细洋布除外。"在这项法律之前,许多不同种类的外国货物在殖民地购买要比在母国购买便宜,有些货物现在可能仍是如此。

有关殖民地贸易的很大一部分的规定中,必须注意到,制定规定的商人是主要的顾问。所以,如果大部分规定里,他们的利益比殖民地或者母国的利益考虑的要多,我们不必奇怪。在他们向殖民地提供他们需要的来自欧洲的所有货物时的垄断权方面,以及在购买不干涉他们在本国进行的贸易的那些殖民地剩余产品的垄断权方面,殖民地的利益被牺牲以用于保护商人的利益。在大部分欧洲和东印度货物向殖民地再出口时,如同向任何独立国家再出口一样,享受的退税,按照重商主义的利益观点,是保护商人的利益而牺牲母国的利益。商人的利益在于,他们送往殖民地的外国货物支付要尽可能少,从而使它们进入英国时缴纳的税收被退还得尽可能多。这样,他们能够在殖民地卖出同样数量的货物而获得高额利润,或者以相同的利润出售更多的数量,因而不管是这种方式还是另一种方式都能获利。同样,殖民地的利益在于,尽可能低价地得到货物,尽可能得到更多的货物。但是这不总是为了母国的利益。它常常会在两个方面受到损失:一是由于退还该货物进口缴纳的大部分税收造成的收入损失,二是由于殖民地市场上,这些外国制造品因为退税便于运输,售价低于母国制造品,而造成的制造业上的损失。人们常说,英国的亚麻布制造业的进步,由于德国亚麻布的再出口到美洲殖民地,被大大影响。

_{由于有利益关系的商人的建议}

国民财富的性质与原理

But though the policy of Great Britain with regard to the trade of her colonies has been dictated by the same mercantile spirit as that of other nations, it has, however, upon the whole, been less illiberal and oppressive than that of any of them.

<small>Except in regard to foreign trade the English colonies have complete liberty.</small>   In every thing, except their foreign trade, the liberty of the English colonists to manage their own affairs their own way is complete. It is in every respect equal to that of their fellow-citizens at home, and is secured in the same manner, by an assembly of the representatives of the people, who claim the sole right of imposing taxes for the support of the colony government. The authority of this assembly over-awes the executive power, and neither the meanest nor the most obnoxious colonist, as long as he obeys the law, has any thing to fear from the resentment, either of the governor, or of any other civil or military officer in the province. The colony assemblies, though like the house of commons in England, they are not always a very equal representation of the people, yet they approach more nearly to that character; and as the executive power either has not the means to corrupt them, or, on account of the support which it receives from the mother country, is not under the necessity of doing so, they are perhaps in general more influenced by the inclinations of their constituents. The councils, which, in the colony legislatures, correspond to the house of lords in Great Britain, are not composed of an hereditary nobility. In some of the colonies, as in three of the governments of New England, those councils are not appointed by the king, but chosen by the representatives of the people. In none of the English colonies is there any hereditary nobility. In all of them, indeed, as in all other free countries, the descendant of an old colony family is more respected than an upstart of equal merit and fortune: but he is only more respected, and he has no privileges by which he can be troublesome to his neighbours. Before the commencement of the present disturbances, the colony assemblies had not only the legislative, but a part of the executive power. In Connecticut and Rhode Island, they elected the governor. ① In the other colonies

---

① [The Board of Trade and Plantations, in a report to the House of Commons in 1732, insisted on this democratic character of the government of some of the colonies, and mentioned the election of governor by Connecticut and Rhode Island: the report is quoted in Anderson, *Commerce*, A. D. 1732.]

但是尽管英国对其殖民地贸易的政策,同与其他国家进行贸易的政策一样,是受到重商主义政策支配的,然而,从整体上来说,它不像其他任何国家的政策那样不自由和具有压制性。

除了对外贸易,英国殖民者在每件事情上以自己的方式处理自己事务的自由是很完全的。这种自由在每个方面都和他们国内臣民的自由相等,也以同样的方式予以保证,即通过人民代表议会,这个议会拥有支持殖民地政府而征税的唯一特权。这个议会的权力使行政权力得以震慑,不论是最卑鄙的还是最令人讨厌的殖民地,只要他遵守法律,就不必担心来自总督或者是省内文武官员对他的憎恶。殖民地议会,尽管和英国众议院一样,不总是完全代表人民,但也接近这种性质;由于行政权力机关没有办法去腐蚀他们,或者由于受到母国的支持而不必这样去做,他们可能总体上会更多地受到选举人意志的影响。殖民地立法机关中的参议院和英国的上议院相当,但不是由世袭贵族组成。在一些殖民地中,就像在新英格兰的三个政府中,这些参议院不是国王任命的,而是由人民代表选出来的。没有一个英属殖民地有世袭的贵族。诚然,在所有殖民地,就像在所有其他自由国家一样,老殖民地家庭的后代,比美德和财产相同的暴发户更受人尊重;但他也只是更受尊重,他没有特权去烦扰邻居。在现在的骚乱开始之前,殖民地议会不仅有立法权,而且还有一部分的行政权力。在康涅狄格和罗得岛,议会选举了总督①。在其他的殖民地,议

> 除了对外贸易,英国殖民地有完全的自由。

---

① 贸易和殖民委员会在 1732 年给下议院的一个报告中,坚持一些殖民地政府的民主特性,并提到了康涅狄格和罗得岛的总督选举:报告在安德森《商业》(1732 年)中被引用。

they appointed the revenue officers who collected the taxes imposed by those respective assemblies, to whom those officers were immediately responsible. There is more equality, therefore, among the English colonists than among the inhabitants of the mother country. Their manners are more republican, and their governments, those of three of the provinces of New England in particular, have hitherto been more republican too.

<small>The absolute governments of Spain, of Portugal, and in a less degree of France, are even more violent in the colonies than at home.</small>

The absolute governments of Spain, Portugal, and France, on the contrary, take place in their colonies; and the discretionary powers which such governments commonly delegate to all their inferior officers are, on account of the great distance, naturally exercised there with more than ordinary violence. Under all absolute governments there is more liberty in the capital than in any other part of the country. The sovereign himself can never have either interest or inclination to pervert the order of justice, or to oppress the great body of the people. In the capital his presence over-awes more or less all his inferior officers, who in the remoter provinces, from whence the complaints of the people are less likely to reach him, can exercise their tyranny with much more safety. But the European colonies in America are more remote than the most distant provinces of the greatest empires which had ever been known before. The government of the English colonies is perhaps the only one which, since the world began, could give perfect security to the inhabitants of so very distant a province. The administration of the French colonies, however, has always been conducted with more gentleness and moderation than that of the Spanish and Portuguese. This superiority of conduct is suitable both to the character of the French nation, and to what forms the character of every nation, the nature of their government, which, though arbitrary and violent in comparison with that of Great Britain, is legal and free in comparison with those of Spain and Portugal.

<small>The sugar colonies of France are more prosperous than the English because they are not discouraged from refining, and slaves are better managed,</small>

It is in the progress of the North American colonies, however, that the superiority of the English policy chiefly appears. The progress of the sugar colonies of France has been at least equal, perhaps superior, to that of the greater part of those of England; and yet the sugar colonies of England enjoy a free government nearly of the same kind with that which takes place in her colonies of North America. But the sugar colonies of France are not discouraged, like those of England, from refining their own sugar; and, what is of still greater importance, the genius of their government naturally introduces better management of their negro slaves.

会任命税务官员，让他们征收议会课征的赋税，直接向议会负责。因此，英国殖民者比他们母国的居民有更多的平等。他们的行为有更多的共和精神，他们的政府，特别是新英格兰的三个省政府，也更有共和精神。

相反，西班牙、葡萄牙和法国的极权政府建立在他们的殖民地上，这种政府普通地授予所有的下级官员独断权，由于相距太远，自然在实施的时候比平时还要暴力。在全部极权政府下，在首都比在本国任何其他地方享有更多的自由。国王自己既没有兴趣也没有倾向去破坏正义秩序，去压迫人民大众。在首都，他的出现多多少少震慑了下级官员。在遥远的省份，人民的疾苦很少可能传达到国王那里，这些官员能更安全地为所欲为。但是在美洲的欧洲殖民地，比曾经知道的最大的帝国里最遥远的省份还要远。英国殖民地政府可能是自有了世界起，唯一能如此好地给予那么远距离省份居民保护的政府。然而，法国殖民地的行政比起西班牙和葡萄牙的行政来说，较为宽宏、温和。这种行为的好处是与法兰西民族的性格和一切民族的性格相适应的，这些民族政府的性质，与英国相比显得专横和暴力，但是与西班牙和葡萄牙相比则比较合法和自由。

然而，在北美殖民地的进步过程中，英国政策的优越性主要地显现出来了。法国蔗糖殖民地的进步，与英国大部分蔗糖殖民地的进步相比，至少是相等的，可能会更胜一筹。但是英国蔗糖殖民地几乎与它在北美殖民地一样享有政治自由。但是，就像英国的那些殖民地一样，法国的蔗糖殖民地精制自产的糖没有受到任何阻碍。更重要的是，政府的精英自然地引进了一种更好的管理黑奴的方法。

国民财富的性质与原理

absolute government being more favourable to the slaves than republican,

In all European colonies the culture of the sugar-cane is carried on by negro slaves. The constitution of those who have been born in the temperate climate of Europe could not, it is supposed, support the labour of digging the ground under the burning sun of the West Indies; and the culture of the sugar-cane, as it is managed at present, is all hand labour, though, in the opinion of many, the drill plough might be introduced into it with great advantage. But, as the profit and success of the cultivation which is carried on by means of cattle, depend very much upon the good management of those cattle; so the profit and success of that which is carried on by slaves, must depend equally upon the good management of those slaves; and in the good management of their slaves the French planters, I think it is generally allowed, are superior to the English. The law, so far as it gives some weak protection to the slave against the violence of his master, is likely to be better executed in a colony where the government is in a great measure arbitrary, than in one where it is altogether free. In every country where the unfortunate law of slavery is established, the magistrate, when he protects the slave, intermeddles in some measure in the management of the private property of the master; and, in a free country, where the master is perhaps either a member of the colony assembly, or an elector of such a member, he dare not do this but with the greatest caution and circumspection. The respect which he is obliged to pay to the master, renders it more difficult for him to protect the slave. But in a country where the government is in a great measure arbitrary, where it is usual for the magistrate to intermeddle even in the management of the private property of individuals, and to send them, perhaps, a letter de cachet if they do not manage it according to his liking, it is much easier for him to give some protection to the slave; and common humanity naturally disposes him to do so. The protection of the magistrate renders the slave less contemptible in the eyes of his master, who is thereby induced to consider him with more regard, and to treat him with more gentleness. Gentle usage renders the slave not only more faithful, but more intelligent, and therefore, upon a double account, more useful. He approaches more to the condition of a free servant, and may possess some degree of integrity and attachment to his master's interest, virtues which frequently belong to free servants, but which never can belong to a slave, who is treated as slaves commonly are in countries where the master is perfectly free and secure.

That the condition of a slave is better under an arbitrary than under

— 1250 —

在所有的欧洲殖民地中,甘蔗都是由黑奴来种植的。出生在欧洲温带地方的人据说是无法承受在西印度的骄阳下从事掘地的劳动;甘蔗的种植,就像现在从事的那样,都是手工劳动,尽管很多人都认为,锥犁的引进是有很大的好处的。但是,正如用牲畜来进行耕种的利润和成功很大程度上取决于对这些牲畜的良好管理一样,所有由奴隶来进行耕种的利润和成功也同样依靠对奴隶的良好管理。而在对奴隶的良好管理上,我认为大家都会承认,法国的种植人要优越于英国种植人。到现在为止,给予奴隶以微弱的保护使其免于他主人的暴力的法律,在一个政府很大程度上专制的殖民地比在一个总体上自由的殖民地被执行得要好。在每一个制定了不幸的奴隶法的国家,当地方长官保护奴隶时,就在某种程度上,干涉了主人对私人财产的管理;在一个自由国家里,主人可能是殖民地议会的成员,或者是这种成员的选举人,地方长官这样做的时候不得不特别的小心和谨慎。他对于主人的尊敬使得他更难以保护奴隶。但是,在一个政府特别专制的国家,地方长官通常干涉个人私有财产管理,如果个人不按照他的意愿去管理,他可能发出传票拘捕他们,所以,他更加容易给奴隶以保护;普通的人性自然地使他这么去做。地方长官的保护使得奴隶在他主人眼中不那么受轻视,因而主人也不得不给予较多的重视,较温和地对待他。这种温和的态度使得奴隶们不仅更加忠诚,而且更加聪明,因而也更加有用。他更加接近一个自由佣人的地位,可能拥有某种程度的诚实和对主人利益的忠诚,这些常常都是属于自由佣人的美德,但从来没有属于一个奴隶,在主人有完全自由和安全的国家,奴隶通常被当作奴隶对待。

我相信,在一个专制政府下,奴隶的状况要好于在自由政府

<small>集权政府比共和政府对奴隶更有利</small>

|国民财富的性质与原理|

<small>as may be seen in Roman history.</small> a free government, is, I believe, supported by the history of all ages and nations. In the Roman history, the first time we read of the magistrate interposing to protect the slave from the violence of his master, is under the emperors. When Vedius Pollio, in the presence of Augustus, ordered one of his slaves, who had committed a slight fault, to be cut into pieces and thrown into his fish-pond in order to feed his fishes, the emperor commanded him, with indignation, to emancipate immediately, not only that slave, but all the others that belonged to him. ① Under the republic no magistrate could have had authority enough to protect the slave, much less to punish the master.

<small>The superiority of the French sugar colonies is the more remarkable inasmuch as they have accumulated their own stock.</small> The stock, it is to be observed, which has improved the sugar colonies of France, particularly the great colony of St. Domingo, has been raised almost entirely from the gradual improvement and cultivation of those colonies. It has been almost altogether the produce of the soil and of the industry of the colonists, or, what comes to the same thing, the price of that produce gradually accumulated by good management, and employed in raising a still greater produce. But the stock which has improved and cultivated the sugar colonies of England has, a great part of it, been sent out from England, and has by no means been altogether the produce of the soil and industry of the colonists. ② The prosperity of the English sugar colonies has been, in a great measure, owing to the great riches of England, of which a part has overflowed, if one may say so, upon those colonies. But the prosperity of the sugar colonies of France has been entirely owing to the good conduct of the colonists, which must therefore have had some superiority over that of the English; and this superiority has been remarked in nothing so much as in the good management of their slaves.

---

① [The story is told in the same way in *Lectures*, p. 97, but Seneca, *De ira*, lib. iii. . cap. 40, and Dio Cassius, *Hist.* , lib. liv. , cap. 23, say, not that Augustus ordered all the slaves to be emancipated, but that he ordered all the goblets on the table to be broken. Seneca says the offending slave was emancipated. Dio does not mention emancipation.]

② [The West India merchants and planters asserted, in 1775, that there was capital worth £ 60000000 in the sugar colonies and that half of this belonged to residents in Great Britain —See the Continuation of Anderson's *Commerce*, A. D. 1775.]

第四篇　第七章

下，这是由各个时代和国家的历史所证明的。在罗马史里，我们第一次读到，地方长官保护奴隶，使其免于主人的暴力，是在皇帝统治的时候。当维迪阿·波利奥在奥古斯都皇帝[1]面前，准备把他犯了一点点错误的奴隶切成小片，然后扔进他的鱼塘来喂鱼的时候，皇帝恼怒地下令马上释放这个奴隶，并且把属于他的奴隶也释放①。在共和制下，没有一个地方长官有足够的权力去保护奴隶，也全部更不能去惩罚主人。

可以从罗马的历史中见到。

应该指出，用来改良法国蔗糖殖民地，尤其是圣多明各的大殖民地的资本，几乎全部来自这些殖民地的逐渐的土地改良和耕种。它几乎完全是殖民者的土地和劳动的产物，或者说是由良好管理而逐渐积累并用来生产更多产物的那部分产物的价格。但是那些用来改良和耕种英国蔗糖殖民地的资本，很大部分都是来自英国，绝不全是土地和殖民地人民劳动的产品②。英国蔗糖殖民地的繁荣，很大程度上是由于英国的财富充盈，一部分流向了（如果我们可以这样说的话）这些殖民地。但是法国蔗糖殖民地的繁荣则完全是由于殖民地人民好的行为，因此这必然比英国殖

法国蔗糖殖民地的优越性在积累自己的资本后变得更明显。

---

① 这个故事在斯密的《关于法律、警察、岁入及军备的演讲》第97页有相同的叙述。但是塞涅卡《愤怒》第3编第40章和狄欧·卡休斯《历史》第54编第23章记载，不是说奥古斯都下令释放所有的奴隶，而是命令将桌上所有的高脚玻璃杯打碎，塞涅卡说犯错的那个奴隶被释放了，狄欧没有提到释放的事。

② 西印度商人和种植人1775年主张，蔗糖殖民地有价值6000万镑的资本，其中半数属于英国居民。参见安德森《商业》续编，1775年。

[1] 奥古斯都(前27~14)：罗马帝国第一任皇帝，尤利斯·恺撒的侄子。他于公元前31年打败马克·安东尼及克娄巴特拉，然后得到了整个帝国的统治权，于公元前29年称皇帝，并于公元前27年被授予奥古斯都荣誉称号。

1253

国民财富的性质与原理

<small>The policy of Europe has done nothing for the prosperity of the colonies.</small>

Such have been the general outlines of the policy of the different European nations with regard to their colonies.

The policy of Europe, therefore, has very little to boast of, either in the original establishment, or, so far as concerns their internal government, in the subsequent prosperity of the colonies of America.

<small>Folly and injustice directed the first project.</small>

Folly and injustice seem to have been the principles which presided over and directed the first project of establishing those colonies; the folly of hunting after gold and silver mines, and the injustice of coveting the possession of a country whose harmless natives, far from having ever injured the people of Europe, had received the first adventurers with every mark of kindness and hospitality.

<small>The more respectable adventurers of later times were sent out by the disorder and injustice of European governments.</small>

The adventurers, indeed, who formed some of the later establishments, joined, to the chimerical project of finding gold and silver mines, other motives more reasonable and more laudable; but even these motives do very little honour to the policy of Europe.

The English puritans, restrained at home, fled for freedom to America, and established there the four governments of New England. The English catholics, treated with much greater injustice, established that of Maryland; the Quakers, that of Pennsylvania. The Portuguese Jews, persecuted by the inquisition, stript of their fortunes, and banished to Brazil, introduced, by their example, some sort of order and industry among the transported felons and strumpets, by whom that colony was originally peopled, and taught them the culture of the sugar-cane. ① Upon all these different occasions it was, not the wisdom and policy, but the disorder and injustice of the European governments, which peopled and cultivated America.

<small>To the actual establishment of the colonies the governments of Europe contributed little,</small>

In effectuating some of the most important of these establishments, the different governments of Europe had as little merit as in projecting them. The conquest of Mexico was the project, not of the council of Spain, but of a governor of Cuba; ② and it was effectuated by the spirit of the bold adventurer to whom it was entrusted,

---

① [Raynal, *Histoire philosophique*, Amsterdam ed. , 1773, tom. iii. , pp. 323、324、326、327, Justamond's English trans. , vol. ii. , p. 442.]

② [Velasquez.]

第四篇 第七章

民者要强;这种优越在他们对奴隶的良好管理上显现出来。

上述内容就是欧洲各国对待他们殖民地的普遍政策。

因此,欧洲的政策在最初的建立阶段或者在美洲殖民地后来的繁荣中(仅就内部管理上说),几乎没有什么可以吹嘘的。

最初建立这些殖民地的计划中,愚蠢和非正义是控制和指导的原则。寻求金银矿山显现出他们的愚蠢,觊觎一个国家的财产,这个国家善良的人民不仅从来没有伤害过欧洲人,而且以善良和友好接待第一批冒险者,足见其不公正。

的确,建立了一些后来殖民地的冒险家,除了寻找金银矿山外,还有比较合理和比较可称颂的动机;但即使是这些动机也不能为欧洲政策增添光彩。

英国的清教徒在国内受限制,为了自由逃到美洲,在那里建立了新英格兰的四个政府。英国的天主教徒,被更加不正义地对待,在马里兰建立了政府,教友派教徒在宾夕法尼亚建立了政府。葡萄牙的犹太人,受到宗教法庭迫害,被剥夺了财产,流亡巴西。通过他们的榜样,在重刑犯和娼妓中,引进了某种秩序和劳动,教导他们如何种植甘蔗①。在所有不同的情况下,使人们侨居美洲并从事耕种的不是智慧和政策,而是欧洲政府的混乱和非正义。

在 些最重要的殖民地的实际建立中,就像在设计一样,欧洲政府没有什么功劳。征服墨西哥,不是西班牙枢密院的计划,而是古巴总督的计划②。实现计划的乃是大冒险家的精神,尽管

---

① 雷纳尔:《哲学史》,阿姆斯特丹版,1773 年,第 3 卷,第 323、324、326、327 页。贾斯特蒙德的英文翻译版,第 3 卷,第 442 页。

② 维拉奎。

in spite of every thing which that governor, who soon repented of having trusted such a person, could do to thwart it. The conquerors of Chili and Peru, and of almost all the other Spanish settlements upon the continent of America, carried out with them no other public encouragement, but a general permission to make settlements and conquests in the name of the king of Spain. Those adventures were all at the private risk and expence of the adventurers. The government of Spain contributed scarce any thing to any of them. That of England contributed as little towards effectuating the establishment of some of its most important colonies in North America.

<small>and discouraged rather than encouraged them after they were established.</small> When those establishments were effectuated, and had become so considerable as to attract the attention of the mother country, the first regulations which she made with regard to them had always in view to secure to herself the monopoly of their commerce; to confine their market, and to enlarge her own at their expence, and, consequently, rather to damp and discourage, than to quicken and forward the course of their prosperity. In the different ways in which this monopoly has been exercised, consists one of the most essential differences in the policy of the different European nations with regard to their colonies. The best of them all, that of England, is only somewhat less illiberal and oppressive than that of any of the rest.

<small>Europe has done nothing except provide the men who founded the colonies.</small> In what way, therefore, has the policy of Europe contributed either to the first establishment, or to the present grandeur of the colonies of America? In one way, and in one way only, it has contributed a good deal. *Magna virûm Mater*! It bred and formed the men who were capable of atchieving such great actions, and of laying the foundation of so great an empire; and there is no other quarter of the world of which the policy is capable of forming, or has ever actually and in fact formed such men. The colonies owe to the policy of Europe the education and great views of their active and enterprising founders; and some of the greatest and most important of them, so far as concerns their internal government, owe to it scarce any thing else.

这位总督不久就后悔不该把事情交给这样一个人，便想尽办法加以阻挠。智利和秘鲁的征服者，以及在美洲大陆上的其他西班牙殖民地的征服者，并没有随他们带去公众的鼓励，而是得到以西班牙国王名义建设殖民地并加以征服的一般允许。这些冒险是由冒险家私人承担风险并支付开支。西班牙政府对他们没有任何资助。英国政府对北美一些重要的殖民地的建设的贡献也非常少。

当这些殖民地建立起来，变得足够强大，引起母国的注意，母国最初对他们颁布的一些规定是为了确保自己对其商业的垄断权，限制他们的市场，以牺牲他们的利益来扩大自己的市场，因此，是妨碍和阻挡他们的繁荣，而不是加速和推动它。这种垄断权行使的不同方式包含不同欧洲国家对待殖民地的政策的最重要的不同。其中最好的是英国的政策，也仅仅是某种程度上比剩下的其他国家少点不自由和压迫。

在他们建立之后是阻碍而不是鼓励。

那么，欧洲政策在哪些方面促进了殖民地的最初建立和美洲殖民地现在的繁荣呢？在一个方面，也仅仅是一个方面，它做出了很大的贡献！它养育和造就了能完成如此伟大的事业、建立如此伟大帝国的人才；世界上没有其他地方的政策能够造就，或者已经实际上造就了这样的人才。殖民地得益于欧洲政策的是他们主动的富有创业精神的创立者所受的教育和远大眼光；一些最大最重要的殖民地，就其内部管理而言，完全要归功于欧洲政策。

欧洲除了提供建立殖民地的人之外什么都没做。

| 国民财富的性质与原理

Part Third Of The Advantages Which Europe Has Derived From The Discovery Of America, And From That Of A Passage To The East Indies By The Cape Of Good Hope

The advantages derived by Europe from America are (1) the advantages of Europe in general, and (2) the advantages of the particular countries which have colonies.

Such are the advantages which the colonies of America have derived from the policy of Europe.

What are those which Europe has derived from the discovery and colonization of America?

Those advantages may be divided, first, into the general advantages which Europe, considered as one great country, has derived from those great events; and, secondly, into the particular advantages which each colonizing country has derived from the colonies which particularly belong to it, in consequence of the authority or dominion which it exercises over them.

(1) The general advantages to Europe are:

The general advantages which Europe, considered as one great country, has derived from the discovery and colonization of America, consist, first, in the increase of its enjoyments; and secondly, in the augmentation of its industry.

(a) an increase of enjoyments,

The surplus produce of America, imported into Europe, furnishes the inhabitants of this great continent with a variety of commodities which they could not otherwise have possessed, some for conveniency and use, some for pleasure, and some for ornament, and thereby contributes to increase their enjoyments.

(b) an augmentation of industry not only in the countries which trade with America directly,

The discovery and colonization of America, it will readily be allowed, have contributed to augment the industry, first, of all the countries which trade to it directly; such as Spain, Portugal, France, and England; and, secondly, of all those which, without trading to it directly, send, through the medium of other countries, goods to it of their own produce; such as Austrian Flanders, and some provinces of Germany, which, through the medium of the countries before mentioned, send to it a considerable quantity of linen and other goods. All such countries have evidently gained a more extensive market for their surplus produce, and must consequently have been encouraged to increase its quantity.

But, that those great events should likewise have contributed to encourage the industry of countries, such as Hungary and Poland,

第三部分 论欧洲从美洲的发现以及由好望角到东印度的通道的发现获得的利益

美洲殖民地从欧洲政策获得的利益就是这些。

欧洲从美洲的发现和殖民地发现获得了什么呢？

这种利益可以分为两种：第一，欧洲作为一个大国，从这些伟大事件中获得的一般利益；第二，每个殖民国家对属于它的殖民地行使权力和进行统治获得的特殊利益。

欧洲作为一个大国，从美洲发现和殖民中获得的一般利益，第一是自己享受的增加，第二是该国的工业得到发展。

从欧洲进口的美洲剩余产品，给这个伟大的大陆的居民提供了除此之外无法得到的丰富多样的产品，有的供方便和使用，有的供娱乐，有的供装饰，因此增加了他们的享乐。

显而易见，美洲的发现和殖民有助于下列国家产业的扩大：第一，与美洲直接通商的国家，比如西班牙、葡萄牙、法国和英国；第二，无法直接通商，但通过其他国家作为中介，将自己的产物送往美洲，例如奥地利的佛兰德以及德国的一些省份，通过这些国家的中介，将大量的亚麻布和其他货物运往美洲。显然，所有的这些国家为他们的剩余产品赢得了一个更为广阔的市场，因此被鼓励去增加这些产品的数量。

但是，这些伟大的事件有利于鼓励比如像匈牙利和波兰等国

| 国民财富的性质与原理

but also in other countries which do not send their produce to America,　which may never, perhaps, have sent a single commodity of their own produce to America, is not, perhaps, altogether so evident. That those events have done so, however, cannot be doubted. Some part of the produce of America is consumed in Hungary and Poland, and there is some demand there for the sugar, chocolate, and tobacco, of that new quarter of the world. But those commodities must be purchased with something which is either the produce of the industry of Hungary and Poland, or with something which had been purchased with some part of that produce. Those commodities of America are new values, new equivalents, introduced into Hungary and Poland to be exchanged there for the surplus produce of those countries. By being carried thither they create a new and more extensive market for that surplus produce. They raise its value, and thereby contribute to encourage its increase. Though no part of it may ever be carried to America, it may be carried to other countries which purchase it with a part of their share of the surplus produce of America; and it may find a market by means of the circulation of that trade which was originally put into motion by the surplus produce of America.

or even receive any produce from America.　Those great events may even have contributed to increase the enjoyments, and to augment the industry of countries which, not only never sent any commodities to America, but never received any from it. Even such countries may have received a greater abundance of other commodities from countries of which the surplus produce had been augmented by means of the American trade. This greater abundance, as it must necessarily have increased their enjoyments, so it must likewise have augmented their industry. A greater number of new equivalents of some kind or other must have been presented to them to be exchanged for the surplus produce of that industry. A more extensive market must have been created for that surplus produce, so as to raise its value, and thereby encourage its increase. The mass of

The exclusive trade of the mother countries reduces the enjoyments and industry of all Europe and America, especially the latter.　commodities annually thrown into the great circle of European commerce, and by its various revolutions annually distributed among all the different nations comprehended within it, must have been augmented by the whole surplus produce of America. A greater share of this greater mass, therefore, is likely to have fallen to each of those nations, to have increased their enjoyments, and augmented their industry.

The exclusive trade of the mother countries tends to diminish, or, at least, to keep down below what they would otherwise rise to, both the enjoyments and industry of all those nations in general, and of the American colonies in particular. It is a dead weight upon the action of one of the great springs which puts into motion a great part of the business of mankind. By rendering the colony produce dearer in

家的工业或许没有那么明显,这些国家或许从来没有将他们任何一件产品送往美洲。然而,这些事件曾经做过这种贡献是毋庸置疑的。美洲的一部分产品在匈牙利和波兰被消费,那里对世界这一新地区也有蔗糖、巧克力、烟草的需求。但是,这些商品一定是用匈牙利和波兰的产品或者是这些产品中的某一部分来购买的。这些美洲产品是新价值、新的等价物,被引进匈牙利和波兰来交换这些国家的剩余产品。通过运到这两个国家之后,它们为两国的剩余产品创造了一个新的更加广阔的市场。它们增加了产品的价值,因而有助于刺激它的增长。尽管没有任何剩余产品可能被运往美洲,但是可以被运往其他国家,这些国家用美洲剩余产品的一部分去购买;它可以通过最初由美洲剩余产品推动的贸易流通去获得一个市场。

其他国家不商品往美国。

那些伟大的事件可能有助于增加人们享乐,也增加国家的产业,这些国家不仅从未把任何商品运往美洲,也没有从美洲收到任何商品。即使是这样的国家,也可能收到来自那些通过美洲贸易使剩余产品增加的国家的大量其他商品。大量的新等价物呈现在他们面前来交换那个产业的剩余产品。对于剩余产品的更加广阔的市场被创造出来,因此增加了它的价值,从而鼓励了它的增长。每年投入欧洲商业系统并通过多样的周转而分配给所有与其有关的国家的商品总量,通过美洲的整个剩余产品得以增加。因此,这一商品的较大份额就有可能分到每一个这样的国家,增加他们的享乐,扩大他们的产业。

甚至从未到美洲产品的国家也是如此。

母国的垄断贸易,会减少或者至少是减弱这些一般国家和特别的美洲殖民地的享乐和产业。这是在推动人类一人部分商业运动的大发条上的一个巨大的重物。通过使得所有其他国家的

母国专营贸易减少了整个欧洲对美乐和勤奋,后者尤其如此。

all other countries, it lessens its consumption, and thereby cramps the industry of the colonies, and both the enjoyments and the industry of all other countries, which both enjoy less when they pay more for what they enjoy, and produce less when they get less for what they produce. By rendering the produce of all other countries dearer in the colonies, it cramps, in the same manner, the industry of all other countries, and both the enjoyments and the industry of the colonies. It is a clog which, for the supposed benefit of some particular countries, embarrasses the pleasures, and encumbers the industry of all other countries; but of the colonies more than of any other. It not only excludes, as much as possible, all other countries from one particular market; but it confines, as much as possible, the colonies to one particular market: and the difference is very great between being excluded from one particular market, when all others are open, and being confined to one particular market, when all others are shut up. The surplus produce of the colonies, however, is the original source of all that increase of enjoyments and industry which Europe derives from the discovery and colonization of America; and the exclusive trade of the mother countries tends to render this source much less abundant than it otherwise would be.

The particular advantages which each colonizing country derives from the colonies which particularly belong to it, are of two different kinds; first, those common advantages which every empire derives from the provinces subject to its dominion; and, secondly, those peculiar advantages which are supposed to result from provinces of so very peculiar a nature as the European colonies of America.

The common advantages which every empire derives from the provinces subject to its dominion, consist, first, in the military force which they furnish for its defence; and, secondly, in the revenue which they furnish for the support of its civil government. The Roman colonies furnished occasionally both the one and the other. The Greek colonies, sometimes, furnished a military force; but seldom any revenue. ① They seldom acknowledged themselves subject to the dominion of the mother city. They were generally her allies in war, but very seldom her subjects in peace.

The European colonies of America have never yet furnished any military force for the defence of the mother country. Their military force has never yet been sufficient for their own defence; and in the different wars in which the mother countries have been engaged, the defence of their colonies has generally occasioned a very considerable

---

① [There is an example of revenue being furnished in Xenophon, *Anab.*, V. , v. , 7, 10.]

产品昂贵,它同样阻碍了所有其他国家的产业,以及娱乐和殖民地的产业。为了某些国家的所谓的利益,这种障碍物使愉快变得尴尬,妨害了其他国家的产业;但是对殖民地的产业比对其他国家的产业妨害更大。它不仅尽可能多地把其他任何国家排除在一个特殊市场之外,而且尽可能地把殖民地限制在一个市场之内;当所有的其他市场是开放时,它被排除在一个特殊的市场之外;当所有的其他市场是关闭时,它被限制在一个特殊的市场之内,这之间的差别是非常大的。然而,殖民地剩余产品是欧洲从美洲的发现和殖民得到的娱乐和产业的增长的最初源泉;而母国的专营贸易使这一源泉不如原来会有的那样丰富。〔(2)殖民地国家的特殊利益是:(a)从省得到的普通利益;(b)从它们得到的特殊利益:〕

每个殖民国家从特别属于它的殖民地得到的特殊利益分为两种:第一,每个国王从在他统治下的省份获得的普通利益;第二,从像欧洲的美洲殖民地那样一种性质非常特殊的省所得到的特殊利益。

每个国王从在他统治下的省份获得的普通利益包括:第一,各省为帝国国防提供的军事力量;第二,他们支持帝国内政提供的收入;罗马殖民地偶尔提供这两者。希腊殖民地有时提供军事力量,但极少提供任何收入①。他们极少承认自己在母市的统治下。在战争中,它们通常是母市的同盟者,但在和平时却不是它的臣民。〔(a)普通利益是提供军事力量和收入,〕

欧洲在美洲的殖民地从未为母国的国防提供过任何军事力量。它们的军事力量还不足以保卫自己;在母国参与的不同战争中,它们殖民地的防卫造成了这些国家的军事力量的非常巨大的〔但是殖民地没提供过军事力量,〕

---

① 色芬尼:《长征记》V.,v.,7,10 中提供了一个有关收入的例子。

distraction of the military force of those countries. In this respect, therefore, all the European colonies have, without exception, been a cause rather of weakness than of strength to their respective mother countries.

and the colonies of Spain and Portugal alone have contributed revenue.   The colonies of Spain and Portugal only have contributed any revenue towards the defence of the mother country, or the support of her civil government. The taxes which have been levied upon those of other European nations, upon those of England in particular, have seldom been equal to the expence laid out upon them in time of peace, and never sufficient to defray that which they occasioned in time of war. Such colonies, therefore, have been a source of expence and not of revenue to their respective mother countries.

(b) the exclusive trade is the sole peculiar advantage.   The advantages of such colonies to their respective mother countries, consist altogether in those peculiar advantages which are supposed to result from provinces of so very peculiar a nature as the European colonies of America; and the exclusive trade, it is acknowledged, is the sole source of all those peculiar advantages.

In consequence of this exclusive trade, all that part of the surplus produce of the English colonies, for example, which consists in what are called enumerated commodities, can be sent to no other country but England. Other countries must afterwards buy it of her. It must be cheaper therefore in England than it can be in any other country, and must contribute more to increase the enjoyments of England than those of any other country. It must likewise contribute more to encourage her industry. For all those parts of her own surplus produce which England exchanges for those enumerated commodities, she must get a better price than any other countries can get for the like parts of theirs, when they exchange them for the same commodities. The manufactures of England, for example, will purchase a greater quantity of the sugar and tobacco of her own colonies, than the like manufactures of other countries can purchase of that sugar and tobacco. So far, therefore, as the manufactures of England and those of other countries are both to be exchanged for the sugar and tobacco of the English colonies, this superiority of price gives an encouragement to the former, beyond what the latter can in these circumstances enjoy. The exclusive trade of the colonies, therefore, as it diminishes, or, at least, keeps down below what they would otherwise rise to, both the enjoyments and the industry of the countries which do not possess it; so it gives an evident advantage to the countries which do possess it over those other countries.

The exclusive trade of each country is a disadvantage to the other countries,

This advantage, however, will, perhaps, be found to be rather

分散。因此,从这方面来说,所有的欧洲殖民地毫无例外是造成母国力量薄弱的一个原因。

只有西班牙和葡萄牙的殖民地,给母国的国防提供过任何收入,或者给予其内政以支持。其他欧洲国家,尤其是英国,对殖民地收的税,极少能跟和平时期的开支相等,就更不可能在战时支付殖民地增加的费用。所以,这些殖民地对它们的母国只是负担不是财源。西班牙和葡萄牙殖民地对贡献。

这些殖民地对它们母国的利益,完全在于假定从像欧洲的美洲殖民地这样一种性质非常特殊的省份得到的特殊利益;人们承认,专营贸易是所有那些特殊利益的唯一源泉。(b)这种专营贸易拥有独一无二的优势。

例如,这种专营贸易使得英国殖民地的包含在列举商品的所有剩余产品,不得送往英国以外的其他国家。其他国家以后从英国购买这些商品。因此,这些商品在英国一定比在其他任何国家更便宜,这对于增加英国的享受比其他任何国家的享受更大。这也有利于鼓励她的产业。英国用来交换列举商品的那一部分自己的剩余产品,比起其他国家用来交换这些列举商品的自己的剩余产品,得到的价格一定会更高。例如,英国的制造品能购买到的它自己的殖民地的糖和烟草,一定比其他国家的相同制造品所能买到的自己殖民地的糖和烟草要多。因此,英国的制造品和其他国家的制造品用来交换英国殖民地的糖和烟草,这种价格上的优越性给予前者一种鼓励,超越了后者在这些情况下所能享受的鼓励。因此,殖民地的专营贸易,会降低至少是阻碍不拥有这种贸易的国家的享受和产业,所以拥有多于其他国家贸易的国家显然得到更明显的利益。每个专营贸易对其他国家来说是不利的。

然而,或许这种利益只会是相对利益而不是绝对利益;给予

rather than an advantage to that country.	what may be called a relative than an absolute advantage; and to give a superiority to the country which enjoys it, rather by depressing the industry and produce of other countries, than by raising those of that particular country above what they would naturally rise to in the case of a free trade.
e, g., England gets tobacco cheaper than France, but not cheaper than it would if there were no exclusive trade.	The tobacco of Maryland and Virginia, for example, by means of the monopoly which England enjoys of it, certainly comes cheaper to England than it can do to France, to whom England commonly sells a considerable part of it. But had France, and all other European countries been, at all times, allowed a free trade to Maryland and Virginia, the tobacco of those colonies might, by this time, have come cheaper than it actually does, not only to all those other countries, but likewise to England. The produce of tobacco, in consequence of a market so much more extensive than any which it has hitherto enjoyed, might, and probably would, by this time, have been so much increased as to reduce the profits of a tobacco plantation to their natural level with those of a corn plantation, which, it is supposed, they are still somewhat above. The price of tobacco might, and probably would, by this time, have fallen somewhat lower than it is at present. An equal quantity of the commodities either of England, or of those other countries, might have purchased in Maryland and Virginia a greater quantity of tobacco than it can do at present, and, consequently, have been sold there for so much a better price. So far as that weed, therefore, can, by its cheapness and abundance, increase the enjoyments or augment the industry either of England or of any other country, it would, probably, in the case of a free trade, have produced both these effects in somewhat a greater degree than it can do at present. England, indeed, would not in this case have had any advantage over other countries. She might have bought the tobacco of her colonies somewhat cheaper, and, consequently, have sold some of her own commodities somewhat dearer than she actually does. But she could neither have bought the one cheaper nor sold the other dearer than any other country might have done. She might, perhaps, have gained an absolute, but she would certainly have lost a relative advantage.
To subject other countries to this disadvantage England has made two sacrifices.	In order, however, to obtain this relative advantage in the colony trade, in order to execute the invidious and malignant project of excluding as much as possible other nations from any share in it, England, there are very probable reasons for believing, has not only sacrificed a part of the absolute advantage which she, as well as every other nation, might have derived from that trade, but has subjected herself both to an absolute and to a relative disadvantage in almost every other branch of trade.

拥有专营贸易的国家的优越地位,是通过降低其他国家的产业和产品,而不是使这个国家的产业和产品提高到在自由贸易的情况下自然会达到的水平以上。

不是对那个国家有利。

例如,马里兰和弗吉尼亚的烟草,因为英国享有垄断权,英国的价格肯定比在法国的价格低,英国通常向法国出售很大一部分的烟草。但是,如果法国和所有其他欧洲国家被允许同马里兰和弗吉尼亚进行自由贸易,那么这些殖民地的烟草这时在所有其他的国家以及英国的价格可能比它实际的价格要便宜。烟草的生产,由于它现在享有比以前更加广阔的市场,增加了不少,烟草种植的利润降到正常的水平,和栽种谷物的利润水平相当,据说还要稍微高一些。此时,烟草的价格可能稍微低于它现在的价格。英国或者那些其他国家的同样数量的商品,可能在马里兰和弗吉尼亚购买到比现在更多数量的烟草,因此,能在它们国内卖一个更好的价钱。所以,烟草的廉价和丰富增加了英国或者是任何其他国家的享乐或者产业,它可能在自由贸易的情况下比在现在产生更大程度的效果。诚然,英国在这种情况不会比其他国家更有利。它可能以更低的价格从它的殖民地购买烟草,从而以高于其实际价格出售一些它自己的商品。但是它不能比其他国家购买得更便宜,或出售得更贵。它或许得到一种绝对利益,但它肯定会丧失一种相对利益。

例如,英国比法国得到烟草便宜,但是不能比没有专营贸易更加便宜。

然而,为了在殖民地贸易中获得这种相对利益,为了要实行将其他国家尽量排除在殖民地贸易之外的招惹恶感的恶毒计划,我们有理由相信,英国不仅牺牲了它以及其他国家可能从贸易得到的一部分绝对利益,而且使自己在贸易的几乎每个方面都处于绝对和相对的不利地位。

为了让其他国家处于这种不利地位,英国做出了两大牺牲。

The withdrawal of foreign capital from the colony trade raised profits in it and drew capital from other British trades and thereby raised profits in them,   When, by the act of navigation, England assumed to herself the monopoly of the colony trade, the foreign capitals which had before been employed in it were necessarily withdrawn from it. The English capital, which had before carried on but a part of it, was now to carry on the whole. The capital which had before supplied the colonies with but a part of the goods which they wanted from Europe, was now all that was employed to supply them with the whole. But it could not supply them with the whole, and the goods with which it did supply them were necessarily sold very dear. The capital which had before bought but a part of the surplus produce of the colonies, was now all that was employed to buy the whole. But it could not buy the whole at any thing near the old price, and, therefore, whatever it did buy it necessarily bought very cheap. But in an employment of capital in which the merchant sold very dear and bought very cheap, the profit must have been very great, and much above the ordinary level of profit in other branches of trade. This superiority of profit in the colony trade could not fail to draw from other branches of trade a part of the capital which had before been employed in them. But this revulsion of capital, as it must have gradually increased the competition of capitals in the colony trade, so it must have gradually diminished that competition in all those other branches of trade; as it must have gradually lowered the profits of the one, so it must have gradually raised those of the other, till the profits of all came to a new level, different from and somewhat higher than that at which they had been before.

and continues to do so.   This double effect, of drawing capital from all other trades, and of raising the rate of profit somewhat higher than it otherwise would have been in all trades, was not only produced by this monopoly upon its first establishment, but has continued to be produced by it ever since.

The colony trade has increased faster than the whole British capital,   First, this monopoly has been continually drawing capital from all other trades to be employed in that of the colonies.

  Though the wealth of Great Britain has increased very much since the establishment of the act of navigation, it certainly has not increased in the same proportion as that of the colonies. But the foreign trade of every country naturally increases in proportion to its wealth, its surplus produce in proportion to its whole produce; and Great Britain having engrossed to herself almost the whole of what may

第四篇 第七章

当英国通过航海法而垄断殖民地贸易时,以前用在这方面的外国资本必然从里面撤走。以前经营一部分贸易的英国资本,现在要经营全部贸易。以前只需要把一部分它们想从欧洲得到的货物供应给殖民地的英国资本,现在要把需要的所有欧洲货物供应给殖民地。但是它不能完全满足需求,于是英国资本供应的货物必然以高昂的价格出售。以前只购买一部分殖民地剩余产品的资本,现在被用来购买全部产品。但是它不能以和原价差不多的价格购买全部产品,因此它买的产品必然是以非常低廉的价格买进的。但是在一种资本使用中,商人卖得非常贵而买得非常便宜,这其中的利润一定是非常巨大的,而且比在贸易的其他方面获得的普通利润要高得多。在殖民地贸易中的利润优越性,一定会从贸易的其他方面吸收一部分原来的资本。但是这种资本转移,由于它一定会逐渐增加殖民地贸易中资本的竞争,所以它一定会逐渐消灭在那些贸易的其他方面的竞争;它也一定会逐渐降低前者的利润,所以也一定会逐渐提高后者的利润,直到所有的利润达到一个新的水平,不同于而且要高于以前的水平。

<small>外国资本从殖民地中撤走,英国本土资本增加了,贸易利润会提高,并从其他贸易中吸引过资本来,这些部门的利润提高。</small>

从所有其他贸易中撤出资本以及使所有贸易的利润比以前要高,这种双重效果,不仅来自于垄断权初建时,而且自此之后一直持续产生。

<small>一直在产生这种影响。</small>

第一,这一垄断持续从所有其他贸易吸引资本,用于殖民地贸易。

尽管大不列颠财富自从航海法制定以来增长得很大,但它的增长和殖民地的增长不是同一个比例。但是每个国家的外国贸易同它的财富,它的剩余产品和它的整个产品,自然呈有比例的增长;英国已经将可以称为殖民地对外贸易的几乎全部据为己

<small>殖民地增长比英国本土资本得全部资本,殖民地贸易增长更快。</small>

1269

be called the foreign trade of the colonies and her capital not having increased in the same proportion as the extent of that trade, she could not carry it on without continually withdrawing from other branches of trade some part of the capital which had before been employed in them, as well as withholding from them a great deal more which would otherwise have gone to them. Since the establishment of the act of navigation, accordingly, the colony trade has been continually increasing, while many other branches of foreign trade, particularly of that to other parts of Europe, have been continually decaying. Our manufactures for foreign sale, instead of being suited, as before the act of navigation, to the neighbouring market of Europe, or to the more distant one of the countries which lie round the Mediterranean sea, have, the greater part of them, been accommodated to the still more distant one of the colonies, to the market in which they have the monopoly, rather than to that in which they have many competitors. The causes of decay in other branches of foreign trade, which, by Sir Matthew Decker,[1] and other writers, have been sought for in the excess and improper mode of taxation, in the high price of labour, in the increase of luxury, &c. may all be found in the over-growth of the colony trade. The mercantile capital of Great Britain, though very great, yet not being infinite; and though greatly increased since the act of navigation, yet not being increased in the same proportion as the colony trade, that trade could not possibly be carried on without withdrawing some part of that capital from other branches of trade, nor consequently without some decay of those other branches.

England, it must be observed, was a great trading country, her mercantile capital was very great and likely to become still greater and greater every day, not only before the act of navigation had established the monopoly of the colony trade, but before that trade was very considerable. In the Dutch war, during the government of Cromwel, her navy was superior to that of Holland; and in that which broke out in the beginning of the reign of Charles II. it was at least equal, perhaps superior, to the united navies of France and Holland. Its superiority, perhaps, would scarce appear greater in the present times;

---

[1] [*Essay on the Causes of the Decline of the Foreign Trade*, consequently of the Value of the Lands of Britain and on the means to restore both, 2nd ed., 1750, pp. 28 – 36, *et passim*.]

有,它的资本却没有同那个贸易的规模成比例增长,所以它只有不断地从其他贸易将以前用在那里的资本的一部分吸引过来,并留住更多的会流向那里的资本,才能进行殖民地贸易。因此,自航海法制定以来,殖民地贸易持续增长,而许多其他的对外贸易部门,特别是对欧洲其他地区的贸易,则在不断萎缩。我们对外销售的制造品,不是像在航海法以前适应欧洲的邻近市场,或者是适应地中海周围国家的更远一些的市场,而是很大一部分适应于殖民地的更远的市场,适应于它们有垄断权的市场,而不是适应它们有很多竞争者的市场。其他部门对外贸易萎缩的原因,马修·德克尔爵士[①]以及其他作家从征税方式的过度和不合适方面去寻找,从劳动力的高价方面去寻找,从奢侈的增长方面去寻找,等等,其实可以全部从殖民地贸易的过度增长中去寻找。英国商业资本尽管数量巨大,但是不是无限的;尽管航海法制定后有了大幅增长,但是却不是和殖民地贸易呈同比增长的,这种贸易不从其他贸易部门吸收一部分资本就无法进行,因而不使其他贸易部门萎缩就无法进行。

必须注意到,英国是一个大的贸易国家,它的商业资本非常巨大,而且有可能每天变得越来越大,而这些不仅是在航海法规定殖民地贸易垄断之前,而且还是在贸易变得非常大之前。在对荷兰的战争中,克伦威尔当政,其海军比荷兰海军要优越。在查理二世即位时爆发的战争中,英国海军的实力与法国和荷兰的联合海军的实力至少相等,或许要更高。可能它的优越性在现在的

[①] 《论由于英国土地价值降低而使对外贸易衰落的原因以及恢复二者的方法》,第 2 版,1750 年,第 28~36 页及以下。

国民财富的性质与原理

and the colonial monopoly has merely changed the direction of British trade.　at least if the Dutch navy was to bear the same proportion to the Dutch commerce now which it did then. But this great naval power could not, in either of those wars, be owing to the act of navigation. During the first of them the plan of that act had been but just formed; and though before the breaking out of the second it had been fully enacted by legal authority; yet no part of it could have had time to produce any considerable effect, and least of all that part which established the exclusive trade to the colonies. Both the colonies and their trade were inconsiderable then in comparison of what they are now. The island of Jamaica was an unwholesome desert, little inhabited, and less cultivated. New York and New Jersey were in the possession of the Dutch: the half of St. Christopher's in that of the French. The island of Antigua, the two Carolinas, Pensylvania, Georgia, and Nova Scotia, were not planted. Virginia, Maryland, and New England were planted; and though they were very thriving colonies, yet there was not, perhaps, at that time, either in Europe or America, a single person who foresaw or even suspected the rapid progress which they have since made in wealth, population and improvement. The island of Barbadoes, in short, was the only British colony of any consequence of which the condition at that time bore any resemblance to what it is at present. The trade of the colonies, of which England, even for some time after the act of navigation, enjoyed but a part (for the act of navigation was not very strictly executed till several years after it was enacted), could not at that time be the cause of the great trade of England, nor of the great naval power which was supported by that trade. The trade which at that time supported that great naval power was the trade of Europe, and of the countries which lie round the Mediterranean sea. But the share which Great Britain at present enjoys of that trade could not support any such great naval power. Had the growing trade of the colonies been left free to all nations, whatever share of it might have fallen to Great Britain, and a very considerable share would probably have fallen to her, must have been all an addition to this great trade of which she was before in possession. In consequence of the monopoly, the increase of the colony trade has not so much occasioned an addition to the trade which Great Britain had before, as a total change in its direction.

时代极少显得巨大;至少是荷兰的海军如果能与现在的商业规模保持相同的情况下是这样。但是这一巨大的海军力量在这两场战争中都不可能是由于航海法。在第一次战争中,那一法律的制定计划刚刚形成;尽管在第二场战争爆发之前,航海法已经由立法机关通过,但没有哪一部分有时间产生任何巨大的效果,而法律中建立与殖民地专营贸易的部分效果更小。当时的殖民地及其贸易同现在的情况相比显得很微不足道。牙买加岛是一个不健康的沙漠,极少有人居住,也很少有人耕种。纽约和新泽西是荷兰的财产,圣克里斯托弗的一半在法国人手中。安提瓜岛、南北卡罗来纳、宾夕法尼亚、佐治亚和新斯科夏还没有殖民。弗吉尼亚、马里兰和新英格兰已经殖民,它们虽然是极其繁荣的殖民地,但是在当时的欧洲或美洲可能没有人能够预见到或者猜测过它们在财富、人口和土地改良方面日后会取得那么快速的进步。简而言之,巴巴多斯岛是唯一的英国殖民地,当时的情况和现在的情况有一些相似。甚至在航海法实施后的一段时间,英国也只享受一部分殖民地贸易(因为在航海法通过之后的头几年里,该法并未被严格执行),殖民地贸易当时也不可能是英国大量贸易和成为由这种贸易所支持的巨大海军力量的原因。当时由巨大海军力量支持的贸易是欧洲的贸易,也是地中海沿岸各国的贸易。但是英国现在享有的那一贸易的份额不能支撑任何巨大的海军力量。要是殖民地不断增长的贸易对所有的国家自由开放,不管落到英国头上的份额是多大,有可能是很大的一部分,那也只是对它以前拥有的巨大贸易的一个增加。由于这一垄断,殖民地贸易的增加没有那么大程度地造成英国以前享有的贸易的增加,而是导致了贸易方向的完全改变。

<small>对殖民地贸易的垄断只是改变了英国贸易的方向</small>

Secondly, this monopoly has necessarily contributed to keep up the rate of profit in all the different branches of British trade higher than it naturally would have been, had all nations been allowed a free trade to the British colonies.

The monopoly of the colony trade, as it necessarily drew towards that trade a greater proportion of the capital of Great Britain than what would have gone to it of its own accord; so by the expulsion of all foreign capitals it necessarily reduced the whole quantity of capital employed in that trade below what it naturally would have been in the case of a free trade. But, by lessening the competition of capitals in that branch of trade, it necessarily raised the rate of profit in that branch. By lessening too the competition of British capitals in all other branches of trade, it necessarily raised the rate of British profit in all those other branches. Whatever may have been, at any particular period, since the establishment of the act of navigation, the state or extent of the mercantile capital of Great Britain, the monopoly of the colony trade must, during the continuance of that state, have raised the ordinary rate of British profit higher than it otherwise would have been both in that and in all the other branches of British trade. If, since the establishment of the act of navigation, the ordinary rate of British profit has fallen considerably, as it certainly has, it must have fallen still lower, had not the monopoly established by that act contributed to keep it up.

But whatever raises in any country the ordinary rate of profit higher than it otherwise would be, necessarily subjects that country both to an absolute and to a relative disadvantage in every branch of trade of which she has not the monopoly.

It subjects her to an absolute disadvantage: because in such branches of trade her merchants cannot get this greater profit, without selling dearer than they otherwise would do both the goods of foreign countries which they import into their own, and the goods of their own country which they export to foreign countries. Their own country must both buy dearer and sell dearer; must both buy less and sell less; must both enjoy less and produce less, than she otherwise would do.

It subjects her to a relative disadvantage; because in such branches of trade it sets other countries which are not subject to the same absolute disadvantage, either more above her or less below her than they otherwise would be. It enables them both to enjoy more and to produce more in proportion to what she enjoys and produces.

第四篇　第七章

第二,这一垄断必然有利于保持英国贸易的不同部门的利润率高于让所有国家同英国殖民地进行自由贸易时自然拥有的水平。

殖民地贸易的垄断,由于它必然会比自然流入情况下更大比例的英国资本吸引到这种贸易中来,以及由于将所有的外资排除在外,必然会使这种贸易中使用的全部资本数量降到自由贸易自然会达到的水平以下。但是,通过减少一个部门贸易的资本竞争,也必然提高在那个部门的利润率。但是减少贸易所有其他部门的英国资本的竞争,必然会增加这些其他部门的利润率。自从航海法制定以来,在任何特殊的时期,不管英国商业资本的情况和大小怎样,在这一情况继续时,殖民地贸易的垄断使得普通的英国利润率高于在那个部门以及其他部门的英国贸易。自航海法制定以来,如果普通的英国资本利润率大量下降,它肯定是下降了,那么,要不是这一法律建立起来的垄断来维持,它一定会下降得更低。

但是在任何国家使普通利润率高于它应有的水平的事物,也必然使其没有垄断权的每个贸易部门具有绝对的和相对的不利。

那种事物使它处于绝对不利:因为在这些贸易部门,它的商人如果不用比原来更高的价格售卖进口到本国的外国商品和它们自己国家出口到外国的商品,就无法得到更大的利润。它们自己的国家必须买得更贵也卖得更贵,必须少买少卖,而它们也必须比以前享受得少生产得少。

那种事物使它处于相对不利:因为在这些贸易部门,那些处于并不是同样绝对劣势的其他国家,要么比它更强,要么也与它相差不远。这使得其他国家与它享受和生产的多少相比,享受更

— 1275 —

It renders their superiority greater or their inferiority less than it otherwise would be. By raising the price of her produce above what it otherwise would be, it enables the merchants of other countries to undersell her in foreign markets, and thereby to justle her out of almost all those branches of trade, of which she has not the monopoly.

<small>High profits raise the price of manufactures more than high wages.</small> Our merchants frequently complain of the high wages of British labour as the cause of their manufactures being undersold in foreign markets; but they are silent about the high profits of stock. They complain of the extravagant gain of other people; but they say nothing of their own. The high profits of British stock, however, may contribute towards raising the price of British manufactures in many cases as much, and in some perhaps more, than the high wages of British labour.

<small>So British capital has been taken from European and Mediterranean trade,</small> It is in this manner that the capital of Great Britain, one may justly say, has partly been drawn and partly been driven from the greater part of the different branches of trade of which she has not the monopoly; from the trade of Europe in particular, and from that of the countries which lie round the Mediterranean sea.

<small>partly attracted by high profit in the colony trade,</small> It has partly been drawn from those branches of trade; by the attraction of superior profit in the colony trade in consequence of the continual increase of that trade, and of the continual insufficiency of the capital which had carried it on one year to carry it on the next.

<small>partly driven out by foreign competition.</small> It has partly been driven from them; by the advantage which the high rate of profit, established in Great Britain, gives to other counries, in all the different branches of trade of which Great Britain has not the monopoly.

<small>While raising British profit, the monopoly has lowered foreign profits.</small> As the monopoly of the colony trade has drawn from those other branches a part of the British capital which would otherwise have been employed in them, so it has forced into them many foreign capitals which would never have gone to them, had they not been expelled from the colony trade. In those other branches of trade it has diminished the competition of British capitals, and thereby raised the rate of British profit higher than it otherwise would have been. On the contrary, it has increased the competition of foreign capitals, and thereby sunk the rate of foreign profit lower than it otherwise would have been.

多生产更多。这使得它们的优越大于或者它们的不利小于本来的情况。通过提高它产品的价格,使其高于原来的水平,其他国家的商人能够在外国市场以更低的价格出售,因此,它就被排挤出了那些不具有垄断地位的贸易部门。

由于我们的商人的制造品在外国市场被低价销售,所以他们频繁地抱怨英国劳动力的高价;但是他们却对资本的高利润只字不提。他们抱怨其他人的奢侈所得,却不提他们自己的所得。然而,英国资本的高利润在很多场合下可能有利于提高英国制造品的价格,就像英国劳动的高工资一样,在有些场合可能提高得更多。

高利润使制造品价格提高高工资高利润比资本高

我们可以说,英国的资本以这样的方式,从它不具有垄断权的不同贸易部门,特别是欧洲贸易以及地中海沿岸各国的贸易中,部分地被抽了出来,部分地被挤了出去。

英国资本从欧洲和地中海贸易中被撤出,

它部分地被从这些贸易部门抽出,是由于殖民地贸易高额利润的吸引,而这种利润是由于那种贸易的不断增长,以及用以贸易的资本一年一年地感到不足。

所以部分是由于殖民地贸易高利润的吸引,

它部分地被从这些贸易部门挤出,是由于在英国建立起来的高利润率在英国不具有垄断权的不同的贸易部门对其他国家的优势。

部分的被外国竞争所排挤。

当殖民地贸易垄断权从其他部门吸引了一部分本来应该用于其中的英国资本时,它就迫使许多从未进去过的外国资本进入这些部门,要是它们不是从殖民地贸易中被排挤的话,它们不会进入的。在这些其他的贸易部门,它减少了英国资本的竞争,因此使英国利润率高于原来的水平。相反,它增加了外国资本的竞争,因此使外国利润率低于原来的水平。不管是这种情况还是另

在提高英国利润的同时,垄断降低了外国利润。

— 1277 —

Both in the one way and in the other it must evidently have subjected Great Britain to a relative disadvantage in all those other branches of trade.

The colony trade is supposed to be more advantageous than others.

The colony trade, however, it may perhaps be said, is more advantageous to Great Britain than any other; and the monopoly, by forcing into that trade a greater proportion of the capital of Great Britain than what would otherwise have gone to it, has turned that capital into an employment more advantageous to the country than any other which it could have found.

but trade with a neighbouring country is more advantageous than with a distant one and a direct trade is more advantageous than a round-about,

The most advantageous employment of any capital to the country to which it belongs, is that which maintains there the greatest quantity of productive labour, and increases the most the annual produce of the land and labour of that country. But the quantity of productive labour which any capital employed in the foreign trade of consumption can maintain, is exactly in proportion, it has been shewn in the second book, to the frequency of its returns. A capital of a thousand pounds, for example, employed in a foreign trade of consumption, of which the returns are made regularly once in the year, can keep in constant employment, in the country to which it belongs, a quantity of productive labour equal to what a thousand pounds can maintain there for a year. If the returns are made twice or thrice in the year, it can keep in constant employment a quantity of productive labour equal to what two or three thousand pounds can maintain there for a year. A foreign trade of consumption carried on with a neighbouring, is, upon this account, in general, more advantageous than one carried on with a distant country; and for the same reason a direct foreign trade of

while the monopoly has forced capital into (1) a distant and (2) a round about trade.

consumption, as it has likewise been shewn in the second book, is in general more advantageous than a round-about one.

But the monopoly of the colony trade, so far as it has operated upon the employment of the capital of Great Britain, has in all cases forced some part of it from a foreign trade of consumption carried on with a neighbouring, to one carried on with a more distant country, and in many cases from a direct foreign trade of consumption to a round-about one.

(1) The trade with America and the West Indies is distant and the returns peculiarly infrequent.

First, the monopoly of the colony trade has in all cases forced some part of the capital of Great Britain from a foreign trade of consumption carried on with a neighbouring, to one carried on with a more distant country.

It has, in all cases, forced some part of that capital from the trade with Europe, and with the countries which lie round the Mediterranean sea, to that with the more distant regions of America and the West Indies, from which the returns are necessarily less frequent, not only on account of the greater distance, but on account of the peculiar circum-

一种情况都明显地使英国在所有其他的贸易部门处于相对不利。

然而，或许可以说，殖民地贸易比其他贸易对英国来说是更为有利；通过迫使比原来会有的更大一部分英国资本进入，垄断权就把那些资本用于对国家更为有利的用途。

> 殖民地贸易被认为比其他贸易更为有利。

任何资本对其所属的国家最有利的用途，是在这个国家维持最大量的生产性劳动和增加那个国家的土地和劳动到最大的程度。但是，在第二章中曾指出，在对外消费贸易中投入的任何资本能维持的生产性劳动数量，是和它的往返次数成比例的。例如，在每年往返一次的对外消费贸易中使用的1000镑的资本，等于在其所属的国家内能经常雇佣的生产性劳动的数量。如果一年有两到三次的往返，它所能经常雇佣的生产性劳动的数量，相当于2000镑或3000镑一年所能维持的劳动数量。所以，一般说来，同邻国进行的对外消费贸易，比对遥远国家进行的这种贸易更加有利；由于同一个原因，直接的对外消费贸易，一般比间接的对外消费贸易更有利，这在第二篇也已经指出了。

> 但是与邻国的贸易比远方国家的贸易更有利，直接贸易也比间接贸易更有利。

但是殖民地贸易的垄断，就其对英国资本用途的影响来说，在所有的情况下，迫使某一部分资本从与邻国的对外消费贸易流入与遥远国家的对外消费贸易，而且在很多情况下，迫使资本从直接的对外消费贸易流入间接的对外消费贸易。

> 而垄断迫使资本进入（1）远方贸易（2）间接贸易。

第一，殖民地贸易的垄断在所有情况下，使一部分英国资本从与邻国的对外消费贸易流向与更为遥远的国家的对外消费贸易。

> （1）与美洲和西印度贸易往返次数特别少，距离遥远，不只是。

在所有的场合下，它使得一部分资本从欧洲以及地中海沿岸的贸易流入更为遥远的美洲和西印度地区的贸易，后者往返的次数必然少，不仅是因为距离太远，而且是由于这些国家的情况特

stances of those countries. New colonies, it has already been observed, are always understocked. Their capital is always much less than what they could employ with great profit and advantage in the improvement and cultivation of their land. They have a constant demand, therefore, for more capital than they have of their own; and, in order to supply the deficiency of their own, they endeavour to borrow as much as they can of the mother country, to whom they are, therefore, always in debt. The most common way in which the colonists contract this debt, is not by borrowing upon bond of the rich people of the mother country, though they sometimes do this too, but by running as much in arrear to their correspondents, who supply them with goods from Europe, as those correspondents will allow them. Their annual returns frequently do not amount to more than a third, and sometimes not to so great a proportion of what they owe. The whole capital, therefore, which their correspondents advance to them is seldom returned to Britain in less than three, and sometimes not in less than four or five years. But a British capital of a thousand pounds, for example, which is returned to Great Britain only once in five years, can keep in constant employment only one-fifth part of the British industry which it could maintain if the whole was returned once in the year; and, instead of the quantity of industry which a thousand pounds could maintain for a year, can keep in constant employment the quantity only which two hundred pounds can maintain for a year. The planter, no doubt, by the high price which he pays for the goods from Europe, by the interest upon the bills which he grants at distant dates, and by the commission upon the renewal of those which he grants at near dates, makes up, and probably more than makes up, all the loss which his correspondent can sustain by this delay. But, though he may make up the loss of his correspondent, he cannot make up that of Great Britain. In a trade of which the returns are very distant, the profit of the merchant may be as great or greater than in one in which they are very frequent and near; but the advantage of the country in which he resides, the quantity of productive labour constantly maintained there, the annual produce of the land and labour must always be much less. That the returns of the trade to America, and still more those of that to the West Indies, are, in general, not only more distant, but more irregular, and more uncertain too, than those of the trade to any part of Europe, or even of the countries which lie round the Mediterranean sea, will readily be allowed, I imagine, by every body who has any experience of those different branches of trade.

(2) It is also largely a roundabout trade.

Secondly, the monopoly of the colony trade has, in many cases, forced some part of the capital of Great Britain from a direct foreign trade of consumption, into a round-about one.

殊。我们说过,新殖民地总是资本不足。它们的资本总是大大少于在它们的有利的土地改良和耕种上所使用的资本。因此,它们有一个对多于自己所拥有的资本的经常性的需要;为了弥补它们的不足,它们试图尽可能多地向母国借钱,因此它们对母国总是处于欠债状态。殖民者最普通的还债方式,不是向母国的富翁立据借款(虽然他们有时也这样做),而是只要来往商人允许,尽可能地拖欠他们的货款,即用欧洲货物供给他们的商人的货款。他们每年的还款常常不到借款的 1/3,有时还达不到他们欠款的这个比例。因此,来往商人垫付的全部资本,极少在三年之内回到英国,有时候四五年都回不去。但是,例如,五年一次回到英国的 1000 镑英国资本,同每年往返一次的全部资本相比,只能雇佣 1/5 的英国劳动;不是 1000 镑每年所能经常维持的劳动数量,而是 200 镑一年能维持的劳动数量。毫无疑问,种植人通过支付欧洲货物的高价,通过他对远期票据支付的利息,通过他对近期票据更新支付的佣金,弥补了,可能更多地弥补了来商人因为遭到延期付款而受的全部损失。但是,尽管他弥补了商人的损失,他也不能弥补英国的损失。在回收非常遥远的贸易中,比其那些回收频繁和很近的贸易,商人的利润可以同样大或者更大一些;但是,他居住的国家的利益,那里经常维持的生产性劳动数量,以及每年的土地和劳动产出一定要少得多。与那些欧洲贸易,甚至是地中海沿岸各国比较,与美洲贸易的往返期限,尤其是对西印度各国的往返期,一般说,不仅更远,而且更不规律,也更不确定,我想这是这些不同贸易部门任何有经验的人都会毫不犹豫承认的。

第二,殖民地贸易的垄断,在很多情况下,使得英国资本的一部分从直接对外消费贸易进入间接对外消费贸易。

(2)它很大程度上是一种间接贸易。

— 1281 —

国民财富的性质与原理

Among the enumerated commodities which can be sent to no other market but Great Britain, there are several of which the quantity exceeds very much the consumption of Great Britain, and of which a part, therefore, must be exported to other countries. But this cannot be done without forcing some part of the capital of Great Britain into a round-about foreign trade of consumption. Maryland and Virginia, for example, send annually to Great Britain upwards of ninety-six thousand hogsheads of tobacco, and the consumption of Great Britain is said not to exceed fourteen thousand. Upwards of eighty-two thousand hogsheads, therefore, must be exported to other countries, to France, to Holland, and to the countries which lie round the Baltic and Mediterranean seas. But, that part of the capital of Great Britain which brings those eighty-two thousand hogsheads to Great Britain, which re-exports them from thence to those other countries, and which brings back from those other countries to Great Britain either goods or money in return, is employed in a round-about foreign trade of consumption; and is necessarily forced into this employment in order to dispose of this great surplus. If we would compute in how many years the whole of this capital is likely to come back to Great Britain, we must add to the distance of the American returns that of the returns from those other countries. If, in the direct foreign trade of consumption which we carry on with America, the whole capital employed frequently does not come back in less than three or four years; the whole capital employed in this round-about one is not likely to come back in less than four or five. If the one can keep in constant employment but a third or a fourth part of the domestic industry which could be maintained by a capital returned once in the year, the other can keep in constant employment but a fourth or a fifth part of that industry. At some of the out ports a credit is commonly given to those foreign correspondents to whom they export their tobacco. At the port of London, indeed, it is commonly sold for ready money. The rule is, *Weigh and pay*. At the port of London, therefore, the final returns of the whole round-about trade are more distant than the returns from America by the time only which the goods may lie unsold in the warehouse; where, however, they may sometimes lie long enough. ① But, had not the colonies been confined to the market of Great Britain for the sale of their tobacco, very little more of it would probably have come to us than what was necessary for the home consumption.

---

① [These four sentences beginning with 'At some of the outports' are not in ed. 1.]

在只能运往英国而不能运往其他市场的列举商品中，有几种商品的数量超过了英国的消费，因此有一部分就必须被运往其他的国家。但是如果不迫使英国资本的一部分进入一个间接的对外消费贸易，这就不可能实现。例如，马里兰和弗吉尼亚每年运往英国的烟草达到了 96000 桶以上，但英国的消费量据说不超过 14000 桶。因此，82000 桶必须被运往其他的国家，如法国、荷兰、波罗的海和地中海沿岸的国家。但是，将 82000 桶烟草运往英国，又将它们从英国运往其他国家，并从那里带回货物或货币的那一部分英国资本，就是使用在间接对外消费贸易中；也必然被迫使进入这种用途以处理那个巨大差额。如果我们要计算全部资本需要多少年才能回到英国，我们必须要在美洲往返期的距离上加上从这些其他国家的往返期。在我们与美洲进行的直接对外消费贸易中，如果被经常使用的全部资本要三四年才能回到英国，那么，在间接对外消费贸易中使用的全部资本则不可能在少于四到五年的时间内返回。如果前者只能经常维持一年往返一次的资本能够维持的 1/3 或 1/4 的本国劳动量，那么后者只能经常维持 1/4 或 1/5 的劳动量。在某些出口港口，通常给予那些出口烟草的外国商人以信用。诚然，在伦敦港，通常是以现钱售卖。这个规则是：现称现付。因此，在伦敦港，整个间接贸易的最终往返期，比美洲贸易的往返期，多了货物存放货仓不曾出售的时间；然而，货物存放的时间有时候可能很长①。但是，要是殖民地在它们的烟草销售上没有被限制在英国的市场，除了国内消费的需要外，极少会有更多的烟草进入我们国内。在这种情况下，

---

① 在以"在某些出口港口"开头的这四句话不在第 1 版中。

国民财富的性质与原理

        The goods which Great Britain purchases at present for her own consumption with the great surplus of tobacco which she exports to other countries, she would, in this case, probably have purchased with the immediate produce of her own industry, or with some part of her own manufactures. That produce, those manufactures, instead of being almost entirely suited to one great market, as at present, would probably have been fitted to a great number of smaller markets. Instead of one great round-about foreign trade of consumption, Great Britain would probably have carried on a great number of small direct foreign trades of the same kind. On account of the frequency of the returns, a part, and probably but a small part; perhaps not above a third or a fourth, of the capital which at present carries on this great round-about trade, might have been sufficient to carry on all those small direct ones, might have kept in constant employment an equal quantity of British industry, and have equally supported the annual produce of the land and labour of Great Britain. All the purposes of this trade being, in this manner, answered by a much smaller capital, there would have been a large spare capital to apply to other purposes; to improve the lands, to increase the manufactures, and to extend the commerce of Great Britain; to come into competition at least with the other British capitals employed in all those different ways, to reduce the rate of profit in them all, and thereby to give to Great Britain, in all of them, a superiority over other countries still greater than what she at present enjoys.

The monopoly has also forced part of the capital of Great Britain into a carrying trade,　　The monopoly of the colony trade too has forced some part of the capital of Great Britain from all foreign trade of consumption to a carrying trade; and, consequently, from supporting more or less the industry of Great Britain, to be employed altogether in supporting partly that of the colonies, and partly that of some other countries.

        The goods, for example, which are annually purchased with the great surplus of eighty-two thousand hogsheads of tobacco annually re-exported from Great Britain, are not all consumed in Great Britain. Part of them, linen from Germany and Holland, for example, is returned to the colonies for their particular consumption. But, that part of the capital of Great Britain which buys the tobacco with which this

and makes her whole industry and commerce less secure owing to its being driven into one channel.　　linen is afterwards bought, is necessarily withdrawn from supporting the industry of Great Britain, to be employed altogether in supporting, partly that of the colonies, and partly that of the particular countries who pay for this tobacco with the produce of their own industry.

        The monopoly of the colony trade besides, by forcing towards it a much greater proportion of the capital of Great Britain than what would naturally have gone to it, seems to have broken altogether that natural balance which would other wise have taken place among all the different branches of British industry. The industry of Great Britain, instead of being accommodated to a great number of small markets,

英国目前用运往其他国家的大量烟草剩余购买的用于自己消费的货物，可能会用它自己产业的直接产品，或者用它自己制造品的一部分去购买。那些产品以及制造品，不是像现在这样几乎完全适合于一个大的市场，而是可能适合于很多的小市场。由于频繁的往返，有一部分，可能只是很小的一部分，也许不超过 1/3 或 1/4 目前用于间接贸易的资本，足够进行所有的那些小的直接贸易，可以经常雇佣同等数量的英国产业，同样支持英国的土地和劳动的年产物。这样，这种贸易的所有目的都已经由非常小量的资本达到，就会有很大的闲置资本用于其他用途；来改良土地，增加制造品，扩大英国的商业，至少同其他的在不同用途中使用的英国资本竞争，减少它们中的利润率，因此使英国在各个方面享有比其他国家现在具有的更加有利的地位。

殖民地贸易的垄断也迫使英国一部分资本从对外消费贸易流入转口贸易；因此，从或多或少支持英国的产业，到被用来部分支持殖民地产业，部分支持其他国家的产业。垄断也迫使英国一部分资本流入转口贸易，

例如，每年将 82000 桶剩余烟草转手后再购买的货物，并不是全部在英国消费，而是转售出去。其中有一部分，例如来自德国和荷兰的亚麻布，又回到各殖民地，供它们消费。但是，那一部分用来购买烟草（后来用来购买亚麻布）的英国资本，必然从支持英国的产业中被抽出，一部分用来维持殖民地产业，一部分用来维持那些用自己国家产业的产品来支付这种烟草的国家的产业。

此外，殖民地贸易的垄断，通过迫使比自然情况下更大比例的英国资本流入殖民地，似乎完全打破了英国产业不同部门间的自然平衡。英国的产业，不是适应于数量众多的小市场，而是主要适应于一个大的市场。它的商业，不是在大量小渠道里流动，由于被赶进一个渠道，这使得它的整个商业不那么安全。

has been principally suited to one great market. Her commerce, instead of running in a great number of small channels, has been taught to run principally in one great channel. But the whole system of her industry and commerce has thereby been rendered less secure; the whole state of her body politic less healthful, than it otherwise would have been. In her present condition, Great Britain resembles one of those unwholesome bodies in which some of the vital parts are overgrown, and which, upon that account, are liable to many dangerous disorders scarce incident to those in which all the parts are more properly proportioned. A small stop in that great blood-vessel, which has been artificially swelled beyond its natural dimensions, and through which an unnatural proportion of the industry and commerce of the country has been forced to circulate, is very likely to bring on the most dangerous disorders upon the whole body politic. The expectation of a rupture with the colonies, accordingly, has struck the people of Great Britain with more terror than they ever felt for a Spanish armada, or a French invasion. It was this terror, whether well or ill grounded, which rendered the repeal of the stamp act, among the merchants at least, a popular measure. In the total exclusion from the colony market, was it to last only for a few years, the greater part of our merchants used to fancy that they foresaw an entire stop to their trade; the greater part of our master manufacturers, the entire ruin of their business; and the greater part of our workmen, an end of their employment. A rupture with any of our neighbours upon the continent, though likely too to occasion some stop or interruption in the employments of some of all these different orders of people, is foreseen, however, without any such general emotion. The blood, of which the circulation is stopt in some of the smaller vessels, easily disgorges itself into the greater, without occasioning any dangerous disorder; but, when it is stopt in any of the greater vessels, convulsions, apoplexy, or death, are the immediate and unavoidable consequences. If but one of those overgrown manufactures, which by means either of bounties or of the monopoly of the home and colony markets, have been artificially raised up to an unnatural height, finds some small stop or interruption in its employment, it frequently occasions a mutiny and disorder alarming to government, and embarrassing even to the deliberations of the legislature. How great, therefore, would be the disorder and confusion, it was thought, which must necessarily be occasioned by a sudden and entire stop in the employment of so great a proportion of our principal manufacturers?

Some moderate and gradual relaxation of the laws which give to Great Britain the exclusive trade to the colonies, till it is rendered in a great measure free, seems to be the only expedient which

而是被引导着主要在一个大的渠道里流动。但是这样一来,它整个工商系统,变得不如以前那么安全,它整个政治组织的状态也不如以前健康。在当前的情况下,英国像一个不太健康的机体,有些重要的部分长得过大,因此,同那些所有的部分的比例都适当的机体相比,更有可能发生危险的情况。大血管被人为地膨胀到超过其自然限度,国家的工商中一个不自然的部分被迫通过它来流通,因此大血管上一个小小的停止就有可能给整个政治组织带来最危险的疾病。因此,英国人民对于预期与殖民地决裂的恐怖大于它们对西班牙无敌舰队或法国人进攻感到的恐怖。不管有无根据,正是这种恐怖使得商人们认为废除印花税是受欢迎的举措。被完全排除在殖民地贸易之外,要是只持续几年时间,我们的大部分商人常常会认为,他们已经预见到了他们贸易的中止;我们大部分的制造业主会认为,他们的生意全毁了;我们的大部分工人会认为,他们的工作全丢了。同我们任何陆上邻邦决裂,尽管有可能引起这些不同阶层的人当中的一些人就业中断,但在预见这种事情时不会引起那么普遍的情感。血液在一些小血管中循环不畅,很容易流到大血管中,而不会引起任何危险性疾病,但是当它在任何大血管中受阻时,其立即和不可避免的结果就是痉挛、瘫痪乃至死亡。如果一种过度膨胀的制造业,由于津贴或者由于国内市场及殖民地市场的垄断,被人为地提到了不自然的高度,稍有小小的中断或阻断,就会造成骚乱或混乱,使政府震惊,甚至使议会难堪。因此,人们会想,当我们的主要的制造业有很大一部分突然完全停止时,它必然会引起的骚乱和混乱会是多大呢?

对给予英国殖民地专营贸易的法律作适当的逐渐地放松,直

| 国民财富的性质与原理

The gradual relaxation of the monopoly is desirable.

can, in all future times, deliver her from this danger, which can enable her or even force her to withdraw some part of her capital from this overgrown employment, and to turn it, though with less profit, towards other employments; and which, by gradually diminishing one branch of her industry and gradually increasing all the rest, can by degrees restore all the different branches of it to that natural, healthful, and proper proportion which perfect liberty necessarily establishes, and which perfect liberty can alone preserve. To open the colony trade all at once to all nations, might not only occasion some transitory inconveniency, but a great permanent loss to the greater part of those whose industry or capital is at present engaged in it. The sudden loss of the employment even of the ships which import the eighty-two thousand hogsheads of tobacco, which are over and above the consumption of Great Britain, might alone be felt very sensibly. Such are the unfortunate effects of all the regulations of the mercantile system! They not only introduce very dangerous disorders into the state of the body politic, but disorders which it is often difficult to remedy, without occasioning, for a time at least, still greater disorders. In what manner, therefore, the colony trade ought gradually to be opened; what are the restraints which ought first, and what are those which ought last to be taken away; or in what manner the natural system of perfect liberty and justice ought gradually to be restored, we must leave to the wisdom of future statesmen and legislators to determine.

The present exclusion from the trade with the twelve provinces would have been more severely felt but for five transitory circumstances.

Five different events, unforeseen and unthought of, have very fortunately concurred to hinder Great Britain from feeling, so sensibly as it was generally expected she would, the total exclusion which has now taken place for more than a year (from the first of December, 1774) ① from a very important branch of the colony trade, that of the twelve associated provinces of North America. First, those colonies, in preparing themselves for their non-importation agreement, drained Great Britain completely of all the commodities which were fit for their

———————————————

① [The date at which the non-importation agreement began to operate.]

到它在很大程度上是自由的,似乎是唯一的权宜之计,它在未来的任何时候可以使英国从危险中解脱出来,使它能,甚至是迫使它将一部分资本从过度增长的用途中抽取出来,并转入其他的用途,尽管利润不太大。通过逐渐减少它产业的一个部门,并逐渐增加其他的部门,可以逐渐地使产业的不同部门恢复到自然、健康和适当的比例,这一比例是完美的自由必然建立的,也只有完美的自由能保持。一次性对所有国家开放殖民地贸易,不仅会造成某种暂时性的不方便,而且会给目前将产业或资本投入其中的大部分人带来巨大的永久性的损失。即使是用来进口 82000 桶烟草的船只来说,烟草数量超过了英国的消费,但是损失了这笔生意,光这一点就会让人非常痛苦。这就是所有的重商主义体系的法规所带来的不幸后果!它们不仅把非常危险的混乱引进了政治组织,而且这种混乱,即使不引起(至少短时间内不引起)更大的混乱,也常常难以矫正。因此,用什么方式逐渐开放殖民地贸易,什么限制应该先消除,什么限制应该后消除,完美的自由和公正应该如何逐渐恢复,我们必须留给未来的聪明的政治家和立法者去决断。

逐渐放松垄断是适宜的。

　　五种不曾预见和想到的事件,非常幸运地发生,使英国没有像一般预期那样强烈地感到从一个非常重要的殖民地贸易部门——北美洲 12 个联邦的贸易中被完全排除出来,这事到现在算来已经超过一年多了(从 1774 年 12 月 1 日起)①。第一,这些殖民地在准备实行它们的不进口协议过程中,将英国所有适合它们市

如果不是由五个暂时性的事件,对目前从12个省的贸易中被排除出来会更为严重感觉到。

---

① 这一天是不进口协议开始生效的日子。

market: secondly, the extraordinary demand of the Spanish Flota ① has, this year, drained Germany and the North of many commodities, linen in particular, which used to come into competition, even in the British market, with the manufactures of Great Britain: thirdly, the peace between Russia and Turkey, ② has occasioned an extraordinary demand from the Turkey market, which, during the distress of the country, and while a Russian fleet was cruizing in the Archipelago, had been very poorly supplied: fourthly, the demand of the North of Europe for the manufactures of Great Britain, has been increasing from year to year for some time past: and, fifthly, the late partition and consequential pacification of Poland, by opening the market of that great country, have this year added an extraordinary demand from thence to the increasing demand of the North. These events are all, except the fourth, in their nature transitory and accidental, and the exclusion from so important a branch of the colony trade, if unfortunately it should continue much longer, may still occasion some degree of distress. This distress, however, as it will come on gradually, will be felt much less severely than if it had come on all at once; and, in the mean time, the industry and capital of the country may find a new employment and direction, so as to prevent this distress from ever rising to any considerable height.

The present exclusion from the trade with the twelve provinces would have been more severely felt but for five transitory circumstances.
　　The monopoly of the colony trade, therefore, so far as it has turned towards that trade a greater proportion of the capital of Great Britain than what would otherwise have gone to it, has in all cases turned it, from a foreign trade of consumption with a neighbouring, into one with a more distant country; in many cases, from a direct foreign trade of consumption, into a round-about one; and in some cases, from all foreign trade of consumption, into a carrying trade. It

① ['For the greater security of the valuable cargoes sent to America, as well as for the more easy prevention of fraud, the commerce of Spain with its colonies is carried on by fleets which sail under strong convoys. These fleets, consisting of two squadrons, one distinguished by the name of the "Galeons," the other by that of the "Flora," are equipped annually. Formerly they took their departure from Seville; but as the port of Cadiz has been found more commodious, they have sailed from it since the year 1720.' W. Robertson, *History of America*, bk. viii. ; in *Works*, 1825, vol. vii. p. 372.]

② [By the treaty of Kainardji, 1774.]

场的商品全部买光;第二,这一年,西班牙船队①的特别的需要将德国和北欧的许多商品,特别是亚麻布,全部买光,这些商品过去常常和英国的制造品竞争,甚至是在英国市场上;第三,俄罗斯和土耳其之间的和平②引起了土耳其市场的特殊需要,当这个国家处于不幸中,而且俄罗斯的舰队在爱琴海巡逻时,这个供应是非常糟糕的;第四,北欧对英国制造品的需要在过去的一段时间年年增加;第五,波兰最近被瓜分完毕,因此带来了局势平定,通过开拓那个大国的市场,这一年除了北欧日益增长的需求外,还带来了很大的市场需求。除了第四点,这些事件在性质上是暂时和偶然的,被排除在如此重要的殖民地贸易部门之外,如果不幸持续的时间更长,还会引起更大程度的痛苦。然而,这种痛苦如果是逐渐来到,那么同立刻来到相比,在感觉上会不那么严重;同时,国家的产业和资本可以找到新的用途和方向,从而防止这种痛苦上升到一个相当的高度。

因此,殖民地贸易的垄断,就其让英国资本比原本会有更大一部分流向这种贸易而言,在所有情况下,使其与邻国的对外消费贸易转到遥远的国家的对外消费贸易;在很多情况下,从直接的对外消费贸易转到间接的对外消费贸易;在一些情况下,从全部的对外消费贸易转到转口贸易。因此,在所有的情况下,都使

不于智事对前二的中除会严果由个事件,且十省易排来为地感觉到如五时于从个贸被出更重觉到

---

① 为了确保运往美洲的贵重货物的更大的安全,以及为了更好地防止造假,西班牙与其殖民地的商业由在强大的护航之下行驶的商船队进行。这些船队分为两种,一种叫做"加利昂斯",另一种叫做"弗洛达",它们每年装备一次。以前它们从赛维尔出发,但是由于发现了更加方便的加的斯港,它们从1720年起便由这里出发。W.罗伯逊:《美洲史》,第八编,见《全集》,1825年,第7卷,第372页。

② 根据凯拿基和约,1774年。

The monopoly is bad,
has in all cases, therefore, turned it, from a direction in which it would have maintained a greater quantity of productive labour, into one, in which it can maintain a much smaller quantity. By suiting, besides, to one particular market only, so great a part of the industry and commerce of Great Britain, it has rendered the whole state of that industry and commerce more precarious and less secure, than if their produce had been accommodated to a greater variety of markets.

but the trade itself is good.
We must carefully distinguish between the effects of the colony trade and those of the monopoly of that trade. The former are always and necessarily beneficial; the latter always and necessarily hurtful. But the former are so beneficial, that the colony trade, though subject to a monopoly, and notwithstanding the hurtful effects of that monopoly, is still upon the whole beneficial, and greatly beneficial; though a good deal less so than it otherwise would be.

The trade in its natural state increases the productive labour of Great Britain.
The effect of the colony trade in its natural and free state, is to open a great, though distant market for such parts of the produce of British industry as may exceed the demand of the markets nearer home, of those of Europe, and of the countries which lie round the Mediterranean sea. In its natural and free state, the colony trade, without drawing from those markets any part of the produce which had ever been sent to them, encourages Great Britain to increase the surplus continually, by continually presenting new equivalents to be exchanged for it. In its natural and free state, the colony trade tends to increase the quantity of productive labour in Great Britain, but without altering in any respect the direction of that which had been employed there before. In the natural and free state of the colony trade, the competition of all other nations would hinder the rate of profit from rising above the common level either in the new market, or in the new employment. The new market, without drawing any thing from the old one, would create, if one may say so, a new produce for its own supply; and that new produce would constitute a new capital for carrying on the new employment, which in the same manner would draw nothing from the old one.

The monopoly of the colony trade, on the contrary, by excluding the competition of other nations, and thereby raising the rate of profit both in the new market and in the new employment, draws produce from the old market and capital from the old employment. To augment our share of the colony trade beyond what it otherwise would be, is the

它从维持更大数量的生产性劳动这一方向变成维持数量更小的生产性劳动的方向。此外,通过使英国工商业很大的一部分只适应一个特殊的市场,这就使得工商业的整个状况,比起使它的产品适应更加丰富多样的市场来,更加不确定、更加不安全。

_{垄断是坏的,}

我们必须小心区分殖民地贸易的影响和那一贸易垄断的影响。前者通常必然是受益的;后者通常必然是有害的。但是前者是如此有利,以至于殖民地贸易虽然被垄断,尽管有这种垄断产生的有害影响,整体来说殖民地贸易却仍然是有利的,而且是大大有利的;尽管远远不如没有垄断那么有利。

_{但贸易本身是好的。}

殖民地贸易在自然和自由的状态下的影响,是给英国产业的邻近市场即欧洲市场与地中海沿岸各国的市场所不能容纳的那部分产品,打开一个巨大却遥远的市场。在自然与自由的状态下,殖民地贸易会鼓励英国不断地增加剩余产品,这是由于殖民地会不断提供新的等价物来和它交换,英国从来没有从这些市场抽出被输入的任何部分的产品。在自然与自由的状态下,殖民地贸易想要增加英国生产性劳动的数量,但是却没有在任何方面改变以前那里使用的生产性劳动的方向。在殖民地贸易自然与自由的状态下,所有其他国家的竞争将会阻碍利润率在新的市场或者在新的用途里上升到普通水平以上。这个新的市场,不会从旧的市场中抽出任何东西,而会创造(如果我们可以这样说的话)一种新产品来供应自己;这种新产品会组成一种新的资本用于新的用途,这同样不会从旧的市场抽出任何东西。

_{在自然状态下的贸易增加了英国的生产性劳动。}

相反,殖民地贸易的垄断,通过排除其他国家的竞争,从而在新的市场和新的用途上提高了利润率,所以它从旧的市场中抽出产品,从旧用途中抽出资本。使我国在殖民地贸易中的份额超过

国民财富的性质与原理

<small>The monopoly diminishes it.</small>
avowed purpose of the monopoly. If our share of that trade were to be no greater with, than it would have been without the monopoly, there could have been no reason for establishing the monopoly. But whatever forces into a branch of trade of which the returns are slower and more distant than those of the greater part of other trades, a greater proportion of the capital of any country, than what of its own accord would go to that branch, necessarily renders the whole quantity of productive labour annually maintained there, the whole annual produce of the land and labour of that country, less than they otherwise would be. It keeps down the revenue of the inhabitants of that country, below what it would naturally rise to, and thereby diminishes their power of accumulation. It not only hinders, at all times, their capital from maintaining so great a quantity of productive labour as it would otherwise maintain, but it hinders it from increasing so fast as it would otherwise increase, and consequently from maintaining a still greater quantity of productive labour.

<small>The natural good effects of the trade more than counterbalance the bad effects of the monopoly.</small>
The natural good effects of the colony trade, however, more than counterbalance to Great Britain the bad effects of the monopoly, so that, monopoly and all together, that trade, even as it is carried on at present, is not only advantageous, but greatly advantageous. The new market and the new employment which are opened by the colony trade, are of much greater extent than that portion of the old market and of the old employment which is lost by the monopoly. The new produce and the new capital which has been created, if one may say so, by the colony trade, maintain in Great Britain a greater quantity of productive labour, than what can have been thrown out of employment by the revulsion of capital from other trades of which the returns are more frequent. If the colony trade, however, even as it is carried on at present, is advantageous to Great Britain, it is not by means of the monopoly, but in spite of the monopoly.

<small>The colonies offer a market for the manufactured rather than the rude produce of Europe,</small>
It is rather for the manufactured than for the rude produce of Europe, that the colony trade opens a new market. Agriculture is the proper business of all new colonies; a business which the cheapness of land renders more advantageous than any other. They abound, therefore, in the rude produce of land, and instead of importing it from other countries, they have generally a large surplus to export. In new colonies, agriculture either draws hands from all other employments, or keeps them from going to any other employment. There are few hands

它原来的程度,是垄断公开宣称的目的。如果我们在贸易中的份额在有垄断时不比在没有垄断时大,那就没有理由要建立这种垄断。但是迫使任何一个国家的资本超出正常比例的资本违反自然趋势流入这种贸易,必然会使那里每年所维持的生产性劳动的总量、每年所生产的土地和劳动的产物的总量,比原来的要少。它使那个国家的居民的收入低于其自然会上升的程度,因而减少它们积累的实力。在所有的时候,它不仅阻碍他们的资本维持其本来能够维持的那么大数量的生产性劳动,而且还阻碍他们的资本以原本能增长的程度快速增长,因此就维持了一个非常大量的生产性劳动。_{垄断会减少它。}

然而,殖民地贸易的自然良好影响,抵消了英国垄断的不良影响后还有剩余,所以,垄断以及即使现在也在进行的贸易,不仅是有利的,而且是大大有利的。由垄断贸易打开的新的市场和新的产业,比由垄断丧失的那一部分旧市场和旧用途范围更大。由殖民地贸易创造的新市场和新产业,如我们可以这么说的话,在英国维持的生产性劳动的数量比从往返期更为频繁的其他贸易抽出资本所能使其失业的生产性劳动的数量大。然而,如果殖民地贸易像现在一样进行,对英国是有利的,这不是通过垄断,而是由于垄断。_{贸易的自然良好影响抵消了垄断的不良影响。}

殖民地贸易开拓了一个新的市场,是为了欧洲的制造品而不是为了它的天然产物。农业是所有新殖民地的合适业务:土地的廉价使其比任何其他部门更加有利。因此,他们的土地天然产物十分丰富,不仅不用从其他国家进口,通常还有大量的剩余供出口。在新的殖民地,农业要么从其他的用途中吸收劳动,要么防止自己的劳动流入任何其他的用途。极少有劳动力可以从事必_{殖民地贸易为欧洲制造品提供一个市场,而不是为天然产物。}

to spare for the necessary, and none for the ornamental manufactures. The greater part of the manufactures of both kinds, they find it cheaper to purchase of other countries than to make for themselves. It is chiefly by encouraging the manufactures of Europe, that the colony trade indirectly encourages its agriculture. The manufacturers of Europe, to whom that trade gives employment, constitute a new market for the produce of the land; and the most advantageous of all markets; the home market for the corn and cattle, for the bread and butcher's-meat of Europe; is thus greatly extended by means of the trade to America.

but the monopoly has not maintained the manufactures of Spain and Portugal,

But that the monopoly of the trade of populous and thriving colonies is not alone sufficient to establish, or even to maintain manufactures in any country, the examples of Spain and Portugal suffiently demonstrate. Spain and Portugal were manufacturing countries before they had any considerable colonies. Since they had the richest and most fertile in the world, they have both ceased to be so.

where the bad effects of the monopoly have nearly overbalanced the good effects of the trade.

In Spain and Portugal, the bad effects of the monopoly, aggravated by other causes, have, perhaps, nearly overbalanced the natural good effects of the colony trade. These causes seem to be, other monopolies of different kinds; the degradation of the value of gold and silver below what it is in most other countries; the exclusion from foreign markets by improper taxes upon exportation, and the narrowing of the home market, by still more improper taxes upon the transportation of goods from one part of the country to another; but above all, that irregular and partial administration of justice, which often protects the rich and powerful debtor from the pursuit of his injured creditor, and which makes the industrious part of the nation afraid to prepare goods for the consumption of those haughty and great men, to whom they dare not refuse to sell upon credit, and from whom they are altogether uncertain of repayment.

In England the good effects of the trade have greatly counteracted the bad effects of the monopoly.

In England, on the contrary, the natural good effects of the colony trade, assisted by other causes, have in a great measure conquered the bad effects of the monopoly. These causes seem to be, the general liberty of trade, which, notwithstanding some restraints, is at least equal, perhaps superior, to what it is in any other country; the liberty of exporting, duty free, almost all sorts of

需品制造,更没有劳动力供装饰品制造。他们发现从其他国家购买这两种制造品的很大部分比自己制造要便宜。主要通过鼓励欧洲的制造业,殖民地贸易间接鼓励了其农业。由殖民地贸易提供用途的欧洲制造业者,构成了一个土地产品的新市场;一个在所有市场中最有利的市场,欧洲的谷物、牲畜、面包和鲜肉的国内市场,而这个市场由于对美洲的贸易而大大扩张了。

但是,人口众多和繁荣的殖民地贸易的垄断,其单独不足以建立甚至不足以维持在任何国家的制造业,西班牙和葡萄牙的例子就足以说明了。西班牙和葡萄牙在他们有任何大块的殖民地之前就是制造业国。自从它们拥有世界上最富裕和最肥沃的殖民地以后,它们就不再是制造业国家了。

但是垄断没有维持西班牙和葡萄牙的制造业。

在西班牙和葡萄牙,垄断的不良影响(由于其他原因而变得更为严重)或许几乎抵消了殖民地贸易的自然的良好影响。这些原因似乎是:其他的垄断;黄金和白银的价值贬低到大部分其他国家之下;由于对出口征收不适当的关税而被排除于外国市场之外,由于货物从一个国家的一个地方运往另一个地方被征收更不适合的税收而引起的国内市场的萎缩;尤其是司法行政的不规则和不公正,常常保护富裕的和有势力的债务人,使之免遭债权人的追讨,它使得国家的工业部门不敢制造产品来供那些傲慢的大人物消费,不敢拒绝向他们赊售,也完全不能肯定他们会偿还欠款。

但是垄断没有维持西班牙和葡萄牙的制造业。

相反,在英国,殖民地贸易的良好影响,加上其他的原因,在很大程度上抵消了垄断的不良影响。这些原因似乎是:普遍的贸易自由,尽管有一些限制,至少是等于或许优于在任何其他国家的情况;出口自由,本国产业生产的几乎各类货物向几乎任何外

英国贸易的良好影响大大抵消了垄断的不良影响。

— 1297 —

goods which are the produce of domestic industry, to almost any foreign country; and what, perhaps, is of still greater importance, the unbounded liberty of transporting them from any one part of our own country to any other, without being obliged to give any account to any public office, without being liable to question or examination of any kind; but above all, that equal and impartial administration of justice which renders the rights of the meanest British subject respectable to the greatest, and which, by securing to every man the fruits of his own industry, gives the greatest and most effectual encouragement to every sort of industry.

<small>The trade has benefited British manufactures in spite of the monopoly, not in consequence of it.</small>   If the manufactures of Great Britain, however, have been advanced, as they certainly have, by the colony trade, it has not been by means of the monopoly of that trade, but in spite of the monopoly. The effect of the monopoly has been, not to augment the quantity, but to alter the quality and shape of a part of the manufactures of Great Britain, and to accommodate to a market, from which the returns are slow and distant, what would otherwise have been accommodated to one from which the returns are frequent and near. Its effect has consequently been to turn a part of the capital of Great Britain from an employment in which it would have maintained a greater quantity of manufacturing industry, to one in which it maintains a much smaller, and thereby to diminish, instead of increasing, the whole quantity of manufacturing industry maintained in Great Britain.

The monopoly of the colony trade, therefore, like all the other mean and malignant expedients of the mercantile system, depresses the industry of all other countries, but chiefly that of the colonies, without in the least increasing, but on the contrary diminishing, that of the country in whose favour it is established.

<small>The monopoly reduces wages in the mother country.</small>   The monopoly hinders the capital of that country, whatever may at any particular time be the extent of that capital, from maintaining so great a quantity of productive labour as it would otherwise maintain, and from affording so great a revenue to the industrious inhabitants as it would otherwise afford. But as capital can be increased only by savings from revenue, the monopoly, by hindering it from affording so great a revenue as it would otherwise afford, necessarily hinders it from increasing so fast as it would otherwise increase, and consequently from maintaining a still greater quantity of productive labour,

国出口时均免税；或许更为重要的是，从我们自己国家的任何部分向任何其他部分运输货物的毫无束缚的自由，不需要向任何国家机关解释，不受任何形式的询问或检查；尤其是，平等和公正的司法行政，使得最卑鄙的英国臣民的权利受到最伟大的英国臣民的尊重，通过保障它产业内每一个人获得自己的劳动成果，它给予了每一种产业最大和最有效的鼓励。

然而，如果英国的制造业由于殖民地贸易而进步（它们肯定会这样），那不是依靠贸易垄断的结果，而是由于垄断以外的因素造成的结果。垄断的影响不是增加英国制造业一部分产品的数量，而是改变它的质量和形状，使其违反自然趋势，适应于往返缓慢和遥远的市场，不是适应于往返频繁和近的市场。因此，它的影响是将一部分英国资本从能维持较大量的制造产业的用途转向维持较少量的制造产业的用途，因此它减少了而不是增加了英国维持整个制造产业的数量。殖民地贸易有利于不列颠的制造业，不是因为垄断，而是因为垄断以外的原因。

因此，殖民地贸易的垄断，像所有其他重商主义体系和所有其他的卑鄙恶毒的办法一样，使所有其他国家的产业萧条，但是主要是殖民地的产业没有丝毫的增长，相反减少了那些为了本国利益而建立的产业。

垄断阻碍了那个国家的资本，不管这种资本在任何特殊时候的大小如何，维持在像原本该维持的那么大数量的生产性劳动，并向产业性居民提供原本应该提供的那么大数量的收入。但是，由于资本只能通过收入的节省才能增加，所以垄断通过阻碍资本提供像原本应该提供的那样大量的收入，必然阻碍了像它原本应该增长的那样快速的增长，因此维持了一个更大数量的生产性劳动，为该国的产业居民提供了一个更大数量的收入。所以，垄断 垄断减少了母国的工资，

—— 1299 ——

and affording a still greater revenue to the industrious inhabitants of that country. One great original source of revenue, therefore, the wages of labour, the monopoly must necessarily have rendered at all times less abundant than it otherwise would have been.

raises-profits, and thereby tends to lower rents and the price of land.

By raising the rate of mercantile profit, the monopoly discourages the improvement of land. The profit of improvement depends upon the difference between what the land actually produces, and what, by the application of a certain capital, it can be made to produce. If this difference affords a greater profit than what can be drawn from an equal capital in any mercantile employment, the improvement of land will draw capital from all mercantile employments. If the profit is less, mercantile employments will draw capital from the improvement of land. Whatever therefore raises the rate of mercantile profit, either lessens the superiority or increases the inferiority of the profit of improvement; and in the one case hinders capital from going to improvement, and in the other draws capital from it. But by discouraging improvement, the monopoly necessarily retards the natural increase of another great original source of revenue, the rent of land. By raising the rate of profit too, the monopoly necessarily keeps up the market rate of interest higher than it otherwise would be. But the price of land in proportion to the rent which it affords, the number of years purchase which is commonly paid for it, necessarily falls as the rate of interest rises, and rises as the rate of interest falls. The monopoly, therefore, hurts the interest of the landlord two different ways, by retarding the natural increase, first, of his rent, and secondly, of the price which he would get for his land in proportion to the rent which it affords.

It reduces the absolute amount of profit,

The monopoly, indeed, raises the rate of mercantile profit, and thereby augments somewhat the gain of our merchants. But as it obstructs the natural increase of capital, it tends rather to diminish than to increase the sum total of the revenue which the inhabitants of the country derive from the profits of stock; a small profit upon a great capital generally affording a greater revenue than a great profit upon a small one. The monopoly raises the rate of profit, but it hinders the sum of profit from rising so high as it otherwise would do.

thus rendering all the original sources of revenue less abundant.

All the original sources of revenue, the wages of labour, the rent of land, and the profits of stock, the monopoly renders much less abundant than they otherwise would be. To promote the little interest of one little order of men in one country, it hurts the interest of all other orders of men in that country, and of all men in all other countries.

必然使收入的一个巨大的初始来源,即劳动工资,在所有的时候都比它原本应该会有的那样富足。

通过提高商业利润率,垄断抑制了土地的改良。改良的利润,取决于土地实际上的产出和通过应用一定数量的资本能使土地产出的数量之间的差额。如果这一差额比同样资本在任何商业用途中得到的利润更大,土地改良将从所有的商业用途中吸收资本。如果这个利润较少,商业用途就会将资本从土地改良中吸收出来。因此,提高商业利润率的事物,要么减少改良的利润,要么使改良利润降到更低;第一种情况阻碍资本进入土地改良,第二种情况从土地改良吸收资本。但是,通过阻碍改良,垄断必然减缓另一巨大的收入初始来源即土地地租的自然增长。垄断也提高利润率,它必然使得市场利息率高于其原本应该有的水平。但是与提供的地租成比例的土地的价格,即通常用若干年地租来计算的价格,必然随着利息率上升而下降,随着利息率下降而上升。因此,垄断从两个不同的方面破坏地主的利益:第一,阻碍他的地租的自然增长;第二,阻碍他从同其缴纳的地租成比例的土地上获得的价格的自然增长。

<small>垄断提高利润,因而试图降低土地地租和价格。</small>

诚然,垄断提高商业利润率,因而稍微提高了我们商人的所得。但是由于它阻碍资本的自然增长,它试图减少,而不是增加国家居民从资本利润中得到的收入总额;巨额资本的少量利润通常比少量资本的大量利润提供更大量的收入。垄断提高了利润率,但却阻碍了利润总额提高到它原本可以达到的高度。

<small>垄断减少了利润的绝对数量。</small>

对于所有的收入初始来源,劳动工资,土地地租和资本利润,垄断使它们远远不如原本情况下富足。为了提升一个国家一小部分人的少量利益,它损害了那个国家所有其他阶层的人的利

<small>因此使所有的收入初始来源不那么富足。</small>

国民财富的性质与原理

More fatal still, it destroys parsimony.

It is solely by raising the ordinary rate of profit that the monopoly either has proved or could prove advantageous to any one particular order of men. But besides all the bad effects to the country in general, which have already been mentioned as necessarily resulting from a high rate of profit; there is one more fatal, perhaps, than all these put together, but which, if we may judge from experience, is inseparably connected with it. The high rate of profit seems every where to destroy that parsimony which in other circumstances is natural to the character of the merchant. When profits are high, that sober virtue seems to be superfluous, and expensive luxury to suit better the affluence of his situation. But the owners of the great mercantile capitals are necessarily the leaders and conductors of the whole industry of every nation, and their example has a much greater influence upon the manners of the whole industrious part of it than that of any other order of men. If his employer is attentive and parsimonious, the workman is very likely to be so too; but if the master is dissolute and disorderly, the servant who shapes his work according to the pattern which his master prescribes to him, will shape his life too according to the example which he sets him. Accumulation is thus prevented in the hands of all those who are naturally the most disposed to accumulate; and the funds destined for the maintenance of productive labour receive no augmentation from the revenue of those who ought naturally to augment them the most. The capital of the country, instead of increasing, gradually dwindles away, and the quantity of productive labour maintained in it grows every day less and less. Have the exorbitant profits of the merchants of Cadiz and Lisbon augmented the capital of Spain and Portugal ? Have they alleviated the poverty, have they promoted the industry of those two beggarly countries ? Such has been the tone of mercantile expence in those two trading cities, that those exorbitant profits, far from augmenting the general capital of the country, seem scarce to have been sufficient to keep up the capitals upon which they were made. Foreign capitals are every day intruding themselves, if I may say so, more and more into the trade of Cadiz and Lisbon. It is to expel those foreign capitals from a trade which their own grows every day more and more insufficient for carrying on, that the Spaniards and Portuguese endeavour every day to straiten more and more the galling bands of their absurd monopoly.

益，以及所有其他国家所有人的利益。

完全是通过提高普通利润率，垄断才证明或者能够证明对任何一个特别的人群是有利的。但是除了对这个国家大体上的所有的不好影响外（已经提到这是高利润率的一个必然结果）或许还有一个比所有这些不好影响加在一起更加严重的后果，但如果我们从经验来判断，它是和高利润率联系在一起的。似乎高利润率在各地都会毁坏在其他情况下商人具有的极度节省的特性。当利润高时，节省的美德似乎变成多余，奢侈才更适合于他的富裕境地。但是大量商业资本的主人必然是每个国家整个产业的领导者和指挥者，他们的作用比任何其他阶层的人对一个国家整个产业部门的生产方式产生的影响要大得多。如果雇主是小心谨慎和过度节省的，他的雇佣工人也非常有可能是这样的；但如果主人是放荡和混乱的，那么听从主人吩咐做事的仆人，也将会根据主人给他树立的榜样来规划自己的生活。这样，在那些自然情况下最容易积累的人手中，积累就无法实现了；用于维持生产性劳动的基金，不能从自然情况下应该使这种基金增加最多的人的收入得到增加。国家的资本，不是增加，而是逐渐消失，维持在其中的生产性劳动的数量每天增长得越来越少。加的斯和里斯本商人的超额利润增加了西班牙和葡萄牙的资本吗？这种利润消除了贫困，促进了它们的产业吗？这两个贸易城市的商业消费的风气是如此，使得这种超额利润远远未能增加国家的一般资本，而且似乎不足以保持原有的资本。如果我可以这样说的话，外国资本每天都在越来越多地自行进入加的斯和里斯本的贸易。为了把外国资本从自己资本每天越来越不够经营的贸易中驱逐出去，西班牙人和葡萄牙人每天都在试图越来越加紧它们的荒谬

更严重的是，它毁坏了非常节俭的习惯。

Compare the mercantile manners of Cadiz and Lisbon with those of Amsterdam, and you will be sensible how differently the conduct and character of merchants are affected by the high and by the low profits of stock. The merchants of London, indeed, have not yet generally become such magnificent lords as those of Cadiz and Lisbon; but neither are they in general such attentive and parsimonious burghers as those of Amsterdam. They are supposed, however, many of them, to be a good deal richer than the greater part of the former, and not quite so rich as many of the latter. But the rate of their profit is commonly much lower than that of the former, and a good deal higher than that of the latter. Light come light go, says the proverb; and the ordinary tone of expence seems every where to be regulated, not so much according to the real ability of spending, as to the supposed facility of getting money to spend.

It is thus that the single advantage which the monopoly procures to a single order of men, is in many different ways hurtful to the general interest of the country.

<small>The policy of the monopoly is a policy of shopkeepers.</small>

To found a great empire for the sole purpose of raising up a people of customers, may at first sight appear a project fit only for a nation of shopkeepers. It is, however, a project altogether unfit for a nation of shopkeepers; but extremely fit for a nation whose government is influenced by shopkeepers. Such statesmen, and such statesmen only, are capable of fancying that they will find some advantage in employing the blood and treasure of their fellow-citizens, to found and maintain such an empire. Say to a shopkeeper, Buy me a good estate, and I shall always buy my clothes at your shop, even though I should pay somewhat dearer than what I can have them for at other shops; and you will not find him very forward to embrace your proposal. But should any other person buy you such an estate, the shopkeeper would be much obliged to your benefactor if he would enjoin you to buy all your clothes at his shop. England purchased for some of her subjects, who found themselves uneasy at home, a great estate in a distant country. The price, indeed, was very small, and instead of thirty years purchase, the ordinary price of land in the present times, it amounted to little more than the expence of the different equipments which made the first discovery, reconnoitred the coast, and took a fic-

的垄断。将加的斯和里斯本的商业风气和阿姆斯特丹的风气相比,你会感觉到商人的行为和特性受到资本高低利润的影响的差异是多大啊!确实,伦敦的商人一般没有成为像加的斯和里斯本那样的杰出的贵族;但是他们通常也不像阿姆斯特丹商人那样小心谨慎和极度节省。然而,通常认为,他们中的很多人,比前者中的很大一部分人要更为富裕,却不如后者中的很多人一样那么富裕。但是他们的利润率常常比前者要低得多,比后者要高得多。俗话说,来得容易,去得也容易;普通的消费方式在任何地方似乎都不是由支付的真实能力决定的,而是受得到钱拿去消费的难易程度决定的。

因此,垄断为某一单独阶层的人们取得的单独的好处,在很多不同的方面对国家的一般利益是有害的。

为了将全体人民培养成顾客这一单独目的而建立一个巨大的帝国,最初可能看起来是一个仅仅适合店主国家的计划。然而,它却是一个完全不适合店主国家的计划,而是极其适合其政府被店主影响的国家。那些政治家,也仅仅只有这些政治家,能够幻想出,他们能用他们人民的鲜血和财富来建立和维持这样一个国家,并获得一些利益。对一个店主说,买我的一块好地产,我将经常在你的商店买衣服,即使我需要以比在别的商店更贵的价格来买这些衣服;你会发现他不是那么情愿去响应你的提议。但是如果其他的人给你买了这一处地产,让你在这个商店中买你需要的所有衣服,店主会对那个人十分感激。英国为它的一些臣民在一个遥远的国家购买了一处巨人的地产,这些臣民在国内感到不是很自在。诚然,价格非常低,不是现在的土地普通价格,即30年的地租,而只是初次发现、勘探海岸和夺取土地的设备费用。

<small>垄断政策是店主的政策。</small>

titious possession of the country. The land was good and of great extent, and the cultivators having plenty of good ground to work upon, and being for some time at liberty to sell their produce where they pleased, became in the course of little more than thirty or forty years (between 1620 and 1660) so numerous and thriving a people, that the shopkeepers and other traders of England wished to secure to themselves the monopoly of their custom. Without pretending, therefore, that they had paid any part, either of the original purchase-money, or of the subsequent expence of improvement, they petitioned the parliament that the cultivators of America might for the future be confined to their shop; first, for buying all the goods which they wanted from Europe; and, secondly, for selling all such parts of their own produce as those traders might find it convenient to buy. For they did not find it convenient to buy every part of it. Some parts of it imported into England might have interfered with some of the trades which they themselves carried on at home. Those particular parts of it, therefore, they were willing that the colonists should sell where they could; the farther off the better; and upon that account proposed that their market should be confined to the countries south of Cape Finisterre. A clause in the famous act of navigation established this truly shopkeeper proposal into a law.

<small>The expenditure of Great Britain on the colonies has all been laid out to support the monopoly, and is enormous.</small>   The maintenance of this monopoly has hitherto been the principal, or more properly perhaps the sole end and purpose of the dominion which Great Britain assumes over her colonies. In the exclusive trade, it is supposed, consists the great advantage of provinces, which have never yet afforded either revenue or military force for the support of the civil government, or the defence of the mother country. The monopoly is the principal badge of their dependency, and it is the sole fruit which has hitherto been gathered from that dependency. Whatever expence Great Britain has hitherto laid out in maintaining this dependency, has really been laid out in order to support this monopoly. The expence of the ordinary peace establishment of the colonies amounted, before the commencement of the present disturbances, to the pay of twenty regiments of foot; to the expence of the artillery, stores, and extraordinary provisions with which it was necessary to supply them; and to the expence of a very considerable naval force which was constantly kept up, in order to guard, from the smuggling vessels of other nations, the immense coast of North America, and that of our West Indian islands. The whole expence of this peace establishment was a charge upon the revenue of Great Britain,

这里土地良好,而且十分辽阔,耕种者有大量的好土地可以耕种,还可以自由地在某个时间在任何地方售卖他们的产品,在三四十年的时间内(1620~1660年),变成了一个人口众多富裕繁荣的民族,因此店主和英国其他的贸易者,希望确保这样一种垄断。所以,他们不装作会开始用货币购买土地,接着用来支付土地改良费用,他们只会向议会请愿,要求美洲耕种者将来只去他们的商店买东西:第一,到他们的商店购买殖民地人民需要的一切欧洲产品;第二,殖民地人民要把他们认为适于购买的那些殖民地产物,全部卖给他们的商店。他们并不认为全部产物都适于购买,因为其中有一部分输入英国可能妨碍他们在国内经营的某些商业部门。这部分产品,他们自然希望移民们尽量对外地售卖,愈远愈好;即由于这个原因,他们提议,把这些产品的销售市场限定在菲尼斯特海角以南各国。这种真正小买卖商人的提议,在有名的航海条例中定为一个正式条款。

英国一直将维持这种垄断作为殖民统治的主要目的,或者更为确切地说,作为唯一的目的。专营贸易被认为是各省最大的财富来源,在支持公民政府或本国国防建设方面,它从未提供任何资金和军事力量。这种垄断是它们依赖性的首要标志,也是这种依赖性的唯一产物。英国为维持该依赖性支付的所有费用实质上都是为了支持这种垄断。在这次骚乱开始前,维持殖民地正常和平状态下的支出总计相当于维持20个步兵团的费用;也相当于维持炮兵储备以及维持他们生活所需的特殊食物的总费用;甚至相当于维持一支大规模海军部队的花费,而这支海军通常肩负着防止他国走私船只入境,保卫北美和西印度群岛广阔海岸线的重任。所有用于维持殖民地正常和平状态的费用都需要由英

英国用殖民地的巨额支出都是为了支持垄断。

| 国民财富的性质与原理

and was, at the same time, the smallest part of what the dominion of the colonies has cost the mother country. If we would know the amount of the whole, we must add to the annual expence of this peace establishment the interest of the sums which, in consequence of her considering her colonies as provinces subject to her dominion, Great Britain has upon different occasions laid out upon their defence. We must add to it, in particular, the whole expence of the late war, and a great part of that of the war which preceded it. The late war was altogether a colony quarrel, and the whole expence of it, in whatever part of the world it may have been laid out, whether in Germany or the East Indies, ought justly to be stated to the account of the colonies. It amounted to more than ninety millions sterling, including not only the new debt which was contracted, but the two shillings in the pound additional land tax, and the sums which were every year borrowed from the sinking fund. The Spanish war which began in 1739, was principally a colony quarrel. Its principal object was to prevent the search of the colony ships which carried on a contraband trade with the Spanish main. This whole expence is, in reality, a bounty which has been given in order to support a monopoly. The pretended purpose of it was to encourage the manufactures, and to increase the commerce of Great Britain. But its real effect has been to raise the rate of mercantile profit, and to enable our merchants to turn into a branch of trade, of which the returns are more slow and distant than those of the greater part of other trades, a greater proportion of their capital than they otherwise would have done; two events which if a bounty could have prevented, it might perhaps have been very well worth while to give such a bounty.

Under the present system of management, therefore, Great Britain derives nothing but loss from the dominion which she assumes over her colonies.

A voluntary separation would be very advantageous.

To propose that Great Britain should voluntarily give up all authority over her colonies, and leave them to elect their own magistrates, to enact their own laws, and to make peace and war as they might think proper, would be to propose such a measure as never was, and never will be adopted, by any nation in the world. No nation ever voluntarily gave up the dominion of any province, how troublesome soever it might be to govern it, and how small soever the revenue which it afforded might be in proportion to the expence which it occasioned. Such sacrifices, though they might frequently be agreeable to the interest, are always mortifying to the pride of every nation,

国的财政收入支付,但与此同时,这些费用仅仅是殖民国为殖民统治付出的最小代价。如果想了解总花销,我们还需加入这样一部分利息数额一起核算,即在英国将殖民地看作是隶属于自己的省份的前提下,针对不同形势对它们进行防卫所需经费的利息。需要特别指出的是,我们还必须加入上一场战争的花销以及此前战争的大部分花销。上一场战争完全是一场殖民地间的战争,所以不论这些钱花在何处,不论是在德意志还是东印度,从公正的角度看来,都应被解释为用于殖民地的花销。总额达9000多万英镑的总花销不仅包括新发行公债,还包括每镑2先令的土地附加税,以及每年从偿债基金借入的金额。始于1739年的西班牙战争首先是一场殖民地战争,主要目的是防止对在西班牙公海内进行走私贸易的殖民地船只进行搜查。这些总花销事实上是为了维持垄断所发放的奖励。鼓励英国的制造商和繁荣商业的目的冠冕堂皇,但实际效果则是为了提高商业利润率,使商人将超过其预想的更大一部分资本投入这样一种贸易部门,这种贸易部门的回报远远落后于其他大部分贸易部门;如果奖励能有效防止上述两种情况发生,那么发放奖励就是值得的。

所以,在现有管理体制下,英国殖民统治一无所获,损失巨大。

建议英国自动放弃对其殖民地的管制,让它们自主选举地方长官,自主立法,自主停战交火,无异于提出一种从未被也永远不会被任何一国采用的提议。没有任何一个国家会主动放弃过对国内任何一省的权力,不论治理该省有多么棘手,不论该省对本国财政做出的贡献和它所带来的国家财政支出是多么不成比例。这种牺牲虽然时常与国家利益相符,但却通常有损国家威信;更

_{自愿分离非常有利。}

and what is perhaps of still greater consequence, they are always contrary to the private interest of the governing part of it, who would thereby be deprived of the disposal of many places of trust and profit, of many opportunities of acquiring wealth and distinction, which the possession of the most turbulent, and, to the great body of the people, the most unprofitable province seldom fails to afford. The most visionary enthusiast would scarce be capable of proposing such a measure, with any serious hopes at least of its ever being adopted. If it was adopted, however, Great Britain would not only be immediately freed from the whole annual expence of the peace establishment of the colonies, but might settle with them such a treaty of commerce as would effectually secure to her a free trade, more advantageous to the great body of the people, though less so to the merchants, than the monopoly which she at present enjoys. By thus parting good friends, the natural affection of the colonies to the mother country, which, perhaps, our late dissensions have well nigh extinguished, would quickly revive. It might dispose them not only to respect, for whole centuries together, that treaty of commerce which they had concluded with us at parting, but to favour us in war as well as in trade, and, instead of turbulent and factious subjects, to become our most faithful, affectionate, and generous allies; and the same sort of parental affection on the one side, and filial respect on the other, might revive between Great Britain and her colonies, which used to subsist between those of ancient Greece and the mother city from which they descended.

<small>The colonies do not furnish nearly sufficient revenue to make them advantageous.</small> In order to render any province advantageous to the empire to which it belongs, it ought to afford, in time of peace, a revenue to the public sufficient not only for defraying the whole expence of its own peace establishment, but for contributing its proportion to the support of the general government of the empire. Every province necessarily contributes, more or less, to increase the expence of that general government. If any particular province, therefore, does not contribute its share towards defraying this expence, an unequal burden must be thrown upon some other part of the empire. The extraordinary revenue too which every province affords to the public in time of war, ought, from parity of reason, to bear the same proportion to the extraordinary revenue of the whole empire which its ordinary revenue does in time of peace. That neither the ordinary nor extraordinary revenue which Great Britain derives from her colonies, bears this proportion to the whole revenue of the British empire, will readily be allowed. The monopoly, it has been supposed, indeed, by increasing the private revenue of the people of Great Britain, and thereby enabling them to pay greater taxes, compensates the deficiency of the public revenue of the colonies. But this monopoly, I have endeavoured to show, though a very grievous tax upon the colonies, and though it may increase the revenue of a particular order of men in Great Britain, diminishes instead of increasing that of the great body of the people; and consequently diminishes instead of increasing the ability of

为严重的影响是,它常与统治集团的私人利益相悖,因而丧失了对许多利润丰厚地区的管理权和获得财富和荣誉的机会,而这种机会恰恰来源于最动乱和广大民众最无利可图的地区。即使是最善于空想的热心人士也不会提出这样的建议,至少不会太过期待这样的建议被采纳。但是一旦该建议被采纳,英国不但会立刻脱身于殖民地每年的建制支出,而且可能和它们订立有效保证自由贸易的通商条约,该条约相比现有的垄断,将会更加有利于民众,损益于商人。友好的分离有利于殖民地迅速恢复对于母国差不多消失殆尽的情感,也有助于迅速缓和与母国间的紧张气氛。这不仅会使殖民地将来遵守与母国分离时所订立的通商条约而且还会使其在战争和贸易中成为母国最忠实、最亲密、最慷慨的同盟而非骚乱制造者。英国和它的殖民地也会恢复类似于古希腊殖民地和它们的母亲城之间那种"母慈子孝"的情感。

为了使一省有利于它所属的帝国,它在和平时期不但应该负担自己和平建设费用,还应该为支持帝国政府做出适当贡献。所有省份都必须或多或少地为政府支出增长做出自己的贡献。如果任何一省没有为财政支出做出任何贡献,那么帝国的其他省份必然会被迫担负不平等的重担。同理,各省在战时上缴国家的收入与帝国财政收入的比例应与和平状态下相同。大家公认的是英国战时和和平状态下的收入都无法与这个比例持平。的确,有人认为这种垄断下人民收入的增长使得英国人民有能力缴纳更多赋税去补偿殖民地公共收入的短缺。但是我试图证明的是,这种垄断虽然对殖民地苛以重税,虽然可以增加英国某些特殊阶层的收入,但对于广大民众而言,他们的收入是减少了而不是增加了;相应的,他们的纳税能力降低了而不是增强了。在这种垄断

殖民地不缴纳足够收入使其有利于帝国。

| 国民财富的性质与原理

the great body of the people to pay taxes. The men too whose revenue the monopoly increases, constitute a particular order, which it is both absolutely impossible to tax beyond the proportion of other orders, and extremely impolitic even to attempt to tax beyond that proportion, as I shall endeavour to shew in the following book. No particular resource, therefore, can be drawn from this particular order.

The colonies may be taxed either by their own assemblies, or by the parliament of Great Britain.

<small>The colonial assemblies will never vote enough,</small> That the colony assemblies can ever be so managed as to levy upon their constituents a public revenue sufficient, not only to maintain at all times their own civil and military establishment, but to pay their proper proportion of the expence of the general government of the British empire, seems not very probable. It was a long time before even the parliament of England, though placed immediately under the eye of the sovereign, could be brought under such a system of management, or could be rendered sufficiently liberal in their grants for supporting the civil and military establishments even of their own country. It was only by distributing among the particular members of parliament, a great part either of the offices, or of the disposal of the offices arising from this civil and military establishment, that such a system of management could be established even with regard to the parliament of England. But the distance of the colony assemblies from the eye of the sovereign, their number, their dispersed situation, and their various constitutions, would render it very difficult to manage them in the same manner, even though the sovereign had the same means of doing it; and those means are wanting. It would be absolutely impossible to distribute among all the leading members of all the colony assemblies such a share, either of the offices or of the disposal of the offices arising from the general government of the British empire, as to dispose them to give up their popularity at home, and to tax their constituents for the support of that general government, of which almost the whole emoluments were to be divided among people who were strangers to them. The unavoidable ignorance of administration besides, concerning the relative importance of the different members of those different assemblies, the offences which must frequently be given, the blunders which must constantly be committed in attempting to manage them in this manner, seems to render such a system of management altogether impracticable with regard to them.

<small>and have no knowledge of what is required.</small> The colony assemblies, besides, cannot be supposed the proper judges of what is necessary for the defence and support of the whole empire. The care of that defence and support is not entrusted to them. It is not their business, and they have no regular means of information concerning it. The assembly of a province, like the vestry of a parish, may judge very properly concerning the affairs of its own particular district; but can have no proper means of judging concerning those of the whole empire. It cannot even judge properly concerning the proportion which its own province bears to the whole empire;

下收入增加的人构成了特殊的阶层,但是对他们的征税绝对不可能高于对其他阶层征税的比例,而且这种做法也是极不明智的,关于这一点我会在下文做出详细解释。所以,这个阶层并不能带来特殊收入。

殖民地所属议会和英国国会都可以向殖民地征税。

要求殖民地议会征收足够的收入以支持所有情况下自己的国民和军事支出并能在必要时为英国一般政府开支贡献自己微薄之力的设想似乎是无稽之谈。虽然在国王的直接监督下,英国国会建立了这样一种管理制度,并且获得足够的费用支持本国的国民和军事建设,但这已经成为历史了。即使是英国国会,也只有在将国民和军事建设中所产生的管理职位和相应的支配权分配给国会特殊议员,才能建立这样一种管理制度。但是由于殖民地议会不受国王直接监督,且数量繁多,位置分散,立法不同,所以即使国王有相同的管理办法也无法用同一种方式去管理他们,更何况国王尚未有相同的管理方案。将国民和军事建设中所产生的管理职位和相应的支配权分配给殖民地议会领导者,让其放弃民众支持,对民众征税支持一般政府支出是完全不可能的,其中全部管理者的报酬都是在陌生人之间分配的。另外,不可避免的是,管理部门对于不同议会间不同成员的相对重要性缺乏了解,这必然会经常引起不满情绪,如果按这种方式管理必然铸成大错,这就使得这种管理体系对于殖民地会议来说成为空想。

_{殖民地不会以投票的方式决定征税,}

另外,人们也并不能认为殖民地会议有权评定何谓保卫和支持整个帝国的必要经费,没有人将这个任务委托殖民地会议办理。这不是他们的职责,而且他们也没有得到相关信息的正常手段。和教区会议相类似的省议会可以合理评定自己辖区内的事务,但是缺乏评定整个帝国事务的合理手段。他们甚至不能评定

_{并且不知道何谓"必要经费"。}

or concerning the relative degree of its wealth and importance, compared with the other provinces; because those other provinces are not under the inspection and superintendency of the assembly of a particular province. What is necessary for the defence and support of the whole empire, and in what proportion each part ought to contribute, can be judged of only by that assembly which inspects and superintends the affairs of the whole empire.

<small>It has been proposed that parliament should tax the colonies by requisition,</small>　　It has been proposed, accordingly, that the colonies should be taxed by requisition, the parliament of Great Britain determining the sum which each colony ought to pay, and the provincial assembly assessing and levying it in the way that suited best the circumstances of the province. What concerned the whole empire would in this way be determined by the assembly which inspects and superintends the affairs of the whole empire; and the provincial affairs of each colony might still be regulated by its own assembly. Though the colonies should in this case have no representatives in the British parliament, yet, if we may judge by experience, there is no probability that the parliamentary requisition would be unreasonable. The parliament of England has not upon any occasion shown the smallest disposition to overburden those parts of the empire which are not represented in parliament. The islands of Guernsey and Jersey, without any means of resisting the authority of parliament, are more lightly taxed than any part of Great Britain. Parliament in attempting to exercise its supposed right, whether well or ill grounded, of taxing the colonies, has never hitherto demanded of them any thing which even approached to a just proportion to what was paid by their fellow-subjects at home. If the contribution of the colonies, besides, was to rise or fall in proportion to the rise or fall of the land tax, parliament could not tax them without taxing at the same time its own constituents, and the colonies might in this case be considered as virtually represented in parliament.

<small>as the King of France taxes some of his provinces,</small>　　Examples are not wanting of empires in which all the different provinces are not taxed, if I may be allowed the expression, in one mass; but in which the sovereign regulates the sum which each province ought to pay, and in some provinces assesses and levies it as he thinks proper; while in others, he leaves it to be assessed and levied as the respective states of each province shall determine. In some provinces of France, the king not only imposes what taxes he thinks proper, but assesses and levies them in the way he thinks proper. From others he demands a certain sum, but leaves it to the states of each province to assess and levy that sum as they think proper. According to the scheme of taxing by requisition, the parliament of Great Britain would stand nearly in the same situation towards the colony assemblies, as the king of France does towards the

本省对帝国所应承担的比例或者是与其他省份相比本省相对富裕程度和重要性；因为其他省份不受某个特定省议会的检查和监督。何谓保卫和支持整个帝国的必要经费以及各自要负担多少，只能由检查和监督整个帝国事务的议会评定。

相应的，有人建议，对于殖民地应该强令征税，英国国会决定每个殖民地应缴税的数量，各省议会以最适合本省的方式评估征收。这样与整个帝国有关的事情就可以有负责检查和监督帝国事务的议会决定；各殖民地议会也可以对关于本省的事务行使自主权。虽然在这种情况下，殖民地在大英帝国国会里不能拥有代表，但是根据经验判断，国会强制征税时绝非无理。英国国会从未在任何场合中表示要给在国会中没有代表的地区加压。根西岛和泽西岛对于国会权威束手无策，但是和英国其他地区相比，他们却税赋较轻。国会试图行使他们对殖民地应有的征税权利，不管这种权利本身是否有根据，但至今所征得的数额甚至低于他们在母国的殖民地所缴纳的合理比例。另外，如果殖民地的贡献要根据地税的涨跌而涨跌，国会就不能在不向自己的选民征税的情况下去向殖民地征税，这些殖民地在这种情况下就可能被认为在国会中有了代表。有人提议国会应对殖民地强行征税，

对帝国的不同地区分别征税（如果可以这样表达）是不乏实例可循；国王决定各省应缴纳的税额，在某些省份国王评估和征收自己认为合适的数额，其他省份他将决定权交给该省各自议会。在法国的某些省份，国王不但强征自己认为合理的税额，而且用自己认为合适的方式去评估和征收。对于其他省，他要求一个固定的数额，并将评估和征收的权利下放到各省议会，让他们决定合理的征收数量。按照这种强制征税的体制，英国国会与殖就像法国国王向某些省份征税一样，

国民财富的性质与原理

states of those provinces which still enjoy the privilege of having states of their own, the provinces of France which are supposed to be the best governed.

<small>but parliament has not sufficient authority,</small> But though, according to this scheme, the colonies could have no just reason to fear that their share of the public burdens should ever exceed the proper proportion to that of their fellow-citizens at home; Great Britain might have just reason to fear that it never would amount to that proper proportion. The parliament of Great Britain has not for some time past had the same established authority in the colonies, which the French king has in those provinces of France which still enjoy the privilege of having states of their own. The colony assemblies, if they were not very favourably disposed (and unless more skilfully managed than they ever have been hitherto, they are not very likely to be so), might still find many pretences for evading or rejecting the most reasonable requisitions of parliament. A French war breaks out, we shall suppose; ten millions must immediately be raised, in order to defend the seat of the empire. This sum must be borrowed upon the credit of some parliamentary fund mortgaged for paying the interest. Part of this fund parliament proposes to raise by a tax to be levied in Great Britain, and part of it by a requisition to all the different colony assemblies of America and the West Indies. Would people readily advance their money upon the credit of a fund, which partly depended upon the good humour of all those assemblies, far distant from the seat of the war, and sometimes, perhaps, thinking themselves not much concerned in the event of it? Upon such a fund no more money would probably be advanced than what the tax to be levied in Great Britain might be supposed to answer for. The whole burden of the debt contracted on account of the war would in this manner fall, as it always has done hitherto, upon Great Britain; upon a part of the empire, and not upon the whole empire. Great Britain is, perhaps, since the world began, the only state which, as it has extended its empire, has only increased its expence without once augmenting its resources. Other states have generally disburdened themselves upon their subject and subordinate provinces of the most considerable part of the expence of defending the empire. Great Britain has hitherto suffered her subject and subordinate provinces to disburden themselves upon her of almost this whole expence. In order to put Great Britain upon a footing of equality with her own colonies, which the law has hitherto supposed to be subject and subordinate, it seems necessary, upon the scheme of taxing them by parliamentary requisition, that parliament should have some means of rendering its requisitions immediately effectual, in case the colony assemblies should attempt to evade or reject them; and what those means are, it is not very easy to conceive, and it has not yet been explained.

民地如同法国国王与那些被认为治理的最好的仍享有殖民地特权的省份关系相同。

但是虽然这样,根据这种体制,殖民地不可能有任何合理的理由惧怕他们对公共负担的份额会超过他们母国的殖民地所负担的合理份额;英国就可能有适当的理由惧怕这个份额可能达不到合理的比例。英国国会过去并未在殖民地确立如法国国王那样在某些拥有特权的省份所有的相同权威。如果殖民地议会不赞同(除非不是用更艺术的方式管理,他们很可能不赞同),他们仍有可能找到很多理由逃避和拒绝国会最合理的强征。如果法国战争爆发,必须有1000万英镑用于保卫帝国领地。这些钱必须用公债筹措,以国会基金作为抵押支付利息。国会提议用在英国征税的方式筹集一部分资金,而另一部分则向美洲和东印度的各个殖民地议会强制征集。人们是否愿意在这种基金的担保下掏钱呢?毕竟这种基金部分依靠远离战争中心的殖民地议会的情绪,并且这些议会有时认为自己与战争无关。依靠这种基金筹措肯定比不上在英国征税的话所可能征收的数额。战争带来的负担就这样会像往常一样落在英国帝国的身上,即落在帝国一部分地区而不是所有地区身上。英国或许是自古以来拓展疆域时开支持续增长,资源不断消耗的国家。其他国家通常通过将保卫国家的可观费用分摊在从属省份的方式为自己减压。英国却将几乎将所有从属省份保卫帝国的费用揽在自己身上,为了使英国站在与他的殖民地平等的位置上,当然从法律上看殖民地从属于英国,看上去有必要通过国会强制征税,如果殖民地议会意图逃避或拒绝,国会应该有使强制命令立即生效的手段;不管这些手段是什么,都难以加以设想和说明。

但是国会没有足够的权威,

国民财富的性质与原理

and resistance breaks out.

Should the parliament of Great Britain, at the same time, be ever fully established in the right of taxing the colonies, even independent of the consent of their own assemblies, the importance of those assemblies would from that moment be at an end, and with it, that of all the leading men of British America. Men desire to have some share in the management of public affairs chiefly on account of the importance which it gives them. Upon the power which the greater part of the leading men, the natural aristocracy of every country, have of preserving or defending their respective importance, depends the stability and duration of every system of free government. In the attacks which those leading men are continually making upon the importance of one another, and in the defence of their own, consists the whole play of domestic faction and ambition. The leading men of America, like those of all other countries, desire to preserve their own importance. They feel, or imagine, that if their assemblies, which they are fond of calling parliaments, and of considering as equal in authority to the parliament of Great Britain, should be so far degraded as to become the humble ministers and executive officers of that parliament, the greater part of their own importance would be at an end. They have rejected, therefore, the proposal of being taxed by parliamentary requisition, and like other ambitious and high-spirited men, have rather chosen to draw the sword in defence of their own importance.

Representation in parliament in proportion to taxation should be offered. Otherwise it seems hopeless to expect submission,

Towards the declension of the Roman republic, the allies of Rome, who had borne the principal burden of defending the state and extending the empire, demanded to be admitted to all the privileges of Roman citizens. Upon being refused, the social war broke out. During the course of that war Rome granted those privileges to the greater part of them, one by one, and in proportion as they detached themselves from the general confederacy. The parliament of Great Britain insists upon taxing the colonies; and they refuse to be taxed by a parliament in which they are not represented. If to each colony, which should detach itself from the general confederacy, Great Britain should allow such a number of representatives as suited the proportion of what it contributed to the public revenue of the empire, in consequence of its being subjected to the same taxes, and in compensation admitted to the same freedom of trade with its fellow-subjects at home; the number of its representatives to be augmented as the proportion of its contribution might afterwards augment; a new method of acquiring importance, a new and more dazzling object of ambition would be presented to the leading men of each colony. Instead of piddling for the little prizes which are to be found in what may be called the paltry raffle of colony faction; they might then hope, from the presumption which men naturally have in their own ability and good fortune, to draw some of the great prizes which sometimes come from the wheel of the great state lottery of British politics.

如果英国国会在未征得各殖民地议会同意的情况下,同时完全确立对殖民地征税的权利,那么这些殖民地议会的权利就会终结,不列颠美洲领袖的权威也会烟消云散。人们渴望对公共事务有些管理权,主要因为这些权利会使他们变得重要。领袖和各国贵族拥有的维持和捍卫他们相对重要性的权利,决定了自由政府每个体系的稳定性和持久性。这些领袖不断对他人重要性发起的攻击,对自己重要性的捍卫,构成了国内派系和野心斗争。美洲的领袖,像其他国家一样,渴望保持他们的重要性。他们感觉或想象如果他们习惯称为国会的被认为是和英国国会拥有相同权威的本国议会降低为英国国会卑微的管家和执行官时,他们的重要性就消失了。所以,他们拒绝了由国会强制征税的提议,像其他充满野心勃勃和高傲的人一样他们宁愿选择拿起武器捍卫自己的重要性。

罗马盟国作为保卫国家和拓展疆域的过程中的主力军,在罗马共和国衰落时要求拥有罗马公民的所有特权。在这种要求被拒绝的时候,社会战争爆发了。在战争过程中,罗马按照他们独立于联盟的程度一个个的赋予了大部分人这些特权。英国国会坚持对殖民地征税;他们拒绝为一个没有自己代表的国会缴税。对于每一个想脱离一般联盟的殖民地,如果英国允许他们按照为帝国公共财政收入所做出的比例来拥有国会议席,和母国缴纳相同份额的赋税,享受补偿性的贸易自由,代表数量根据贡献比例有所增减,那么每个殖民地的领袖就会看到一种获得重要性新方法,发现一个新的激动人心的目标。他们再也不会为在殖民地派系斗争中获得蝇头小利而浪费时间,而期望凭借人们对于他们能力和幸运的期望,在英国政治斗争的国家大奖中中头彩。除非有

国民财富的性质与原理

Unless this or some other method is fallen upon, and there seems to be none more obvious than this, of preserving the importance and of gratifying the ambition of the leading men of America, it is not very probable that they will ever voluntarily submit to us; and we ought to consider that the blood which must be shed in forcing them to do so, is, every drop of it, the blood either of those who are, or of those whom we wish to have for our fellow-citizens. They are very weak who flatter themselves that, in the state to which things have come, our colonies will be easily conquered by force alone. The persons who now govern the resolutions of what they call their continental congress, feel in themselves at this moment a degree of importance which, perhaps, the greatest subjects in Europe scarce feel. From shopkeepers, tradesmen, and attornies, they are become statesmen and legislators, and are employed in contriving a new form of government for an extensive empire, which, they flatter themselves, will become, and which, indeed, seems very likely to become, one of the greatest and most formidable that ever was in the world. Five hundred different people, perhaps, who in different ways act immediately under the continental congress; and five hundred thousand, perhaps, who act under those five hundred, all feel in the same manner a proportionable rise in their own importance. Almost every individual of the governing party in America, fills, at present in his own fancy, a station superior, not only to what he had ever filled before, but to what he had ever expected to fill; and unless some new object of ambition is presented either to him or to his leaders, if he has the ordinary spirit of a man, he will die in defence of that station.

and resistance will be as obstinate as that of Paris.

It is a remark of the president Henaut, that we now read with pleasure the account of many little transactions of the Ligue, which when they happened were not perhaps considered as very important pieces of news. But every man then, says he, fancied himself of some importance; and the innumerable memoirs which have come down to us from those times were, the greater part of them, written by people who took pleasure in recording and magnifying events in which, they flattered themselves, they had been considerable actors. How ob stinately the city of Paris upon that occasion defended itself, what a dreadful famine it supported rather than submit to the best and afterwards the most beloved of all the French kings, is well known. The greater part of the citizens, or those who governed the greater part of them, fought in defence of their own importance, which they foresaw was to be at an end whenever the ancient government should be re-established. Our colonies, unless they can be induced to consent to a

其他方法（似乎没有比这种方法更明显的方法）来维护重要性和满足美洲领袖的野心，他们应该不会屈从于我们；我们应该意识到为了迫使他们屈从于我们而付出的每一滴血都来自于我们国民的，或者是我们的准国民。那些持有能在状况发生时单凭武力征服殖民地的想法的人是愚蠢的。那些现在对于他们所谓的大陆会议有决定权的人们在此刻感到他们的重要性，而这种重要性也许欧洲的伟人都未曾体会过。他们从店主、商人和律师变成政治家和立法者，并且被委以为正在扩张的帝国设计新政府形式的重任，而这个帝国将成为他们认为的或许说是确实很有可能成为世界最强大和最令人敬畏的大国之一。500个不同的人可能用不同方式在大陆会议下工作，或许还有在他们之下工作的另外50万人，但这些人都可能以同样的方式感觉到他们日益增强的重要性。几乎每一个美洲统治集团都以一种优越感满足他们的想象的地位，这种优越感不但强于他曾经得到过的地位，更强于他期望得到的地位。除非有一种新的目标出现在他或者他的领袖面前，否则每一个普通人都会为捍卫这种地位而拼命。

亨诺主席曾说我们现在喜欢读关于同盟间小事的描述，这些事情发生时也许被认为是不值得一提。但是，每个人都想象他们的有一定重要性，从那些时候开始的无数回忆大部分都是由那些钟情于记录和放大事件本身的人撰写的，而这些人通常夸耀自己在实践中扮演了重要角色。对于巴黎在那次事件中所表现的坚定，在噩梦般的饥荒面前不向最好和后来最受人爱戴的法国国王低头的历史，人们了然于胸。大部分民众，或者说大部分民众的管理者，都为维护旧政府重新建立时而消亡的重要性而战。我们的殖民地，除非在诱导下与我们结盟，否则他们就会为保卫自己

抵抗将会像巴黎一样坚决。

> union, are very likely to defend themselves against the best of all mother countries, as obstinately as the city of Paris did against one of the best of kings.

The discovery of representation makes the case different from that of Rome and Italy.

> The idea of representation was unknown in ancient times. When the people of one state were admitted to the right of citizenship in another, they had no other means of exercising that right but by coming in a body to vote and deliberate with the people of that other state. The admission of the greater part of the inhabitants of Italy to the privileges of Roman citizens, completely ruined the Roman republic. It was no longer possible to distinguish between who was and who was not a Roman citizen. No tribe could know its own members. A rabble of any kind could be introduced into the assemblies of the people, could drive out the real citizens, and decide upon the affairs of the republic as if they themselves had been such. But though America were to send fifty or sixty new representatives to parliament, the door-keeper of the house of commons could not find any great difficulty in distinguishing between who was and who was not a member. Though the Roman constitution, therefore, was necessarily ruined by the union of Rome with the allied states of Italy, there is not the least probability that the British constitution would be hurt by the union of Great Britain with her colonies. That constitution, on the contrary, would be completed by it, and seems to be imperfect without it. The assembly which deliberates and decides concerning the affairs of every part of the empire, in order to be properly informed, ought certainly to have representatives from every part of it. That this union, however, could be easily effectuated, or that difficulties and great difficulties might not occur in the execution, I do not pretend. I have yet heard of none, however, which appear insurmountable. The principal perhaps arise, not from the nature of things, but from the prejudices and opinions of the people both on this and on the other side of the Atlantic.

The American representatives could be managed.

> We, on this side the water, are afraid lest the multitude of American representatives should overturn the balance of the constitution, and increase too much either the influence of the crown on the one hand, or the force of the democracy on the other. But if the number of American representatives were to be in proportion to the produce of American taxation, the number of people to be managed would increase exactly in proportion to the means of managing them; and the means of managing, to the number of people to be managed. The monarchical and democratical parts of the constitution would, after the union, stand exactly in the same degree of relative force with regard to one another as they had done before.

> The people on the other side of the water are afraid lest their distance from the seat of government might expose them to many oppressions. But their representatives in parliament, of which the number ought from the first to be considerable, would easily be able to protect

第四篇　第七章

与最好的母国开战,就像巴黎在与最好的国王的斗争中所表现得一样坚决。

在古代是没有代表制的。当一国的人被允许加入别国国籍时,他们只能在与别国公民投票和讨论国事时行使这种权利。赋予意大利大部分居民罗马公民的特权,彻底毁了罗马共和国。想要分清楚谁是谁不是罗马公民已经不太可能了。部落再也认不清自己的成员,任何一个暴民都可能加入人民议会,驱逐真正的公民,就像自己是公民一样决定共和国事务。但是即使美洲人将50个或60个代表选入国会,众议员掌门也会轻而易举的区分成员与非成员。因此,虽然罗马宪法被罗马和意大利联盟破坏,但是英国宪法绝不会被英国和其殖民地联盟破坏。恰恰相反,该宪法会因联盟而更完全,会因为没有联盟而变得不完整。地区国会负责讨论和决定帝国地区事务,为了使他们得到信息的渠道更顺畅,国会中应该有地区代表。我不敢自称这个联盟将会轻易生效,顺利实现。我从来都没听说过有不可克服的困难。最主要的困难可能不是来自于事情本身,而是来自于大西洋两岸的人们的偏见和态度。

代表制的发现使得这件事情不同于意大利和罗马。

在大西洋这边的我们大量的美洲代表涌入会推翻宪法的平衡,使得统治者或者是民主的力量膨胀。但是,如果美洲代表的和美洲赋税数量成比例,那么需要管理的人数就会相应增长到和管理他们的手段成比例;管理他们的手段也会相应的和需要管理的人数成正比。宪法中的君主部分和民主部分在联盟结成后彼此的力量强弱和以前并无不同。

美洲代表可以被管理。

在大西洋彼岸的人们担心过度远离政府席位会让他们面临挑战。但是他们在国会的代表(从一开始数量就是可观的),很容

them from all oppression. The distance could not much weaken the dependency of the representative upon the constituent, and the former would still feel that he owed his seat in parliament, and all the consequence which he derived from it, to the good-will of the latter. It would be the interest of the former, therefore, to cultivate that good-will by complaining, with all the authority of a member of the legislature, of every outrage which any civil or military officer might be guilty of in those remote parts of the empire. The distance of America from the seat of government, besides, the natives of that country might flatter themselves, with some appearance of reason too, would not be of very long continuance. Such has hitherto been the rapid progress of that country in wealth, population and improvement, that in the course of little more than a century, perhaps, the produce of American might exceed that of British taxation. The seat of the empire would then naturally remove itself to that part of the empire which contributed most to the general defence and support of the whole.

The discovery of America, and that of a passage to the East Indies by the Cape of Good Hope, are the two greatest and most important events recorded in the history of mankind. Their consequences have already been very great: but, in the short period of between two and three centuries which has elapsed since these discoveries were made, it is impossible that the whole extent of their consequences can have been seen. What benefits, or what misfortunes to mankind may hereafter result from those great events, no human wisdom can foresee. By uniting, in some measure, the most distant parts of the world, by enabling them to relieve one another's wants, to increase one another's enjoyments, and to encourage one another's industry, their general tendency would seem to be beneficial. To the natives, however, both of the East and West Indies, all the commercial benefits which can have resulted from those events have been sunk and lost in the dreadful misfortunes which they have occasioned. These misfortunes, however, seem to have arisen rather from accident than from any thing in the nature of those events themselves. At the particular time when these discoveries were made, the superiority of force happened to be so great on the side of the Europeans, that they were enabled to commit with impunity every sort of injustice in those remote countries. Hereafter, perhaps, the natives of those countries may grow stronger, or those of Europe may grow weaker, and the inhabitants of all the different quarters of the world may arrive at that equality of courage and force which, by inspiring mutual fear, can alone overawe the injustice of independent nations into some sort of respect for the rights of one another. But nothing seems more likely to establish this equality of force than that mutual communication of knowledge and of all sorts of improvements which an extensive commerce from all countries to all countries naturally, or rather necessarily, carries along with it.

易保护他们远离压迫。距离不会削弱代表对选民的依赖性,而且代表们仍然会感觉到他们在国会中始终占有一席之地,选民的认同仍然是他们的力量和利益所在。所以,代表通过利用立法成员的权威,通过控诉文武官员在遥远的地区可能犯下的罪行去培养选民对他们的认同感。另外,美洲本土居民有理由乐观认为美洲和政府中心的距离不可能永远这样遥远。美洲一向在诸如财富,人口和进步方面进展迅猛,或许在一个世纪之内,美洲的纳税额就会超过英国。帝国的中心位置也就会自然而然的随之移动在帝国防卫和支持中贡献最大的地区。

美洲大陆和由好望角通往东印度通路的发现是人类有史以来两个最伟大最重要的事件。他们的影响已经非常明显了,但是这些发现之后两三个世纪内还是不可能发现他们的全部影响的。没人可以预见这些伟大发现给人类带来的利益和灾难。通过某种方式联结世界上最远的地区,使他们满足彼此的需要,增加彼此的乐趣,激励彼此的工业,整体趋势应该是有利于这些地区的。对于东印度和西印度本土居民来说,这些事件所造成的灾难已经完全抹杀了他们所带来的商业利益。但是这些事件看上去似乎不是这些事件本身造成的,而是偶然。这些发现出现时正是欧洲力量占优势的时期,所以他们在这些偏远国家犯下的恶行有了堂而皇之的借口。从此以后,这些国家的本土居民可能会变得强大,或者这些欧洲人会变得弱小,世界上所有不同地区的居民会变得拥有平等的力量和勇气,这样就会产生相互畏惧,这种畏惧足可以震慑一个国家去尊重另一个国家的权利。但是没有什么事情能像这种互相间的交流一样建立这种平等,而且这种交流的效果自然而然体现在各国间商业的繁荣上。

| 国民财富的性质与原理

<small>Meantime the discovery has exalted the mercantile system.</small>   In the mean time one of the principal effects of those discoveries has been to raise the mercantile system to a degree of splendour and glory which it could never otherwise have attained to. It is the object of that system to enrich a great nation rather by trade and manufactures than by the improvement and cultivation of land, rather by the industry of the towns than by that of the country. But, in consequence of those discoveries, the commercial towns of Europe, instead of being the manufacturers and carriers for but a very small part of the world (that part of Europe which is washed by the Atlantic ocean, and the countries which lie round the Baltic and Mediterranean seas), have now become the manufacturers for the numerous and thriving cultivators of America, and the carriers, and in some respects the manufacturers too, for almost all the different nations of Asia, Africa, and America. Two new worlds have been opened to their industry, each of them much greater and more extensive than the old one, and the market of one of them growing still greater and greater every day.

<small>The countries which possess America and trade to the East Indies appear to get all the advantage, but this is not the case.</small>   The countries which possess the colonies of America, and which trade directly to the East Indies, enjoy, indeed, the whole shew and splendour of this great commerce. Other countries, however, notwithstanding all the invidious restraints by which it is meant to exclude them, frequently enjoy a greater share of the real benefit of it. The colonies of Spain and Portugal, for example, give more real encouragement to the industry of other countries than to that of Spain and Portugal. In the single article of linen alone the consumption of those colonies amounts, it is said, but I do not pretend to warrant the quantity, to more than three millions sterling a year. But this great consumption is almost entirely supplied by France, Flanders, Holland, and Germany. Spain and Portugal furnish but a small part of it. The capital which supplies the colonies with this great quantity of linen is annually distributed among, and furnishes a revenue to the inhabitants of those other countries. The profits of it only are spent in Spain and Portugal, where they help to support the sumptuous profusion of the merchants of Cadiz and Lisbon.

<small>The monopoly regulations sometimes harm the country which establishes them more than others.</small>   Even the regulations by which each nation endeavours to secure to itself the exclusive trade of its own colonies, are frequently more hurtful to the countries in favour of which they are established than to those against which they are established. The unjust oppression of the industry of other countries falls back, if I may say so, upon the heads of the oppressors, and crushes their industry more than it does that of those other countries. By those regulations, for example, the merchant of Hamburgh must send the linen which he destines for the American market to London, and he must bring back from thence the tobacco which he destines for the German market; because he can neither send the one directly to America, nor bring back the other directly from thence. By this restraint he is probably obliged to sell the

第四篇 第七章

　　同时,这些发现的最大影响是将重商主义提升到一个在其他情况下不可能达到的显著地位。这个体系旨在通过发展贸易和制造业而非农耕,城市而非农村来繁荣国家。但是,这些发现使得欧洲商业城市不再是世界范围内的制造和供应商(大西洋沿岸的欧洲地区,波罗的海和地中海周边国家),而成为了美洲无数农耕者的制造商,亚洲、非洲、美洲几乎所有国家的经营商和一定意义上的制造商。这样,两个更大更广阔的新世界就向欧洲商业城市敞开了大门,其中一个市场正日益茁壮成长着。

同时,这些发现激励了重商主义。

　　那些拥有美洲殖民地并直接与东印度进行贸易的国家确实享受着这个伟大的商业带来的所有假象和光荣。但是其他国家虽然想排除所有的不公平限制,但是还是享受了一大部分真正的利益。举例来说,西班牙和葡萄牙的殖民地,给其他国家产业比本国产业更大的鼓励。据说这些殖民地仅亚麻布一项的消费就高达300多万英镑,当然我不确定这个数字正确与否。但是这种大量的消费几乎全部由法国、佛兰德、荷兰和德意志提供,西班牙和葡萄牙只提供一小部分。负责殖民地数量巨大的亚麻布的资金每年都在居民中分配并为他们创收。资本利益仅在西班牙和葡萄牙消费,大部分用来支持加的斯和里斯本商人的无度挥霍。

拥有美洲与东印度进行贸易的国家看上去得到了所有利益,但事实并非如此。

　　即使是每个国家竭力保护自己殖民地专有贸易的规章,比起所要损害的国家,通常会更大的损害所要保护的国家。对其他国家产业不公平的压制,如果我可以这样说的话,会反作用于压迫者,更大的破坏其自身产业。举例说明,这些规章规定汉堡商人必须将欲送往美洲的亚麻送到伦敦,从伦敦带回提供给德意志的烟草;因为他既不能将亚麻直接送往美洲,也不能从那里将烟草运回。由于这种限制,他可能会相对廉价销售亚麻,并且会用别

垄断章家受害最深,订立规章时其有国。

— 1327 —

one somewhat cheaper, and to buy the other somewhat dearer than he otherwise might have done; and his profits are probably somewhat abridged by means of it. In this trade, however, between Hamburgh and London, he certainly receives the returns of his capital much more quickly than he could possibly have done in the direct trade to America, even though we should suppose, what is by no means the case, that the payments of America were as punctual as those of London. In the trade, therefore, to which those regulations confine the merchant of Hamburgh, his capital can keep in constant employment a much greater quantity of German industry than it possibly could have done in the trade from which he is excluded. Though the one employment, therefore, may to him perhaps be less profitable than the other, it cannot be less advantageous to his country. It is quite otherwise with the employment into which the monopoly naturally attracts, if I may say so, the capital of the London merchant. That employment may, perhaps, be more profitable to him than the greater part of other employments, but, on account of the slowness of the returns, it cannot be more advantageous to his country.

The mother countries have engrossed only the expence and inconveniences of possessing colonies.

After all the unjust attempts, therefore, of every country in Europe to engross to itself the whole advantage of the trade of its own colonies, no country has yet been able to engross to itself any thing but the expence of supporting in time of peace and of defending in time of war the oppressive authority which it assumes over them. The inconveniencies resulting from the possession of its colonies, every country has engrossed to itself completely. The advantages resulting from their trade it has been obliged to share with many other countries.

The monopoly of American trade is a dazzling object.

At first sight, no doubt, the monopoly of the great commerce of America, naturally seems to be an acquisition of the highest value. To the undiscerning eye of giddy ambition, it naturally presents itself amidst the confused scramble of politics and war, as a very dazzling object to fight for. The dazzling splendour of the object, however, the immense greatness of the commerce, is the very quality which renders the monopoly of it hurtful, or which makes one employment, in its own nature necessarily less advantageous to the country than the greater part of other employments, absorb a much greater proportion of the capital of the country than what would otherwise have gone to it.

The mercantile stock of every country, it has been shewn in the second book, naturally seeks, if one may say so, the employment most advantageous to that country. If it is employed in the carrying trade, the country to which it belongs becomes the emporium of the goods of all the countries whose trade that stock carries on. But the owner of that stock necessarily wishes to dispose of as great a part of those goods as he can at home. He thereby saves himself the trouble,

的时候不会出的高格收购烟草;他的利润可能会相对变小。在汉堡与伦敦的贸易中,他当然会比与美洲直接通商更快的收回资金,虽然我们可能假设美洲的付款与伦敦一样准时,但这种假设绝不会成立。所以在这些受规章所限的汉堡商人的贸易中,比起他被排斥在外的贸易,他的资金能保证长期雇用更大数量的德国劳动力。所以一种贸易看上去利润小于另一种贸易,但是这对他的国家来说两者相同。请允许我这样说,对于垄断自然吸引的伦敦商人的资本进入,则是完全另一种情况。那种雇佣对他来说可能会比其他雇佣更有利,但是,由于回报的缓慢,对于他的国家则是不利的。

所以,经过欧洲各国将本国殖民地的全部贸易利润归己有的这些不公尝试后,没有一个国家能得到他们想要的东西,除了在和平时期支持以及战乱时期保卫对于殖民地的压迫。相反的,他们却完全得到了拥有殖民地带来的不便。他有义务与其他国家分享殖民贸易的成果。

> 只有地销不到拥民的开母国得了殖民的和便。

毫无疑问,对于美洲巨大商业的垄断第一眼看上去自然有着最高价值所得。在目光短浅的野心家看来,这种垄断在纷乱的政治斗争中必然会以一种让人为之奋斗的炫目的争抢目标形式出现。但是这种炫目的目标和无比巨大的商业,恰恰赋予了垄断有害的性质,也就是说,垄断使一种产业给国家带来少于其他产业的利益,却吸引了比原来更多的国家资本。

> 对美洲贸易垄断是炫目的一种目标。

在第二篇中我提到过,各国商业资本自然会寻求(请允许我这样说)对最本国最有利的投资。如果用于货运贸易,所属国就会变成以此投资所经营的各国货物中心市场。但是资本所有者当然会希望能像在本国抛售最多的货物。这样做他就会省掉出

国民财富的性质与原理

The stock of a country naturally seeks the employment most advantageous to the country, preferring the near to the more distant employments,

risk, and expence, of exportation, and he will upon that account be glad to sell them at home, not only for a much smaller price, but with somewhat a smaller profit than he might expect to make by sending them abroad. He naturally, therefore, endeavours as much as he can to turn his carrying trade into a foreign trade of consumption. If his stock again is employed in a foreign trade of consumption, he will, for the same reason, be glad to dispose of at home as great a part as he can of the home goods, which he collects in order to export to some foreign market, and he will thus endeavour, as much as he can, to turn his foreign trade of consumption into a home trade. The mercantile stock of every country naturally courts in this manner the near, and shuns the distant employment; naturally courts the employment in which the returns are frequent, and shuns that in which they are distant and slow; naturally courts the employment in which it can maintain the greatest quantity of productive labour in the country to which it belongs, or in which its owner resides, and shuns that in which it can maintain there the smallest quantity. It naturally courts the employment which in ordinary cases is most advantageous, and shuns that which in ordinary cases is least advantageous to that country.

unless profits are higher in the more distant, which indicates that the more distant employment is necessary.

But if in any of those distant employments, which in ordinary cases are less advantageous to the country, the profit should happen to rise somewhat higher than what is sufficient to balance the natural preference which is given to nearer employments, this superiority of profit will draw stock from those nearer employments, till the profits of all return to their proper level. This superiority of profit, however, is a proof that, in the actual circumstances of the society, those distant employments are somewhat under-stocked in proportion to other employments, and that the stock of the society is not distributed in the properest manner among all the different employments carried on in it. It is a proof that something is either bought cheaper or sold dearer than it ought to be, and that some particular class of citizens is more or less oppressed either by paying more or by getting less than what is suitable to that equality, which ought to take place, and which naturally does take place among all the different classes of them. Though the same capital never will maintain the same quantity of productive labour in a distant as in a near employment, yet a distant employment may be as necessary for the welfare of the society as a near one; the goods which the distant employment deals in being necessary, perhaps, for carrying on many of the nearer employments. But if the profits of those who deal in such goods are above their proper level, those goods will be sold dearer than they ought to be, or somewhat above their natural price, and all those engaged in the nearer employments will be more or less oppressed by this high price. Their interest, therefore, in this case requires that some stock should be withdrawn from

第四篇　第七章

口的麻烦、风险和花费，所以尽管在国内售价较低，他也愿意在国内小利润销售，而不是出口国外。所以他自然会竭尽所能将这种货运贸易变成国外消费贸易。如果他再一次将资本投资在对外消费贸易上，他会出于同样的理由竭尽所能的在国内销售准备销往国外市场上的大部分货物，他也会相应的竭尽所能将对外消费贸易转变成为国内贸易。各国商业资本都会找寻近的市场而避开远的用途；找寻回报快而避开回报漫长的方式；找寻能维持所属国最人劳动力市场的方式而避开仅能维持最小劳动力的投资领域。他会自然而然的找寻通常情况下对国家最有利的方式而避开最不利的。

资本当然寻求有利可图的投资，更接近不远的用途，国家会寻有本国的资喜欢而不是远的用途。

一般情况下，远距离的贸易对一个国家不是那么有利，但是如果某种贸易的利润大于近距离贸易的收益，则这种高收益就会将资本从近距离贸易中吸引过来，直至所有利润水平都恢复正常。但是这种高利润证明了在真实社会状况下，这些远距离的贸易资本比起其他业务略有欠缺，社会资本在各种用途中并未按最合理的方式分配。这证明有些东西与实际相比收购价较高而售价较低，某些特殊阶层的公民或多或少的都被压迫了，有的表现为花更多的钱，有的表现为获得比公平情况下更少的东西；这些阶层应该得到平等，而且这种平等是理所当然的。虽然相同的资本在远距离贸易中维持的劳动量不如近距离贸易维持的劳动量，但它们对于社会公益福利来说都是必要的。远距离贸易的货物可能是近距离贸易所需的。但是如果经营者的利润高于正常水平，这些货物就会以比平常或者说比他们自然价格更高的价格出售，所有参与近距离贸易的人都会或多或少的受这种高价的压迫。所以在这种情况下，他们的利益要求将一些资本从近距离贸

在离中也远贸易更重要，非远距离贸易高，说明距离贸易的重要性。

those nearer employments, and turned towards that distant one, in order to reduce its profits to their proper level, and the price of the goods which it deals in to their natural price. In this extraordinary case, the public interest requires that some stock should be withdrawn from those employments which in ordinary cases are more advantageous, and turned towards one which in ordinary cases is less advantageous to the public; and in this extraordinary case, the natural interests and inclinations of men coincide as exactly with the public interest as in all other ordinary cases, and lead them to withdraw stock from the near, and to turn it towards the distant employment.

If too much goes to any employment, profit falls in the employment and the proper distribution is so restored.

It is thus that the private interests and passions of individuals naturally dispose them to turn their stock towards the employments which in ordinary cases are most advantageous to the society. But if from this natural preference they should turn too much of it towards those employments, the fall of profit in them and the rise of it in all others immediately dispose them to alter this faulty distribution. Without any intervention of law, therefore, the private interests and passions of men naturally lead them to divide and distribute the stock of every society, among all the different employments carried on in it, as nearly as possible in the proportion which is most agreeable to the interest of the whole society.

The mercantile system disturbs this distribution, especially in regard to American and Indian trade.

All the different regulations of the mercantile system, necessarily derange more or less this natural and most advantageous distribution of stock. But those which concern the trade to America and the East Indies derange it perhaps more than any other; because the trade to those two great continents absorbs a greater quantity of stock than any two other branches of trade. The regulations, however, by which this derangement is effected in those two different branches of trade are not altogether the same. Monopoly is the great engine of both; but it is a different sort of monopoly. Monopoly of one kind or another, indeed, seems to be the sole engine of the mercantile system.

The Portuguese attempted at first to exclude all other nations from trading in the Indian Seas, and the Dutch still exclude all other nations from trade with the Spice Islands.

In the trade to America every nation endeavours to engross as much as possible the whole market of its own colonies, by fairly excluding all other nations from any direct trade to them. During the greater part of the sixteenth century, the Portugueze endeavoured to manage the trade to the East Indies in the same manner, by claiming the sole right of sailing in the Indian seas, on account of the merit of having first found out the road to them. The Dutch still continue to

易中吸引出来,转向远距离贸易,这样才能将他们的利益减至正常水平,货物的价格减至自然水平。在这个特殊的例子里,公共利益要求一些资本从在一般情况下对公众更有利的贸易中吸引出来,转向一般情况下对公众不太有利的贸易中。在这些特殊的例子里,人们的自然利益和倾向于其他时候的公共利益恰巧一致,并引导他们将资本从短距离贸易中吸引出来转向远距离贸易。

所以个人私利和激情自然而然地使他们将资本转向一般情况下对社会最有利的贸易中去。但是如果因为这种自然的喜好而将过量的资本转入这种贸易,利润下降和其他贸易中利润的提升会立刻转变这种错误的分配。所以,人们的私利和激情在毫无法律干涉的情况下自然的引导他们按照最有利于社会整体利益的方式将在所有贸易中分割和分配社会资本。

> 过量的资本转向一种贸易,利润的下降和其他贸易中利润的提升会在短时间内重建合理的分配方式。

重商主义体系所有的规章,必然或者说多少打乱了这种自然的和最有利的资本分配。但是和对美洲和东印度贸易有关的规章中,这种分配的影响最大;因为与这两个大洲的贸易吸引了比其他两个贸易分支更大量的资本。但是造成两个贸易分支混乱的规章并不完全相同。垄断是两者的"发动机";但这是一种不同的垄断。确实,这样的或者是那样的垄断,看上去是这种重商主义体系的唯一"发动机"。

> 重商主义体系扰乱分配,特别是对美洲和东印度贸易。

在对美洲的贸易中,每一个国家都尽最大努力垄断本国殖民地贸易,彻底将其他国家与殖民地间的直接贸易排除在外。在16世纪的大部分时间内,葡萄牙人按相同的方法管理对东印度的贸易,声称由于它们最早找到了通向印度海岸的道路,所以对这些海岸享有独占权。荷兰人仍旧将所有欧洲国家排除在与香料岛

> 葡萄牙人起初试图将所有国际贸易交易所有排除在海岸外,荷兰人仍将所有国家排除在香料岛贸易之外。

| 国民财富的性质与原理

exclude all other European nations from any direct trade to their spice islands. Monopolies of this kind are evidently established against all other European nations, who are thereby not only excluded from a trade to which it might be convenient for them to turn some part of their stock, but are obliged to buy the goods which that trade deals in somewhat dearer, than if they could import them themselves directly from the countries which produce them.

<small>Now the principal ports are open, but each country has established an exclusive company.</small>

But since the fall of the power of Portugal, no European nation has claimed the exclusive right of sailing in the Indian seas, of which the principal ports are now open to the ships of all European nations. Except in Portugal, however, and within these few years in France, ① the trade to the East Indies has in every European country been subjected to an exclusive company. Monopolies of this kind are properly established against the very nation which erects them. The greater part of that nation are thereby not only excluded from a trade to which it might be convenient for them to turn some part of their stock, but are obliged to buy the goods which that trade deals in, somewhat dearer than if it was open and free to all their countrymen. Since the establishment of the English East India company, for example, the other inhabitants of England, over and above being excluded from the trade, must have paid in the price of the East India goods which they have consumed, not only for all the extraordinary profits which the company may have made upon those goods in consequence of their monopoly, but for all the extraordinary waste which the fraud and abuse, inseparable from the management of the affairs of so great a company, must necessarily have occasioned. The absurdity of this second kind of monopoly, therefore, is much more manifest than that of the first.

<small>Monopolies of the American kind always attract, but monopolies of exclusive companies sometimes attract, sometimes repel stock.</small>

Both these kinds of monopolies derange more or less the natural distribution of the stock of the society: but they do not always derange it in the same way.

Monopolies of the first kind always attract to the particular trade in which they are established, a greater proportion of the stock of the society than what would go to that trade of its own accord.

Monopolies of the second kind may sometimes attract stock towards the particular trade in which they are established, and sometimes repel it from that trade according to different circumstances. In poor countries they naturally attract towards that trade more stock than would otherwise go to it. In rich countries they naturally repel from it a good deal of stock which would otherwise go to it.

---

① [The monopoly of the French East India Company was abolished in 1769. See the Continuation of Anderson's *Commerce*, 1801, vol. iv., p. 128.]

进行直接贸易之外。这种垄断的建立明显的有损于其他欧洲国家的利益,是他们必须以比直接从产地购入时更高的价格购买这些货物。

但是自从葡萄牙衰败之后,再没有欧洲国家声称对印度海岸的独占权,这些海岸的主要港口现在已经对所有的欧洲国家船只开放。但是除了葡萄牙以及这些年在法国①之外,所有欧洲国家对东印度的贸易已经由一家专营公司开展。这种垄断直接违反了设置垄断的国家的利益。该国的人部分国民不但被排除在一种有利可图的贸易之外,而且必须以更比对所有国民开放时更高的价格去购买垄断贸易经营的货物。自从英国东印度公司建立以来,举例来说,英国其他的居民不但无法从事这种贸易,而且须以更好的价格购买消费掉的东印度货物。这种垄断使得该公司取得高额利润,而且本国消费者除这种高额利润外还必须承担起公司经营过程中无法避免的浪费和造假的代价。这第二种垄断比起第一种来更加无理。

这几种形式的垄断都多少打乱了社会资本的自然分配,但是这种打乱通常不是以同样的方式进行的。

第一种形式的垄断通常不按常理出牌,而把大量的社会资本吸引到享有特殊垄断权的贸易中。

第二种形式的垄断在不同情况下可能有时会把大量的社会资本吸引到享有特殊垄断权的贸易中,有时可能会排斥这种资本。在贫穷的国家,垄断自然会将比本来更多的资本吸引到贸易

旁注:现在重要港口都开放了,但是各国立营专司。所要都但国家建了公司。

旁注:美洲的垄断总是吸引资本,但专营公司有时吸引资本,有时排斥资本。

---

① 法国东印度公司垄断于1769年被取消。参见安德森《商业》续编,1801年,第4卷,第128页。

国民财富的性质与原理

In poor countries they attract.

Such poor countries as Sweden and Denmark, for example, would probably have never sent a single ship to the East Indies, had not the trade been subjected to an exclusive company. The establishment of such a company necessarily encourages adventurers. Their monopoly secures them against all competitors in the home market, and they have the same chance for foreign markets with the traders of other nations. Their monopoly shows them the certainty of a great profit upon a considerable quantity of goods, and the chance of a considerable profit upon a great quantity. Without such extraordinary encouragement, the poor traders of such poor countries would probably never have thought of hazarding their small capitals in so very distant and uncertain an adventure as the trade to the East Indies must naturally have appeared to them.

in rich they repel.

Such a rich country as Holland, on the contrary, would probably, in the case of a free trade, send many more ships to the East Indies than it actually does. The limited stock of the Dutch East India company ① probably repels from that trade many great mercantile capitals which would otherwise go to it. The mercantile capital of Holland is so great that it is, as it were, continually overflowing, sometimes into the public funds of foreign countries, sometimes into loans to private traders and adventurers of foreign countries, sometimes into the most round-about foreign trades of consumption, and sometimes into the carrying trade. All near employments being completely filled up, all the capital which can be placed in them with any tolerable profit being already placed in them, the capital of Holland necessarily flows towards the most distant employments. The trade to the East Indies, if it were altogether free, would probably absorb the greater part of this redundant capital. The East Indies offer a market both for the manufactures of Europe and for the gold and silver as well as for several other productions of America, greater and more extensive than both Europe and America put together.

Both effects are hurtful.

Every derangement of the natural distribution of stock is necessarily hurtful to the society in which it takes place; whether it be by repelling from a particular trade the stock which would otherwise go to it, or by attracting towards a particular trade that which would not

---

① [Raynal, *Histoire philosophique*, ed. Amsterdam, 1773, tom. i. , p. 203, gives the original capital as 6,459,840 florins.]

中。在富国,垄断将本来会进入的大量资本排除在贸易之外。

举例来说,像瑞典和丹麦这样贫穷的国家,如果不将贸易交由专营公司来作,可能从未向东印度派过一艘船。这样一个公司的建立鼓励了冒险者。他们的垄断权保护他们在本国市场的竞争中立于不败之地,在外贸中与其他国家的交易者拥有同样的机会。他们的垄断权显示了他们在相当大数量的货物上享有巨额利润的确定性和能在大量货物上获取利润的机会。如果没有这样的特别的激励,穷国的贫穷交易者可能永远不会用他们少量的资金去像东印度那样遥远的不确定的地方进行冒险。

<small>穷国,垄断吸引资本。</small>

相反的,荷兰那样的富国在自由贸易中可能会派比实际情况下更多的船只去东印度。荷兰东印度公司①的有限的资本可能将许多可能会进入这种大商业的资本排斥在外。荷兰的商业资本,如果可以这么说的话,经常满溢,又是流入外国公共基金,有时流入私人交易者和国外冒险家的贷款,又是流入最间接的消费品对外贸易,有时流入货运贸易。他们的资本占据了所有近距离贸易,只要是有利可图的贸易都有这种资本,所以荷兰的资本必然会转向距离最远的贸易。与东印度的贸易如果完全自由,可能会吸收绝大部分这种过剩资本。东印度为欧洲制造业,美洲的黄金白银以及许多其他产品提供比欧美加起来更广阔的市场。

<small>在富国,垄断排斥资本。</small>

对这种资本分配的打乱必然会伤害产生这种混乱的社会;不管是将本来会流入的资本排除在某种贸易之外还是将本不会流入的资本吸引到某种贸易中去。如果没有专营公司,荷兰对东印

<small>这两种效果都是有害的。</small>

---

① 雷纳尔:《哲学史》,阿姆斯特丹版,1773年,第1卷,第203页所载原始资本为6459840弗洛林。

otherwise come to it. If, without any exclusive company, the trade of Holland to the East Indies would be greater than it actually is, that country must suffer a considerable loss by part of its capital being excluded from the employment most convenient for that part. And in the same manner, if, without an exclusive company, the trade of Sweden and Denmark to the East Indies would be less than it actually is, or, what perhaps is more probable, would not exist at all, those two countries must likewise suffer a considerable loss by part of their capital being drawn into an employment which must be more or less unsuitable to their present circumstances. Better for them, perhaps, in their present circumstances, to buy East India goods of other nations, even though they should pay somewhat dearer, than to turn so great a part of their small capital to so very distant a trade, in which the returns are so very slow, in which that capital can maintain so small a quantity of productive labour at home, where productive labour is so much wanted, where so little is done, and where so much is to do.

A country which cannot trade to the East Indies without an exclusive company should not trade there.

Though without an exclusive company, therefore, a particular country should not be able to carry on any direct trade to the East Indies, it will not from thence follow that such a company ought to be established there, but only that such a country ought not in these circumstances to trade directly to the East Indies. That such companies are not in general necessary for carrying on the East India trade, is sufficiently demonstrated by the experience of the Portugueze, who enjoyed almost the whole of it for more than a century together without any exclusive company.

The idea that the large capital of a company is necessary is fallacious.

No private merchant, it has been said, could well have capital sufficient to maintain factors and agents in the different ports of the East Indies, in order to provide goods for the ships which he might occasionally send thither; and yet, unless he was able to do this, the difficulty of finding a cargo might frequently make his ships lose the season for returning, and the expence of so long a delay would not only eat up the whole profit of the adventure, but frequently occasion a very considerable loss. This argument, however, if it proved any thing at all, would prove that no one great branch of trade could be carried on without an exclusive company, which is contrary to the experience of all nations. There is no great branch of trade in which the capital of any one private merchant is sufficient, for carrying on all the subordinate branches which must be carried on, in order to carry on the principal one. But when a nation is ripe for any great branch of trade, some merchants naturally turn their capitals towards the principal, and some towards the subordinate branches of it;

度的贸易就会比实际更广泛,也会由于一部分资本被排除在最方便的贸易之外而蒙受巨大的损失。同理,如果没有专营公司,瑞典和丹麦对东印度的贸易会比实际贸易范围小,更可能会不存在,那么两国也会因为一部分资本被吸引到一种多少不适合现在状况的贸易中而蒙受巨大损失。他们在现在的状况下最好的办法是向别国购买东印度的货物,即使购买价格更高也强于将小资本的一大部分投入到距离远,回报慢的贸易中去,这种贸易所投入的资本在对于劳动力的需求量极大的情况下仅能维持国内少量的劳动力,而且进展很小,后续工作量很大。

所以,虽说一个国家不能在没有专营公司的情况下直接与东印度通商,但这也不能作为建立一个专营公司的理由,只能说这样的一个国家在这种情况下不适合与东印度直接通商。总体上来说,葡萄牙的经历能够证明与东印度通商不需要专营公司,因为它在东印度一个多世纪的贸易中并没有专营公司的存在。

一个在没有专营公司的情况下无法与东印度通商的国家根本不应该与东印度通商。

没有听说过有任何私人商人能为了给偶尔派往东印度的船只提供货物而用足够的资本支持东印度各港口的商业和代理商;除非他能做到,否则寻找货船的困难经常会使他的船只耽误回程日期,这种长期的延误不仅会吃掉所有冒险所得利润,而且经常造成巨大损失。但是这种论点如果还能证明任何事情的话,那么也只能证明每个贸易分支在没有专营公司的情况下是无法进行贸易的,这与所有国家的经验都是相悖的。经营一个大的贸易分支必然经营它的所有附属部门,但是没有任何私人商人的资本足够支撑这些附属贸易部门的运转。但是当一个国家为了一个大贸易分支做好准备的时候,一些商人就会自然地把资本投注到这个大的分支中来,还有一些人也会把资本投注在大贸易分支的附

有一家大公司的资本的想法是荒谬的。

国民财富的性质与原理

and though all the different branches of it are in this manner carried on, yet it very seldom happens that they are all carried on by the capital of one private merchant. If a nation, therefore, is ripe for the East India trade, a certain portion of its capital will naturally divide itself among all the different branches of that trade. Some of its merchants will find it for their interest to reside in the East Indies, and to employ their capitals there in providing goods for the ships which are to be sent out by other merchants who reside in Europe. The settlements which different European nations have obtained in the East Indies, if they were taken from the exclusive companies to which they at present belong, and put under the immediate protection of the sovereign, would render this residence both safe and easy, at least to the merchants of the particular nations to whom those settlements belong. If at any particular time that part of the capital of any country which of its own accord tended and inclined, if I may say so, towards the East India trade, was not sufficient for carrying on all those different branches of it, it would be a proof that, at that particular time, that country was not ripe for that trade, and that it would do better to buy for some time, even at a higher price, from other European nations, the East India goods it had occasion for, than to import them itself directly from the East Indies. What it might lose by the high price of those goods could seldom be equal to the loss which it would sustain by the distraction of a large portion of its capital from other employments more necessary, or more useful, or more suitable to its circumstances and situation, than a direct trade to the East Indies.

There are not numerous and thriving colonies in Africa and the East Indies, as in America.

Though the Europeans possess many considerable settlements both upon the coast of Africa and in the East Indies, they have not yet established in either of those countries such numerous and thriving colonies as those in the islands and continent of America. Africa, however, as well as several of the countries comprehended under the general name of the East Indies, are inhabited by barbarous nations. But those nations were by no means so weak and defenceless as the miserable and helpless Americans; and in proportion to the natural fertility of the countries which they inhabited, they were besides much more populous. The most barbarous nations either of Africa or of the East Indies were shepherds; even the Hottentots were so. ① But the natives of every part of America, except Mexico and Peru, were only hunters; and the difference is very great between the number of shepherds and that of hunters whom the same extent of equally fertile territory can maintain. In Africa and the East Indies, therefore, it was more difficult to displace the natives, and to extend the European plantations over the greater part of the lands of the original inhabitants.

① [Raynal, *Histoire philosophique*, 1773, tom. i. , p. 178.]

属部门中；虽然所有的分支都在以这种方式运转，但是很少出现由单独的私商资本经营的情况。所以如果一个国家与东印度交易的条件成熟，它的一部分资本自然会在那种贸易的不同分支中分配。有些商人会认为住在东印度有利，可以利用自己的资本为住在欧洲的其他傻瓜女人派往东印度的船只提供货物。欧洲各国在东印度的殖民地，如果从专营公司中脱离出来直接归君主管理，那么就会变成对殖民地所属国商人来说既安全又便宜的住所。请允许我这样表述，如果一国一部分资本在某些时间内不足以经营一个贸易分支，那就证明该国缺乏经营这种贸易的条件，那么即使价格高些，也应该从其他欧洲国家购入东印度货物，而不是自己直接从东印度进口。这种高价所造成的损失不会等同于将自己大部分资金从其他更必要、更有用、更合适的贸易中抽出来而从事东印度直接贸易而造成的损失。

虽然欧洲人拥有大量的非洲和东印度沿岸的殖民地，他们从未像在美洲群岛和大陆一样在这些国家中建立无数繁荣的殖民地。但是，非洲和其他统称为东印度的国家都居住着野蛮民族。但是这些民族绝非像悲惨无助的美洲人一样软弱好欺负；和他们国家的自然富庶程度相称，他们的人口数量更多。非洲或者是东印度的大部分野蛮国家都是游牧民族；霍屯督族①也是如此。但是除墨西哥和秘鲁之外的美洲每个地区的土著都是单纯的狩猎者。等量的肥沃程度相同的土地所能维持的牧民和狩猎者的数量有着极大的差异。所以，在非洲和东印度，很难将土著人赶走而在他们的土地上扩大欧洲的种植园。另外，有人已经注意到专

与美洲不同，非洲和东印度没有大量的繁荣的殖民地。

---

① 雷纳尔：《哲学史》，1773 年，第 1 卷，第 178 页。

国民财富的性质与原理

The genius of exclusive companies, besides, is unfavourable, it has already been observed, to the growth of new colonies, and has probably been the principal cause of the little progress which they have made in the East Indies. The Portugueze carried on the trade both to Africa and the East Indies without any exclusive companies, and their settlements at Congo, Angola, and Benguela on the coast of Africa, and at Goa in the East Indies, though much depressed by superstition and every sort of bad government, yet bear some faint resemblance to the colonies of America, and are partly inhabited by Portugueze who have been established there for several generations. The Dutch settlements at the Cape of Good Hope and at Batavia, are at present the most considerable colonies which the Europeans have established either in Africa or in the East Indies, and both these settlements are peculiarly fortunate in their situation. The Cape of Good Hope was inhabited by a race of people almost as barbarous and quite as incapable of defending themselves as the natives of America. It is besides the half-way house, if one may say so, between Europe and the East Indies, at which almost every European ship makes some stay both in going and returning. The supplying of those ships with every sort of fresh provisions, with fruit and sometimes with wine, affords alone a very extensive market for the surplus produce of the colonists. What the Cape of Good Hope is between Europe and every part of the East Indies, Batavia is between the principal countries of the East Indies. It lies upon the most frequented road from Indostan to China and Japan, and is nearly about mid-way upon that road. Almost all the ships too that sail between Europe and China touch at Batavia; and it is, over and above all this, the center and principal mart of what is called the country trade of the East Indies; not only of that part of it which is carried on by Europeans, but of that which is carried on by the native Indians; and vessels navigated by the inhabitants of China and Japan, of Tonquin, Malacca, Cochin-China, and the island of Celebes, are frequently to be seen in its port. Such advantageous situations have enabled those two colonies to surmount all the obstacles which the oppressive genius of an exclusive company may have occasionally opposed to their growth. They have enabled Batavia to surmount the additional disadvantage of perhaps the most unwholesome climate in the world.

The English and Dutch companies, though they have established no considerable colonies, except the two above mentioned, have both made considerable conquests in the East Indies. But in the manner in which they both govern their new subjects, the natural genius of an exclusive company has shown itself most distinctly. In the spice islands the Dutch are said to burn all the spiceries which a fertile sea-

The Dutch exclusive company destroys spices and nutmeg trees, and has reduced the population of the Moluccas. The English company has the same tendency.

营公司的特点对于殖民地发展不利,也可能是造成他们在东印度取得极小进展的主要原因。葡萄牙人在没有专营公司的情况下开展对非洲和东印度的贸易,他们在刚果,安哥拉和本格拉的殖民地以及在东印度果阿的殖民地虽然由于迷信和政府不良行为受损,但是他们和美洲的殖民地有些许共同点,即部分居民为已经在那里定居几代的葡萄牙人。好望角和巴达维亚的荷兰殖民地现在是欧洲人在非洲和东印度建立的最大殖民地,这些地方地理位置得天独厚,非常幸运。好望角的居民就像美洲土著人一样野蛮沉默,无力进行自我防卫。此外,请允许我这样表述,它是欧洲与东印度之间的驿站,几乎所有的欧洲船只来回途中都在此停留。而为这些船只提供新鲜食品、水果、葡萄酒就为殖民地的剩余生产物提供了广阔的市场。就像好望角位于欧洲和东印度各地区的中间一样,巴达维亚位于东印度各地区之间。它处在从印度斯坦到中国和日本的道路上,而且几乎正在中间位置。几乎全部穿行于欧洲和中国的船只都要经过巴达维亚,它也号称东印度城市贸易中心和主要市场,同时又与欧洲人和印度土著贸易;在这个港口可以经常看到中国人、日本人、越南人、东京人、马六甲、交趾支那和西里伯岛居民航行的船只。这种地理优势使这两个殖民地克服了专营公司时常加之于他们的压迫造成的不利于他们成长的所有困难,也使巴达维亚克服了由于世界上最糟糕的气候所造成的不利因素。

除了上述两个殖民地外,英国和荷兰的公司虽然没有建立大规模殖民地,但是都在东印度征服了很多地区。但他们在管理新属地的方式中,专营公司的自然特性明显暴露。据说荷兰人在香料岛烧毁了所有丰收季节里过剩的、可能有损于利润的香料。在

son produces beyond what they expect to dispose of in Europe with such a profit as they think sufficient. In the islands where they have no settlements, they give a premium to those who collect the young blossoms and green leaves of the clove and nutmeg trees which naturally grow there, but which this savage policy has now, it is said, almost completely extirpated. Even in the islands where they have settlements they have very much reduced, it is said, the number of those trees. If the produce even of their own islands was much greater than what suited their market, the natives, they suspect, might find means to convey some part of it to other nations; and the best way, they imagine, to secure their own monopoly, is to take care that no more shall grow than what they themselves carry to market. By different arts of oppression they have reduced the population of several of the Moluccas nearly to the number which is sufficient to supply with fresh provisions and other necessaries of life their own insignificant garrisons, and such of their ships as occasionally come there for a cargo of spices. Under the government even of the Portugueze, however, those islands are said to have been tolerably well inhabited. The English company have not yet had time to establish in Bengal so perfectly destructive a system. The plan of their government, however, has had exactly the same tendency. It has not been uncommon, I am well assured, for the chief, that is, the first clerk of a factory, to order a peasant to plough up a rich field of poppies, and sow it with rice or some other grain. The pretence was, to prevent a scarcity of provisions; but the real reason, to give the chief an opportunity of selling at a better price a large quantity of opium, which he happened then to have upon hand. Upon other occasions the order has been reversed; and a rich field of rice or other grain has been ploughed up, in order to make room for a plantation of poppies; when the chief foresaw that extraordinary profit was likely to be made by opium. The servants of the company have upon several occasions attempted to establish in their own favour the monopoly of some of the most important branches, not only of the foreign, but of the inland trade of the country. Had they been allowed to go on, it is impossible that they should not at some time or another have attempted to restrsin the production of the particular articles of which they had thus usurped the monopoly, not only to the quantity which they themselves could purchase, but to that which they could expect to sell with such a profit as they might think sufficient. In the course of a century or two, the policy of the English company would in this manner have probably proved as completely destructive as that of the Dutch.

Nothing, however, can be more directly contrary to the real interest of those companies, considered as the sovereigns of the countries which they have conquered, than this destructive plan. In almost all countries the revenue of the sovereign is drawn from that of the people. The greater the revenue of the people, therefore, the greater the annual produce of their land and labour, the more they can afford

没有殖民的岛上,他们把奖金发给那些采集丁香和豆蔻树的花蕾与绿叶的人,但据说这些植物已经在这种野蛮政策下绝种了。即使是在拥有殖民地的岛上,据说他们的做法也大大减少了这些植物的数量。如果他们自己岛上的产量超出他们市场的需求许多,他们就会认为土著人可能会想方设法将一部分运到别的国家;他们于是认为保持垄断的最好方法是注意抑制生长以低于他们销往市场的数量。通过不同的压迫手段,他们减少了马鲁古群岛中几个群岛的人口,使得其只能给自己的少数守备队和时常来运香料的船只提供最低限度的新鲜食物和其他生活必需品。但是,即使是在葡萄牙这样的统治下,这些岛的居民数量还是可观的。英国公司还没有时间在孟加拉建立这样一种堪称完美的破坏制度。但是他们的政府目标却有着出奇一致的趋势。我坚信工厂头目有时会以打着缺粮的幌子命令农场主除去地里的罂粟而种植稻米或其他粮食。但是其不可告人的真实目的却是高价出售大量鸦片现货。有时他会因预见到鸦片热销带来的超额利润而命令农场主除去水稻和粮食而种植罂粟。公司的职员经常试图在对外和本地贸易的重要分支建立有利于他们的垄断。如果允许他们这样做,他们绝对可能会限制他们意图垄断的特殊商品的生产,控制在他们有能力购买以及能在足够利润基础上售出的数量之内。在一两个世纪内,事实证明英国公司的政策在这种方式下与荷兰一样具有完全破坏性。

但是,作为被征服国家的统治者,没有什么比这种破坏性计划更直接的违背他们的真实利益了。几乎所有的国家里,统治者的收入都来自于人民的贡献。所以,人民的收入越多,他们的年度土地和劳动力产出就更多,从而对国家财政的贡献就更多。因

This destructive system is contrary to their interest as sovereigns, to the sovereign. It is his interest, therefore, to increase as much as possible that annual produce. But if this is the interest of every sovereign, it is peculiarly so of one whose revenue, like that of the sovereign of Bengal, arises chiefly from a land-rent. That rent must necessarily be in proportion to the quantity and value of the produce, and both the one and the other must depend upon the extent of the market. The quantity will always be suited with more or less exactness to the consumption of those who can afford to pay for it, and the price which they will pay will always be in proportion to the eagerness of their competition. It is the interest of such a sovereign, therefore, to open the most extensive market for the produce of his country, to allow the most perfect freedom of commerce, in order to increase as much as possible the number and the competition of buyers; and upon this account to abolish, not only all monopolies, but all restraints upon the transportation of the home produce from one part of the country to another, upon its exportation to foreign countries, or upon the importation of goods of any kind for which it can be exchanged. He is in this manner most likely to increase both the quantity and value of that produce, and consequently of his own share of it, or of his own revenue.

but they prefer the transitory profits of the monopolist merchant to the permanent revenue of the sovereign. But a company of merchants are, it seems, incapable of considering themselves as sovereigns, even after they have become such. Trade, or buying in order to sell again, they still consider as their principal business, and by a strange absurdity, regard the character of the sovereign as but an appendix to that of the merchant, as something which ought to be made subservient to it, or by means of which they may be enabled to buy cheaper in India, and thereby to sell with a better profit in Europe. They endeavour for this purpose to keep out as much as possible all competitors from the market of the countries which are subject to their government, and consequently to reduce, at least, some part of the surplus produce of those countries to what is barely sufficient for supplying their own demand, or to what they can expect to sell in Europe with such a profit as they may think reasonable. Their mercantile habits draw them in this manner, almost necessarily, though perhaps insensibly, to prefer upon all ordinary occasions the little and transitory profit of the monopolist to the great and permanent revenue of the sovereign, and would gradually lead them to treat the countries subject to their government nearly as the Dutch treat the Moluccas. It is the interest of the East India company considered as sovereigns, that the European goods which are carried to their Indian dominions, should be sold there as cheap as possible; and that the Indian goods which are brought from thence should bring there as good a price, or should be sold there as dear as possible. But the reverse of this is their interest as merchants. As sovereigns, their

此，统治者的意图是尽量增加这种年产量。如果这是每一个统治者的利益所在，那么相对于孟加拉这样的主要靠地租收入支持国家财政的国家更是如此。租金必须与产品的数量和质量成比例，数量和质量都必须取决于市场大小。数量多少都依赖于有购买力的人的消费，而他们支出的价格都会和他们的竞争的欲望成比例。因此，统治者出于利益考虑为自己国家的产品开拓最广阔的市场，准许最大的贸易自由，尽量增加购买者的人数和竞争；所以，除废除一切垄断之外，还应该废除强加于本国产品在本国范围内的运输、出口运输以及能和本国产品交换的进口运输的垄断。这样他就可能增加那种物产的数量和价值，从而增加自己的份额及增加自己的收入。

但是一群商人即使变成了统治者，也无法进入统治者的角色。他们仍旧把贸易或者说是为了再销售而买进的行为看作是自己的主要业务；令人惊讶的是，他们将统治者地位看作是商人地位的附属品，前者应服务于后者，使他们能在印度低价购入，在欧洲高价售出，从而获取利润。为此，他们竭力排斥所有受制于本国政府的商人于市场之外，将这些国家的过剩产品减少到仅能维持他们基本生存需要的水平，或者说在欧洲出售利润能达到他们自己认为合理的水平。他们作为商人的思维定式让他们在所有场合都宁肯获得垄断者的暂时的小利润，而舍弃统治者的永久的大收入；同时这种习惯也让他们像荷兰人处置马鲁古那样对待自己统治的国家。作为统治者，东印度公司的利益是运送到他们印度殖民地内的欧洲货物应该在那里以尽可能低的价格出售，而从印度出口的货物则应该以最有利、最高的价格在欧洲售出。但是作为商人，他们的利益与此相反。作为统治者，他们的利益与

interest is exactly the same with that of the country which they govern. As merchants, their interest is directly opposite to that interest. But if the genius of such a government, even as to what concerns its direction in Europe, is in this manner essentially and perhaps incurably faulty, that of its administration in India is still more so. That administration is necessarily composed of a council of merchants, a profession no doubt extremely respectable, but which in no country in the world carries along with it that sort of authority which naturally over-awes the people, and without force commands their willing obedience. Such a council can command obedience only by the military force with which they are accompanied, and their government is therefore necessarily military and despotical. Their proper business, however, is that of merchants. It is to sell, upon their masters account, the European goods consigned to them, and to buy in return Indian goods for the European market. It is to sell the one as dear and to buy the other as cheap as possible, and consequently to exclude as much as possible all rivals from the particular market where they keep their shop. The genius of the administration, therefore, so far as concerns the trade of the company, is the same as that of the direction. It tends to make government subservient to the interest of monopoly, and consequently to stunt the natural growth of some parts at least of the surplus produce of the country to what is barely sufficient for answering the demand of the company.

All the members of the administration, besides, trade more or less upon their own account, and it is in vain to prohibit them from doing so. Nothing can be more completely foolish than to expect that the clerks of a great counting-house at ten thousand miles distance, and consequently almost quite out of sight, should, upon a simple order from their masters, give up at once doing any sort of business upon their own account, abandon for ever all hopes of making a fortune, of which they have the means in their hands, and content themselves with the moderate salaries which those masters allow them, and which, moderate as they are, can seldom be augmented, being commonly as large as the real profits of the company trade can afford. In such circumstances, to prohibit the servants of the company from trading upon their own account, can have scarce any other effect than to enable the superior servants, under pretence of executing their masters order, to oppress such of the inferior ones as have had the misfortune to fall under their displeasure. The servants naturally endeavour to establish the same monopoly in favour of their own private trade as of the public trade of the company. If they are suffered to act as they could wish, they will establish this monopoly openly and directly, by fairly prohibiting all other people from trading in the articles in which they chuse to deal; and this, perhaps, is the best and least oppressive way of establishing it. But if by an order from Europe

他们所统治的国家利益完全相同。两种角色下的利益是相冲突的。

但是如果说政府的这种倾向在对欧洲的管理本质上或许可以说是不可挽回的错误,那么在对印度的管理上则更是如此。那个统治机构必然等同于一个商人协会,这个职业无疑是极受人尊重的,但是这个职业在世界上任何国家都不具有震慑人民,使之自愿服从的权威。这样一种商人协会对人民只能以武力相逼,所以他们的政府必然是军事和专制的。他们正当的职业是商人。他们的本来职业是受主人之托去售卖欧洲货物,购入欧洲市场所需的印度货物。换句话说,就是高价出售欧洲货物而低价购入印度货物,从而将所有竞争者尽量排除在特定市场之外。因此,就公司贸易而言,统治机构和管理部门的倾向一致。它使政府服从垄断利益,从而阻止某些国家过剩产物至少是一部分的自然生长,使其达到仅够维持公司需求。

另外,统治机构的所有成员,多少都有自己的生意,想阻止他们这么做是不会奏效的。这些职员有贸易手段,而且在远离主人监督的地方办公,所以想靠一纸命令让他们放弃一切计划,放弃发财梦,满足于主人支付的有限的不可提升的薪酬(这种薪酬通常和公司贸易的实际利润所能提供的相等),这简直是极端愚蠢的想法。在这种情况下,禁止公司职员从事私人生意只能令高级职员打着执行主人命令的幌子去压迫触犯他们的初级职员,别无其他效果。这些职员会效仿公司贸易建立有利于他们个人贸易的垄断。如果放任自流,他们就会公开的直接建立这种垄断,禁止其他人经营他们所要经营的货物贸易,这或许是建立垄断最好的、压迫性最小的方法。但是如果欧洲那边下令禁止他们从事

they are prohibited from doing this, they will, notwithstanding, endeavour to establish a monopoly of the same kind, secretly and indirectly, in a way that is much more destructive to the country. They will employ the whole authority of government, and pervert the administration of justice, in order to harass and ruin those who interfere with them in any branch of commerce which, by means of agents, either concealed, or at least not publicly avowed, they may chuse to carry on. But the private trade of the servants will naturally extend to a much greater variety of articles than the public trade of the company. The public trade of the company extends no further than the trade with Europe, and comprehends a part only of the foreign trade of the country. But the private trade of the servants may extend to all the different branches both of its inland and foreign trade. The monopoly of the company can tend only to stunt the natural growth of that part of the surplus produce which, in the case of a free trade, would be exported to Europe. That of the servants tends to stunt the natural growth of every part of the produce in which they chuse to deal, of what is destined for home consumption, as well as of what is destined for exportation; and consequently to degrade the cultivation of the whole country, and to reduce the number of its inhabitants. It tends to reduce the quantity of every sort of produce, even that of the necessaries of life, whenever the servants of the company chuse to deal in them, to what those servants can both afford to buy and expect to sell with such a profit as pleases them.

The interest of the servants is not, like the real interest of the company, the same as that of the country.

From the nature of their situation too the servants must be more disposed to support with rigorous severity their own interest against that of the country which they govern, than their masters can be to support theirs. The country belongs to their masters, who cannot avoid having some regard for the interest of what belongs to them. But it does not belong to the servants. The real interest of their masters, if they were capable of understanding it, is the same with that of the country, and it is from ignorance chiefly, and the meanness of mercantile prejudice, that they ever oppress it. But the real interest of the servants is by no means the same with that of the country, and the most perfect information would not necessarily put an end to their oppressions. The regulations accordingly which have been sent out from Europe, though they have been frequently weak, have upon most occasions been well-meaning. More intelligence and perhaps less good-meaning has sometimes appeared in those established by the servants in India. It is a very singular government in which every member of the administration wishes to get out of the country, and consequently to have done with the government, as soon as he can, and to whose interest, the day after he has left it and carried his whole fortune with him, it is perfectly indifferent though the whole country was swallowed up by an earthquake.

I mean not, however, by any thing which I have here said, to throw any odious imputation upon the general character of the servants

这种私人贸易，他们就会以一种更加有害于国家的手段秘密地，间接的建立这种垄断。他们会发挥政府的全部权利颠倒黑白，控制和毁灭妨碍他们的人，这些人以代理人为媒介或者是至少不公开承认利用代理人经营的商业部门。但是职员的私人贸易比公司集体贸易种类多得多。公司集体贸易仅限于欧洲贸易，只包括国外贸易的一部分。但是职员的私人贸易可以推广到国内外一切贸易部门。公司垄断只能阻碍自由贸易条件下出口欧洲的剩余产物自然增长。职员垄断却将会阻碍他们经营的一切产物的自然增长，不管是用于本国内需消费还是出口需要；因此，会损害全国的农耕，减少人口。它会将公司职员所要经营的产品和生活必需品数量降至他们有能力购买并期望获得的利润出售水平。

统治机构的职员由于所处的地位，会用比他们主人更严苛的手段维持他们的利益并危害统治国家的利益。国家是他们的主人，这些人也需要考虑属国的利益。他们主人的真实利益，如果他们能够了解，是与属国利益一致的。无知卑鄙的重商偏见使得主人压迫属国。但是职员的真实利益与属国不同，所以即使知识完全，他们也会压迫属国。欧洲发出的条例有时不甚完美，但大多数情况下都是善意的。印度的职员所订立的条例有时看上去是明智的，但是却缺乏善意。这个政府着实奇怪，职员都想尽快离开本国，和政府脱离关系。当他们带着财产离开之时，即使地震毁掉整个国家，他们也无动于衷。_{公司利益不同，职员利益和国家利益也不同。和公司实益同，职员利益和国家利益不同。}

以上一番话绝无意诋毁东印度公司职员的一般品行，更绝非

<small>The evils come from the system, not from the character of the men who administer it.</small> of the East India company, and much less upon that of any particular persons. It is the system of government, the situation in which they are placed, that I mean to censure; not the character of those who have acted in it. They acted as their situation naturally directed, and they who have clamoured the loudest against them would, probably, not have acted better themselves. In war and negociation, the councils of Madras and Calcutta have upon several occasions conducted themselves with a resolution and decisive wisdom which would have done honour to the senate of Rome in the best days of that republic. The members of those councils, however, had been bred to professions very different from war and politics. But their situation alone, without education, experience, or even example, seems to have formed in them all at once the great qualities which it required, and to have inspired them both with abilities and virtues which they themselves could not well know that they possessed. If upon some occasions, therefore, it has animated them to actions of magnanimity which could not well have been expected from them, we should not wonder if upon others it has prompted them to exploits of somewhat a different nature.

<small>Exclusive companies are nuisances.</small>   Such exclusive companies, therefore, are nuisances in every respect; always more or less inconvenient to the countries in which they are established, and destructive to those which have the misfortune to fall under their government.

针对某个人。我指责的是政府体制和职员的地位,而不是他们的品行。他们的行为受体制和环境所限,大声责难他们的行为也不见得多光彩。在战争和谈判中,马德拉斯和加尔各答市议会很多次表现的果断明智,足以和罗马共和国鼎盛时期的元老院媲美。可是,这些议会议员接受的是与战争和政治距离很远的职业教育。但是,他们的环境本身就可以陶冶他们所需要的品质;没有教育,经验和榜样的力量,他们也会不知不觉中具备能力与德行。所以,如果某些场合使他们做出预见不到的高尚行为,那么在其他场合在这种环境中做出的多少不相称的行为也不足为怪。

> 罪恶的源泉是制度,而非推行制度的人的品行。

因此,专营公司每一方面都令人厌恶;对于设立这种公司的国家,总会造成不便;对于受其统治的国家,它具有毁灭性的意义。

> 专营公司让人厌恶。